QUEBEC SOCIETY
Critical Issues

QUEBEC SOCIETY
Critical Issues

Marcel Fournier
University of Montreal

Michael Rosenberg
Dawson College

Deena White
University of Montreal

Prentice Hall Canada Inc.
Scarborough, Ontario

Canadian Cataloguing in Publication Data

Fournier, Marcel, 1945–
      Quebec society: critical issues

ISBN 0-13-158551-7

1. Quebec (Province)–Social conditions 1960–
I. Rosenberg, M. Michael. II. White, Deena. III. Title.

HN110.Q4F68   1997 971.4′04   C96-930865-5

© 1997 Prentice-Hall Canada Inc., Scarborough, Ontario
A Viacom Company

Prentice-Hall, Inc., Englewood Cliffs, New Jersey
Prentice-Hall International (UK) Limited, London
Prentice-Hall of Australia, Pty. Limited, Sydney
Prentice-Hall Hispanoamericana, S.A., Mexico City
Prentice-Hall of India Private Limited, New Delhi
Prentice-Hall of Japan, Inc., Tokyo
Simon & Schuster Asia Private Limited, Singapore
Editora Prentice-Hall do Brasil, Ltda., Rio de Janeiro

ISBN 0-13-158551-7

Acquisitions Editor: Rebecca Bersagel
Production Editor: Kelly Dickson
Copy Editor: Carol Glegg
Editorial Assistant: Shoshana Goldberg
Production Coordinator: Jane Schell
Cover Design: Kyle Gell
Page Layout: Arlene Edgar

1 2 3 4 5   RRD   01 00 99 98 97

Printed and bound in the USA

Every reasonable effort has been made to obtain permissions for all articles and data used in this edition. If errors or omissions have occurred, they will be corrected in future editions provided written notification has been received by the publisher.

We welcome readers' comments, which can be sent by e-mail to
collegeinfo_pubcanada@prenhall.com

Page 45: "Quebec and the Ideal of Federalism," from the journal *Annals of the American Academy of Political & Social Science*, by Louis Balthazar, page(s) 40–53. Reprinted by permission of Sage Publications, Inc.

Charter of French Language and Charter of the Human Rights and Freedoms reproduced with permission from des Publications du Québec.

Canadian Charter of Rights and Freedoms from the Department of Canadian Heritage reproduced with the permission of the Minister of Canadian Heritage and the Minister of Public Works and Government Services.

Table of Contents

Preface

In 1943, sociologist Everett Hughes published a book on Quebec Society which he entitled *French Canada in Transition*. Today, well over fifty years later, Quebec still remains very much "in transition." Quebec is a society which continues to evolve and to change. What kind of society Quebec will become is not clear, however, because, as the extremely close vote in the 1995 referendum on sovereignty showed, Quebecers have not yet agreed on what kind of society they want. This makes Quebec fascinating to those who live outside it, and sometimes exhausting to those who live within it. In either case it makes Quebec highly relevant as a topic both to sociologists and to the general public.

Given this rapid pace of change, this book is not intended to provide a comprehensive and detailed portrait of Quebec society. Such a book would be much larger and cost substantially more than this one, and would quickly be out of date. Instead, our goal is to examine a number of key issues which we believe to be crucial to the understanding of contemporary Quebec society. Some of these issues are political ones, but we have also included other important areas to ensure that the book encompasses more than just the political and constitutional issues that dominate much of the discourse on Quebec.

While many excellent books on Quebec have appeared in recent years, these have tended to be primarily political or historical in context, dealing with the evolution of Quebec society and, in particular, its political development. Such books are important and informative, and it is certainly true that both politics and the influences of history do play a crucial role in contemporary Quebec. But such books tend to ignore or pay insufficient attention to other issues that Quebecers also see as central to their lives, such as the changing role of the family, the ability of the education system to integrate the children of immigrants into the francophone milieu, or the debate on how to change the health care system. Thus, while the political implications of the constitutional changes and choices facing Quebecers do permeate these issues, and past history continues to provide the context for understanding these changes and choices, the reality is that contemporary Quebec is a society which is preoccupied with much me than constitutional issues and political debates. If English-speaking North Americans are to understand Quebec society and the direction in which it is moving, they must look beyond constitutional issues to examine the transformations affecting Quebec society itself.

This book is intended as an accessible introduction to contemporary society, one which identifies the issues viewed as critical according to Quebecers themselves and which places these issues into a context that is understandable to others. For this reason, we invited social scientists living and working in Quebec to write the contributions to this text. Moreover, we asked that their contributions not only present the issues in a general way, but that they also include data taken from their ongoing research and intellectual interests. This, we hope, will provide the reader with an overview of some key aspects of Quebec social science as well as of Quebec society.

Several chapters of this book were written in French and we would like to thank Benoit Ouellette for his excellent work in translating them into English. We would also like to thank Isabelle Billett for her invaluable assistance in preparing the manuscript. Finally, we would like to thank the authors of the individual chapters for putting aside their own research to prepare the material for this book. All of them took on the task of writing their chapters with enthusiasm, recognizing that such a book has not previously been available to an English-speaking audience, and that it can serve a useful role in making Quebec society more understandable to those who live outside it, and perhaps even to some who live within it.

AN INTRODUCTION
TO QUEBEC SOCIETY

To understand Quebec means to understand the social relationships, institutions, and experiences out of which Quebec society is composed. This is no easy matter for several reasons. One is that Quebec is a distinct society whose traditions, institutions, and concerns are different from those of many who are reading this book. Moreover, it is always difficult to get a grasp of just what the concerns of Quebecers are at any given moment because of the volatility of Quebec society. Few would have imagined in 1976 that Quebec would have a referendum on sovereignty in 1980; few would have imagined in 1990 that there would be another referendum in 1995, or that the vote supporting sovereignty in 1995 would be greater than in 1980. While change seems to have become a constant feature of modern life everywhere, no other part of North America has undergone so dramatic a set of changes as has Quebec since the "Quiet Revolution" of the 1960s.

A paradox of Quebec society is, however, the extraordinary link which persists between an ever-changing present and an ever-present past. Politically, culturally, ideologically, and even institutionally Quebecers remain tied to their history. A good example, discussed later in this book, is the persistence of the division of public schools in Quebec along religious lines (Protestant and Catholic) 30 years after education was largely secularized. Today, Catholic and Protestant public schools are fundamentally identical in terms of curriculum and even clientele, with Catholic children attending Protestant schools and Protestant children attending Catholic schools, and both being attended by children who fit into neither category. Whereas Protestant schools used to be English schools and most Catholic schools used to be French, even that difference has disappeared, as 40% of students currently attending Protestant schools are attending ones that function in French. Yet the distinction between Protestant and Catholic schools not only persists, it is entrenched in Canada's constitution.

To understand Quebec society it is essential to recognize how and why Quebec is a distinct society, to have some familiarity with its past, and to know some of the issues and concerns with which it is preoccupied at present. All three issues will be briefly discussed in the following pages. In this introduction particular attention will be paid to political issues and changes since the casual reader is likely to be more familiar with Quebec politics than with other aspects of Quebec society. Politics can thus serve to orient the reader to the issues discussed in the other chapters of this book. Also, since political action and political change do not determine a society but rather reflect what people are experiencing, thinking and feeling, they serve as an index to the broader sets of changes happening in a society.

QUEBEC AS A DISTINCT SOCIETY

Whatever the political outcome of the current debate among Canadians about whether Quebec is a province of Canada like any other, or whether it is a distinct society and should be treated differently from other provinces, there is little question that from a sociological standpoint, Quebec is very much a distinct society, one which differs in fundamental ways from the rest of North America.

Some of these distinctions are obvious, as in the case of language or politics. Quebec's population is over 80% francophone, with many other Quebecers able to speak French. In this respect, Quebec is a fundamentally French society and most Quebecers are determined that this will remain the case.

The "French face" of Quebec is not just a matter of language, however, but of culture. Perhaps because they see their culture as threatened, "culture" to the Québécois is more intimately linked with identity than tends to be the case for anglophone North Americans. This is because the Québécois culture is about who they are and how they relate to others. In contrast, "culture" for anglophone North Americans tends to be more "material," i.e. it tends to be focused on things: books, art, music, films, objects and the activities related to these. In terms of *content*, the culture of the Québécois is not all that different from that of other North Americans: Quebecers love to buy Elvis Presley albums just as Americans love to buy Céline Dion albums. Yet the Québécois feel their francophone culture to be distinct, and that sense of themselves as different is an important part of their identity.

Politically, too, Quebec is distinct, if for no other reason than that it currently has in power a government committed to removing Quebec from the existing Canadian federation. Or, to take another example, consider how very different the actions of the Quebec government have been on the issue of reducing Quebec's budget deficit from what we have seen in Alberta or Ontario. In those provinces, unilateral government action provoked dramatic and sometimes violent responses from many segments of the population. In Quebec, matters proceeded very differently. A two-day "socio-economic summit" was held in the spring of 1996 which included business, labour, and even the official political opposition in the National Assembly. After intensive debate and discussion, an agreement was made among all parties on how the government was to proceed. Conflicts and disagreements will emerge over time, of course, but the government is seen as acting on the basis of a widespread consensus rather than a partisan ideological stance. This gives the government's actions an inherent legitimacy which is lacking in the other provinces.

Quebec is distinct, as well, in terms of many of its institutions, as the example of Quebec's dual confessional public school system mentioned above shows. But there are many others. One excellent example is the *caisses populaires*, which were founded in 1900 as an alternative to the banks. The *caisses populaires* were designed as decentralized, cooperative structures which promoted savings, provided credit to workers and farmers, provided mortgages, and financed residential construction (Linteau, Durocher, Robert and Ricard, 1991).

These institutions, which were promoted by the Catholic Church, were seen as an alternative to the "materialistic" banks which many francophones saw as overly concerned with profits and oriented to serving the needs of big business.

What really makes Quebec distinct, however, is not simply its collection of cultural or political or institutional characteristics or traits. It is that Quebec is distinct as a totality, as a *society* which is more than the sum of its parts. Francophone Quebecers identify themselves as a single people—the Québécois—with their own sets of social relationships, their own experiences, and their own interests and desires. This makes Quebec very different from the rest of Canada, which has tended to define itself in recent decades as a pluralistic, multicultural society composed of many diverse groups.

It also poses something of a problem for some Quebecers, such as anglophones or recent immigrants, many of whom wonder if they are included within the category of "Québécois." Quebec's politicians have often asserted that all Quebecers are a part of the Québécois community and many non-francophone do identify themselves as Québécois. René Lévesque, the first Parti Québécois premier of the province (quoted in *The Montreal Star*, June 6, 1977) stated that "Each and every person who lives in Quebec is a Québécois, ...(all) who earn their living here, all who pay their taxes here, all who have the right to vote, or are awaiting it—all those who are recognized as citizens or waiting to be so—all of these people are Québécois."

Nevertheless, statements such as that of former Premier Jacques Parizeau in 1995 following the defeat of the sovereignty option in the referendum, where he said that "we" (meaning the francophone Québécois) voted in favour of sovereignty but were defeated by an alliance of "money and the ethnic vote" make many members of ethnic minorities nervous. Indeed, immigration has become a controversial issue in Quebec society, seen by some as a threat to the French character of the society.

Regardless of whether Quebec is recognized as distinct by other Canadians or by Canada's constitution, it is distinct by virtue of its people's perception of themselves as distinct and different. This is a reality of Quebec's political, cultural, and social life with which other Canadians will, at some point, have to come to terms.

QUEBEC BEFORE THE QUIET REVOLUTION

It may well be argued that the British conquest of New France was the most fateful event in Canadian history. Certainly, this is unquestionably the case for Quebec to date. As the motto of the province of Quebec, "Je me souviens" ("I remember"), makes evident, francophone Quebecers have never forgotten that Quebec was once a French nation with its own culture, history, and heroes (Rioux, 1978). Nor have they forgotten the ensuing 200 years of struggle to preserve their culture, their language, their institutions, and their religion despite the British conquest.

Their success in that struggle is all the more remarkable because they were under the political and economic domination of another group, the British, with whom they had to compete for control over their society. Moreover, throughout the nineteenth and early twentieth centuries the rest of North America was modernizing and industrializing in ways which were incompatible with the preservation of the traditional way of life of francophone Quebecers which centered on agriculture and the rural community.

An important force in preserving the culture and way of life of the French was the Catholic Church. The influence of the Church was a consequence of several factors. One was that the Church provided a broad range of educational, charitable, and social services which had a significant impact upon the daily life of many Quebecers. This made the local priest an important figure in the community, one who had broad influence and commanded respect. In addition, the Church promoted a policy of isolation, ruralism, and conservatism which was compatible with the desire of the British elite to retain their economic and political control over the province. Supported both by the ordinary citizen and by the elites, the Church itself became a dominant spiritual, political, and social force in the province of Quebec.

Quebec's isolation from the currents of change in North America, its delayed modernization, was also supported by the institutional self-segregation (Guindon, 1967) of the British and French communities. Both communities remained separate from each other, so much so that novelist Hugh MacLennon's phrase, the "two solitudes" is often used to summarize the state of relations between British and French communities in Quebec before the Quiet Revolution. Moreover, it was not only the French who sought to remain separate from the British in order to preserve their language and way of life. As "conquerors," the British, too, sought to separate themselves from the Catholic French inhabitants whom many viewed as inferiors (Lower, 1977). Porter (1965) has suggested that ethnic segregation can be seen as an aspect of social control, for example, "the control potential inherent in ethnic segregation ...(could) ...enhance the position of both ethnic leaders and the leaders of the charter groups" (Porter, 1965: 73). In any case, the division of Quebec into separate French and British communities ensured that both groups would be in a constant state of conflict and competition, a condition which helped promote francophone nationalism.

Nonetheless, given the dynamics of modernization in North America, it was inevitable that the isolation of Quebec should end. The breakdown of Quebec as a rural society was effected by the industrialization of the province and its concomitant urbanization. Quebec lacked sufficient arable land to support its total population in agriculture. Approximately 5% of Quebec's land area is suitable for farming and "(it) has been estimated that from 1871 to 1901 the proportion of young males leaving farm life rose from 40 to 56%" (Morris, Lanphier, 1977: 136). The abundance of cheap labour stimulated industrialization which in turn promoted the exodus from the farms. At the same time, the political development of the province increased the size, services, and complexity of the government bureaucracy.

Lévesque (1976: 738) suggests that World War II was the decisive "midwife" in this change:

> Wartime service, both overseas and on the industrial home-front, dealt a mortal blow to the old order, gave an irresistible impetus to urbanization and started the breakup of the traditional rural-parish ideal, yanked women by the thousands into war-plant industry and as many men into battle-dress discovery of the great wide world.

The war also resulted in a dramatic growth of both the federal and provincial bureaucracies. Once begun, such bureaucratic growth tends to take on a life of its own and spreads its control over ever greater sectors of society. In this respect, the increasing provincial government involvement in education in the 1950s was significant, especially as it wrested control of education away from the Catholic Church.

Industry, bureaucracy, and education are institutional carriers of modernity (Berger, Berger, Kellner, 1974). Although Quebec modernized after most of the rest of North America, this delay did not alter the typical consequences of modernization. The first major change could be seen in the dramatic collapse of the Catholic Church's influence. It is, of course, a well-observed feature of modernity that organized religion loses much of its significance in modern societies (Berger, 1969, 1979; Luckmann, 1967) as a consequence of the relativization which characterizes the modern experience of the world. In such a situation the Church ceased to constitute the taken-for-granted plausibility structure of Quebec society.

In the case of the Catholic Church in Quebec, however, several other factors were also at work. One was the growth in importance and power of the state which diminished the role the Church played in the community and in the lives of ordinary Quebecers. As more and more services were taken over by the government and removed from clerical control, the influence of the local priest diminished, as did the influence of the Church in Quebec society as a whole. Moreover, the Quebec government in the 1950s, under Premier Duplessis, showed itself capable of controlling and even manipulating the Church for partisan political interests, which again diminished the stature of the Church. Also, Duplessis proved effective at using the state apparatus as a means of promoting the interests and powers of Quebec's francophones, so that during the 1950s the state, rather than the Church, became the dominant ideological force in Quebec.

In retrospect, then, it is clear that the changes usually attributed to the Quiet Revolution did not begin in 1960 but were already developing in the 1940s and 50s. Moreover, legislative and social change did not end in 1966 but in fact accelerated and continues today.

THE QUIET REVOLUTION

The period between 1960 and 1966 did, nevertheless, mark the beginning of a new era in Quebec society. The term "Quiet Revolution" is usually taken to refer to this period during which a whole series of legislative changes gave new powers to the Quebec state and inspired many other social changes in Quebec society.

A new political alliance came into power in 1960 which included several groups with a vested interest in a strong and financially viable Quebec state (A. Breton, 1964; Guindon, 1967, 1968; Renaud, 1984). Foremost among these groups were the "new middle class," whose ties to the state were direct and intimate; newly emerging francophone business elites whose interests were tied to state expansion; and parapublic employees, such as teachers and health care workers, whose jobs were a product of the dramatic increase in the scope and size of the parapublic sector initiated by the government and whose salaries were paid from the provincial treasury. Linteau, Durocher, Robert and Ricard (1991: 408) also mention in this context "intellectuals" such as social scientists, teachers and journalists with strong personal and ideological commitments to the state, and "career trade union officials, many of them university-educated" (Linteau, Durocher, Robert, Ricard, (1991: 408).

The new political alliance also included a new generation of politicians, some motivated by the desire for social reforms, others inspired by a new nationalism. Quebec in the 1950s had been a breeding ground for a generation of political activists personally committed to overcoming the Duplessis era's legacy of political corruption and state inaction. This new generation of politicians was impatient to begin the process they referred to as *"rattrapage,"* the accelerated modernization and democratization of Quebec society, and they began to work on significant legislative initiatives almost immediately upon coming into office.

These initiatives were of two types. One of them had to do with structural reform, such as the establishment of a Ministry of Education and the Office de la Langue Française, and the implementation of the Quebec Pension Plan. The impact of these structural reforms was enormous, not only in terms of expanding the role of the state but also in expanding the size of its bureaucratic apparatus. Between 1960 and 1971 the number of people employed in Quebec's public and para-public sectors increased from 36,000 to 350,000, which meant that government employees increased from 2% to 15% of the total labour force (Renaud, 1984: 151).

The second type of change was ideological, expressing a new conception of the state and its goals. The state now came to be seen as the leading player in the process of transforming Quebec into a new, modern, self-assured and democratic society capable of controlling its own destiny. This meant altering the role of the state within Quebec, and altering, as well, relations between Quebec and the federal government.

The Quebec society which emerged from the Quiet Revolution in 1966 was substantially different from the traditional society which had preceded it. Quebec's key institutions—in particular the Catholic Church and the state—had been radically transformed in a remarkably short period of time. The rapid secularization of Quebec society had diminished the role and authority of the Church while the newly activist state was expanding its influence into almost every sector of Quebec society. During this period, much of Quebec's francophone population had come to equate the promotion of their collective identity with the empowerment of the state. The Québécois, as they now began to call themselves, felt that in the state and its agencies they at last had the collective tools with which to build their future society. But what type of society would it be? How would it fit into Canada's political and economic structure? Was a fully developed Quebec society even possible within the confines of the Canadian federation? These questions raised new debates and generated new disagreements within the Québécois community about the nature of Quebec society and its future within Canada, causing the issues of nationalism and language to take on a new and urgent priority. The result was a breakdown of the ideological and political alliances which had initiated the reforms of the early 1960s along with the rise of various competing forms of state-centered nationalism (Moniere, 1981).

THE ROLE OF LANGUAGE

The issue of language played a significant role in these debates for a number of reasons. As Marcel Fournier (1990: 44) has noted, the "representation of identity does not rest only on inherent characteristics, but is also ... a function of the balance of power within which the group or collectivity exists, which determines the ease with which it may transform these traits into a collective identity." In this respect, the French language has always been a key part of the francophone community's collective sense of self, the symbolic marker which identifies them as a distinct and coherent collectivity, differentiating them from most other Canadians and indeed from the rest of North America. The preservation of the French language despite 200 years of British domination was a major accomplishment of francophone Quebecers, a shared source of pride in the past and a collective point of concern for the future. Magnuson (1981) has argued that, with the modernization of Quebec, the French language took on an even more important symbolic role as the significance of other traditional elements of francophone identity, such as religion and life style, were reduced. One point on which almost all francophone Quebecers agreed, then, was that the new Quebec society being built should be a French society. The issue of language and nationalism were thus intertwined, whatever the form of nationalism being formulated.

Another factor which made the role of language a contentious issue in Quebec society beginning in the 1960s was the demographic changes affecting the francophone population. The high birth rates which had characterized the francophone community for 200 years went into a steep decline and the Québécois ceased to reproduce themselves at a rate that would maintain their population. This demographic decline caused widespread public concern because it seemed to pose a threat to the continued survival of Quebec as a French society—a serious issue to a people which had fought so hard for so long to ensure the survival of their language and institutions. Given that the Québécois now felt that they had the tools with which to take complete control of their society, this perceived demographic threat to the very survival of their society provoked a powerful emotional reaction.

Reinforcing the proportionate decline of the francophone Québécois population was the linguistic choice made by immigrants, most of whom chose English as their language of work and education. Immigrants seemed to view Canada as an English country and believed that job opportunities and higher status were more accessible to English-speakers as opposed to French-speakers. Yet if it was to survive as a French society, many nationalists believed that Quebec would have to increase the use of French by immigrants. In this respect, the preference of most immigrants for English seemed, to nationalist Québécois, to be a rejection of their vision of Quebec as a French society and, given the significant number of immigrants coming to Quebec at that time, posed a further threat to the possibility of establishing such a society.

Language was thus an issue on which most francophone Quebecers agreed. However, on other issues there was much less unanimity. Indeed, the identification of the year 1966 as the end of the Quiet Revolution is not because it marked the end of reforms but because the defeat of the Liberal government in the election of that year marked the end of the consensus around which the Quiet Revolution had been built. Quebec's political turbulence ever since is a sign that no new consensus has yet emerged.

NEW SOCIAL CONCERNS AND THE RISE OF THE PARTI QUÉBÉCOIS

As noted earlier, political action and political change do not determine a society; rather, they reflect what people are experiencing, thinking, and feeling. The changes in Quebec society after 1960 rendered traditional Quebec politics obsolete and raised new issues which required new solutions. Now that Quebec had built up a huge new state apparatus, who could best administer that apparatus and ensure that it continued to reflect the popular will? Now that Quebec's economy had modernized and expanded dramatically, who could best control industry so that it would function in tune with the collective project of building a francophone society? What about the huge new public sector unions that had been created as a result of government expansion? Who could integrate these and other unions into a new consensus that would include business and the state? Then, of course, there was Quebec's population that was being educated at unprecedented levels. Who could best provide career opportunities to ensure that the new generation got to use the skills they had been taught? Nor could women's new demands be ignored any longer. But who could best ensure that they would achieve their goals and take an equal place in society?

The traditional parties, the Liberals and the Union Nationale, were at a disadvantage because they *were* traditional. They expressed ideologies and sought solutions which many Quebecers perceived as divorced from the new issues. The Parti Québécois, formed in 1968, was a new party dedicated to creating a new society, one which campaigned for sovereignty, but also for good government. "Good" not only in the sense of competent, but good as well in the sense of being attuned to the needs of Quebecers. Under the leadership of popular politician René Lévesque, the Parti Québécois showed remarkable strength as early as the 1970 provincial election when it obtained 24% of the popular vote. By 1976 enough Quebecers were convinced that the Parti Québécois would provide good government that they voted the Parti Québécois into office.

The creation of the Parti Québécois was the result of a new kind of *independantiste* ideology and new social support for the idea of sovereignty. Rejecting violence, the Parti Québécois, as its very name indicated, sought independence through the development of a broadly based, active political party with support from all sectors of Quebec society, including anglophone and ethnic groups. For the intellectual leadership of the Parti Québécois, the independence of Quebec was inevitable. Their role was not to speed up the process by violence but to develop the political institutions which would be needed by the new state. This latter goal, it was argued, could be done even while Quebec was still a part of Canada.

From one point of view the election of a Parti Québécois government in November of 1976 was purely a political event: the transfer of power from one political party to another. In formal terms nothing had really changed in Quebec either politically or socially. There was no revolution, no mass arrests, no dawning of a millennial era, no real fundamental alteration in the ongoing lives of ordinary Quebecers.

Yet this is certainly not how the election results were understood at the time by many Quebecers. The victory of the Parti Québécois was of enormous symbolic significance, one which signaled a shift in the public's understanding of what Quebec had become and what their own position in it would now be. Indeed, for many Quebecers, the election seemed to mark the end of one world and the beginning of another.

To its committed supporters, the Parti Québécois victory was a sign that the Québécois had at last "matured," were at last "grown up" enough to take on responsibility for their own lives and to form their own nation. The victory was a surprise because it had come so "soon," but the fact that victory would come was nevertheless "inevitable," a "natural" ending to 200 years of national development which had forged a sovereign Quebec in fact, if not in law.

Still, it was understood that the struggle for an independent Quebec had not yet ended. Many were afraid that sovereignty would still be thwarted or delayed by dirty tricks and the financial manipulations of the "English." The extraordinary elation displayed by Parti Québécois supporters on election night was their response to a distant—however "inevitable"—dream that had somehow come true that day.

To its opponents, especially the anglophones of Montreal, the Parti Québécois victory was an "aberration," a sign that Quebec—gone "mad"—was no longer "home."

The election of the Parti Québécois, then, was an unprecedented event in modern Canadian history, a dramatic turnabout from the often expressed "banality" of Canadian politics. The election of a party committed to the destruction of the Canadian confederation naturally created shock waves throughout Canada, but particularly in English-speaking Quebec. Anglophone Quebecers were disoriented, confused, and above all fearful of what the future might hold. Articles in Montreal's English-language newspapers immediately following the election carried repeated calls for the public to "remain calm." Clearly, 1976, like 1960, was a crucial turning point in the evolution of Quebec society.

THE ACTIVIST STATE

Given the high degree of state activism in Quebec, politics not only reflects social change, it helps create it. The Parti Québécois made choices which affected business and labour, the status of the French language, women, ethnic minorities, and the health and education systems; indeed, almost no facet of Quebec society was left untouched. Between 1976 and 1986 the Parti Québécois initiated an extraordinary program of state intervention in the lives of its citizens which was unprecedented in North America. This involved intervention in the economy, as in the takeover of Asbestos Corporation; in education with Bill 101 which required the majority of children to attend French language schools; in culture with the elimination of English signs in stores and public places; and intervention in many other sectors of society as discussed in the various chapters in this book.

Yet, the referendum on sovereignty held in 1980 resulted in a federalist win and Quebec remained a part of Canada. Then, to many people's surprise, the Parti Québécois was re-elected in 1981 and, although defeated in 1986, was eventually elected again in 1994, with yet another referendum defeat in 1995 for sovereignty. Clearly, the Parti Québécois was not and is not being elected on the basis of its sovereignty platform, although a significant number of Quebecers support that platform. What the Parti Québécois represents to many Quebecers is a commitment to retaining the achievements of the Quiet Revolution and to continuing with the collective project of building Quebec as a modern, democratic, francophone society. Its sovereignist position is supported to the extent that people are able to see it as representing Quebec's best chance for building on past achievements and maintaining significant control over the future. Furthermore, in times of increasing economic uncertainty, hope for the latter tends to become increasingly compelling. But Quebecers' expectations of their state go well beyond the kind of simple crisis management that has gotten neo-conservative parties elected in other societies. The fortunes of the two major political parties in Quebec are tied to their relative ability to promote a collective *"projet de société"*— what the former American president George Bush once called "the vision thing."

QUEBEC SOCIETY: CRITICAL ISSUES

Within Quebec society, this collective project has developed on two fronts. It is evoked by a vision of Quebec's distinctive identity as opposed to that of "others," a vision which often takes political form and is promoted by the state through legislation, regulation and the discourse of confrontation with Ottawa. It is this vision with which this introduction has so far been preoccupied and which most other books on Quebec treat as central. But there is another vision of Quebec's identity, one which is affirmed within the society, through the promotion of certain patterns of social relations and certain ways of getting things done. It is this second, more neglected (and more sociological) vision which this book hopes to bring to the attention of those seeking to understand Quebec society.

This approach is shown clearly in the opening chapter on the state. The Quebec state is not merely a political entity; rather, as Deena White shows, the state has become a significant social player since Quebecers chose to invest "their" state with both the expertise and the political will to promote the *"projet de société."* The result is not an authoritarian state that stands above the society, but rather a democratic state that is strategically situated at the hub of social institutions and social relations. As a consequence, social groups see the state not only as a source of order, but also as a source of power for them.

Here, then, lies an important dimension of social relations and social change in Quebec society: social groups tend to be successful in promoting their own agendas to the extent that they can find a way to work through the state. The consequence is a relatively politicized, highly volatile society. On the other hand, the Quebec state itself is empowered to the extent that social groups perceive that there are structural opportunities for them to participate within it, and thus to "see" themselves in the state. Thus, in spite of the tensions created within the society by the presence of an activist state, this internal dynamic contributes to the affirmation of a collective identity embodied in the state.

In his chapter on the "idea of federalism," Louis Balthazar characterizes this dynamic as "a network of communications," a term which describes very well the loose, internal coherence of Quebec society. In his chapter, Balthazar shifts the focus to Quebec's external relations with Canada and with the other provinces. Balthazar distinguishes between Quebec's own, coherent, national self-image and the fragmented or individualistic self-image that is common in other parts of Canada. He points out that Canadians are encouraged to view themselves either as individual, right-bearing citizens, or secondarily, as members of non-territorial groups such as visible minorities or women. In contrast, the Quebec identity is that of a national and provincial community. This view encourages Quebec to take a radically federalist stand in its relations within Canada, to defend a vision of Canada as a true political federation between collectivities, rather than a melting pot or mosaic of multiple individual identities.

This notion of "a network of communications" is reflected as well in Christopher McAll's discussion of language in Quebec society. In contrast to Balthazar's macro-level approach, McAll defines a community as "a network of potential communicators and action partners." He looks at language at the micro-level of individual interactions to try to understand the dynamics of bilingualism in Quebec. The issue is not so much that English is becoming the dominant language worldwide, but rather that "similar things are happening in the Quebec private sector workplace as are happening elsewhere in bilingual environments where one of the two languages is English." He gives us a feeling for the fluidity of the boundaries of language communities in Quebec today, where the majority of people are able to speak both languages (which was not the case in the past). While language, McAll says, is reified in Quebec—has become a thing in itself—languages cannot really be separated from the people who speak them, from the relations between people themselves, and from the contexts in which they (one or another language) are spoken in everyday life.

Greg Nielsen's chapter on culture provides an analysis of Quebec's critique of federal communication policy which combines the macro- and micro-levels of analysis. By exploring the intimate link between culture and identity which characterizes the Québécois, Nielsen explains why Quebecers have been critical of federal communication policy and its agencies such as the Canadian Broadcasting Corporation. The issue, Nielsen explains, is not one of competition between Quebec and Ottawa for control of communication agencies and technologies, but the survival of Quebec's culture and its ability to control its own future. Because they fail to recognize the link between culture and identity which the Québécois take for granted, English Canadians fail to understand the real nature of Quebec's concerns, a failure which, Nielsen argues, strengthens support for sovereignty in Quebec.

Having placed such importance on preserving their own culture and developing their own identity, Quebecers in the past were not very sensitive to the needs and concerns of immigrants or ethnic minorities. This has changed in recent years, as many francophone Quebecers have begun to confront the issue of determining the place of ethnic minorities in the national community they have sought to create. The challenge that minority groups pose to Quebec and its collective project is discussed in the chapter on ethnic relations in Quebec. The authors argue that rather than adopting either the melting pot image of American society, or the multicultural mosaic image of Canada, Quebec has been seeking a compromise between the two. Ethnicity, including French-Canadian or Québécois ethnicity, is a social construction and an ongoing process, constantly open to transformations. In this light, we understand the development of Quebec's national identity as proceeding hand in hand with the recognition of Quebec's pluralism. The boundaries of the national community are not static, firmly anchored to an unchangeable "ethnic" identity. National identity not only survives, but in fact remains a dynamic social force insofar as its boundaries are continually challenged by the changing pluralism of Quebec society.

The influence of this dynamic on the constitution of Quebec's institutional infrastructure is illustrated in Marcel Fournier and Michael Rosenberg's chapter on education. As a society which is still in the process of forming, Quebecers look to education both to solve their current problems and to create the society of the future. By placing so much importance on education, however, Quebecers have made it one of the most contentious issues in Quebec society. In many ways, the example of education shows the limits of state control and the inability of the state either to legislate a new social order or to bring it about by rational planning. By looking to the state to democratize education it led instead to the subordination of the education system to bureaucratic concerns and controls; by looking to legislation on the language of education to francize immigrants it led instead to people who may speak French well but who fail to identify with the aspirations of the Québécois. In the face of such structural contradictions, there is a new awareness that the social contract between the state and civil society in Quebec must be broadened to accommodate more groups, and must be attuned to the concerns not only of the majority but of minority groups as well. There is also a new caution in Quebec over the future of education exemplified by the formation of an Estates General to study the issue of education from as many points of view as possible. Educational reforms marked the beginning of the Quiet Revolution and the curious combination of utopian zeal and rational planning which characterized it. The new caution which has shown up in the case of education—a new recognition that the state by itself may not be able to solve every problem with which it deals—may also presage a new social dynamic in Quebec society.

All of the chapters discussed so far have identified a collectivist orientation among Quebecers which, as we noted earlier, results in the promotion of certain patterns of social relations and certain ways of getting things done. The remaining chapters examine such relations within specific domains of Quebec society while at the same time showing that any notion such as that of a collectivist orientation is a shorthand term for very complex sets of social processes.

The chapter by Mona-Josée Gagnon on the labour movement suggests that the impact of Quebec's collectivist national character on social institutions is sometimes more indirect than direct. Gagnon refuses to reduce the parapolitics of union relations in Quebec to cultural particularities. Nonetheless, the distinct history of Quebec's labour movement, coloured by the emergence of Catholic unionism as well as American-style unions, has left its mark. On the one hand, current anti-labour economic and political tendencies are posing similar challenges to unions in Quebec as elsewhere in the Western world. On the other hand, the fragmented organization of the Quebec labour movement leads to a dynamic that seriously complicates the development of a common stand. Quebec union federations are always in the public eye. Like political parties, they must court the media in order to maintain their relative strength vis-à-vis each other, and to promote their differing views of labour organization: one that is similar to the highly decentralized, American model and the other a more centralized, cohesive, national model. It has therefore been impossible for the union federations to separate labour's aspirations from the aspirations of Quebec society as a whole.

In her chapter on the Quebec family, Hélène Belleau also rejects a number of myths, one being that the Quebec family was different historically from that found in any other rural society, though its modernization admittedly took longer. Another widely held belief is the domination, in the past, of the Catholic Church over family life. That, too is a myth, because despite the "public" hold of the Church on the society, people were making clear distinctions in their lives between what they chose to adhere to and what they rejected. Looking at the Quebec family today, Belleau identifies two images: a collectivist image within which the family is seen as an extension of community and as a guarantor of social solidarity; and an individualist image which emphasizes the family as an autonomous unit and the role played by individual members of the family.

Yolande Cohen and Marie-Blanche Tahon suggest that the individualist image is closer to the reality of Quebec women today. They focus on the growing independence of women vis-à-vis the family, and on the participation of women in sociopolitical and economic institutions, for example, as head of the provincial chamber of commerce, and at the head of several important ministries, and so on. Their approach diverges from that of many others presented in this book in highlighting the individual as opposed to collective participation of women in the society. They claim that the impressive position of women in Quebec society as compared to some others has less to do with the organized feminist movement than with sociopolitical factors (such as a high rate of common-law relations, a low birth rate, and the impact of the Charter of Rights). They also suggest that "popular feminism" (by which they mean "lived" feminism) is more important in Quebec than any theoretically based and politically organized forms of feminism. In addition, Cohen and Tahon reject the myth of the submissive women of the past in stating how women have taken a leading role in social development in Quebec throughout much of its history. For example, they are the leaders in the community movements mentioned in Deena White's chapter.

The chapter by Lamarche, Brunet and Rossi, focusing on Quebec's health system, confirms that Quebec is currently facing the same challenges as other provinces, and indeed, other societies throughout the West: how to maintain the gains that have been made during the development of the welfare state. In the past, Quebec built up a record of dealing with special problems in special ways, with its innovative health network held up as a model by many other nations in the throes of rapid modernization. The question remains as to what extent, as a full-fledged member of a globalizing political economy, Quebec will manage to retain its distinctive style that seeks to combine the ideals of technocratic efficiency and collective action.

Finally, we come to the chapter on social movements. There is a certain irony in including such a chapter in a collection such as this one. In what sense can we talk about social movements in a society which is collectively oriented to a *projet de société*? Is not the society as whole a kind of social movement? Certainly, it makes little sense to talk about nationalism as a social movement in a society where almost everyone is a nationalist, or of political movements in a society which is so politicized. Nevertheless, new issues and new concerns do arise in Quebec as in any other society. This is shown in Liliane Cotnoir, Louis Maheu, and Jean-Guy Vaillancourt's chapter which focuses on the ecological movement in Quebec. They examine the development of processes of negotiation and *concertation* between different ecological groups that are very different with respect to ideology and priorities, in their effort to present a common front to work through the state. Here, as elsewhere in Quebec society, we see the formulation of a "collective" approach with the aim of developing a cohesive network, as opposed to be being content with fragmentation and individualistic efforts. This is similar in some ways to the community movement discussed in White's chapter and the labour movement in Gagnon's chapter, complete with a move from being an external opponent of the state to an internal participant in its national projects.

Quebec is very much still a society which is under construction. Quebecers are still learning about each other, about their diverse visions of what their society should be, and about how to get where they want to go. This makes Quebec fascinating in itself, but it also raises significant questions for social scientists that have not yet been answered. Is the national community to which most Quebecers aspire still possible within a modern world in which the nation-state is rapidly losing its autonomy and perhaps even its legitimacy? Is Quebec out of step with the currents of change which are sweeping the world? Or is it Quebec rather than Canada which is in tune with contemporary global changes which have seen the break-up of states as different as Czechoslovakia and the Soviet Union? Are we possibly heading for a world in which ever-larger global alliances are formed among ever-smaller political units?

None of the editors of this work are so rash as to predict what the future will bring. Historical contingencies almost never show up in advance, as the break-up of the Soviet Union proved so well. As we have mentioned repeatedly throughout this introduction, however, Quebec is a society, not just a political entity. It is the understanding of that society that is the goal of this work.

REFERENCES

Berger, Peter 1969. *The Sacred Canopy*. Garden City: Doubleday.

Berger, Peter 1979. *The Heretical Imperitive*. Garden City: Doubleday.

Berger, Peter, Berger, B., Kellner, H. 1974. *The Homeless Mind*. New York: Vintage Books.

Breton, Albert 1964. 'The Economics of Nationalism'. *Journal of Political Economy*, 72: 376-386.

Cook, Ramsay 1986. *Canada, Quebec, and the Uses of Nationalism*. Toronto: McClelland and Stewart.

Fournier, Marcel 1990. 'Quebec and its Cultural Specificity Or the Construction of an Identity,' Pp. 43-69 in R. Breton et al (eds.), *National Survival in Dependent Societies: Social Change in Canada and Poland*. Ottawa: Carleton University Press.

Gagnon, Alain, Montcalm, M. 1990. *Quebec: Beyond The Quiet Revolution*. Scarborough: Nelson Canada.

Guindon, Hubert 1967. 'Two Cultures: An Essay on Nationalism, Class, and Ethnic Tension,' Pp. 33-59 in R. Leach (ed.), *Contemporary Canada*. Durham, N.C.: Duke University Press.

Handler, Richard 1988. *Nationalism and the Politics of Culture in Quebec*. Madison, Wisconsin: The University of Wisconsin Press.

Levesque, René 1976. 'For An Indepentent Quebec'. *Foreign Affairs*, 54: 734-744.

Linteau, Paul-André, Durocher, R., Robert, J-C, and **Ricard, F.** 1991. *Quebec Since 1930*. Toronto: James Lorimer.

Lower, Arthur R.M. 1977. *Colony To Nation*. Toronto: McClelland and Stewart.

Luckmann, Thomas 1967. *The Invisible Religion*. New York: Macmillan.

Magnuson, Roger 1980. *A Brief History of Quebec Education: From New France to Parti Quebecois*. Montreal: Harvest House.

McRoberts, Kenneth 1988. *Quebec: Social Change and Political Crisis*. Third Edition. Toronto: McClelland and Stewart.

Monière, Denis 1981. *Ideologies in Quebec*. Toronto: University of Toronto Press.

Morris, Raymond, Lanphier, C.M. 1977. *Three Scales of Inequality*. Don Mills: Longmans.

Porter, John 1965. *The Vertical Mosaic*. Toronto: University of Toronto Press.

Renaud, Marc 1984. 'Quebec's New Middle Class in Search of Social Hegemony,' Pp. 150-185 in A. Gagnon (ed.), *Quebec: State and Society*. Toronto: Methuen.

Rioux, Marcel 1978. *Quebec in Question*. Toronto: Lorimer.

QUEBEC STATE AND SOCIETY

INTRODUCTION

Everywhere, state-society relations are in transition. While transnational production and marketing have taken on a breadth and depth previously beyond the imagination, states of all sorts are facing serious challenges. The neo-liberal and neo-conservative scripts that they follow lead to policies that are making the rich richer, the poor, poorer. Politicians and activists who call for policies to protect domestic industries, or to protect the victims of "economic restructuring," are marginalized by the press and the political establishment. Even as misery spreads within affluent societies, governments are expected to eliminate deficit spending and to wipe out enormous public debts, regardless of how this affects its most vulnerable citizens. The "entitlement mentality" bred by the welfare state must be dispelled, we are told; individuals, families and communities will simply have to learn to fend for themselves. In this context, Canada's Prime Minister Jean Chretien recently admonished Quebec's leaders to stop blaming Ottawa for its socioeconomic problems, when it is the only province that has not (yet) subjected its citizens to draconian cuts in the areas of health and welfare.

In fact, figures reported by the federal government in 1994 suggested that the state of Quebec's fiscal health was not significantly different from that of Ottawa itself or the other provinces. Economic growth was accelerating, and the level of employment rose more than in any other province that year, due in part to a provincial programme for subsidizing job creation (Statistics Canada, 1994). Quebec politicians naturally find it useful to blame Ottawa for the province's economic ills. Economic policy is, after all, a federal responsibility. Yet, while success would be impossible to predict, there is reason to believe that economic and fiscal policy made in Quebec would be far more bold, comprehensive and strategically designed than Canada's has been, because that is Quebec's style.

In areas under its own responsibility, Quebec has a history of implementing sweeping, innovative policies on a scale that would be unimaginable in most other provinces. Its history of radical reform—sometimes verging on the social democratic, sometimes neo-liberal—dates from the Quiet Revolution of the 1960s when the state undertook a series of massive modernization projects. The political style developed then still distinguishes Quebec in important ways from other Canadian provinces. In recent years, both of Quebec's major political parties toe a line between neo-liberalism and neo-conservatism that would in many ways be familiar to most Western societies. Yet in other ways, Quebec's approach would be considered strange. While other governments are paring down the public sphere through privatization and brutal cuts to public services, the Quebec state gives no appearance of seeking to do the same. Though Quebec's governments are not adverse to user fees, welfare crackdowns and other common responses to the fiscal crisis, the tentacles of the state actually seem to be spreading further and deeper into Quebec society. More and more social groups are being drawn into collaboration with the state in efforts to construct what so many only advocate: a welfare *society*.

This chapter aims to both describe and explain this peculiarity of the state-society relation in Quebec. I will first seek to dispel or correct a certain number of myths and in so doing, clarify a fundamental difference between the way in which the state is *thought about* in Quebec, compared to Anglo-Saxon societies such as England, the U.S. and most of Canada. Then, I will illustrate the mutual embedding of the state in society, and society in the state, through a discussion of the place of expertise in Quebec's public domain. Finally, I will trace the history of an almost emblematic dimension of reform in Quebec—the emphasis on "communities" and "community participation"—showing how it has evolved in a pattern of reflexive renewal of the relation between the so-called state and social "actors" or participants. Now, at a time when investments in individual citizens are being curtailed and expertise has become an unaffordable luxury for the state, the "community" is being actively developed as a primary agent of social management.

STATE AND SOCIETY

The use of the term "state" to refer to the formal institutions of the provincial government in Quebec is not casual. The state refers to a set of organizational actors claiming a monopoly of legitimate control over a given territory and its population, and over the means of coercion. The word "claim" is perhaps the most significant in this definition (Hoffman, 1995). It indicates that control, even in the hands of state actors, is never complete. It is constantly challenged by other authorities within the society who claim control over specific social spheres, such as corporate actors in the economic sphere, professionals in the health sphere, union leaders, grass-roots activists, managers, and even the individual citizen in the sphere of private life. A shared political rationality is likely to define a society's notions about which aspects of economic, social and cultural life are legitimate objects for governance, and by which types of authorities (expert or moral, public or private), and so on.

Another important challenge to a state's monopoly of control could come from rivals for jurisdiction over a territory and its population as a whole. In the Canadian case, such rivalry between provincial and federal governments has been endemic, for under the terms of confederation, Canada has a valid claim in areas such as the economy and foreign affairs. But at least since the end of World War II, it also legislates in areas formally under provincial control, such as health and welfare. The situation is complicated by the fact that the boundaries between federal and provincial domains are fuzzy: at what point does unemployment change from being an economic problem under federal jurisdiction, to a welfare problem under provincial jurisdiction? Indeed, the emergence of a modern, assertive Quebec state in the 1960s was closely tied to the accumulation and concentration of authority at the federal level during the post-war construction of the Canadian welfare state, when such issues of jurisdiction came to the forefront. If tensions around these issues developed earlier in Quebec than in other provinces, this was because the Quebec state was actively engaged in laying claim to its own authority in these same spheres, with its own well-developed plans, tailored to its own peculiar circumstances.

To speak of the Quebec state is now common idiom within the province. But for years prior to the Quiet Revolution, any use of that term would clearly have been an exaggeration. This is because the conservative Union Nationale government, under the long-standing leadership of Maurice Duplessis, never claimed a monopoly of control within the territory.[1] In his view, formal organizations of government were to be confined to administrative tasks relating to the management of the territory, for example, the distribution of public funds to local elites for spending on public works. Their limited mandate also included a vigilant defense of the constitutional division of powers between federal and provincial governments, so that federal incursions into the areas of education, health, welfare and culture were adamantly rebuffed. But this did not mean that the provincial government claimed its own authority in these domains. On the contrary, in matters pertaining to culture and the people's welfare, the Catholic Church's authority, and its monopoly over service provision, was never contested by government leaders even if rumblings could be heard within many sectors of the society from the 1940s on. Moreover, economic issues were also deemed to be quite beyond the authority of the government, falling under the competence of English Canadian and foreign corporate and financial authorities. Prior to Duplessis' death in 1959, the government of Quebec was committed to maintaining this internal division of authority.

The Quebec state was effectively constituted through the Quiet Revolution. The objective of the elite group of francophone intellectuals, professionals and other experts who led the Liberal Party to power in 1960 was to fabricate a

---

[1] Maurice Duplessis, leader of the now-defunct, conservative Union Nationale party, was premier of Quebec almost continuously for 23 years, from 1936 to 1939, and again from 1944 to his death in 1959. From the standpoint of post-Quiet Revolution Quebec, those years are sometimes referred to as *la grande noirceur*—the dark ages.

rational, modern institutional infrastructure, in line with the province's urban industrial, social and economic needs, and capable of propelling Quebec into the twentieth century and beyond. This meant transforming a passive administrative apparatus into an activist state, able to claim its authority in a vast array of newly defined policy domains. The year 1960 is marked as the jumping-off point for a fifteen-year marathon of frenetic expansion of the government bureaucracy and the public sector. No area of the social fabric remained untouched. First and foremost, the educational system was taken over from the Church, expanded, restructured and modernized. Energy companies were nationalized to better serve industry, and an array of para-public financial and investment institutions were created to support the growth of indigenous capital. Then, all church-owned (and, in the case of minority groups, community-owned) establishments in the health and social service spheres were integrated into a new public network, restructured, extended, and consolidated under direct government authority and coordination. According to one estimate, the Quiet Revolution generated 23 new government departments, 55 consultative bodies, 63 economic management agencies, and 34 autonomous, or para-public organizations including a variety of state-owned enterprises (Lachapelle *et al*, 1993: 79).

Today, just under 150,000 people are employed in government administration alone, and this number fails to include the tens of thousands of teachers, university professors, health professionals, social workers, engineers, managers and other specialists who work in the public sector.

The ambitions of the reforming elite were sustained by enthusiastic support from members of the educated, francophone middle class, whose career paths, truncated in the anglophone-dominated private sector, comfortably merged with the bureaucratic development of the state and its growing numbers of public and parapublic organizations and enterprises (Guindon, Renaud). But popular support for the radical modernization of familiar institutions could hardly be taken for granted. Indeed, the alternation between progressive (Liberal) and conservative (Union Nationale) governments during the 1960s testifies to the precarious legitimacy of the reform movement. Until this time, government had been a remote affair for most people. Political bonds were strongest at the local level, where familiar *"notables"* (the curé, the doctor, the notary, small businessmen and the deputé) constituted the influencial figures in the community. They in turn were endorsed by Church leaders who claimed "dictatorial" power within both the religious and lay communities (Desbarats, 1965).

By dismantling traditional institutions or targeting them for radical modernization, the reforming elite risked alienating more people than it satisfied.

In the early days of the Quiet Revolution, then, consensus building was a major challenge for the reforming elite. A major strategy in this effort involved the redirection of the powerful national identity of Quebec's population. The cultural identity of the French-Canadian people had been embodied in and nourished by the Church for a hundred years. It was expressed not only through religion, but also through language and custom—the stuff of all national communities. Furthermore, this cultural community was institutionally complete. It had generated its own distinctive health, education and welfare establishments, a unique, cooperative banking network, an independent union movement, local political elites and an abundance of parish-based voluntary associations. In all these secular areas, the Church leadership had played an influential and often controlling role. The authority of the Church, particularly outside the spiritual realm, was increasingly coming under attack within the society as a whole. Still, the new state elite did *not* aspire to take over from the Church. It rather aspired to transform the relations of authority within the province by radically democratizing public participation in social, cultural and political affairs through the creation of a broad, dynamic public sphere.

This meant transforming an inward-looking community into a outward-looking one. Two different images of this new political identity vied for dominance. One was liberal and individualistic, notably promoted by Pierre Elliott Trudeau and others in the influential review, *Cité-Libre*. The aim expressed by this movement was to create the conditions for French-Canadians to become equal and unexceptional citizens of Canada, participating in the prosperity of the emerging Canadian welfare state. The Church was rebuked for preaching against such participation. Nationalism, because of its close association to traditional, Church-supported values, was anathema to these intellectuals. But the image of the secular, free-standing citizen in a faceless, mass society, especially one in which French-Canadians felt themselves to be foreigners due to language and customs, never captured the imagination of the general population. It allowed no place at all for the self-image of a people whose identity as members of a solid, separate national community was unquestionable.

This alien political image was rivalled by another that instead translated national identity into a modern form. It was taken up by Quebec's ascending state elite in its efforts to forge a bond with the people. For even as they hacked away at traditional institutions, they saw little point in trying to destroy the enduring collective identity of the French-Canadian people. To build consensus and social solidarity in times of rapid and radical change, they could adopt no more common or efficient strategy than "to appeal for their authority to already crystallized national identities" (Cerny, p.98). Recycling certain symbols of collective identity such as language, they banished other more traditional and moralistic symbols promoted by the Church in favour of an activist, participative, forward-looking identity, embodied in the state. Thus, Premier Jean Lesage argued in 1961:

> The current situation forces us to rethink our traditional positions. We need powerful means, not only to meet the inevitable challenges that we will face in the coming years, but also to put the French-Canadian people in tune with the present-day world. Now, the only powerful means that we have is the Quebec State, *our* state. We cannot afford the luxury of not using it. (quoted in Pelletier, 1992: 617, translated by the author.)

This transformed nationalism was reinforced not by moralistic exhortations, but by new forms of knowledge. Historical and sociological interpretations of Quebec's place in the modern world (Dofny, Rioux) were deployed, as were federal and provincial statistics that documented the systematic socioeconomic inequality of, and discrimination against French-speaking Canadians, both inside and outside Quebec (Bernard, Boisjoly, 1992). If religion and tradition were gradually shed as the hallmarks of a collective identity, these new forms of knowledge ensured that language, at least, would persist in symbolizing the boundaries of a structurally distinct and defensive social collectivity within Canada. They also ensured that in the emerging new political rationality, Quebec's welfare would not be blindly entrusted to Canadian authorities; Quebecers would become, as Lesage declared, "maîtres chez nous"—masters in their own home.

The Quebec state has thus been, from its inception, a nationalist state, or, to use the more familiar term, a "nation-state." Its territorial boundaries symbolically correspond to the boundaries of national identity. The society that it represents, or embodies, is bounded by national symbols such as language and culture, and bonded by national identity. In this way, it is far more similar to European nation-states such as England, France and Germany than it is to the United States or to other Canadian provinces. The state apparatus that burgeoned during the Quiet Revolution has a wholly francophone face, for it is over the public sphere that the francophone majority has, since the 1960s, asserted its "ownership." This public homogeneity in what is essentially a pluralistic society, has been a source of considerable political tension, and will be discussed at length in the chapter relating to ethnic relations. But it is no accident that in the present discussion, where the state-society relationship is the focus, minorities will be conspicuously absent. This is a reflection of the concrete absence of non-francophones from the public sphere. Indeed, the very knowledge base that has supported the development of the Quebec state and society since the 1960s has been based on perspectives which confound the concepts of nation, society and state.

Precisely because Quebec is decidedly not a uniform society, despite the cultural homogeneity of its public authorities, its political culture is characterized by an unusual mix of individualist and collectivist images. Both images exist in most modern societies, of course. In the Anglo-Saxon tradition, upheld in societies such as the English and American, for example, the pre-eminence of the individual, of the private sphere over the state, is most vivid in the public imagination. Indeed, the state and civil society are typically understood as facing off against each other in a contest where a limited state and extensive individual liberty are the ideal outcome. Of course, this does not preclude the existence of powerful collective idioms such as "Uncle Sam" or simply, "the national interest." Nevertheless, their collective sense is less strong than in non-Anglo-Saxon, continental European societies such as the French and German—and in Quebec— where the collective dimension of society is more powerful in the public imagination. These societies reflect a more organic concept of the state-society relation, where the state is seen as a legitimate, dynamic component of a complex social order, but one which nonetheless has an inherent unity. Private citizens, whether they support or oppose the existing order, are likely to work *through* the state to achieve their ends. To empower the state is to empower the society as a whole. This collectivist predisposition is not likely to disappear in Quebec, embedded as it is in a long-standing national identity. It adds an interesting twist to an otherwise conventional, liberal-democratic political culture.

Claims to a monopoly of authority within Quebec by provincial political elites have been sufficiently successful to forge a robust state in Quebec, thanks to the consensus-building power of a national identity, though the nature and extent of its sovereignty remains ambiguous and a prominent subject of political contention. The state derives its strength not only by virtue of such claims, however, but also by virtue of their enactment. One finds in Quebec a mutual investment of the state in the society, and the society in the state, in accordance with an "organic" political rationality. Growing emphasis over the years on relations between the provincial and federal governments has served to reinforce the collectivist tendency, since it is in its relations with "others" that the state most evidently represents the society as a whole. In its internal relations, this tendency is also evident in the mutual mobilization of private citizens or social groups and state actors in grand, collective projects—*projets de société*. The various strategic mechanisms by which people are linked up with the state (and vice versa) are the subject of the remaining sections of this chapter.

EXPERTISE IN AND AROUND THE STATE

Why does Quebec tend to formulate and adopt policies that often appear radical and utopian, and to develop wall-to-wall structures for their rational and thorough implementation? Quebec's capacity for continuous self-renewal, well beyond the Quiet Revolution, is generally attributed to the authority of the state, supposedly the motor of social change. Through its many public and para-public agencies, establishments and enterprises, the state has indeed developed its capacity to play a leading role in shaping the society. On the one hand, people with the intellectual, professional or technical authority to develop coherent, ambitious social programs and to put them in practice, choose to invest in the state. They do so in part because that is how they think about the state-society relation but also, on a more pragmatic level, because the Quebec state has systematically created the structural opportunities for them to promote their ideas and practices in the public domain, i.e. to "make things happen." On the other hand, the harnessing of expertise to the state is common to welfare states everywhere, and although it may be exceptionally well developed in Quebec, the simple presence of experts in and around the state does not explain their policy style. For, in contrast to most other welfare states, Quebec's policies tend to be more comprehensive than incremental, more strategic than reactive, and more sweeping than piecemeal, disjointed or partial.

One answer lies in the conditions surrounding the emergence of the state. We have seen that Quebec embodies an important consensus-building potential that is shared by many nation-states: the ability to appeal to a robust collective imagination, and to symbolize policies in terms of national character and pride. This is a valuable resource for politicians and technocrats, yet while the Americans, for example, share the capacity to call on "patriotism," for a whole host of reasons they still find it almost impossible to adopt and enact comprehensive reforms (Marmor, 1992). In the United States, Canada and other societies, development has occurred over a long period, and there has been an accumulation of entrenched policy inconsistencies, constantly reinforced by particular and *ad hoc* interests within the society. In contrast, social development in Quebec has been an exceptionally rapid and reflexive process.

Giddens (1994) has drawn a distinction between simple and reflexive modernization. He argues that the processes documented and analyzed by the classical sociologists such as Weber and Durkheim reflected a past time of simple modernization in which new social structures emerged through complex but generally unintentional sociopolitical and economic processes. Efforts to control development through reform tended to be modest, narrow, and hesitant. In contrast, recent welfare state development has been a more intentional process. It has been able to benefit from the birth of the social sciences, for example. It has been influenced to a greater or lesser extent by the international diffusion of statistical and other information concerning ongoing social, political, cultural and economic processes, and by various theories of social change in general. On the basis of accumulated knowledge and interpretations of past events, policy-making emerges as a teleological process, that is, a process directed towards certain aims and ends. It is reflexive in so far as social authorities come to contemplate and act upon their own societies in intentional ways. Unlike the piecemeal, reactive reforms of simple modernization, reform takes on a more rational and utopian character. Quebec's policy style can almost serve as the archetypal case.

As far back as the 1930s, a number of renowned American sociologists from the University of Chicago came to study social change in French Canada. Uniquely in North America, Quebec society afforded them a context in which to gather rich ethnographic data on a time supposedly gone by, on ways of life just then being ruffled by the forces of industrialization and urbanization, and on a traditional society feeling the reverberations of the secular, modern world surrounding it. Their books, including, for example, Horace Miner's *St. Denis: A French Canadian Parish* (1939) and Everett C. Hughes' *French Canada in Transition* (1943), were widely studied in Quebec's intellectual circles and heavily influenced the development of the social sciences in the province's francophone universities. Quebec's early sociologists carried out their own studies along similar lines, arguing that the Church's moral and conservative interpretations of French-Canadian society had to be replaced by more rational, scientific forms of analysis (Falardeau, 1944, 1953, 1964), which was a theme echoed in non-academic reviews, such as

Cité Libre, as well. In the universities, the image of a slowly transforming French-Canadian community rather quickly gave way to more complex and subtle analyses in which it was argued that Quebec was an already modern, complex, industrial society whose traditional institutions were inadequate to deal with contemporary social and economic realities (Dumont, Rocher, 1961). This preoccupation with social scientific analysis contributed as much to defining the means and ends of the Quiet Revolution as did any political ideology.[2]

The consequence of this unusual set of circumstances was the emergence of a highly intellectual, technocratic political style that included a penchant for the elaboration of highly rational, comprehensive policies, justified by social scientific theory and logical analysis.[3] For example, note the neutral, sociological terminology and tone in this excerpt from the report of the Castonguay-Nepveu Commission of Enquiry into Health and Welfare, which served as the blueprint for the construction of the massive health network mentioned above:

> Change provokes rapid urbanization which uproots a great number of citizens, transplanting them within vast centres where they suffer from isolation and solitude. The accelerated technical evolution rejects a mass of workers from the labour force and the displacement of industrial production demands increasingly greater employment mobility. These phenomena contribute to the disorientation of citizens, bring about profound repercussions on the relations of men among themselves and provoke alienation, isolation and solitude. It is therefore important the society set up a development policy which neutralizes as much as possible the negative effects of change and which adjusts itself to the realities of a complex life. (Commission, 1970, Part I, Vol. 3, No. 1: 18)

This faith in the power of social science also had the consequence of encouraging an attitude bordering on arrogance (Renaud, Doré, White, 1989). In the same report, it is claimed that "social development must shape society *as a sculptor shapes a block of stone ...*" (Commission, 1971: 19, author's italics). Success was to be assured by "science and modern technique" (p. 199) on the one hand, and on the other, by "the power and resources of the state to initiate such a vast undertaking" (p. 227). As an American advisor to the Commission of Enquiry noted:

---

[2] The political ideologies vying for influence at the time of the quiet revolution still represent the principal ideological divide in Quebec today: at one pole, liberal individualism and at the other, collectivist nationalism. But the nationalism emerging in the years prior to and during the Quiet Revolution was itself an intellectual product of the social sciences. Strongly opposed to the traditional and conservative ideology preached by the Church, it was formulated during the 1950s on the basis of a secular reinterpretation of Quebec's history, and a structural interpretation of its current social and economic problems. See for example, Behiels, 1984.

[3] It may or may not be considered pertinent to mention that the early reformers in Quebec had all benefited from a classical education—the only kind available in Quebec *colleges* before the Quiet Revolution—which fostered proficiency in a highly deductive, Cartesian form of reasoning. Their policy-making style may be considered an excellent example of this.

The extraordinary opportunity presented to a small group of dedicated individuals to study the problems, devise proposed solutions and then endeavour to implement them from positions of power is probably without parallel elsewhere in the world (Lee, 1979: 53).

This is very likely true. It might explain, in part, the utopianism inherent in the sweeping reforms that continued in the same vein right up to the end of the 1970s. Utopianism was also sustained, however, by the social scientists' obsession with the tremendous potential of the state to enact the aspirations of social movements: first, the modernization movement that brought about the Quiet Revolution, and later, the nationalist movement, particularly in its social-democratic guise promoted by the Parti Québécois in the early 1970s. In fact, when the Parti Québécois first came to power in 1976, an important portion of the intellectual community in Quebec, of which sociologists were a significant element, "took power." New blood in the state bureaucracy was to a large extent drawn from university departments, and individuals with social science training took up positions as cabinet members, heads of government enterprises, and even as deputy minister (Renaud, Doré, White, 1989).

At the same time, serious questions were beginning to be posed by many Quebec sociologists (Fortin, 1981). Analyzing the reform processes of the Quiet Revolution, some began to accuse the state of bureaucratic and technocratic overdevelopment, and even of authoritarianism (Renaud, 1977). Yet, as an indication of the extent to which the social sciences have become the idiom of Quebec politics, those very same indictments have turned up in recent government reports (e.g. Rochon, 1988) in which the inefficiency of the public sector is attributed in part to inter-professional and inter-organizational rivalry. Reforms are then developed simply to restructure social relations that characterize the public system, be they relations between professions, between organizations, or between citizens and the system. Thus, even though change is attempted based on the basis their critique, technocratic tendencies persist. A new mental health policy adopted in 1989 temporarily impeded the ongoing *ad hoc* development of community resources by setting up committees to spend a year assessing regional needs, and elaborating comprehensive, regional service organizational plans.

Social, economic and cultural development in Quebec has clearly been highly technocratic, with changes in almost any domain passing, either directly or indirectly, through the state. But despite a policy style engineered by the state, it would be a misconception to view the Quebec state as autocratic, or even to see Quebec reforms as unilaterally "top-down." Indeed, compared to recent cost-saving policies unilaterally imposed by the governments of Alberta and Ontario, for example, Quebec's more reflexive style means that policies tend to require meticulous justification in terms of their long-term impact on different social groups, in addition to consultation with the full range of interested experts both in and around the state. Now, this style can be as paralyzing as it is enabling. The reason its paralyzing effects are far less apparent is that reflexive social development and social management is not an exclusive domain of state authorities.

The Quiet Revolution was far more than an assertion and expansion of the authority of the state. Not only did the reforming elite begin its intellectual campaign long before the state's new form was even imagined, but at the same time, militant, grass-roots groups were mushrooming in urban neighbourhoods, initiating local action for change from the bottom up. They influenced future government programmes through the establishment of popular clinics and other community action projects, and, as we shall see in the following sections, similar grass-roots movements have had a major influence on seemingly top-down reforms to this very day. In fact, the mutual embeddedness of state and society has resulted in a certain common ground and relatively fluid movement between "lay experts" in social activist groups and certain "radical" professionals in the public sector. So while Quebec can undoubtedly be characterized as a highly technocratic society, this is countered by it also being a highly politicized, rather than a passive society.

STATE AND COMMUNITY: THE EVOLUTION OF AN INTIMATE RELATION

In this section, the relation between state and lay or "community" authorities is analysed as an illustration of the diverse mechanisms by which the local and central, state and non-state actors are linked up in Quebec. Similar analyses might have been presented with reference to the economic sphere (Smith) or the cultural sphere (Bélavance, Fournier, 1992), for example. For in these areas and others, the mutual investment of the private and public sectors—indeed, the absence of a clear distinction between them in some cases—is equally outstanding. But the "community" has provided one of the most prominent political idioms in Quebec. Its particular power in Quebec may lie in its ability to translate traditional heritage and collective identity into political action. It recalls the central social and cultural role played by the rural parish in the already mythical near-history of the society—mythical because analysts do not all agree with the Chicago School's original portrayal of pre-war French Canada as an ideal-typical "folk community" (Garigue, 1958).

The parish was one of the dominant organizing institutions in urban as well as rural Quebec. In the big city, it guaranteed a certain level of local social cohesiveness and personal identification with the *quartier* or neighbourhood, while organizing nearly all of the local institutions, from schools and hospitals to voluntary associations and recreational facilities. Indirect ties between parish life and the world of work were also constructed through the Church's role in organizing unions. But links to a wider public or political sphere were almost nonexistent. With the Quiet Revolution, this was to change (Godbout, 1985). The state and its centralized institutions took on a more salient role in peoples' lives. Familiar figures no longer served to bind local institutions, such as the school, to the community; they were gradually replaced by experts and bureaucrats *acting* at the local level, but clearly not indigenous. But not all those ties that were to bind the local functions to the centre originated in the state. Rather, there was an almost parallel invasion of both state and community by the new, progressive, professional and para-professional middle class.

Even before the new state could absorb many of the graduating university students trained, during the late 1950s and early 1960s, in innovative forms of social analysis and social work, these restless experts were plying their trade at the local level, which was the only level where the opportunities could be created. They were "radical" to the extent that they bypassed traditional local elites and the Church, and set their objectives well beyond conventional philanthropy and social casework. Their aims were analogous to those of the state reformers: they sought to replace conservative, parish-based associations with more progressive, activist groups working to bring about social change. Community organizers, like other early reformers, were inspired by the Chicago School tradition of joining the sociological analysis of communities with social activism, such as the development of local leadership and institutions. But their organizing techniques and skills were ultimately perfected through the study of more aggressive American models of community action. These included Saul Alinsky's confrontational approach to self-empowerment for citizen groups (Alinsky, 1969, 1972), and the War Against Poverty, which had also become increasingly confrontational in character until the early termination of its funding.[4] What these models of community organizing had in common was that, despite a discourse emphasizing self-empowerment, self-help, and the development of local institutions, the advancement of local interests was seen to be guaranteed only through confrontation (or occasionally, cooperation) with authorities *outside* the community. Indeed, Quebec's new middle class militants themselves came from outside the working class communities they organized. They constituted some of the first links between local social groups and a public sphere of social management.

No wonder a certain affinity has always seemed to exist between state and community rhetoric, particularly in the broad areas of health and welfare. But the ties are much more profound than that, as demonstrated by the history of social reform in Quebec, reinforced by the very recent discourse of the Minister of Income Security:

> Some (community initiatives and practices) are extraordinarily innovative and illustrate particularly well the new logic of poverty as well as new forms of action. Led by community organizations, these new practices are centred on new fields of activity, in response to newly emerging needs; they are founded on

---

[4] The American War Against Poverty was a short-lived federal project initiated by President Lyndon B. Johnson in the mid-1960s. Borrowing an idea from community development in the Third World, it involved the funding of community projects organized by local groups having no official status or connections to any "establishment" organizations. Community organizers disseminated information within needy neighbourhoods and provided help in developing projects, applying for funds and implementing programmes.

novel partnerships with local collectivities. Their originality lies in their basing themselves on the daily practices of the population and on the relations that constitute the fabric of local life... *It is therefore essential that the state provide them all the support they need.* (Blackburn, 1995: 169 (italics added))

COMMUNITY ORGANIZATION, SYSTEM INTEGRATION AND DEPENDENT PARTICIPATION

One of the most significant infrastructural reforms in Quebec was the Health and Social Service Social reform of 1972. It integrated all general and specialized hospitals, social service centres, most convalescent and rehabilitation facilities, and all major social service agencies. It also introduced an entirely new type of small, participatory, socio-health care establishment, the CLSC (Centre Local de Services Communautaires, or Local Community Service Centre). The Commission of Enquiry that developed the blueprint for this reform began its work in 1966. By this time, community action was already well developed in both urban and rural regions of the province. It was to have a significant impact on the new policy rhetoric as well as the structuring of the new health and social service network and its evolution.

One of the earliest forms that community action took during the time of the Quiet Revolution was the *comité de citoyens* (citizens' committee). These committees emerged in deteriorating, urban working class neighbourhoods and rural areas facing rapid modernization and threats to independent forms of production. They would consist of 20 or 30 local people receiving guidance and training from "radical" professionals, disaffected with the traditional role assigned to social work by the Church-run bureaucracies. They would sometimes be financed through charitable organizations or donations and federal local initiative grants when these became available in the early 1970s. In some cases, as many as 300 citizens would participate in the activities organized by these committees around such issues as housing, health or urban renewal. Some would offer direct services to the community, such as health care, legal aid, tenants' rights protection, food co-ops and day care. The committees' objectives went beyond local organizing, however, to include advocacy and the lobbying of public authorities for such collective services as parks and recreation facilities for youths, or more and better schools. Individual *comités de citoyens* might group together to reinforce the authority of their demands.

While the citizens' committees presented themselves as radical alternatives to traditional social services, they greatly interested some members of the reforming elite who were involved in elaborating health and social service policy. In fact, the reform eventually introduced a specific response to community action: the CLSC. The CLSCs were to be an original type of public establishment: small, non-bureaucratic and geared to respond to locally expressed needs. They were to focus on community development and prevention rather than traditional casework and medical services, and they were to to encourage accessibility and citizen participation. Eventually, 160 of these organizations were established in communities across the province. Through the CLSCs, it was believed that citizens' autonomous activities could be integrated with public health and social service activities.

Extensive citizen participation in the CLSCs was foreseen by the reform. Not only were citizens awarded seats on the management committees of the CLSCs, but even more, the establishment of each CLSC was delegated to existing or new coalitions of citizens' committees, working with a professional community organizer appointed by the state. The real power of the citizens was to prove illusory, however. Instead, community organizers revelled in their new, official professional status. Instead of "organizing" the community, they turned to "organizing" (unionizing) the CLSCs themselves. Furthermore, the activists-turned-professionals now developed their own definitions of community needs and the programmes required to meet those needs. Citizen members of the boards were left in a dependent, powerless position in relation to the assertions of organizational and professional ambitions. Most withdrew; a few remained in an ineffectual, token or subordinate role. The turbulent first five years of CLSC development thus pitted citizens against professionals, and professionals against administrators and the state, resulting in the unofficial banishment of community organization as a primary CLSC activity, and a turn towards less radical, though nonetheless innovative forms of socio-health service delivery. The implications of integration into the public sphere were finally confirmed by the Ministry of Social Affairs:

> I don't think you are expecting excuses from me for the government's control over CLSCs. This control is the normal and inseparable counterpart of our responsibilities, which are challenged much less frequently ... the State defines the goals of a programme like the CLSCs and provides the means for carrying them out. The responsibility delegated by the State concerns the way these means are used to achieve the goals ... participation must be seen in this context. Let there be no confusion: participation does not mean that the State abdicates its role; it merely shares it ... the proportions in which it is shared can of course be challenged, but not the basic idea. (quoted in Lesemann, 1994: 260).

Within the public sector, the CLSCs are clearly "community" organizations, differing in size, mandate, structure and organizational style from any other public establishment. The type of professionalism that they embody is still less medicalized, specialized, bureaucratic and technocratic than any large health organization or social service agency. To the groups that continue to emerge through autonomous action, however, CLSCs are now considered mini-institutions.

As the CLSCs were "tamed," they eventually came to be used by the state to implement universal programmes at the local level, including, for example, health services in the schools and workplace, para-natal services and home-care services. Their role within the public sector also shifted: the CLSCs were reinforced as primary health and social service organizations, a relatively inexpensive alternative, for minor health problems, to emergency wards or the doctor's office. Some CLSCs have managed to retain a fairly high level of community involvement, while others, particularly those established in a second wave of development in the 1980s, are far less engaged. But all of them now provide at least some technical support for the creation and administration of local, non-profit organizations and self-help groups. They remain a highly innovative and flexible component of the public health and social service network, and an important, accessible public presence at the local level, especially in rural areas and working class neighbourhoods.

But because the CLSC mandates are tightly regulated by the state, and their budgets fixed accordingly, the limitations of the state's "integrationist" strategy have become increasingly apparent. As new problems emerge in local communities resulting from social changes such as rising unemployment and poverty, the deinstitutionalization of the mentally ill, the public exposure of domestic violence and so on, it is always autonomous community action that responds first. Disorderly, *ad hoc* social development and social management persist, then, on the margins of the comprehensive, rationalized, integrated public service network.

LIGHT STRUCTURES: *LA CONCERTATION* AND PARTNERSHIP

The integration of social experts into a structured public sphere such as the CLSC network was effective in so far as it made it possible for the state to harness, and to rationalize the deployment of this vast expertise to broad objectives of social management. But it was inefficient in many ways, and incomplete. On the one hand, the rigid structuring of professional roles and organizational mandates and relations has led to internal rivalries between different professional groups and between different sorts of establishments. One analysis declared that the system was being held "hostage" by the various interest groups it integrated (Rochon, 1988). On the other hand, it left numerous structural "holes" in the system—"unmet needs" in the health and social service jargon—and inhibited the kind of flexibility and innovation that would otherwise have permitted professionals and other experts to be more responsive to emerging problems and changes in the social environment. In contrast, flexibility and continued innovation became the hallmarks of the self-renewing, autonomous community sector.

A study published in 1975 counted 138 *groupes populaires*[5] in the Montreal region alone (Collin, Godbout, 1975). This represents considerable activity at the grass-roots level, during a period when professionals who were integrated into the public sphere were working to establish their own authority in areas such as

---

[5] *Groupes populaires*, meaning grass-roots groups, refers to voluntary associations that provide or promote autonomous, user-run, alternative forms of community development or social service that both supplement and challenge the form and content of public and private for-profit services. They do not include more traditional voluntary associations such as Golden Age Clubs, sports and leisure clubs, philanthropic organizations, unions and professional associations.

community health and community organizing (for example, in the CLSCs). By 1990, over 1,000 more *groupes populaires* had been created throughout the province. Of course, the notorious instability of such organizations, particularly due to funding problems, has meant that most have relatively short or erratic lifespans, sometimes reincarnating themselves several times over. Most of these organizations actively resist the status of "complementary" or "auxiliary" services in relation to the existing public network of services. They define themselves instead as user-controlled alternatives to the medical and para-medical establishment and street-level bureaucracies of the public network. From the perspective of public authorities, however, these independent organizations provide services that nicely complement those offered in the public sector, especially in times of austerity when expensive public services cannot be expanded. The challenge is to link them up to public programmes.

La concertation, a buzzword in Quebec since the 1970s, refers to a strategy for harmonizing activities in the public and private spheres without subordinating one to the other. While this discussion focuses on state-community relations, *la concertation* as a model of participation actually originated in a series of economic "summits" organized by the government during the 1970s, with a view to achieving some level of consensus between union, business and state authorities. Unlike corporatism, *la concertation* is not a formal structure of participation but depends instead on the willingness of various authorities to participate. In the health and social service field, its aim is not to directly structure the organization and activities of social actors, nor to directly control their objectives through, for example, contracting. It aims, instead, to align independent social action with policies being promoted by the state, and to coordinate the activities of autonomous community groups and public social support in the pursuit of those policies. *La concertation* takes place at the level of national, regional and local planning in fairly narrowly defined domains such as mental health or youth protection. The autonomy and equal position of each group of organizational participants is ostensibly respected, regardless of status, size, qualifications of the staff or its ideology. Consensus, often stated to be the ultimate objective of *la concertation*, is an elusive goal (Billette, 1995). Nonetheless, *la concertation* has recently come to be touted by politicians as the "Quebec model."

The implementation of Quebec's first official mental health policy, adopted in 1989, provides an excellent example of *la concertation* and partnership planning. An objective of the policy was to develop non-profit community support organizations for the non-institutionalized mentally ill to complement the more specialized and expensive services offered in the public sector, usually by hospital clinics. The policy required the regional health and social service authorities to draw up regional plans for the provision of a full range of mental health services in their territories. They were to do this *in concert* with three identified "partners" or stakeholders: 1) the psychiatric establishment, 2) autonomous non-profit organizations offering alternative mental health resources, and 3) representatives of the "community at large," usually consisting of delegates from municipalities, police forces, welfare offices or educational institutions, and occasionally from independent, voluntary associations serving, for example, women, addicts or youth. For the first time, traditional professionals found themselves forced to debate and negotiate, face to face, with an equal number of lay experts who did not share their definitions of mental illness and its treatment, nor their definition of the proper means and basis for discussion and planning. The exchange of pithy data and executive decision-making were foreign to the independent participants, who were themselves more at ease with debates on fundamental issues, and decision-making by hard-won consensus. The confrontation of these two universes under the auspices of the technocratic regional authorites was experienced by community participants to be a case of "culture shock" (Guay, 1992). Regional plans were produced, though the respective roles assigned to the different partners with respect to service delivery were rarely satisfying for any of the participants. They did occasionally succeed in shifting the principal focus of mental health services in a region, however, from public sector establishments to independent, non-profit establishments.

The result of this and a multitude of similar experiences of *concertation* in Quebec has been the emergence of a state-community relation in which confrontation and cooperation coexist as two sides of an ongoing relation. The Quebec literature on the subject of *la concertation* has identified this paradoxical relationship through such terms such as "cooperative conflict" (Dommergues, 1988; Doré, 1990; Lévesque, Mager, 1992), "contradictory participation" (Maclouf, 1985; Gagnon, Klein, 1991), or "critical cooperation" (Panet-Raymond, Bourque, 1991; Lamoureux, 1994). Social groups both confront the state, opposing its controlling, technocratic inclinations, and participate in debates and negotiations about the ways and means, as well as the ends of social management and development. In fact, *la concertation* may indeed be a "Quebec model" in so far as it blends the Anglo-Saxon tradition of autonomous social groups versus the state, and the Continental tradition of autonomous social groups working through the state.

Like all technocratic strategies, *la concertation* seeks to manage political and ideological differences within the society, to smooth the way for developing creative, cooperative solutions to social problems. But it also carries a risk of depoliticizing communities through participation in groups that are drawn into sterile, "managed" exercises, for example, to "prioritize" needs within a community, which masquerade as discussion, debate and negotiation. The more that the corridors of communication between social participants and the state are structured and institutionalized through the increased use of *tables de concertation*, the more social groups are indirectly integrated into the public sphere. The recent formation of a Secretariat de l'Action Communautaire (Secretariat of Community Action), affiliated directly with the premier's office, illustrates the problem. The mandate of the Secretariat is to facilitate access to government resources by community groups. According to the government communiqué announcing this move,

> Madame Lapointe [special advisor to the premier on community action] envisaged that the creation of the Secretariat would provide more direct access by the community sector to government, and also respond to the government's need to be better informed on the concerns and needs of community organizations.... Amongst the mandates of the secretariat [are]... *to elaborate a global policy of government support for community action* in a spirit of decentralization, to favour concerted action between the ministries and the organizations concerned with community affairs, and to support innovative projects. .. [The government] wants to create a *light structure* but one whose *official character* will give real credibility to this sector at the governmental level (Leclerc, 1995: 26; author's translation, italics added).

A profusion of "light structures" for linking independent social authorities to the state, and vice versa, has thus been added to the "heavy," rigid structures of the public network. However, while *la concertation* establishes lines of communication and increases the level and varieties of social participation in the formulation and implementation of state policies, it is not clear that it produces the consensus and coordination that state authorities, since the Quiet Revolution, have considered essential to the promotion of rational and efficient social management.

INTERMEDIARY STRUCTURES AND THE SOCIAL ECONOMY

The integration of expertise into public networks on the one hand, and the establishment of indirect links with autonomous "lay experts" through *la concertation* on the other, seem to represent opposite poles on the spectrum of state-society links. In the first situation, the state has fairly direct control over social expertise through its participation in public organizations, and can steer their practices towards state policy ends, as was the case with the CLSCs; in the second, control is minimal, and depends upon the capacity of the state to orchestrate cooperative encounters between its own authorities and relatively autonomous groups of participants in the society. But links between the public and private spheres are also woven without the benefit of technocratic involvement. This is where professionals harnessed to the state pursue their private work around the structures that control their activities, in order to pursue private, professional or organizational objectives. In so doing, they meet up with independent authorities such as ethnic community leaders, social advocates or non-profit organizations that either share their objectives, or require what the public sector has: funds and clientele. The result is the "intermediary structure:" an administratively independent, non-profit organization linked by contract or service agreement to the public sector. In this arrangement, public sector professionals or bureaucrats will usually retain clinical or other forms of indirect authority over practices within the intermediary structure. They may even create new non-profit organizations that are nominally independent, but function entirely under their authority.

Health and welfare are the two areas in which this type of indirect linkage between public and private spheres is most prominent. For example, in the mental health field, deinstitutionalization created insurmountable problems for hospital-bound professionals who had, first, to find non-institutional housing for former patients, and second, ensure continuity between their own, medically oriented interventions and those innovative forms of social support that their former patients would need in the community milieu. These challenges were met by contracting with para-professionals outside the public sector to provide specific services for former in-patients who, although no longer hospitalized, were still under the care of the hospital's out-patient staff. The traditional prototype for this kind of structural relationship is the foster home, a private enterprise accepting residents who remain under the clinical authority of a hospital's psychiatric or social work staff. But Quebec's professionals and para-professionals have greatly diversified the intermediary model. The foster home and other traditional profit-making models have been almost entirely abandoned in favour of a wide variety of non-profit structures and mutual arrangements between public professionals and lay authorities. They include housing for former psychiatric patients, providing different kinds and levels of staff support according to need, as well as day centres offering various types of skill development or leisure activities. Sometimes, these organizations are developed as mini-networks, providing an interlocking range of community programs. Contracting arrangements usually mean that certain regulations that apply to the public institution must be maintained in the non-profit organization. For example, a minimum staff-client ratio must be maintained, and staff responsibility for the client is clearly defined. Intermediary structures in the mental health field therefore differ in important ways from autonomous, user-controlled community groups that may provide somewhat similar services (White, Mercier, 1991).

In the area of social assistance, the same strategy has taken on a far more systematic orientation. A new welfare policy adopted in 1989 required that employability-development programmes be made available to all welfare recipients who wanted to participate. Because of the prevailing spirit of suspicion and distrust with respect to people on welfare, public authorities were intent on maintaining a high level of control over services provided to this group. Yet the fiscal crisis prevented the extension of the public sector to provide employability services under the direct authority of the state. Instead, intermediary models were adopted in a systematic fashion. Programmes were developed by state authorities working in the Ministry of Income Security; existing community groups that had worked for years in the area of employability were drawn into the programmes, attracted the funding and the steady flow of clients referred by the welfare offices. These same attractions led to the development of many new non-profit organizations that came into existence solely on the basis of the new welfare programmes. All these non-profit groups are linked to the state by means of contracts with local welfare offices or with the central ministry. While they remain administratively independent, and work with their clients in their own fashion, the contracts impose policy objectives and regulations on these organizations. These include, for example, rules of accessibility to the various employability programmes, limits to the duration of programmes, and quotas for job placement at the end of a client's participation (McAll, White *et al*, 1996).

Contracting out with non-profit groups for the delivery of public services is hardly unique to Quebec. In fact, in the U.S., this is the principal means by which states provide public social services for their citizens. What is characteristic of Quebec is rather the strategic, comprehensive and almost utopian vision that frames the development of the community sector. The formulation and implementation of "community-based" social policy that is epitomized by the development of the public CLSC network represents an enduring bias that takes diverse forms, including the indirect integration of community groups through contracting, and their arm's length integration through *la concertation*. But the inclination towards community integration in the public sphere is taking on new, more sweeping dimensions as a means of combating the negative social effects of repeated recessions and economic restructuring. For example, in 1994 the government put in motion a plan to create 800 intermediary structures to provide short-term work experience for people on welfare. And in 1995, the Secretariat for Community Action, mentioned above, was launched to encourage the establishment of independent self-help or collective, voluntary action groups. The Quebec state is not simply investing in community action, but is actively and systematically developing a substantial non-profit sector, which it calls the *économie sociale*.

This model for adapting to the local, destabilizing effects of the global economy has its roots in the French literature on social policy (Lipietz, 1990; Laville, 1994; Vienney, 1994) which has been less available, perhaps, to Anglo-Saxon societies. The social economy refers to a community sector of non-profit organizations involved in producing services in the collective interest. Indeed, it differs from the public sector only with respect to the nature of its links to the state. Although formally independent of the state, organizations of the social economy are indirectly sustained by the state through funding, with or without contracts. The social economy would become the principal provider of socially useful services previously provided by the state. At the same time, it would provide employment, albeit at a humble income level, for all those surplus workers excluded from the increasingly competitive private sector labour market, and indeed, from the public service sector. In face of the devastating effects of economic restructuring on the security and stability of many local populations and vulnerable social groups, the development of the social economy is seen as a means of actively generating social solidarity. The community organizations that would constitute the social economy would tend to be motivated not by profit nor, ostensibly, by professional ambition, but by shared experiences and the conviction that through collective action, ordinary people can make things better for themselves.

The idea of the social economy has been fermenting at the grass-roots level for several years. Now, in 1996, it is beginning to appear that the deliberate development of the *économie sociale* has an excellent chance of becoming more than a utopian dream in Quebec. For, like most other "good ideas" that emerge within the society, it is rapidly gaining legitimacy within state circles. Certainly, it is a vision that is currently circulating amongst authorities *around* the state. This process of osmosis between society and the state is greatly facilitated by the systematic structuring of multiple avenues of communication between social authorities, including grass-roots leaders, and state authorities. For example, in the wake of a massive demonstration by Quebec women in the spring of 1995, the government set up a committee that included the leaders of the principal womens' and other community groups in Quebec, as well as representatives of several government ministries, to investigate the feasibility of systematically developing the social economy as a means of creating jobs in the service sector. The notion of the social economy is cropping up in union circles as well, and is rapidly taking hold of the public imagination as it is picked up by the press. How is it that Quebec considers such broad and seemingly utopian projects at a time when other states are tearing away at social programmes in a dogged effort to clear the public debt?

CHANGE AND SOLIDARITY

In the final analysis, Quebec is not a neo-liberal state alongside Britain's Thatcherite model, where public services have been privatized, and those that remain in the public sector, such as health care and education, have been restructured according to a quasi-market model. On the contrary, the Quebec state is considered an indispensable instrument for economic and social development. Neither is it neo-conservative in the way that the U.S. state is—or, for that matter, the governments of various Canadian provinces—where individual responsibility, backed by family and community, is held up to be the pillar of the "good society" and where state support is considered inappropriate. The reluctance (so far) to make crippling cuts to the health and welfare systems as some other provinces have done, despite its persistent deficit, is evidence of this. Quebec has traced a path between the neo-liberalism and neo-conservatism of most Anglo-Saxon states, a path that has its origin in a fundamentally different view of the state-society relation and in the perception of the state's responsibilities.

Still, Quebec's leadership, like others, has taken a decidedly neo-liberal turn since the heady days of the Quiet Revolution and the building of the welfare state. The sea change affected both major political parties. The once-social democratic Parti Québécois, which had done much to empower the unions during the 1970s, went on the offensive during the recession of the early 1980s. Using its legislative power, it limited their right to strike, imposed a collective agreement, and rolled back salaries to the tune of 20%. The Liberal party, swept into power in the wake of the draconian anti-union measures taken by the PQ, immediately set up three major committees to study and make recommendations regarding 1) the privatization of public enterprises, 2) the deregulation of industry, and 3) the streamlining of the public bureaucracy. It even appointed a Minister of Privatization. One observer has referred to this period as the counter-Quiet Revolution (Tanguay, 1988). But that was not the whole story.

Another part of the story is all about the systematic, state-supported development of Quebec's economic sector. While the PQ was assailing the unions, it was simultaneously reinforcing and expanding the host of programmes designed to promote the growth of an indigenous business class, providing venture capital for entrepreneurs, and tax breaks for those who would buy stocks in Quebec companies. Hardly a single important Quebec corporation has emerged without some form of participation in a state-sponsored investment relationship with such agencies as the Caisse de Depot, leading some to refer to the booming businesses of the 1980s as "Quebec Inc." Furthermore, no concerted effort was made to act upon the privatization, deregulation and bureaucratic streamlining reports published by the Liberal party in the mid-1980s; they were more or less abandoned. Indeed, this government's major focus during that period was the construction of the massive James Bay hydro-electric power plant (phase II) under the auspices of Hydro-Quebec, a para-public corporation. But if, for a time, it appeared that the rise of the Quebec business class would pressure the state to adopt a more clearly neo-liberal path to development, downplaying the role of the public sector, this expectation was not long-lived. After all, private industry was itself so tightly bound up with public investment that the boundary between public and private, state and society, was as blurred in the economic arena as it was in the arena of social development.

Both major political parties in Quebec have consistently been staunch supporters of free trade and the restructuring of industry to meet the demands of a global economy. They have not been adverse to controlling the fiscal purse by capping public expenses and imposing cuts. As early as 1984, a neo-liberal analysis of Quebec's fiscal problems was put forward in a White Paper that laid the plans for reforms very closely related to those proposed in the federal Macdonald Commission report a year later (Gouvernement du Quebec, 1984; Government of Canada, 1985). While the White Paper had been prepared by a Parti Québécois government, similar tones, bordering on neo-conservatism, characterized the Liberal Party's subsequent reforms in the area of welfare:

> It is important to reiterate that welfare payments and the full range of advantages related to social assistance must not, for any reason, rise above the revenues of minimum wage workers, and the gap between them must be an

obvious one. The new income security system must also impose upon those people eligible for assistance the same responsibilities as those incurred by any other low-income household. (Ministere de la main-d'oeuvre et de la securite du revenu, 1987:19)

Despite its tendencies towards both neo-liberalism and neo-conservatism, the high level of authority enjoyed by the Quebec state would likely evaporate if today, under dire economic conditions, it were to argue in favour of its own disengagement from social and economic problems. Instead, Quebec's leadership argues for a *change* in the state's role. It aims to ensure that other, supposedly more competent and efficient means are used to respond to the growing needs of the population during hard times. But the state's responsibility to ensure that these other means exist, and that they are geared to take up the challenge, is never questioned.

This is the context in which the concept of the "social economy" is taken very seriously by Quebec's leadership. Threats of privatization of social services are being displaced by a commitment to, and investment in, their *communitarization*. Furthermore, this is being accomplished in *concertation* with the leadership of the community movement. The objective is not only to provide a means for the containment and even reduction of the public sector, but also, to do so in a way that promotes social solidarity rather than social unrest. At the same time, the *communitarization* of health and welfare reduces the absolute cost of services, for community groups are inexpensive alternatives to the public sector. They depend more on semi-professional or non-professional labour; their employees are poorly paid and non-unionized and they can even be staffed to a large extent by volunteers and welfare recipients. Thus, even in divesting itself of direct responsibility for the care of the society's most vulnerable and marginal groups, the Quebec state is appearing to adopt a reflexive, rational, comprehensive stance.

The state will therefore remain at the hub of the society. Groups and elites continue to work through the state rather than without it or against it. It may be difficult to argue that this pattern works better than any other (the American lobby system, for example) but it is equally difficult to argue that it works less well. For, if it means that Quebec is a more bureaucratic and technocratic society, it also means that it is a highly politicized society with a wide variety of social groups mobilized to shape the processes of social change. This in turn means that, while social development appears to be rational and systematic, it is also more turbulent and imaginative. But the structuring of multiple avenues of communication between social and state authorities at the local, regional and national levels ensures that "good ideas" are rapidly and systematically diffused throughout the province. It almost seems as if Quebec is a society that has more solutions than it has problems. But the problems, of course, are plenty.

Quebec's unemployment rate is consistently higher than the Canadian average, standing at 11.3% in February of 1996 (compared to Canada's 9.6%), while another 6.4% of the population is on welfare. So far, the 1990s have known slower economic growth, less job creation and a higher average unemployment rate than the previous four decades (Aubrey, Charest, 1996). These figures translate into misery for hundreds of thousands, and are repeated to various degrees across Canada. In some provinces, the response has been a "tough love" disengagement of the state, in which poverty is treated as an individual defect which must not be supported through government programmes. The massive strikes in Ontario in 1996 may presage further and deeper social unrest wherever this path is followed. So far, Quebec's path has been somewhat different. Its dependence on the investment of expertise in policy formation and social programming continues, though the new state authorities are now graduates of business schools, not social science departments. Yet, Quebec has not slashed its social programmes as much as many other provinces have. The provincial budget, which has not shown a surplus since the Quiet Revolution, now has a deficit standing at over fifty million dollars.

Lucien Bouchard, the new premier, has vowed to devote the remaining years of his mandate to eliminating this deficit. The painful measures that the government was unwilling to undertake before the referendum on sovereignty may now be imminent. Quebec may not ultimately avoid the sociopolitical protests boiling up in other provinces and often directed against the federal government as well. It may only have put them off for a while. However, those few years have also given the society time to generate a significant support infrastructure at the community level, with the state's endorsement and investment. While the ideas and organizations were born of collective action, the state has devised quasi-formal channels to hear, discuss and disseminate those ideas at decision-making levels, and may be prepared to institutionalize them in a relatively systematic fashion.

Although concepts such as the social economy may seem promising, in reality, they are unlikely to provide much more than a weak palliative in harsh times (White, 1994). Social unrest may be inevitable, and the current government may very well lose the next election on the basis of the path it chooses to take. But if the state's actions come to be seen as reactionary and harmful to the collective good, this is likely to be construed in Quebec as a lack of imagination and will within the society as a whole.

REFERENCES

Alinsky, S. 1969. *Reveille for Radicals,* New York: Vintage Press.

Alinsky, S. 1972. *Rules for Radicals,* New York: Random House.

Aubrey, F., Charest, J. 1996. Orientations de la CSN: Developper l'economie solidaire. *Interaction communautaire,* No. 36-37:17-19.

Behiels, M.D. 1984. Québec: Social Transformation and Ideological Renewal, 1940-1976, in Cross, M.S. & Kealey, G. eds., *Modern Canada 1930s-1980s,* Toronto: McClelland and Stewart.

Bélanger, P.R., Lévesque, B. 1992. Le mouvement populaire et communautaire: de la revendication au partenariat (1963-1992), in Daigle, G., Rocher, G., eds (1992) *Le Québec en jeu,* Montréal: Les presses de l'Université de Montréal.

Bellavance, G., Fournier, M. 1992. Rattrapage et cirages: dynamismes culturels et interventions étatiques dans le chap de production des biens culturels, in Daigle, G., Rocher, G., eds (1992) *Le Québec en jeu,* Montréal: Les presses de l'Université de Montréal.

Bernard, P., Boisjoly, J. 1992. Les classes moyennes: en voie de disparition ou de réorganisation? in Daigle, G., Rocher, G., eds (1992) *Le Québec en jeu,* Montréal: Les presses de l'Université de Montréal.

Billette, I. 1995. *Les rapports dynamiques du processes partenarial. Un regard dans le domaine de la santé mentale,* Master's Thesis, Department of Sociology, Université de Montréal.

Blackburn, J. 1995. "Nouvelles pratiques et nouvelles perspectives face à la pauvreté des individus et des collectivités: l'action du gouvernement québécois," *Nouvelles pratiques sociales,* Vol.8, No.1:161-171.

Boucher, J. 1992. Les syndicats: de la lutte pour la reconnaissance à la concertation conflictuelle, in Daigle, G. & Rocher, G., eds (1992) *Le Québec en jeu,* Montréal: Les presses de l'Université de Montréal.

Castonguay, C. 1967. *Report of the Commission of Enquiry on Health and Social Welfare,* Québec: Gouvernement du Québec.

Cerny, P.G. 1990. *The Changing Architecture of Politics: Structure, Agency and the Future of the State,* Newbury Park, CA: Sage.

Cohen, Anthony P. 1985. *The Symbolic Construction of Community,* Chichester: Ellis Horwood.

Collin, J-P, Godbout, J. 1975. Les organisations popularies en milieu urbain: contre-pouvoir ou nouvelle pratique professionnelle, Montréal: Institut national de recherche sociale.

Confédération des syndicats nationaux, and Centrale de l'enseignement du Québec. 1987. *The History of the Labour Movement in Québec,* Montreal: Black Rose Books.

Desbarats, P. 1965. *The State of Quebec.* Toronto: McClelland & Stewart.

Dofny, J., Rioux, M. 1962. "Les classes sociales au Canada français," *Revue française de Sociologie,* 3, 3: 295-300.

Domergues, P. 1988. *La société du partenariat,* Paris: Anthropos.

Doré, G. 1990. *L'enjeu de la "coopération conflictuelle" pour les groupes communautaires.* Paper presented at the conference on Politiques économiques et politiques sociales: 18 mois après le libre-échange, Montréal: Université de Montréal.

Dumont, F., Rocher, G. 1961. "Introduction à la sociologie du Canada français," in *Le Canada français aujourd'hui et demain.* Paris: Librairie A. Fayard.

Eme, B. 1990. Développement local et pratiques d'insertion, *Economie et Humanisme,* 315: 28-37.

Falardeau, J-C. 1949. The Parish as an Institutional Type, reprinted in Blishen, B., Jones, F., Naegele, K., Porter, J. (1968) *Canadian Society,* Toronto: Macmillan.

Falardeau, J.C. (ed.), 1953. *Essais sur le Québec contemporain.* Québec: PVC.

Falardeau, J.C. 1964. *L'essor des Sciences sociales au Canada français.* Québec: Ministère des affaires culturelles.

Fortin, G. 1981. "Sociologie et/ou politique," in M. Mayer-Renaud, A. Le Doyen, eds., *L'intervention sociale.* Actes du colloque de l'Association canadienne des sociologues et anthropologues de langue française, Montréal: éditions coopératives Albert Saint-Martin.

Fréchette, P. 1992. Croissance et changements structurels de l'économie, in Daigle, G., Rocher, G., eds (1992) *Le Québec en jeu,* Montréal: Les presses de l'Université de Montréal.

Gagnon, C., Klein, J.L. 1991. "Le partenariat dans le développement local: tendances actuelles et perspectives de changement social," *Cahiers de géographie du Québec,* Vol. 35, No. 95: 239-258.

Garigue, P. 1958. *Études sur le Canada français,* Montréal.

Giddens, A. 1994. *Beyond Left and Right,* Cambridge: Polity Press.

Girard, C. 1995. Tour d'Horizon: Québec, *Canadian Review of Social Policy,* 36:108-110.

Godbout, J. 1985. Les relation central-local ou le rende-vous manqué, *Revue internationale d'action communautaire,* 13/53: 125-130.

Gouvernement du Québec. 1984. *White Paper on the Personal Tax and Transfer Systems.* Ministère des Finances.

Government of Canada, 1985. *Report of the Royal Commission on the Economic Union and Development Prospects for Canada* (MacDonald Report) Ottawa: Supply and Services Canada.

Gow, J.I. 1992. La vie mouvementée de l'administration publique québécoise, in Daigle, G., Rocher, G., eds (1992) *Le Québec en jeu,* Montréal: Les presses de l'Université de Montréal.

Guay, L. 1992. "Le choc des cultures: bilan de l'expérience de participation des resources alternatives à l'élaboration des plans régionaux d'organisation de services en santé mentale," *Nouvelles pratiques sociales,* 4,2:43-58.

Guindon, H. 1988. *Québec Society: Tradition, Modernity and Nationhood,* Toronto: University of Toronto Press.

Hoffman, J. 1995. *Beyond the State,* Cambridge: Policy Press.

Lachapelle, G., Bernier, G., Salée, D., Bernier, L. 1993. *The Quebec Democracy,* Montreal: McGraw-Hill Ryerson.

Lamoureux, J. 1994. *Le partenariat à l'épreuve,* Montréal: Éditions St-Martin.

Langlois, S. 1990. *La société québécoise en tendances, 1960-1990,* Montréal: Institut québécois de recherche sur la culture.

Laville, J-L. 1990. L'insertion par l'économique, *Economie et Humanisme,* 315: 18-27.

Laville, J-L. 1994. *L'economie solidaire. Une perspective internationale.* Paris: Desclee de Brouwer.

Leclerc, Y. 1995. "Là où l'initiative locale est stimultée, le Québec grandit", *Nouvelles pratiques sociales*, Vol. 8, No.1: 13-27.

Lee, S.S. 1979. *Québec Health System: A Decade of Change 1967-1977.* L'Institut d'Administration Publique du Canada, monographie no. 4.

Lefebre, P. 1992. La sécurité du revenu, in Daigle, G., Rocher, G., eds (1992) *Le Québec en jeu,* Montréal: Les presses de l'Université de Montréal.

Lesemann, F. 1994. *Services and Circuses,* Montreal: Black Rose Books.

Lesvesque, B. Mager, L. 1992. "Vers un nouveau contrat social? Éléments de problématique pour l'étude du régional et du local," in Klein, J.L. and Gagnon, C. (eds). *Les partenaires du développement face au défi du local.* Chicoutimi, Québec: GRIR, Université du Québec à Chicoutimi.

Lipietz, A. 1990. Apres fordisme et democratie. Les temps modernes, 524: 97-121.

Lipietz, A. Pour la communauté-providence, in *Choisir l'audace,* 101-118.

Maclouf, P. 1985. "Les restructuration économiques et l'ancrage territorial de la crise de l'État-providence," *Revue internationale d'action communautaire*, 13-53.

Marmor, T.R. 1992. *American Medical Care Reform: Are We Doomed to Fail?* Daedalus, 121, 4: 175-194.

Ministère de la main d'oeuvre et de la sécurité du revenu. 1987. *Pour une politique de sécurité du revenu* (Rapport Paradis) Québec: Gouvernement du Québec.

Ministère de la main d'oeuvre et de la sécurité du revenu. 1987. *Pour une politique de sécurité du revenu (Rapport Paradis)* Québec: Gouvernement du Québec.

Pelletier, R. 1992. La Révolution tranquille, in Daigle, G. & Rocher, G., eds (1992) *Le Québec en jeu,* Montréal: Les presses de l'Université de Montréal.

Renaud, M. 1977 Réforme ou illusion? Une analyse des interventions de l'Etat québécois dans le domaine de la santé, *Sociologie et Sociétés*, 9, 1: 149.

Renaud, M. Doré, White, D. 1989. "Sociology and Social Policy: From a Love-Hate Relationship with the State to Cynicism and Pragmatism," *Canadian Review of Sociology and Anthropology*, State of the Art Edition: Francophone Québecois Sociology, 26, 3: 426-456.

Report of the Royal Commission on the Economic Union and Development Prospects for Canada (MacDonald Commission) 1985. Ottawa: Supply and Services Canada.

Rochon, J. et al. 1988. *Rapport de la Commission d'enquête sur les Services de Santé et les Services Sociaux,* Québec: Les Publications du Québec.

Rodrigue, N. 1995. La communautairisation: vecteur de changement social, *Nouvelles pratiques sociales*, 8, 1: 230-234.

Rose, N., Miller, P. 1992. Political power beyond the state: problematics of government, *British Journal of Sociology*, 43: 2.

Saint-Pierre, C. 1963. *Étude des associations volontaires dans une communauté canadienne-française,* Masters thesis, Department de sociology, Université de Montréal.

Smith, M. 1994. "L'impact du Québec inc. Repartition des revenues et essicacité éqonomique," *Sociologie et Sociétés,* 22:2, 91-110.

Statistics Canada, 1994.

Tanguay, B. 1988. Business, labour and the state in the new Quebec, *American Review of Canadian Studies,* 17, 4: 395-407.

Vaillancourt, Y. 1995. Éléments de problématique concernant l'arrimage entre le communautaire et le public dans le domaine de la santé et des servcies sociaux, *Nouvelles pratiques sociales,* 8, 1: 227-277.

Vienney, C. 1994. *L'economie sociale.* Paris: La decouverte.

White, D. 1994. "La gestion communautaire de l'exclusion," *Lien Social et Politiques,* 32: 37-51.

White, D. Mercier, C., 1991. Coordinating Community and Public-Institutional Mental Health Services: Some Unintended Consequences," *Social Science and Medicine,* 33, 6:729-739.

QUEBEC AND THE IDEAL
OF FEDERALISM[1]

It is difficult to conceive of any raison d'être for Canada apart from its being an alternative to the United States. Canadians may share a lot of values with their American neighbours and maintain very friendly ties, but their very existence as a country is predicated upon a refusal to join the American republic. Quebec's French Canadians were the first to say no to the American Revolution in 1776 because they considered, more or less explicitly, that their identity was better protected within the British Empire than within an American nation. Loyalists joined them later.

When modern Canada was created in 1867 by British colonies coming together, the motivation behind the new project was still the desire to counter the forces of American integration. John A. Macdonald, the first prime minister, had hoped the new country would be a legislative union like Great Britain but he had to yield to strong pressures, especially from Quebec, to form a federation. Hence, Canada was bound to be at once a federal entity and one that would be very different from the United States. Contrary to its neighbour, Canadian federalism would not be cemented by a strong national myth such as the idea of an indivisible union that became almost a religion after the Civil War.

French Canadians living in Quebec have been traditionally faithful to this non-American form of decentralized federalism, as it allowed them to maintain a distinct society within Canada. The case can be made that they were the best defenders of federalism and of the British parliamentary system. Ironically, these French Canadians in Quebec may break from the Canadian federation precisely because recent developments have made the federation alien from its original intent and more similar to the American concept of national union.

I will try to show how the modernization of Quebec institutions has reinforced this will to maintain decentralization, and how resistance to it has put more distance between Quebec and the rest of Canada. Instead of addressing

---

[1] This is a revised version of an article published under the same title in *The Annals of the American Academy of Political and Social Science*, March 1995, pp. 40-53.

Quebecers' claims, the Trudeau government squarely put forward a quasi-American concept of Canadian union. The latter has become so popular among English-speaking Canadians that recent efforts to reinstate the kind of federalism that would be suitable to Quebec have been in vain. It seems now that there is little hope of realizing the modern ideal dear to most Quebecers: to keep alive their basic identity as well as their allegiance to Canada.

MODERNIZATION AND NETWORKING

It has been a fateful error of modern social science to assume that modernization would abolish barriers between nations and would always facilitate integration into larger entities. While it is undeniable that modernity has made peoples closer and more similar to one another, it has, in the same process, given a new twist to nationalism, regionalism or the assertion of collective distinctiveness. This is noticeable as well in what is called "post-modernity." Karl Deutsch, among others, has shown convincingly that social mobilization, as it progresses more rapidly than assimilation, tends to foster nationalism and the reinforcement of linguistic identity.[2]

Quebec is a case in point. A Quiet Revolution unfolded in the early 1960s as a new provincial government brought about long-needed reforms to the Quebec society at all levels: cultural, social, political, and economic. This was applauded by most Canadians and considered as a good omen for a new, more homogeneous Canadianism. As Quebec was catching up with the modern world and the rest of the country, it was thought that it would become more like the other provinces.

In fact, Quebecers had been subjected to industrialization, urbanization and modernization since World War I. Modern ways of living had become prevalent since the end of World War II and the traditional structure was falling apart gradually. But many old institutions had been maintained by a conservative provincial government up to 1959. The federal government of Canada, however, in the course of an unprecedented era of prosperity, was actively promoting modern Keynesian concepts and producing policies intended "for the welfare of all Canadians," often at the expense of provincial jurisdictions. Quebec first resisted in a mostly negative way. One could think that, with a French-speaking prime minister from Quebec like Louis Saint-Laurent (1948-1957), Canadianism would eventually triumph over provincialism. As Ottawa intervened more and more in fields of provincial competence, it even contributed to the enhancement of culture in francophone Quebec as well as in other provinces. The Canadian Broadcasting Corporation (CBC), the National Film Board and the Canada Council for the Arts and Sciences are good examples of such federal activity.

---

[2] See *Nationalism and Social Communication*. Cambridge, MA: M.I.T. Press, 1966; and *Tides Among Nations*. New York: The Free Press, 1979.

But Ottawa's contribution to the modernization of Quebec would not fulfil its original goal. It would end up, in many cases, feeding the very collective identity that it was set to transcend. This is very well illustrated by the phenomenon of television. The CBC was the only transmitter of TV shows in Canada from 1952 to 1960. Naturally, CBC's goal was to make Canadians closer to one another. But, as it had to set up two networks, one in English and one in French, and as the French-speaking population was highly concentrated in Quebec and adjacent areas, it could not but reinforce Canadian duality. Because the French network was, for all practical purposes, a Quebec network (for it was not extended, for many years, much beyond the Quebec borders), the CBC contributed heavily to one result: making French-speaking Quebecers closer to one another, reinforcing Quebec consciousness and Quebec nationalism. For the first time in their history, French Canadians living in Quebec were watching, day after day, a picture of themselves transmitted from one end of the province to the other.

Moreover, television became a fantastic outlet for cultural talents in the performing arts, journalism and other fields. In contrast to the English network that could rely on American production (and had to do so to respond to public demand), the French network had to produce everything on its own. To make things even more dramatic, the TV studios, where most of this production took place, were located in the western part of downtown Montreal, an almost totally anglophone area. Thus, a new generation of dynamic and proud French Canadians, making a living out of using their French language, were confronted on a daily basis with a social setting that was alien to them. As they moved to bars and restaurants in their own city (predominantly French-speaking), they could not be waited on in their language. A perfect scenario had been created for a nationalist movement.

The CBC, among other institutions, thus paved the way for the Quiet Revolution. It was, of course, totally independent from the Church which had been so influential in the past. It was a window to the outside world. One of the most popular shows in the 1950s was René Lévesque's "Point de mire" dealing mainly with international events. This same René Lévesque would become one of the architects of the Quiet Revolution and, eventually, the leader of the secessionist party, the Parti Québécois (PQ).

Under such conditions, Quebec's modernization did not make Quebecers more integrated with the rest of Canada. On the contrary, Quebec evolved in an atmosphere of rivalry with the federal government as the provincial government of Quebec created its own welfare, cultural and economic programs, and expressed a fresh new will to regain the jurisdictions it had lost to Ottawa over the years. Quebec governments had always expressed opposition to the tendency of the federal government to behave as the leader of the game, as the main possessor of sovereignty and the center of a Canadian "nation." But never before had Quebec acted in such a decisive and positive way.

A philosophy was articulated around a concept of federalism that allows for the divisibility of sovereignty and the sharing of power between two levels of government, coordinated but not subordinated to one another, each exercising supreme sovereignty in its constitutional prerogatives. Other provincial governments were obviously not so keen on the exercise of sovereignty, but Quebec had special reasons to jealously safeguard its competence. In the words of its premier, Jean Lesage, it had become "the political expression of French Canada" and was claiming all the power needed to fulfill this mission. Obviously this could not mean a perfect equation between French-Canadians and Quebec, since about 12% of Quebecers are English-speaking and almost one million francophones live outside Quebec. It could mean, however, that the territory of the province of Quebec was the only one in which it was possible to build a modern network of communications[3] in the French language. French-speaking people outside Quebec could speak their language to a certain extent but they could not really make it public. Conversely, the English-speaking population of Quebec, while maintaining its institutions, had to come to terms with the French language becoming the main public instrument of communications in the province.

The most tangible results of the Quiet Revolution are the creation of this all-purpose communications network and of particular networks in cultural activities and also, more gradually, in the economy. Economic instruments created by the Quebec government in the 1960s, for example, Hydro-Quebec, the General Investment Society, the Quebec Deposit and Investment Fund, contributed to the advent of a dynamic network of private enterprises controlled by French-speaking Quebecers.

Thus, the transition was set between the old concept of French-Canadian belonging based on ethnicity to a new modern civic conception of a Quebec community based on the existence of a French language network of communications. Ethnic feelings did not disappear at once, of course. But they could not be the basis, any longer, for political claims on the part of Quebec.

ESSENTIAL QUEBEC CLAIMS

These claims could be summarized in the strict federalist formula expressed previously. Should federalism be understood in this sense of shared sovereignty, it would not be paradoxical to affirm that Quebecers are the best defenders of the Canadian federation. The constitutional cleavage would not then be understood as between federalists and separatists but between unitarian Canadian nationalists and Quebec federalists. Even Michael Ignatieff, who certainly could not be suspected of having sold out to Quebec nationalism, has written:

---

[3] This corresponds to the definition given by K. Deutsch of a people: "A large, general-purpose communication net of human beings," *Tides Among Nations*, p. 301.

> Federalism ... is just a particular way of *sharing political power among different peoples* within a state ... Those who believe in federalism hold that different peoples do not need states of their own in order to enjoy *self-determination*. Peoples ... may agree to share a single state, *while retaining substantial degrees of self-government over matters essential to their identity as peoples.*[4]

If we extract the phrases I have italicized (not unfairly, I hope) from the preceding text, we find exactly what Quebec has been seeking from the 1960s to this day. Representing a communications network of its own, the province of Quebec claimed to constitute a "different people" and, for that reason, wanted to "share political power" with Ottawa in the framework of the Canadian state. Quebecers would thus "enjoy self-determination" within Canada. That would allow them, while sharing a certain number of values and institutions with other Canadians, to retain "substantial degrees of self-government over matters essential to their identity." If all other provinces had concurred with that claim, that would have made the Canadian federation quite decentralized indeed. If, on the contrary, as all indications have shown, no other province would seek to retain as much self-government as Quebec, especially in matters related to identity, it would have resulted in an asymmetric federalism. In other words, Quebec would be granted "special status." This latter phrase was always badly received in English Canada. It carried a connotation of privilege. It does not mean anything, however, but difference and particular distribution of power to meet that difference.

To the oft-repeated question, "What does Quebec want?," Premier Daniel Johnson (1966-1968) replied in 1966:

> As a basis for its nationhood, it wants to be master of its own decision-making in what concerns the human growth of its citizens—that is to say education, social security and health in all their aspects—their economic affirmation—the power to set up economic and financial institutions they feel are required—their cultural development—not only the arts and letters, but also the French language—and the Quebec community's external development—its relations with certain countries and international bodies.[5]

This was an impressive list and it was received in Ottawa with a mixture of shock and scepticism. It meant an important devolution of power. But this proposal was undoubtedly conceived in a spirit of federalism. Quebec would be content to leave vital responsibilities in the hands of the central government, such as defense and the armed forces, foreign policy in general, the central bank, commercial banks, currency and exchange rates, customs and international trade, the postal service, citizenship, and transport. Quebec would also agree to share powers in agriculture, immigration, communication and broadcasting.

---

[4] *Blood and Belonging.* (Toronto, New York, London: Viking, Penguin Books, 1993), p. 110.

[5] Speech to the Tax Structure Committee in Ottawa, quoted by Claude Morin, *Quebec versus Ottawa: The Struggle for Self-Government.* Toronto: University of Toronto Press, 1976, p. 97.

Since other provinces did not call for so much autonomy, this left no other alternative to Quebec but to claim special status, which would entail a dualist concept of Canada. The preliminary report of the Royal Commission on Bilingualism and Biculturalism (created in 1963 by Prime Minister Lester B. Pearson and known as the B&B Commission) had already depicted Quebec as a global society:

> ... the French-speaking Canadians of Quebec ... belong ... to a society ... which in various important fields is already master of its own activities ... But at the same time most of those with whom we talked were of the opinion that this society had less than complete control over a number of crucial sectors in which it is active.[6]

The federal commissioners then stated bluntly that Canada was confronted with a crisis and that "the chief protagonists, whether they are entirely conscious of it or not, are French-speaking Quebec and English-speaking Canada."[7]

The federal government appeared for a time somewhat receptive to this kind of thinking. But with the advent of Pierre Elliott Trudeau as prime minister in 1968, it endeavoured to counter Quebec with a Canadian nationalism of its own. Quebec premiers continued nonetheless to call for stronger autonomy for their province. Robert Bourassa, facing a secessionist opposition between 1970 and 1976, fought for more power in matters of health and welfare, communications and culture. Just as bilingualism was becoming policy in Ottawa, he made French the official language of Quebec in 1974. The following year, a Charter of Rights was adopted by the National Assembly.

As the Parti Québécois came to power in 1976 with the mandate to govern Quebec within the Canadian federation's framework and to conduct a referendum later on its "sovereignty-association" project, another federal commission of enquiry was created to look for ways to keep Canada together. In 1979, it issued a report that stated even more firmly than the previous B&B Commission the need for recognition of Quebec:

> ... we believe that the distinctive role of the Quebec government as the single province containing a French-speaking majority must be recognized ...
>
> Let us put our conviction strongly: Quebec is distinctive and should, within a viable Canada, have the powers necessary to protect and develop its distinctive character; any political solution short of this would lead to the rupture of Canada.[8]

---

[6] *A Preliminary Report of the Royal Commission on Bilingualism and Biculturalism.* Ottawa: Queen's Printer, 1965, pp. 112-113.

[7] *Ibid.*, p. 135.

[8] *The Task Force on Canadian Unity, A Future Together, Observations and Recommendations.* Ottawa: Supply and Services Canada, 1979, p. 87.

Such a statement, from a Commission representative of diverse elements in all of Canada, was well received in Quebec. Even members of the PQ government commented positively while, paradoxically, the government that had commissioned the report did not respond to it in any way, shape or form.

Interestingly enough, a secret report of the U.S. State Department, prepared in Washington in the summer of 1977, offered a better recognition of Quebec aspirations than the Canadian government itself. The document was a briefing paper, not a policy statement. It was just circulated among officers interested in Canada and we don't know if it was ever officially approved. But it represented a fair and balanced analysis of the Quebec situation. It concluded with the following:

> A devolution of power to Quebec only, particularly in cultural and social affairs—which have a human rights aspect, could well be less disruptive to U.S. interests than a general devolution of powers to all the provinces ... There is also no question regarding the basic long-term viability of an independent Quebec in the economic sense or in regards to its ability to be a responsible member of the family of nations.[9]

No devolution of power, nor any other proposal, came from Ottawa. In the course of the 1980 referendum campaign, vague promises were made to Quebecers that changes would be brought to the Constitution that would allow them to keep and consolidate their double identity. The slogan of the campaign to reject sovereignty-association was "Mon NON est québécois:" "My NO is Quebecer" ("NON" sounds like "name" in French). We will see in the following section how these federal promises were not only unfulfilled but contradicted.

The history of Quebec claims for increased sharing of power in the two decades following the beginning of the Quiet Revolution is a very sterile one indeed, especially if we consider, as a respected jurist has written, that "relatively modest reforms ... would have accommodated most of the Quebec demands as they were then presented."[10]

TRUDEAU COUNTERATTACKS

Pierre Trudeau dedicated his career as Prime Minister of Canada to the struggle against the idea of a Quebec global society. He always presented himself as a champion of federalism. But to him, a federal system did not imply a sharing of sovereignty and allegiances. Quebec was a province like the others. The Quebec government was a regional government with some prerogatives; but, for

---

[9] Quoted in Jean-François Lisée, *In the Eye of the Eagle*. Toronto: Harpers Collins, 1990, p. 301.

[10] Edward McWhinney. "English-Canadian Intellectual Responses to Quebec's Quiet Revolution," in *Être contemporain*, ed. J.W. Lapierre, V. Lemieux, J. Zylberberg. Québec: Presses de l'Université du Québec, 1992, p. 292.

Quebecers like all other Canadians, the essential political authority, the one responsible for global welfare, was the Ottawa government. He repudiated dualism, the concept of two nations or of a binational Canada, and even biculturalism, as advocated by the B&B Royal Commission, especially in the preliminary Report quoted earlier. In order to unite the country and make French-speaking Quebecers feel as comfortable in all of Canada as in Quebec, he promoted bilingualism in all federal services across the Canadian "nation;" he never doubted that Canada was one indivisible nation. He was implicitly asking his fellow Quebecers to trade their identity as a people against the promise of bilingualism.

He advanced the concept of multiculturalism, implying the recognition of various ethnic cultures in Canada, thus reducing the global culture of French-speaking Quebec to one ethnic component of the Canadian mosaic. After the passage of the Official Languages Act in 1969 came the policy of multiculturalism in 1971 to satisfy all ethnic groups that were feeling left out by bilingualism.

Quebecers welcomed the Official Languages Act as a long-awaited policy to redress the wrongs they had suffered in a practically unilingual civil service in Ottawa. But that did not make them give up their identity as Quebecers. To them it was only fair that federalism would allow both bilingualism in the central government and a sense of community at the provincial level. They would have accepted multiculturalism if it had not confused their own global culture with the ethnic cultures of immigrants.

After the 1980 Quebec referendum in which 40% of Quebecers voted to give a mandate to their government to negotiate sovereignty-association (that is, political sovereignty coupled with economic association), along with a good number of the 60% who voted "no" who were hoping for a renewal of federalism with some degree of devolution, Trudeau brilliantly maneuvered to patriate the British North America Act from Westminster, first unilaterally, then by excluding Quebec from a deal with other provinces.

In April 1982, less than two years after the contested referendum, Queen Elizabeth was in Ottawa to proclaim a new Canadian Constitution which completely ignored the idea of Quebec as a global society and the home of a specific people. The Charter of Rights attached to the Constitution created a new citizenship, a new Canadianism in which the federalist principle was diluted by the recognition of individual rights and the rights of many groups, all sanctioned by provincial appellate Courts and a Supreme Court with judges appointed by the federal government.

The National Assembly of Quebec did not and could not ratify such a constitution. Not only did the members of the governing party (the PQ), vote against it but so did most of the members of the Liberal opposition, who even spurned the invitation to attend the ceremony of proclamation. Thus the Constitution of Canada, although having force of law in Quebec, is denied of any legitimacy, as it was brought about without any mandate from the population or from its representatives in the Quebec legislature. The federal Parliament members from Quebec who voted for it had been elected in February 1980, in an election in which the constitutional scheme was very vaguely evoked. In contrast, the Quebec National Assembly was elected in April 1981 on a mandate to defend Quebec autonomy in the constitutional debate.

Ironically, Pierre Trudeau, who went into politics to enhance his fellow Quebecers' attachment to Canada, was much more successful in giving life to the old John A. Macdonald dream of a Canadian legislative union. As Kenneth McRoberts has written,

> it is in English Canada that the new Canadian identity has taken root, thanks in particular to the constitutional revision of 1982 ... As a consequence, Québécois and English Canadians are more divided than ever before, separated not just by different constitutional preferences but by mutually exclusive notions of political community.[11]

Many Canadians were nonetheless hopeful that Quebecers would resign themselves to the loss of their collective identity and would eventually appreciate the benefits of the new Canadianism. The late Donald Smiley, a renowned political scientist not the least suspected of being biased toward Quebec, did not agree. He wrote:

> In general, then, an exercise in constitutional review and reform whose alleged objectives were to create more harmonious relations between Quebec and the wider community has involved a betrayal of the Quebec electorate, a breach of fundamental constitutional convention, a recrudescence of Quebec nationalism, and an even more serious Quebec challenge than before to the legitimacy of the Canadian constitutional order.[12]

MEECH LAKE, CHARLOTTETOWN AND THE BLOC QUÉBÉCOIS

Obviously, something had to be done to save Canada and legitimize the Constitution among Quebecers. It is therefore difficult to blame Brian Mulroney, who promised to do everything he could to bring Quebec back to the fold upon becoming prime minister. This commitment earned him great success in Quebec. Even the PQ government welcomed his Progressive Conservative administration in the fall of 1984. But serious negotiations with Quebec would not really move ahead before the provincial election of December 1985 that returned Robert Bourassa's Liberal party to power.

---

[11] "Disagreeing on Fundamentals: English Canada and Quebec," in *The Charlottetown Accord, the Referendum and the Future of Canada*, ed. K. McRoberts and Patrick Monahan. Toronto: University of Toronto Press, 1993, p. 260.

[12] "A Dangerous Deed: The Constitution Act, 1982," in Keith Banting and Richard Simeon, *And No One Cheered: Federalism, Democracy and the Constitutional Act*. Toronto: Methuen, 1983, p. 78.

Bourassa and Mulroney were men of compromise. By the spring of 1986, Quebec had set five minimal conditions that would make the Canadian Constitution acceptable to the National Assembly:

- recognition of Quebec as a distinct society;
- limitation of the federal government's spending power in fields of provincial jurisdiction;
- a guarantee of increased powers in immigration matters;
- provincial participation in the appointment of judges of the Supreme Court;
- a veto right for Quebec.

In August of that same year, all provincial premiers, gathered in Edmonton for their annual meeting, agreed to negotiate on Quebec's five conditions. They reinforced their resolution in another meeting in Vancouver a few months later. In late April 1987, they were ready for an official conference that took place at the prime minister's residence at Meech Lake. They unanimously agreed on a slightly revised version of Quebec's conditions: the veto right was transformed into the requirement of unanimous consent on important constitutional amendments. After a month of public debate that allowed former prime minister Trudeau to register his opposition, provincial premiers met with the leader of the federal government in Ottawa and finally signed the accord. The day of June 3, 1987 was an historic moment, one of the rare occasions in Canadian history when all the federation's governments agreed.

The agreement never took effect because two provincial legislatures failed to ratify it after a deadline of three years. There are many technical reasons to explain that terrible failure. But none of them would have remained if Canadian public opinion had been favorable to the agreement. In fact, outside Quebec, the accord became, with time, less and less agreeable, mainly because it did not fit with the new Canadianism created by the 1982 Constitution. Thus Meech Lake's failure was a victory of Canadian citizenship over federalism.

One of the most reputed analysts of the constitutional debate, Alan Cairns, has described the accord as a "counterattack to reinstall the dominance of governments, and to reassert the primacy of federalism." Canadians were addressed "in terms of membership in national and provincial communities ... rather than as aborigines, visible minorities, women, right bearers, and related constitutional categories indifferent to federalism's spatial construction of communities."[13] This is where the gap has widened between Quebec and the rest of Canada. Quebecers still see themselves within the spatial construction of a federated community

---

[13] Alan C. Cairns. *Disruptions: Constitutional, Struggles, from the Charter to Meech Lake*. Toronto: McClelland and Stewart Inc., 1991, p. 166.

whereas more and more Canadians see themselves either in terms of their large citizenship or as members of groups that have nothing to do with their province. In other words, the only *real* and meaningful province in Canada is Quebec.

Quite naturally, Quebecers felt rejected by the rest of Canada after these three years of good will on their part. Many of them had concluded that this was the final failure of Canadian federalism. Hence a good majority of them, in the summer of 1990, were ready to opt for sovereignty. A group of Progressive Conservative members of Parliament from Quebec left their party to manifest their disenchantment. With Lucien Bouchard, Environment Minister in the Mulroney Cabinet, as their leader, they formed a new party, the Bloc Québécois, advocating sovereignty as the only remaining viable option for Quebec.

Premier Bourassa, on his part, declared that Quebec was still a distinct society in any case and that "Quebecers are free to assume their own destiny, to determine their political status and to assure their economic, social and cultural development." In a rare atmosphere of consensus between the two major parties, a commission was created to advise the government on the future of Quebec. The Bélanger-Campeau Commission, known by the names of its two co-chairmen (typically, two persons belonging to the financial milieu) issued a report in the winter of 1991 that again called for a renewed federalism as a first option for Quebecers. It stressed "the necessity of creating a new relationship between Quebec and the rest of Canada, based on the recognition and respect for the identity of Quebecers and their right to be different."[14] It set a deadline for constitutional change. This was seen by many outside Quebec as unwarranted impatience. But how not to be impatient after thirty years of unfulfilled efforts? The National Assembly endorsed the Commission's deadline of October 1992. If satisfactory changes were not brought forward by then, Quebecers would be consulted on the option of sovereignty.

There was intense constitutional activity in the federal government and elsewhere in Canada during these years. But no visible sign was shown that the two exclusive notions of political community could be reconciled or even put together. On July 7, 1992, the nine premiers of the rest of Canada came to an agreement that seemed to satisfy all Canadian groups and constitutional players but still fell short of Quebec demands. A few weeks later, Premier Bourassa, who had opted to stay away from multilateral negotiations until the rest of Canada offered something viable, became a victim of his own strategy. Frightened by the very deadline he had set, he rejoined the conference table. The result was a series of hasty discussions leading to vague and irrational compromises mixed with a few good proposals like the recognition of

---

[14] *Report of the Commission on the Political and Constitutional Future of Quebec.* Quebec: National Assembly, 1991, p. 48.

self-determination for the aboriginal populations. This was the Charlottetown accord, finally concluded in the capital of Prince Edward Island. It was submitted to a referendum in all of Canada in October 1992.

In spite of a vigorous campaign on the part of all political leaders, the population remained unresponsive. Quebecers thought, with good reason, this was too little, too late. Other Canadians, especially westerners, also thought they were confronted with a bad deal, an incomplete Senate and unacceptable guarantees for Quebec; in fact, there would have been a minimum of Quebec seats in the House of Commons, something that had never previously been asked for.

The Bloc Québécois campaigned along with the PQ opposition in Quebec for the rejection of the Charlettetown accord. It was also quite successful in the federal election of October 1993, electing 54 members, representing almost all ridings that have a high proportion of French-speaking Quebecers. There was one main reason for this success: the obvious failure of Canadian federalism to articulate itself in a meaningful way. The two major federal parties, for the first time in recent history, had nothing to offer Quebecers in terms of the renewal of federalism. Jean Chrétien, the Liberal leader who won a decisive victory and became Prime Minister, conducted his campaign without hardly mentioning the words "Quebec" or "Quebecers," as if Canada were a unitary country, that is, a country with all governing authority held by a central government.

THE PQ IN POWER AND THE REFERENDUM ON SOVEREIGNTY

In 1994, the same scenario was more or less repeated in the provincial election. On September 12, the Parti Québécois was returned to power in Quebec City after campaigning on a commitment to bring about sovereignty after a referendum to be held in 1995. The PQ victory was not, however, as decisive as had been expected. Only 45% of the population voted for Jacques Parizeau's candidates, while 7% voted for a third party, Action Démocratique du Québec (ADQ), which advocated a real confederation with the rest of Canada.

The Quebec Liberal Party, with a new leader, Daniel Johnson (son of the late premier mentioned above) remained strong in the opposition. The PQ government was therefore fighting an uphill battle to rally a majority to the cause of sovereignty. It needed the support of the third party, ADQ, led by the young and skillful Mario Dumont. Dumont delayed his decision but agreed to participate in extraparliamentary commissions set up in the winter of 1995 to consult the population, all over the province, on the future of Quebec. The Quebec Liberal Party refused to join this exercise because it saw it as presenting the population with the "fait accompli" of Quebec sovereignty. In spite of the Liberals' absence, the result of the consultation was not as positive as the government would have wished. People manifested vividly enough their dissatisfaction with the Canadian federal system and the status of Quebec, but a majority remained somewhat reluctant to embrace the ideal of sovereignty pure and simple. In order to connect with the population's mood and win the referendum, the government had to pay heed to the popular desire to maintain some form of Canadian union.

An agreement was reached, on June 12, 1995, between Premier Jacques Parizeau, Bloc Québécois leader Lucien Bouchard and ADQ head, Mario Dumont. The sovereignty project would be associated with a formal offer of partnership with the rest of Canada to be submitted after a referendum victory. The partnership formula did include a political as well as an economic union. The political union that would be offered, taking the European union as a model, was not elaborated in detail since it would be the object of negotiation: a ministerial council with equal representation; a common parliament with proportional representation; and a tribunal. Premier Parizeau, who was known to be a strict sovereigntist for a long time, agreed to be bound by a negotiation committee who would be composed of people representing the whole spectrum of political alignment in Quebec.

Thus, even though the proposal was immediately rejected by all political leaders outside Quebec and by all federalists in Quebec, it had some credibility in the population at large. It seemed that the Quebec government would do everything to obtain an arrangement with the rest of Canada that would limit the exercise of sovereignty and maintain a Canadian union. Sovereignty would not be declared until a year after the referendum. It was difficult to think that other Canadian provinces, especially Ontario and the Maritimes, already so intensely and tightly linked to Quebec by trade and other exchanges, would not accept to negotiate at least some economic agreements.

The referendum was scheduled for October 30, 1995 and the question was phrased as follows:

> Do you agree that Quebec should become sovereign, after having made a formal offer for a new economic and political partnership, within the scope of the Bill Respecting the Future of Quebec and of the agreement signed on June 12, 1995?

This was a rather long and convoluted question. For many outside Quebec, it was even described as dishonest. For Quebecers, however, even among those who would answer "No," it was seen as sufficiently clear. It included the two main elements of deep-rooted aspirations of the French-speaking majority: sovereignty as the expression of identity and the willingness to maintain a form of Canadian union. The references were also widely known. The Bill Respecting the Future of Quebec was the sovereignty project adopted in principle by the National Assembly. Both the Bill and the Agreement were distributed in every household and were available in English as well as in French.

The campaign took a curious twist as the "Yes" forces insisted on the moderation of the project and on its partnership component while the "Nos" would label their opponents as "separatists" and stick posters on every pole available in the province with the words "Non à la Séparation" in large letters. Thus, ironically enough, sovereignists were talking about partnership, and federalists were offering no other choice but Canada as it stood versus complete separation of Quebec from it.

The lack of any constructive proposal for a reformed Canada that would correct the perceived inequities of the 1982 Constitution and the Meech Lake debacle fed into the "Yes" campaign. So did incredibly catastrophic scenarios that were foreseen if the "Yes" should win, like the loss of one million jobs. The Yes campaign, on the other hand, was taken over in September by charismatic leader Lucien Bouchard who was appointed chief negotiator of the contemplated partnership in the advent of a "Yes" victory.

Only at the very end of the campaign, when the polls correctly predicted a close vote, did Prime Minister Jean Chrétien commit himself to bringing about recognition of Quebec as a distinct society and the granting of a veto concerning future constitutional changes. Six days before the vote, from a man who had spent his whole career touting the virtues of a tight-knit Canadian nation, this promise was received as "too little, too late." Huge rallies in Montreal with thousands coming from all parts of Canada to urge Quebecers "not to leave" were not much more successful in converting Yesses into Nos. Since those Canadians had nothing to offer but their words of love, they gave Quebecers the image of an all-inclusive Canada that did not allow for the recognition of Quebec's uniqueness.

The result was terribly close: 50.6% for the "No," 49.4% for the "Yes." Popular participation in the vote reached an impressive 94%. Such an outcome could not but transform the victory into a nerve-racking exercise and a fragile relief whereas the defeat could be seen as moral victory. Obviously it did not settle the issue.

The vote was also a dramatic illustration of Quebec's ethnic cleavage as the huge majority of non-francophones voted "No." That made the Montreal area look like a federalist bastion. This was an illusion produced by the heavy concentration of English-speaking people and ethnic communities in the metropolitan region. Francophones in this region (including a proportion of recent-stock Quebecers who have adopted French as their main language) voted more heavily for the Yes than other regions of Quebec, more than Quebec City and surrounding rural areas.

Jacques Parizeau's speech acknowledging defeat on referendum night reinforced the impression that Quebec nationalism was basically ethnic. In a bitter and disenchanted mood, the sovereignist leader attributed his misfortune to "money and some ethnic votes" and he urged his supporters to take a future revenge in which francophones would raise their 60% support to 65 or 70%. This unfortunate speech was repudiated by several "Yes" advocates who had always gone out of their way to emphasize the pluralistic and multiethnic nature of Quebec. Mr. Parizeau himself, partly apologizing for "his choice of words," submitted his resignation the following day. But the bad impression remained. It did not, however, cause any defection among "Yes" supporters, not even within the ethnic communities. Although the latter are just a few, they are more numerous in some milieux. For example, in the Latin American community, the vote had been around 40% for the "Yes."

WHAT LIES AHEAD?

The Quebec referendum has produced both negative and positive effects. On the negative side, it has hardened the position of those who advocate strong measures to reinforce control over Quebec, like making referenda on sovereignty either illegal or ruled by the federal government, and threatening Quebecers with harsh measures in the advent of secession. The partition of Quebec is even contemplated. All of this, of course, is totally counterproductive. It does nothing to reconcile Quebecers and other Canadians nor to improve Canada's political structure. Moreover, it sends an ugly image of Canada abroad as it emphasizes antagonism, hostility and eventual trouble within the country.

But there are also positive signs. The House of Commons hastened to adopt, one month after the referendum, a motion recognizing Quebec as a distinct society and granting a veto to large Canadian provinces on future constitutional change. The federal government also committed itself to some degree of devolution. In the February 1996 Throne Speech, opening a new session of Parliament, the Governor General announced a new governmental willingness to entrench a "distinct society" clause into the Constitution. All of this is still vague and not very reassuring for Quebec, but it is enough to open the possibility of an eventual resolution of the Canadian riddle.

Quebec Premier Lucien Bouchard, on his part, is more flexible than his predecessor. Although he is still devoted to the ideal of sovereignty, he is determined not to call a referendum too soon and concentrates on addressing Quebec's public finances and economy. The door is not completely closed to further federal-provincial negotiations.

Quebec's dream of Canadian federalism may still be realized, at least partly. Either considerable devolution, leaving small provinces free not to abide by it, or asymmetrical federalism would allow Quebec and English Canada to come to terms with their exclusive concepts of community.

For the time being, Quebec is still a unique network of communications. But the Quebec identity, like any other, is a dynamic phenomenon, and it is changing quite rapidly as this century draws to a close. The old French-Canadian allegiance is almost gone. Younger Quebecers feel now much closer to their fellow citizens living in the province, whatever their ethnic origins, than to French-speaking Canadians of other provinces. The new Quebec identity includes immigrants and anglo-Quebecers as well as long-established francophones. This is still valid even in the post-referendum troubled atmosphere. This identity is also compatible with a new partnership with aboriginal peoples who seek self-determination. At the moment, one of the most remarkable writers in Montreal is a French-speaking young woman by the name of Ying Chen who was born in China. The president of the "Conseil de la langue française" is a woman of Greek origin, Nadia Assimopoulos.

Quebecers are also more outward-looking than ever. They are sensitive to the necessities of economic interdependence and they favor greater integration. This means a North American sense of belonging that goes much beyond Canada. In this context, an interesting movement is growing favouring a non-nationalist approach to sovereignty. The Quebec collective identity would not be so much a matter of language and culture as a matter of aesthetic and ethical choice.[15] Quebec would be a viable space to live in a North American way without falling prey to all the trappings of the American way of life.

Quebec might very well be the last bastion of a real alternative to the United States system in the framework of a British parliamentary regime. Quebecers deeply want to be themselves as well as Canadian, North American and citizens of the world. It would be unfortunate if they couldn't achieve this goal within a Canadian union.[16] But if sovereignty (which in any case could hardly be understood in a classical sense) is necessary for them to maintain their identity, one may hope they will have the courage to opt for it in a democratic and peaceful way.

---

[15] See Martin Masse. *Identités collectives et civilisation: Pour une vision non nationaliste d'un Québec indépendant.* Montréal: VLB Éditeur, 1994.

[16] According to a poll released on February 14, 1996, Quebecers still highly value the Canadian connection but don't think Quebec is "master of its own destiny within Canada" (60.5%) and see the federal system as not "sufficiently flexible to respond to the aspirations of Quebecers" (51.9%). There would still be 54.3%, among those decided, who would vote "Yes" in a referendum on sovereignty. *The Globe and Mail*, Feb. 24 1996, p. A5.

THE BREAKING POINT: LANGUAGE IN QUEBEC SOCIETY

The oft-heard phrase "language in Quebec society" is a somewhat superfluous one. If societies tend to have defining characteristics, then Quebec society is itself defined through language. Few textbooks in sociolinguistics or in the sociology of language fail to bring up the Quebec case in the litany of societies that are riven by linguistic tensions and divisions. It is also, however, somewhat inaccurate to refer to "Quebec society" as if it were a homogeneous entity in which the language game is played out according to the same rules from one end of the province to the other. Quebec is really composed of two distinct societies: the Montreal region, in which 68% of the population listed French as its mother tongue in 1991, and the rest of Quebec, where the same category made up 93.5% of the population at the same period (CLF, 1994: 3). Not only are English-speakers concentrated in the Montreal area (making up 15.5% of the population in 1991), but "other" language groups (of mainly immigrant origin) also tend to live in, or in the vicinity of, the metropolis. Although French-language politicians tend to appeal for solidarity around the language issue as if all francophones were living in the same linguistic environment, the reality is otherwise. Montreal's housing and labour markets, shopping malls and city centre, public thoroughfares and leisure sites, public services and media networks are crisscrossed by language frontiers which make the city quite unlike the rest of Quebec and, indeed, generally unlike any other city anywhere else.

The intention in this chapter is to look more closely at these multiple language frontiers. What do they mean? How are they constructed? Are they disappearing gradually (along with the native-English-speaking population of the Montreal region which declined from 26.5% of the population in 1951 to 15.5% in 1991), or, on the contrary, are they being reinforced?

I will conclude the argument by suggesting that Quebec society has in fact arrived at a breaking point—but not one that might be imagined. In order to get to that breaking point, however, I will first provide certain ways of looking at language from a sociological perspective.

A SOCIOLOGICAL PERSPECTIVE ON LANGUAGE

Language plays a central role in social relations. Not only are the interactions between people explained and understood in terms of language, but those inter-actions themselves, more often than not, take on a linguistic form. If society is seen as the coming together of different categories of people to appropriate, organize, produce, distribute, subsist, and, in some cases, exclude and oppress other groups, language is central to all these activities. Not only does acting together mean talking together (for everything from planning to doing), but the community-in-action that tends to emerge in the doing of things in a collective way also becomes, inevitably, a community of talk.[1] This does not just mean that in order to be able to act together people have to be able to understand each other. It also means that being able to understand each other, sharing the same language or way of talking, comes to be part of the way in which a community-in-action thinks about itself. The idea expressed as "we are the people who act in such-and-such a way" (with respect, for example, to appropriating, producing and excluding) can come to mean one and the same as the idea that "we are the people who talk in such-and-such a way."

Beyond the simple (or not so simple) use of language as a tool for doing things, there is, thus, also the use of language as a way of understanding who we are. Language is not just a question of doing but of being: who I am is inti-mately connected with the way I talk, and the way I talk is directly linked to a larger collective "who" that talks in the same way that I do. If the way we talk is part of belonging to a larger community-in-action, and comes into being in the process of communal action, it is also, by definition, the way in which people in other communities-in-action don't talk. A community-in-action defines itself as a community, that is, it sets up boundaries around itself as a community, by identifying other communities outside itself and its boundaries. The "way" it talks, or the way it comes to talk, is only a "way" insofar as the people on the other side of the boundary don't talk in that way.

Different ways of talking (whether dialects of one language or different lan-guages) are thus not only the result of different people at different places and times developing different ways of communicating with each other, but can also emerge in the interaction between communities. These are two distinct but

---

[1] I use the term "community" to refer to the product of "communalization" in the Weberian sense (*Vergemeinschaftung*) (cf. Weber 1978, pp.41ff. & 341ff. and more especially Weber 1985, pp.21 & 201f. since the specific meaning attached by Weber to the concept *Gemeinschaft* is frequently lost in translation). According to Weber, collective social action oriented towards the realization of a com-mon objective tends to produce a feeling of belongingness and a sense of common identity among those who participate in the action. It is thus that "community" arises out of collective action or, more accurately, accompanies that action and allows it to happen (among other things, by identify-ing those who belong to the collectivity in question and those who do not). I do not, however, limit myself to the Weberian conception, but take it as a starting point for addressing the broader issue of language and collective action.

interlinked processes: living apart from other groups can lead to increasing dissimilarity in the way the members of those groups talk. However, members of groups can also increase the distance between themselves and others by increasing the dissimilarity. More often than not, both these things happen at once: social distance allows and creates dissimilarity of talk (through lack of contact) but dissimilarity can also be actively fostered as a way of increasing or maintaining the social distance which in turn reinforces dissimilarity.

Left to itself, this constant feedback can lead to total language difference and the impossibility of communication across community frontiers. Within a given society, however, there tend to be pressures that push in the opposite direction. A society only exists insofar as it is also, to some extent, a community-in-action, for example, a community that is prepared to defend itself and its territory against other external communities. The existence of that society thus presumes a degree of shared language among members of the society sufficient to allow it to act as a community when the occasion requires. Indeed, I define community as a network of potential communicating and acting partners. But within any society, multiple sub-communities form with the intention of appropriating different kinds of spaces, and multiple ways of talking develop as part of that appropriation and boundary construction. This process of differentiation is held in check, however, by the existence of the overarching society as a potential community-in-action and therefore as a language community. Differentiation can go to the extremes of dialectal difference (the point at which people can still understand each other), but cannot go beyond those extremes without calling into question the existence of the society.

This is what happened after the colonization of Western Scotland by the Irish in the early Middle Ages. The Irish that was spoken in the areas of colonization gradually diverged from the dialects on the Irish mainland to the point where mutual comprehension became impossible. It is at this point that linguists define the emergence of a new language, Scottish Gaelic (Jackson 1951, Thompson 1983). The emergence of this new language is symptomatic of the fact that the society no longer existed in which the Irish and the Scottish of Irish origin belonged to the same potential (or real) community-in-action. In this case, sheer physical distance destroyed the links. Within a society, separate languages do not emerge unless there is a breakdown of the overarching community-in-action which, in any event, signals the end of the original society. What is normal, within a society—particularly in an inegalitarian society—is the emergence of any number of communities building up difference and distance from each other in their ways of talking. The more extreme the inequality, the more such difference and distance moves towards (but not beyond) the limit of mutual comprehension.

Distinct both from the unitary society with more or less pronounced dialectal differences within itself and the juxtaposition of two societies speaking different languages, is a third kind of society which may not be a society at all. In this case, two or more communities, with mutually incomprehensible languages, coexist within the same social framework. Classically, such societies have been the product of conquest and colonialism, where an incoming dominant community-in-action, with its own language, comes into what is already socially appropriated territory and carves out a space for itself. What really happens in such circumstances is not the creation of a new society but rather of two hierarchically opposed societies within the same territory. The community-in-action which is nonetheless necessary for the functioning of the colony, and therefore requires the capacity to communicate which is the precondition for such a community, is ensured by the emergence of an interstitial group of bilinguals who carry messages from one level to the other (generally in a downward direction in the form of commands and in an upward direction in the form of information gathered). Such hierarchically opposed societies—whose dominant group can claim and believe it to be a single, unitary community-in-action—are inherently unstable. The maintenance of language-difference can facilitate exclusionary action on the part of the dominant group, but it can also facilitate redressive action on the part of the subordinated population whose existence as an opposed and potential community-in-action is reinforced by the maintenance of a separate language.

Language thus emerges as a key factor not only in the way social relations, and ultimately societies, are constructed, but also in allowing us to chart appropriated territories and boundaries within those societies. But it is not simply a signpost or boundary marker showing us where to look for the social relations that are somehow supposed to happen "outside" language. Nor is language a "being" in itself that can survive, be under threat, and even die, as current usage would have it. Language is indissociable from the people who speak it, and the people who speak it are indissociable from language. Saying is also doing, as Austin would say, and not just in the more ritualized settings where people declare themselves, hereby, to be doing something even as they say it (getting married, for example, or swearing allegiance to the crown). Every time anyone communicates they are also placing themselves on the map of social relations, declaring, to anyone who cares to listen, who they are, or who they think they are, by what they say and the way they say it. Saying, like any other form of action, is thus a doing and a making, not just a reflection or an echo of other things happening elsewhere.

In the present context I look at saying and doing, at communities-in-action and communities-in-talk, and at dialectal and language differences in the appropriation of social space and boundary construction, in a society in which language is not so much seen as a secondary reflection of something that is happening elsewhere, but ends up displacing everything else as (apparently) the key social issue around which everything else revolves. In Quebec society, the idea that language can exist as a thing in its own right is taken to such extremes that ultimately the whole society is subsumed into the vortex of language-difference, much as Northern Ireland is reduced to Catholicism and

Protestantism. In the following sections I look more closely at the why's and wherefore's of this ultimate form of reification (language as the "thing" in itself) in which the complexity of social relations comes to be reduced to language. First, I return to the scene in which current communities-in-talk and -action in Quebec interrelate with each other; second, I analyze some of the results from ongoing research projects on language in the Montreal private-sector workplace. Finally, I come back to the questions raised in the opening section: what is the meaning of all this "saying" and "doing" in Quebec society?

SETTING THE SCENE

In Quebec society—if it is a society—we find several of the above-mentioned tendencies operating at once. From the sixteenth century onwards, colonialism initially opposed French-speaking colonists against indigenous peoples speaking a variety of languages, the latter being subjected to varying degrees of marginalization and subordination. In some cases, native peoples disappeared (through assimilation) into the surrounding colonial society. In others, their existence as separate societies was consolidated by the setting up of reservations that were specifically designed to maintain distance and difference, and still do. There was no one society which combined the colonists and the colonized; rather, there was an uneasy juxtaposition of a commercially and agriculturally based colonial society, and a number of fragmented, marginalized, and subsistence-orientated indigenous societies.

A second wave of colonialism subsequently opposed English-speaking merchants and settlers (from the late eighteenth century onwards) against French-speaking colonial society (in its different agricultural, commercial and religious dimensions). Where the French had set up their own hierarchical arrangement of colonial and indigenous societies, the British added another layer by occupying the space which they took over from French commercial interests. They left the French-speaking farming population, religious hierarchy and professional classes in the splendid isolation from which they were to emerge only in the 1960s.

From the mid-nineteenth century, the strategic position of Montreal as a port of entry into the rest of Canada and the northern United States contributed to its rapid development as a commercial and industrial centre. Grain from the Canadian west was brought in railroad trucks (many of which were built and maintained in Montreal) to Montreal's docks for shipment across the Atlantic, while immigrants from Europe arrived in their thousands at those same docks, either to remain in the city or to move west into the new industrial heartlands around the Great Lakes or to plant and harvest the grain that they met coming in the opposite direction. This hive of industrial and commercial activity in Montreal was built up around British capital and British companies and—in its early stages—around a skilled workforce largely imported from Britain. It was thus that in 1870, the majority of the population of Montreal was English-speaking and of British and Irish extraction, although increasingly, French Canadians were moving in from the countryside into mainly blue-collar employment.

Even as Montreal's urban workforce became increasingly French-speaking, Quebec society retained its essentially colonial characteristics, as I have defined them here. What had been the juxtaposition of two relatively distinct commercially and agriculturally based societies, each with its own language (with certain regional exceptions), came increasingly to take on the form of a hierarchically ordered, industrial urban society (itself split into two societal language-groups) and a French-speaking agricultural workforce producing mainly for its own subsistence. From the late nineteenth century onwards, internal migrants coming to Montreal from the surrounding countryside found themselves in increasing competition, not only with the first generation of British skilled workers, but also with unskilled immigrant labour from Ireland, China and elsewhere. Montreal thus came to be made up of a series of territories occupied by groups of different languages and origins—much along the lines of other North American cities—but with the French-speaking population rapidly increasing in numerical dominance and the English-speaking population consolidating its hold over large-scale commerce and industry.

This arrangement was to be fundamentally transformed in the 1960s with the (partial) emancipation of French-speaking Quebec from the hold of the Catholic Church and its increasing control over the apparatus of the state. As Guindon has pointed out, alongside the continuing dominance of English-speakers (whatever their maternal language might have been) in the private sector, the 1960s and 1970s saw the emergence of a public sector (including the nationalized production and distribution of electricity, as well as the full panoply of health, social and educational services) under the control of, and largely staffed by, French-speakers, with the exception of those services and institutions that existed to cater to the English-speaking population. Public-sector employment created openings for social advancement and upward mobility for French-speakers that had not hitherto existed on the same scale.

By the end of the 1970s, the average income of male, native-language French-speakers had caught up with that of their English-speaking counterparts (Vaillancourt, 1988), this being due in part to public-sector employment. But French-speakers were also moving into the private sector (in some cases, with the help of the state). The presence of French-speakers among those owning and controlling companies in the various commercial and industrial sectors increased in all sectors except mining. This increasing economic and political power accruing to the French-speaking population (or part of it) was won mainly at the expense of English-speaking Canadian interests. It also gave rise to a series of laws that sought to consolidate the position of French not only as Quebec's official language, but also as the language of everyday usage in the public domain (signposts and advertizing), in the workplace and in education (for those born in Quebec to French-speaking parents, or born outside Quebec, whatever their maternal language might be).

The enactment of fully fledged language legislation was one of the first gestures of the new separatist government of Quebec (elected in 1976). From 1978 onwards, most large and medium-sized private-sector companies were supposed to move from English-only operation (where this was the case) to bilingualism and, if possible, to the exclusive use of French; immigrants arriving in Quebec were no longer allowed to send their children to English-speaking schools (as they had traditionally done), but were obliged to enroll them in the French-speaking system; and the "face" of Quebec was transformed by the requirement that French be the only language on signs and billboards. During the 1980s and 1990s, some of the provisions of this legislation were watered down. The Supreme Court of Canada declared in the 1980s, for example, that immigrants to Quebec from the rest of Canada could send their children to English-speaking schools, while the Quebec government, in recent legislation, has permitted some degree of bilingualism on commercial signs (other than billboards).

On the political front, from the late 1960s onwards, the French-speaking population of Quebec has been wooed by two implacable suitors. The first, consisting of the federal government and the Quebec federalist parties, has attempted to convince Québécois that their best future lies in a bilingual Canada, in which all citizens have the right (theoretically) to live and be served in their own language. The second, made up of Quebec separatist parties in and out of government, suggests that the only viable future consists of a territorially unilingual Quebec within its own frontiers and separated from the rest of Canada. For both suitors, language is the key, and with respect to both of their offers, the French-speaking population of Quebec (that constituted, in 1991, 82% of the population of the province) remains in a state of indecision.

From the 1970s to the 1990s, the future of Quebec and the future of the French language have been intertwined. It is impossible to think about language-use in Quebec without seeing it in light of the political wrangling over the relations between Quebec and the rest of Canada. Every legislative gesture with respect to language tends to be seen as part of an overall confrontation, an endgame, a fight to the finish between the forces of light and darkness (depending on which side one is looking from). The gradual decrease in the population with English as its maternal language, from 14% of the population of the province in 1951 to 9% in 1991, only reinforces the idea that Quebec is in some way being linguistically cleared of its non-French-speaking elements. All of this is grist to the mill for politicians who prefer thinking in terms of stark contrasts rather than shades of grey. But alongside the linguistic confrontations in the political arena, there are other things happening in language use which can be equally confrontational, but which seem to have little to do with the strong messages bravely shouted by each side from behind the barricades.

In the private-sector workplace in Montreal, for example, in spite of the increasing presence of French-speakers as owners, managers and technical experts, and in spite of the decreasing proportion of the population of the province having English as its mother tongue, the use of English has not declined since the 1970s other than in services and blue-collar work (CLF 1994, Monnier 1983, Béland, 1991). In 1989, for example, it has been calculated that more than 50% of all linguistic interaction among white-collar workers in Montreal's key private sector was in English. This represents, if anything, a slight increase relative to the situation ten years beforehand (Béland, 1991). There are indications that the reinforcement of English as an international language of science and business is as much of a threat to the continuing use of French as the old English-speaking community once was. Beneath the stark realities of political discourse, the ground seems to be shifting, or not shifting in the way that the discourse suggests it is. In what follows, I look more closely at this shifting or non-shifting ground on the basis of recently completed and ongoing research projects. The first series of projects relates to the use of language in the workplace; the second, to the linguistic integration, or non-integration, of immigrants.

THE PEOPLE FROM DOWN BELOW: LANGUAGE IN THE WORKPLACE

The workplace is a key social site to examine if we seek to understand the way in which social relations are constructed. Not only do most people spend most of their lives at work, but in an industrial, market-oriented society, access to paid work or the ability to hire and profit from the work of others is the key to survival (at other than bare subsistence levels) and enrichment. Thus, the struggle for the appropriation of social space by different communities-in-action with the express purpose of increasing the benefits accruing to the community (at the expense of others) is linked first and foremost to the workplace and the work process. Montreal's language frontier is frequently seen in residential terms, with the English-speaking population being heavily concentrated in areas west of the city centre. However, the highly visible (and audible) language frontiers between the different urban areas, along with the mixed-language frontier zones, are in many ways less significant in terms of the processes underlying the construction of boundaries than the more complex, less visible, but omnipresent frontiers that run through the Quebec workplace.

This language frontier was studied in the 1940s by Everett Hughes. Hughes did research on a small town in the centre of Quebec and on its British-owned textile mills. The picture that emerges of the town, with the two language groups occupying separate spaces in everything from golfing to churchgoing, is still relevant for our understanding of the role played by language in the occupation of social space. Hughes' account is particularly interesting for the light it throws on the language frontier in the workplace itself. Most of the managers in the principal textile mill were incapable of speaking French and most of the blue-collar workers were incapable of speaking English. The mill only managed to function because of an intermediary group of supervisors who acted as interpreters and go-betweens. The mill thus corresponds to what I have described as the colonial model of language use; in essence, two hierarchically ordered societies coexist within the same social space (albeit occupying different territories within that space) and only manage to come together to some extent as a community-in-action for the purposes of production, given the presence of bilinguals who carry commands across the frontier within the workplace.

The situation as described by Hughes in the 1940s is not dissimilar to that still prevailing in many Montreal workplaces in the 1990s. As mentioned above, more than 50% of all interaction among white-collar workers and management in Montreal's key private sector in the late 1980s is estimated to have been in English, in spite of the fact that those with English as their maternal language represent less than 10% of the population (Béland, 1991). The surveys of language use in the Montreal workplace since the 1970s suggest that parts of the old language frontier are still alive and well. One of the problems, however, is to know exactly what is happening in these key social sites which are, by definition, private and relatively inaccessible to research.

What is known about the workplace language frontier is largely based on the answers to questionnaires done over the telephone about language behaviour at work. Given the politically sensitive nature of all information relating to language use in Quebec, however, it is not clear to what extent respondants of either language group can be expected to provide a detached overview of their language use within the space of a short telephone interview. The opinions expressed in such interviews are liable to be subject to varying degrees of over- and underestimation, depending on the characteristics of the person being interviewed and his or her perception of the goals of the research (almost exclusively funded by Quebec government agencies responsible for the application of the law that requires the use of French in the workplace).

There is another problem with such research, however. The use French or of English at work means little if we do not know how language itself is used in the workplace. In many kinds of factory work, people are not required to talk much and, in fact, may have little opportunity to talk, write or read during work time. Their work, on an assembly line, for example, may thus have low language content, and they may even be prohibited from talking or reading. For such people, "working in French" may mean little more than the use of French for the few oral exchanges between themselves and supervisors or co-workers during the working day and the perusal of French pay-slips at the end of the week. Most white-collar work, on the other hand, revolves around language use. Managers, receptionists, secretaries, clerks, accountants, and sales representatives (among others) spend their workdays talking to each other in meetings, answering

callers, reading documents, giving orders, explaining to clients, and writing letters and reports. White-collar work is, in large part, language work. Language is
taken in its raw state and worked up into different kinds of product, different
forms of "text." While blue-collar workers transform blocks of raw material into
component parts and assemble them into products, white-collar workers spend
their time mining their word-stores and hammering out phrases.

The production process thus brings together two different worlds: one built
around the transformation of language, and the other built around the transformation of other kinds of raw material. What is known about the Montreal private-sector workplace is that English tends to occupy a disproportionate place
(in terms of the number of native-language English-speakers in the population)
in the first of these two worlds, that is, where language is at the heart of the production process. The use of French, on the other hand, is predominant in the
second world, where language is peripheral to the production process, and may,
in certain cases, be completely absent. Hughes did not look at the language frontier in this way, but others since Hughes (Laponce, Monnier and Béland, for
example) have recognized the importance of linking research on the use of different languages at work to the question of the relative amount of language
being used. What has not been done, however, is to look closely at the way in
which language is used in the work process before asking the question as to how
the different languages themselves are used.

LANGUAGE AND THE RECONSTRUCTED WORKDAY

The problem is to develop a research method that allows us to get close enough
to the work process and the use of language to be able to analyze it. Since 1992
we have been experimenting with a method that is based on the reconstruction
of the workday through the use of an interview.[2] Interviews are held at the end
of the workday, and the interviewees are asked to provide a detailed, chronolog-
ical account of everything they did during the day in terms of work, the use of
oral or written language in relation to work, and the use of English and French.
Each of these moments of the interview is kept separate. The goal is first to
understand exactly what the person did during the day in terms of work and
how the work they do fits in to the overall production process. For those who

---

[2] The different research projects on language in the Quebec workplace which are discussed in this
text have been conducted by my research team in the Sociology of language at the University of
Montreal. The members of the team are Louise Tremblay, Catherine Montgomery, Carlos Teixeira,
and Frédérique Le Goff. More than 100 interviews have been conducted in a variety of work settings. Research has been funded by the *Office de la langue française* (Quebec), the Secrétariat à la politique linguistique (Quebec), the Institut de recherches appliquées sur le travail, the Fédération des
travailleurs et travailleuses du Québec, the Social Sciences and Humanities Research Council of
Canada, and the Secretary of State for Multiculturalism (Canada). Further information on our
research methods and results can be obtained from McAll, Montgomery & Tremblay (1994).

are involved in language work, receptionists for example, this first part of the interview already includes a strong language component. For non-language workers, it is necessary to understand the extent to which language is or is not used in relation to work. It is only when the activities of that day in terms of work and language have been understood by the interviewer that the interviewee is asked to specify which language was used for the different work-related language tasks performed during the day. And it is only when the working day has been fully grasped by the interviewer that more general information is sought on whether or not what happened during that particular day is typical of what the person normally does.

Throughout the interview we thus make a distinction not only between the use of language as such and the use of which particular language, but also between the use of language in relation to work (the "professional" use of language) and its use for more social purposes (the "social" use). The principal benefit in meeting people at the end of the working day is that the information provided relates to recent events. In the course of the interview, the tendency to generalize ("I normally use French when I speak to the supervisor") can be countered by specific questions linked to what happened during the day ("Did you speak to your supervisor today, and if so, what did you say?"). Interviewees can thus be confronted by a gap between what they think they normally do and what they actually do. The tendency to underestimate or overestimate certain kinds of language behaviour can thus be corrected (to some extent) by asking detailed questions concerning recent and recalled events.

Another advantage of the method is that it can allow the working day to be reconstructed without the researcher having to gain the company's permission to do so (since the interviewee can be interviewed off company premises and outside working hours). Given the politically sensitive nature of all information relating to the use of French and English in the Quebec workplace, and the hostility of many employers to the language legislation, access to the workplace can be difficult (as it is for research on many other socially sensitive issues). The use of the reconstructed workday by interview, for all its shortcomings, is, in our opinion, the next best thing to being there. In some cases, research can be done in collaboration with the unions, and access to the workplace can be negotiated, or interviewees can be seen at work in the context of company open days. We have used both of these strategies in our research. In many cases, however, neither strategy is possible, and the reconstructed workday has to be relied upon as the only source of information. The idea is to conduct a large number of randomly selected reconstructed workdays for different categories of worker and management in different sectors of industry.

Between 1992 and 1995 we reconstructed randomly selected workdays for more than 100 people working in pharmaceuticals, aeronautics, transportation, the garment industry, and in a variety of public- and private-sector services. On the basis of these interviews we concluded that the private-sector workplace seems to be split into three main, socially defined territories. At the lower end of the labour market, among, for example, low-paid workers in the garment indus-try, there may be little or no language content in the work process itself (Montgomery, 1994). Sewing-machine operators spend their days doing repeti-tive detail work on the basis of pre-established models. The noise of the machines and the layout of the different worksites can make communication difficult. Not only is there little need for talk, but the piece-rate system discour-ages time-wasting interaction and conversation. Such workplaces have high concentrations of immigrant workers, and the brief exchanges that can be heard every now and again against the background of machine noise may be in Spanish, French, Creole, Italian, Greek, Vietnamese, English or a mixture of these and other languages. During the breaks, workers sit in distinct language groups, or resort to broken English or French as a way of communicating across language barriers. The very existence of such a profusion of languages and half-understood snatches of conversation underlines the marginality of language use in this particular work process: it doesn't really matter if people do not under-stand each other. In fact it may even be more convenient if they don't, given the possibility of shared grievances with respect to working conditions.

If sewing-machine operators in the garment industry work in an environment in which, paradoxically, they are both reduced to silence and surrounded by noise—the one being linked to the other—and in which whatever communication there is tends to take place in a variety of different languages, the "language-sur-round" of the better-paid blue-collar workers in the aerospace industry is different. Most of these workers are French-speakers, and the general working environment has more language content than that of sewing-machine operators in the garment industry. Given the complexity of the work process and the high levels of preci-sion involved, there is a greater need for communication and discussion.

The specifications for the machining of component parts, for example, are read from instruction sheets or computer screens, thus requiring language use, even if the noise of the machines may make oral communication difficult. Away from the noisier machines, there is also the possibility of more prolonged socially oriented conversations on anything from house-buying to windsurfing—conver-sations that run in parallel to the work process without interrupting it. At the various airframe and aircraft engine plants that we researched, the "blue-collar language-surround" tends to be French. French sentence structure and French vocabulary are interlaced, however, with local plant or workshop jargon (incomprehensible to the uninitiated), strings of acronyms, and English technical terms for everything from tools and parts to processes. The closer that language use is linked to the production process and to the materials that are being trans-formed, the more French is relegated to a supporting, syntactical role, and the more the central carriers of meaning are English technical terms.

With regard to written texts (instruction manuals, inspection reports, com-puter operating languages, and scribbled notes), the use of English is almost uni-versal. Written texts accompany, define and record all aspects of production. As the product moves through the plant, it may start as a gleam in an engineer's (or the company's) eye, but it is subsequently "written down" in mathematical, graphical and natural language in order to be communicated to those who will transform that written text into something real and three-dimensional (three-dimensional, that is, in other than cyberspace). It is at this key moment of coming-into-existence that the product is thought about and represented symbolically in English. As it moves from virtual to non-virtual reality, English symbols are replaced by the objects and processes they represent. Those doing the replacing and transforming—according to instructions—may be French-speakers, and may bring French into the oral language-surround, but French is absent as a written language in the central production-stream linking the symbolic and material representations of the product.

In these high-technology workplaces in Montreal, French-speakers are numerically dominant and the use of French is technically on the increase as a result of the language legislation that seeks to reinforce the use of French as the working language in Quebec. However, that increase in the use of French in, for example, the oral language-surround of blue-collar workers and on company security notices and pay cheques in the aerospace industry, is not necessarily accompanied by any greater presence of French at the heart of the manufacturing process, where products are conceptualized and defined. That does not mean that there is not a greater presence of French-speakers among engineers and managers. On the contrary, more and more qualified engineers with French as their maternal language are moving into aerospace and comparable sectors. As they move across the threshold into the new workplace, however, they move into an environment where English has traditionally dominated, and as with anyone moving across a societal language frontier, they have little choice but to operate in the local language.

But wherein lies this absence of choice? Why the paradoxical maintenance of the language frontier when native-speakers of French are increasingly present on both sides? Our interviews with engineers and low-level management provide some clues to the unravelling of this paradox. We will begin by moving from the shop floor with its large open spaces, high roofs, ventilation fans, and row upon row of chattering machines, ovens and acid baths, through the double doors into the world where the products are only symbolically present. In doing so, we leave behind the world where raw materials and symbolic representations are transformed into products, and in which the use of French is omnipresent but largely relegated to the oral language-surround, and enter the third type of private-sector territory that is to be considered here, where everything revolves around the use of language.

The reconstructed workdays of French-speaking white-collar workers in a pharmaceuticals company are in some ways not dissimilar to those of blue-collar workers in the aerospace industry (Tremblay 1993). Work-related language use (filling in forms for example, or reading documents) is punctuated by social exchange ("at 10 o'clock this morning I went to department X to talk about last night's hockey results"). As in the case of blue-collar work, the closer that language use is to the work process itself, the greater its English content. However, whereas English content in blue-collar language use among native-language French-speakers tends to be limited to technical terms and set phrases, (with French providing the syntactical support), among white-collar workers interviewed whose mother tongue in French, the use of French recedes more or less completely into the social background.

Paradoxically, in this latter case, the professional and social uses of language are both hopelessly intertwined and yet clearly marked linguistically. Formal, work-related meetings tend to be in English, even where French-speakers constitute the majority and where English-speakers present are known to be bilingual. Informal exchanges and off-the-record remarks during the meeting may be in French (between French-speakers) but English holds the floor as the official, working language. Unlike blue-collar workers, these white-collar workers do not thus have one code with the two languages mixed together—one providing the syntactical support and the other the lexical content—but tend to operate with two separate codes. They switch from one to the other, thereby signalling the work- or non-work-related character of the exchange. Coffee-breaks come to be the main French-speaking events.

In the randomly selected reconstructed workdays there were some exceptions, however. For example, the white-collar workers interviewed are housed in an office block (the administration building) connected to, and built alongside, the company's main manufacturing plant. While English is the working language for management, research and white-collar work, French is the language of the factory. Whenever the interviewees' tasks brought them closer to, or into contact with, the "people from down below" (*les gens d'en bas*)—as the people in the factory are referred to by those in the administration building—French content noticeably increases. French is used not only for telephone calls to the shipping department, but is also the predominant language in a meeting involving the factory manager and various people from administration. French is thus not just the "social" language for French-speaking white-collar workers, but is also the "factory" language, the language to be used when talking to blue-collar workers or their representatives, i.e. to the "people from down below." When asked why they tend to use English even with other French-speakers for administration work, interviewees suggested both that English was simpler and more efficient as a means of communication and that they felt embarrassed when using French in such contexts.

It is clear from these reconstructed workdays that the interviewees are subject to strong pressures as far as language use is concerned. The confining of French to social and factory-linked communication and the almost exclusive use of English in white-collar (language) work is linked to the historical dominance of English-speakers among those owning and running private companies in Quebec. However, with the partial shift of ownership to French-speakers, and their increasing presence among those in white-collar work and management, the historically based argument is no longer adequate to explain the use of English by white-collar workers. Nor is it adequate to suggest that such clearly defined language territories within the workplace are simply the reflection of the increasing predominance of English as an international language. While both of these factors evidently come into play in defining the overall context, there are nonetheless factors originating within the workplace itself that are linked to the division between workers and management and the overall control of the work process.

The feeling of embarrassment expressed by the French-speaking white-collar workers when they use French for work-related tasks reflects the strong norms imposing the use of English at all levels of the company bureaucracy. Bureaucracies are based on the hierarchical organization of language work, information processing, storage and transmission. Orders and requests for information move down through the hierarchy, and oral and written reports of different kinds move upwards in response. Information has to be accessible to the upper levels. There are limits to the extent that those working at such levels would tolerate the speaking of "other" languages among subordinates whose only aim in life (or at least, in work) is to pass on information downwards and feed information upwards. I would suggest that all bureaucracies are founded on the principle of "open access to information from below."

It is equally clear, however, that bureaucracies, as information-gathering and decision-making machines, have an interest in not making certain kinds of information available to those outside the bureaucracy. In the context of private industry, for example, product information has to be sent to those who will eventually transform the drawings and written specifications into objects. However, the company may have no interest in providing production workers with supplementary information relating to company accounts, marketing decisions, personnel cutbacks, planned product lines and plant closures. If one law (open access to information from below) requires white-collar workers to work in the language of management, another (restricted access to information from above) can be a reinforcing factor in any situation where the people down below (on the factory floor) do not actually speak or fully understand management's language.

Hence, the paradox of the survival of the bilingual private-sector workplace in Quebec may not really be a paradox at all, but the working out in practice of two opposing laws. If it was the colonial character of Quebec's social structure and the historical presence of the two language groups that set the system in motion, there seems to be no reason why it should not continue moving in the same direction, in spite of the gradual demise of native-language English-speakers as an indentifiably dominant "community." Given such a conclusion, the hypothesis that workplace bilingualism is simply the reflection of the predominance of English as an international language needs to be reconsidered. It is, in any event, inadequate to explain what is happening anywhere as being just the reflection of what is happening elsewhere. Were this the case, nothing would ever happen. It is more reasonable to think that *similar* things are happening in the Quebec private-sector workplace as are happening elsewhere in bilingual environments where one of the two languages is English. The use of one language, English, is gradually becoming predominant for language-work linked to the defining and conceptualization of products and other management and research activities. Other languages are relegated to the social background and to what I describe as the "blue-collar language-surround." The social frontier within the private-sector workplace between decision-makers and information-processors on the one hand, and production workers on the other, is increasingly defined in linguistic terms. What the Quebec situation suggests is that this emerging linguistic frontier is, in large part, internally generated within the workplace.

If the two territories of white-collar language-work and relatively well-paid blue-collar production-work can be seen as exemplifying the two laws that I have referred to as "open access to information from below" (explaining unilingualism within management hierarchies) and "restricted access to information from above" (explaining the maintenance of bilingualism in the overall work context), the question remains as to what, if any, law underlies the multilingual situation in the first kind of territory considered here, of which the garment industry is the classic example. This kind of territory is characterized by low rates of pay, low levels of unionization, and little if any language content as far as the work itself is concerned. Insofar as people can communicate with each other, they do so in a variety of different languages, given the high proportion of immigrant workers. Not only do such workers have difficulty communicating with each other, given noise and language barriers , but they are often not allowed to communicate at all during work time. The law operating in this territory would seem to be "restricted access to information from whatever direction" and completes the triad of laws that underlie the use of languages in the three types of workplace territory.

OF MINDS AND MARKETS

Fishman has suggested that there are two sociolinguistic models that are useful for understanding cases of societal bilingualism: the first he describes as the "urban French-Canadian nationalist" model, and the second, the "urban American migrant" model (Fishman, 1972: 153). According to the first model, a historically subordinate group gradually extends the use of its language to areas from which it had hitherto been excluded; according to the second, the languages of immigrant communities are gradually confined to local and private usage before eventually disappearing altogether. The complexity of the situation in Montreal can be attributed in part to the coming together of these two models: the use of French has been gradually expanding, and at the same time the constant stream of immigrants into the Montreal area has brought with it a variety of language groups and the more or less localized speaking of those languages for as long as the first generation of immigrants survives.

The situation is more complex than these models would suggest, however. Our reconstructed workdays reveal three socially defined territories in the private sector, each of which contributes to the maintenance of certain patterns of multilingualism, bilingualism and unilingualism. While the use of French has become predominant in public-sector employment at all levels in Quebec, in the private sector (particularly in the Montreal area) it is incorporated into a system of language frontiers that shows few signs of change. What is more, immigrants, traditionally, have tended to learn English rather than French. This has given rise to a situation where immigrants can be seen as threatening the survival of French and, by extension, the survival of the community that speaks it.

From the 1970s onwards, considerable efforts have been made to make French-language courses available to immigrants. Since 1990, Quebec immigration policy has included, as one of its three main objectives, the reinforcing of the French language. Refugees and immigrants who sign up for social welfare and therefore come under Quebec's income security law are required to sign employability-development contracts. According to these contracts, they agree to complete their secondary education or take training courses in order to improve their chances of finding work. If they do not already speak French, then the learning of French is the first stage in the process. Although they are required to sign these contracts, Canadian federal law, at present, does not allow provincial governments to make the receipt of welfare conditional on participation in education or work programmes. The contracts are thus only morally binding, although non-participation can lead to a reduction in the amount of welfare received. The message, however, is clear: immigrants are expected to learn the language of the (numerical) majority and thereby contribute to the increasing use of French in the various work- and non-work-related activities in which they will eventually be involved.

The subsequent experience of immigrants in the labour market can be bewildering. Many go to great lengths to learn French (in order to escape from low-paid work with low language content) only to emerge onto a labour market in which employers frequently require competence in English as well as, or rather than, French. In my own research on a random sample of 62 asylum-seekers who arrived in Montreal between 1986 and 1991, English was the predominant language in 52% of the 71 workplaces they ended up in, as opposed to French in 35%.[3] Their experience is similar to that of highly qualified, non-immigrant university graduates (in engineering, for example) who can emerge on to the labour market only to find that the main private-sector job opportunities require competence in English.

Immigrants are thus brought directly into contact with two distinct and conflicting realities. In terms of the percentage of Quebecers with French as their maternal language, Quebec is an overwhelmingly French-speaking society. In light of that fact, and in the Canadian political context, Quebec defines itself, officially,

---

[3] See: McAll, Christopher. *Les requérants du statut de réfugié au Québec: un nouvel espace de marginalité?* (in press).

as French-speaking. Depending on the viewpoint adopted, the province is either presented as an integral part of a bilingual Canada or as carrying within itself the seeds of an independent state. From both of these viewpoints, however, the factor that binds Quebec society together as a community-in-action (whether inside or, potentially, outside the Canadian state), is language. The political rhetoric of solidarity and belongingness, the joining of people across class, sex, age and regional boundaries in the common purpose of furthering Quebec's cause within or outside Canada, is glued together by language.

Outside the domain of political rhetoric and the forging of collective identities as patterns-for-action, though, in the day-to-day realm of workplace routine and cultural consumerism, there are other ways of talking and acting. The three socially defined territories in the Montreal private-sector workplace discussed in this chapter are alive and well; "other" language immigrants continue to acquire minimal competence in English and French in order to get by in multilingual workplaces; public-sector work, in which the use of French is predominant, is feeling the cold wind of budget cuts; many university researchers in the pure sciences (in the French-language universities) have long since given up reading and publishing in French; and increasing numbers of engineers, with French as their maternal language, also work in the language of the international marketplace.

The official definition of Quebec as a French-speaking province, along with the demographic fact that the vast majority of the population have French as their maternal language, thus coexists with another kind of reality in the Montreal private-sector workplace. In spite of the apparent contradiction to which this situation gives rise, however, the shared use of the French language still holds as the binding force. The community-in-action still sees itself primarily as a community-in-talk. Ultimately it seems necessary to see language in Quebec society as being linked to two distinct realms of meaning and experience. Immigrants and non-immigrants alike are asked to live in both of these two realms at once: the country of the mind, in which language binds and in which there is no breaking of the ranks, and the country of the market in which anything goes, including language. As time goes on, the link between these two communities in thought and in action stretches to the breaking point.

BIBLIOGRAPHY

Austin, J.L. 1962. *How to do things with words*, Cambridge: Harvard University Press.

Béland, Paul 1991. *L'usage du français au travail, situation et tendances (Synthèse)*, Québec, Conseil de la langue française.

Bouchard, Pierre 1991. *Les enjeux de la francisation des entreprises au Québec (1977-1984)*, Québec, Office de la langue française.

Bourdieu, Pierre 1977. "L'économie des échanges linguistiques", *Langue française*, vol. 34, 1977, pp. 17-34.

Bourdieu, Pierre 1982. *Ce que parler veut dire*, Paris: Fayard, 1982.

Brazeau, Jacques 1992. "L'évolution du statut de l'anglais et du français au Canada", *Sociologie et Sociétés*, 24(2), 103-116.

CLF 1986. *Avis, L'état de la francisation des entreprises*, Québec, Conseil de la langue française.

CLF 1992. *Indicateurs de la situation linguistique au Québec*, Québec: Conseil de la langue française.

CLF 1994. *Indicateurs de la langue du travail au Québec*, Québec: Conseil de la langue française.

Fishman, Joshua A. 1972. *The Sociology of Language: An Interdisciplinary Approach to Language in Society*, Rowley, Mass.: Newbury House Publishers.

Gendron 1972. *Rapport de la Commission d'enquête sur la situation de la langue française et sur les droits linguistiques au Québec* Québec, Gouvernement du Québec.

Guindon, Hubert 1978. "The modernization of Quebec and the legitimacy of the Canadian state", in Guindon, H., *Quebec Society* Toronto: University of Toronto Press, 1988, pp. 60-93.

Habermas, Jürgen 1979. "What is Universal Pragmatics?" in *Communication and the Evolution of Society* , Boston: Beacon Press, pp. 1-68.

Heller, Monica 1989. "Aspects sociolinguistiques de la francisation d'une entreprise privée" in *Sociologie et sociétés*, 21(2), pp. 115-28.

Hughes, Everett C. 1943. *French Canada in Transition*. Chicago: University of Chicago Press.

Jackson, Kenneth 1951. "Common Gaelic: The Evolution of the Gaelic Languages", *Proceedings of the British Academy* 37.

Labov, W. 1972. *Language in the Inner City*, Philadelphia: University of Pennsylvania Press.

Laponce, J.A. 1984. *Langue et territoire*, Québec, Les Presses de l'Université Laval.

Maurais, Jacques 1987. "L'expérience québécoise d'aménagement linguistique" in *Politique et aménagement linguistiques*, Québec: Conseil de la langue française, pp. 361-411.

McAll, Christopher 1990. *Class, Ethnicity and Social Inequality*, Montréal, McGill-Queen's University Press; (2nd. edition, 1992).

McAll, Christopher 1991. *Beyond Culture: Immigration in Contemporary Quebec*, Ottawa, Economic Council of Canada, 1991.

McAll, Christopher 1992. "Langues et silence: les travailleurs immigrés au Québec et la sociologie du langage", *Sociologie et Sociétés* , 24(2), pp. 117-130.

McAll, Christopher 1993a. "Comment se fait la francisation", *Relations* May 1993.

McAll, Christopher 1993b. "L'utilisation du langage et des langues dans quatre milieux de travail à Montréal", in McAll, Christopher (1993) (ed.), pp. 1-23.

McAll, Christopher 1993c. (ed.) *Langues et langage dans quatre milieux de travail à Montréal*, Research report submitted to the *Office de la langue française*, Quebec, 1993.

McAll, Christopher 1994. "Identités, inégalités, territoires: une société à déconstruire", in Jean-Marie Fecteau, (ed.) *La condition québécoise*, Montréal: VLB Éditeur.

McAll, Christopher, Montgomery, Tremblay, 1994. "Utilisation du langage et des langues au travail: la reconstruction de la journée du travail et la cartographie sociolinguistique d'entreprise", in *Terminogramme* , 74, pp. 1-7.

Milroy, Lesley 1987. *Language and Social Networks*, (2nd Ed.), Oxford, Blackwell.

Monnier, Daniel 1983. *L'usage du français au travail*, Québec, Conseil de la langue française.

Montgomery, Catherine 1993. "Une journée typique dans la "cité de la mode": l'utilisation des langues et du langage au travail", in McAll, Christopher, (1993c) (ed.), et langage dans quatre milieux de travail a Montreal, p. 24-53.

Paillé, Michel 1989. *Nouvelles tendances démo-linguistiques dans l'île de Montréal 1981-1996*, Québec: Conseil de la langue française.

Piché, Victor 1992. "Le discours démo-politique au Québec: inclusion ou exclusion?", in *Sociologie et Sociétés*, 24(2), p. 143-150.

Québec 1990. *Au Québec: pour bâtir ensemble: Enoncé de politique en matière d'immigration et d'intégration*, Québec: MCCI.

Reynolds, Lloyd G. 1935. *The British Immigrant: His Social and Economic Adjustment to Canada* . Toronto: Oxford University Press.

Rocher, François, Rocher, G. 1991. "La culture québécoise en devenir: les défis du pluralisme", in Ouellet, F., Pagé, M., (eds.), *Pluralisme, ethnicité et société: Construire un espace commun* , Québec: IQRC, pp. 43-76.

Thompson, Derick S., 1983. *The Companion to Gaelic Scotland* , Oxford: Blackwell, 1983.

Tremblay, Louise 1993. "L'utilisation du langage et des langues dans une entreprise du secteur biomédical", in McAll, Christopher, (1993c) (ed.), Langues et langage dans quatre milieux de travail a Montreal, pp. 54-86.

Vaillancourt, François 1988. *Langue et disparités de statut économique au Québec, 1970-1980*, Québec, Conseil de la langue française.

Vaillancourt, François 1991. *Langue et statut économique au Québec, 1980-1985*, Québec: Conseil de la langue française, 1991.

Veltman, Calvin; Polèse, Mario, et al. 1987. *Structure résidentielle et linguistique des groupes ethniques dans la région métropolitaine de Montréal 1971-1981*, Montréal: INRS-Urbanisation.

Weber, Max 1978. *Economy and Society* . Berkeley: University of California Press.

Weber, Max 1985. *Wirtschaft und Gesellschaft* (1921). Tübingen: J.C.B.Mohr 1925; 5. Auflage, Johannes Winkelmann, (ed.), Tübingen: J.C.B.Mohr, 1985.

CULTURE AND THE POLITICS OF BEING QUÉBÉCOIS: IDENTITY AND COMMUNICATION

When Quebec's politicians insist that Quebec needs to assume control of certain areas of federal jurisdiction such as manpower training or communications, this claim is typically seen by Canadians outside Quebec as an attempt by the Quebec government to grab as much power for themselves as possible. Yet, if this were the case, why is it that Quebec does not seek to control all areas of federal jurisdiction? Most sovereignists, for example, seek a partnership with the rest of Canada in order to retain the Canadian dollar, monetary policy, Canadian citizenship and a wide variety of economic ties. Only certain areas of control are considered essential. Specifically, both sovereignists and federalists in Quebec believe that control over communications policy, technology, and institutions is essential to the survival of Quebec's French culture and the ability of Quebec to articulate its own identity. One of the reasons that support for sovereignty has been growing is the refusal of English Canada to accept this belief as legitimate and to see in it nothing more than a ploy for more power. More and more federalists are wondering whether Quebec can really develop to its full potential within the Canadian confederation.

This chapter is about the intimate link between culture and identity prevalent in Quebec and the way in which Quebecers have sought to retain control over their culture in order to maintain and develop their collective identity. That this is a problem will be shown by considering the critique of federal communications policy made by Québécois researchers. The Canadian Broadcasting Corporation and its French-language network, la Société Radio-Canada, are presented as an example of the cultural difference between Canadian and Quebec societies. We choose this example to demonstrate the depth of the difference that distinguishes Québécois from Canadians. First, however, we need to explain a few things about Québécois identity within the Quebec context itself.

The main argument in this chapter is that the politics that would allow recognition of the Québécois identity are becoming so muddled in negative reactions that we forget to respect the positive choice of the identity itself. Regardless of our personal political position, we need to recognize the *indépendantiste* identity as an important, dignified and legitimate expression of social solidarity. Without getting into the debate between those Québécois who wish to remain within Canada and those who do not, it is important to try and understand the solidarity that comes from the choice of being Québécois. In the space available, this chapter can only give a very preliminary and incomplete presentation of this solidarity. Nevertheless, it is important to show that the more Canadians fail to recognize the positive aspects of this identity the stronger it becomes.

IDENTITY AND DIFFERENCE

It is not easy to define what identity means to someone. Indeed, identity is one of those terms which social scientists have great difficulty defining.[1] Our identity is our understanding of who we are, with whom we identify, and how we expect other people to treat us. If I identify myself to others as a doctor, doing so tells people certain things about me and how, under certain circumstances, we will interact with one another. But our identity is also our understanding of who and what we are not, and who we are different from. Canadians, for example, see themselves as different from Americans, and part of Canadian identity is this sense of being different. On the other hand, most Canadians are also not the same as Brazilians or Papuans or Danes, but those differences are not part of what Canadians typically see as relevant to their identity. What becomes relevant to people, and becomes a part of their identity, has to do with the social relationships through which they deal with those "others" they consider the same as themselves and with those "others" whom they consider to be different.

There is one more crucial issue to be addressed when trying to understand identity, which is the issue of "recognition." In a way, our identity is a claim about ourselves whereby we tell others what makes us distinctive. That claim is validated when it is recognized, i.e. when others acknowledge us and accept us as being what we claim to be. Being "ourselves" becomes difficult when our difference is not acknowledged. When Americans say Canadians are pretty much the same as them, Canadians become surprised and sometimes a little angry at such a failure to recognize the distinction. After all, if Canadians cannot be different from Americans, who can they be? The failure to recognize one's distinctive identity then, is a challenge to our sense of who we are. Such misrecognition generates resentment, frustration, sometimes anger, and it certainly threatens the ongoing social relationships among people.

---

[1] For more on the complexities of the question see Craig Calhoun (ed.) *Social Theory and the Politics of Identity*. Cambridge: Blackwell Publishers, 1994.

What is true for Canadians vis-à-vis Americans is true as well for many Québécois. If the Québécois cannot be different from Canadians, who can they be? For many Québécois there is a sense in which Quebec is not only different from Canada but is already a separate country.

Perhaps there really is no satisfactory definition of what exactly it means to be Québécois or Canadian for that matter. Too rigid a definition of either identity risks unfair exclusion. After all, it is possible to live in a country without taking on its identity. Some go so far as to argue that in the new global economy, nation-states as we now know them are becoming redundant. On the other hand, some sociologists have argued for at least a century that too weak an attachment to national identity weakens the solidarity needed to maintain a society. Given that there is still no alternative to the nation-state, one must admit that social disintegration is still a very real danger, as the breakup of Yugoslavia shows. Disintegration can occur not only as a consequence of social control breaking down, when loyalties are too strong and identities are too exclusive but also as a consequence of a lack of attachment to a nation and the absence of a strong collective identity. The more widespread the apathy concerning a sense of belonging to a country, the less citizens are willing to participate in the democratic process and the greater the risks to that country of social disintegration.

The sense of belonging to a larger collectivity, some "we," is an important sociological component of identity. In this respect, the larger Québécois "we" and the larger Canadian "we" are very different. Québécois identity is that of a people who see themselves as having a unique history, one language and a common culture. A stronger version of this definition would be one in which they see themselves as fundamentally different and distinct from Canadians. However, one could consider oneself to be Québécois and not subscribe to either of these positions. Canadian identity is more problematic, as Canadians are seen as having had a diverse history, two languages, and so many cultures that no single culture (not even one of the native cultures) claims to be the original or founding one. The stronger version of this identity would be to see the Québécois as only one of many groups who make up Canada. Again, though, one could consider oneself Canadian and not subscribe to these definitions either.

This is all a little confusing if you do not keep in mind that these definitions of identity are ideal types. Nevertheless, they are useful because they help us understand some of the contradictory aspects of the difference between Quebec and Canada. However, they do not explain why politically and morally we should recognize either society as sovereign or distinct.

In this sense, the ideal-type definition of identity carries the same limitation found in the sociology of the nineteenth-century French sociologist Emile Durkheim. Durkheim tried to show that if individuals were not integrated enough, or if they were too well integrated into the collective identities of their societies, they would suffer and eventually the societies themselves would be weakened. The problem with an approach such as Durkheim's is that the exact balance of integration and difference cannot be determined. For Durkheim, identity was what he called a social fact. This means that one's identity is formed by external forces like ethnicity, religion, social class or gender. Identity is explained as a function of some other determining cause and cannot be explained from its own point of view.

In Durkheim's theory, social order should be maintained regardless of how identities may evolve or how people's understanding of their identity might change. Yet, the world around us today is filled with change as new countries come into being and old nations fall apart. Ignoring the dynamic of such change in favour of some abstract notion of social order poses the risk that change, when it comes, finds us unprepared, generating violence, misery, and chaos for the people involved.

This raises an important problem for our definition of national identity. How can we know when a new country should be created except by understanding the evolution of identification toward some "we" from its own point of view? This question places us back into the familiar but even more difficult problem concerning the contradictory claims that are made by different groups with distinct identities that occupy the same territory, as in the case of natives and non-francophones in Quebec, for example.

Durkheim's sociology was developed toward the end of the colonial period as European societies were becoming more and more aware of other cultures and different identities. The large-scale transcultural migration of the twentieth century is an unparalleled historical phenomenon. A broad consensus has been growing that the best kind of country is the one that looks for ways of sharing as many different individual and collective identities as possible.[2] At the same time, however, it remains an unavoidable fact that nations or countries continue to exist. And if a nation is to exist, it cannot simply be a collection of multiple individual and group identities, for such a collection is not a nation. To be a nation means to have some common identity and culture which can serve as a reference point for all members of the society.

This is not seen positively by all Quebecers. Among non-francophone minorities in Quebec, there is often a perception that the Québécois have their "own" institutions and their "own" culture that excludes others from entering. Some minorities are publicly denouncing their membership in Quebec society out of fear of losing their Canadian citizenship following some future referendum that would lead to Quebec sovereignty. The perception is that over the last 30 years the once desperately poor and marginalized white francophone majority in Quebec has become a dominant and even repressive political force. This is a perception that is sometimes claimed in the name of the estimated 60,000 anglophones who left Quebec in this period. It should be pointed out, though, that the exodus of the anglophone middle class can also be explained by economic trends that have little to do with questions of identity.

---

[2] James Tully traces this ideal in terms of the history of constitutional documents in *Strange Multiplicities: Constitutionalism in an Age of Diversity*. Cambridge: Cambridge University Press, 1995.

These mixed perceptions between so-called anglophones and francophones (so-called because it is not so easy to sociologically define the population in linguistic terms given the high level of bilingualism on both sides) is both historical and political and is almost exclusively centred in Montreal. It sets a context that creates a lot of confusion for new arrivals who are trying to figure out who can and who cannot be Québécois. The ideal and, perhaps, the real answer is that anyone can be Québécois who chooses to become Québécois. But this is obviously a matter of perception and therefore many would disagree. These days when Québécois sit down to try and discuss what it is that they share or what it is they want to protect in terms of the definition of their society and how they would like to be understood, anxiety and frustration are not far from the surface. Despite this unease, there is a consensus that the Quebec identity exists and will continue to grow regardless of the politics that lie ahead.

And so here is our dilemma. Not all Canadians want to be Canadians, though most do. Not all Québécois want their own country but many do and, perhaps soon, most will. A united sovereign Canada is possible only by imposing unity on a significant minority of Québécois who want their own country. A united sovereign Quebec would be possible only by imposing unity on a significant minority of Canadians who want to remain tied to Canada. As it stands, Quebec shares Canadian institutions and yet each culture has very different interpretations of what it means to share those institutions. This is where we are now.

THE POLITICAL SOCIOLOGY OF RECOGNITION

Despite massive opposition to Quebec independence from outside Quebec and from minorities inside Quebec, the *indépendantiste* identity is stronger than it has ever been. All signs suggest that the choice of being Québécois and having one's own country increases the more the rest of Canada refuses to recognize this choice of identity. The "Yes" side in the 1995 sovereignty referendum had far less support outside Quebec than it did in the 1980 period. Yet the "Yes" vote in 1980 was much stronger both numerically and symbolically. For *indépendantistes* the referendum result demonstrates that to be Québécois means to be recognized in terms of a political community who, as a nation or perhaps as a new federation, could itself enter into agreements with other nations and federations, including Canada.

We have already suggested that the failure to acknowledge someone's identity can lead to negative effects. This problem of non-recognition is a very large part of the conflict between Quebec and Canada today. Two broad reasons for non-recognition by the rest of Canada of Quebec's aspirations are readily discernible. One is a profound difference in historical interpretation of the founding event of Quebec society and the other is a legal turn in the political cultures of Quebec and Canada that took place in 1982 with the repatriation of the Canadian Constitution from the British Privy Council and the subsequent imposition of the Charter of Rights and Freedoms.

The first confusion between Québécois and Canadian identities has to do with a major difference in interpreting history, particularly the reluctance on the part of Canadians to accept the importance of the Conquest of New France by the British in 1759 as a founding moment of Quebec's political identity. The British conquering of Quebec was an important moment that helped establish Quebec as a nation or distinct people. But the Quebec nation is in fact much older. Its own culture, traditions and sense of forming a strong collectivity can be traced back to New France at least a century or more prior to the Conquest.[3]

The word "Canada," which means village, is handed down from the Huron and Iroquois First Nations. "Quebec" is a word that comes from another First Nations linguistic family that includes Algonquin. The Algonquin inhabited the region before the Huron and the Iroquois. The word Quebec signifies a passage or strait like the Saint Lawrence River in front of Quebec City. For more than a century before the British Conquest, the inhabitants of New France referred to themselves as "Canadiens" in order to distinguish themselves from the French. Gradually, as the English and American settlers in Ontario and Quebec began to refer to themselves as Canadians, the roughly 65,000 inhabitants of Quebec (1763) started calling themselves "Canadiens-Français." This is a grammatically incorrect term and possibly one of the first anglicisms used in Québécois French. Originally, the term "Québécois" referred only to the inhabitants of Quebec City. Its first reference to the people of Quebec appeared about 100 years ago.[4] Use of the term Québécois only came into widespread practice in the 1950s and emerged as a term that was associated with those who endorsed a will to self-determination or sovereignty. While most anglophones in Quebec prefer the term "Quebecer" or simply "Canadian," there are signs amongst some allophones that this could be changing. Ironically, the term Québécois can actually include non-francophones and English-speaking Quebecers, while it excludes the Canadiens-Français who live outside Quebec and who increasingly refer to themselves as Franco-ontariens, Acadiens, Fransaskois, etc.

Today, a common historical attitude amongst English-speaking Canadiens is that the British had the foresight to allow another religion and language to flourish in their own territory. Canadian historians downplay the importance of the Conquest and few citizens celebrate the achievement of the British and their collaboration with French-speaking Canadians in the founding of Canada on July first. In the context of this kind of understanding of the historical background of the Conquest and the awareness of a sense of being a people whose origins stretch back more than three centuries, Québécois *indépendantistes* interpret today's hardline federalist arguments concerning the illegal nature of any unilateral declaration of independence from Canada as a reflection of the worst of the British colonial mentality. Few *indépendantistes* today see Quebec as a

---

[3] See Fernand Dumont. *La génése de la société québécoise*. Montreal: Boréal, 1993.

[4] See Marcel Rioux. *Les Québécois*, Paris, Seuil, 1975, pp. 11-13.

colony of Britain or Canada. But an entire generation of Québécois have now been socialized in what we can call the politics of being Québécois. Like previous generations, they are taught about British colonization, the 1837 Patriot Rebellion for independence, the Riel Rebellion in the west, forced conscription during the Boer War at the turn of the century and again in the two World Wars, the imposition of the War Measures Act in 1970 that included massive arrests of artists, intellectuals, and political activists, and the broadly perceived betrayal of René Lévesque by the other premiers in the constitutional negotiations that led to the repatriation of the British North America Act in 1982, commonly referred to as "the night of the long knives." Furthermore, this generation knows that Quebec provincial governments have opposed federal intrusion into Quebec jurisdiction in dozens of areas since 1867. Above all, this generation has been taught that there is a solution to Quebec's differences with Canada: sovereignty. The political socialization also teaches that Quebec has a national culture equal to that of English Canada and that it should have its own independence or at least be formally recognized in the constitution. This collective claim has been maintained, historically, and points to a second cause of the root of Canada's present non-recognition of Québécois identity.

Charles Taylor argues that Quebec and Canada have each developed different political and legal cultures, especially since the repatriation of the Canadian constitution in 1982.[5] He suggests that Canada is much influenced by the American model of liberal-individualism. This liberalism emphasizes a procedural definition of justice in which the rights of individuals take precedence over the rights of collectivities. The procedural approach guarantees each person the same rights by making sure the law treats individuals with exactly the same procedures.

On the other hand, Québécois identity has, in large part, been defined by its collectivist quest to secure protection for its language and culture. Such protection was only partially secured under British rule and then in the Canadian constitution of 1867. This collectivist or communitarian approach to rights clashes with the individualist approach. Since the entrenchment of the Canadian Charter of Rights, the Canadian state has proven ready to contradict Quebec's communitarian ideal of two founding nations. Quebec's language Law 101 was declared to be illegal under the new Charter of Rights and Freedoms, a Charter which Quebec never signed. In the meantime, those supporting the liberal rights model have anxiously sought to reconcile a variety of other groups seeking historical compensation for their non-recognition. All the while, Quebec slips further down a growing list of pressing demands for group recognition.

The protection of minority language rights in the Charter, the turn toward federal bilingualism and the fostering of French immersion programs throughout English Canada have not been able to silence Québécois identity politics.

---

[5] Charles Taylor. "The Politics of Recognition." in *Multiculturalism.* Edited by Amy Gutmann. Princeton New Jersey, Princeton University Press, 1994, pp.25-73.

How can we understand the dignity of this choice when we are told that the universal problem is about language? English Canada has come to see Quebec as a region that should act like other regions. As a province it should expect no privileges or special status. After all, haven't Canadians given up enough to solve its language problems? In the 1960s Daniel Johnson demanded "equality or independence." How did this get interpreted in Canada as putting French on the backs of cereal boxes and churning out a generation of quasi-competent bilingual anglophones?

In a world where the English language has become the lingua franca, it is not surprising that Canadians outside Quebec maintain a pragmatic attitude toward language. It is difficult to sense the threat to the culture of a group of people who speak another language when your own language is spoken everywhere in the world. It leads one to the very false and insensitive notion that language is little more than a neutral means of communication. But when the first voice that greets a student at today's university is a computer voice phone, how can we expect people to be sensitive to language? Language is not seen as an oppressive force by English Canada and there is no historical reason why it should empathize with Quebec's concerns on this issue. There is a deep sense in which Canadians see themselves as having gone along with Quebec's demands and therefore should be seen as being quite generous (like the British). For most of Canadian history though, at least until 1969, the French language had no official status outside Quebec.

If Canadians have not been able to come to terms with Quebec's "special status," they have been even less understanding of Quebec's claim to have become a fully modern, pluralist society. Quebec's Quiet Revolution brought about a fundamental shift from an ethnic or racial form of nationalism to a civic form of nationalism. While many Canadians supported the remarkable transformation of Quebec society, the new claim for a progressive nationalism has fallen on deaf ears. While historically some intellectuals in English-speaking Canada have been receptive to Quebec's apparent will to self-determination, most fail to look beyond the sociological explanation of nationalism as simply a representation of state, class, or especially homogeneous ethnic interest. As a result, understanding Quebec identity "in itself," incorporating the concept of its own autonomy, is very difficult.

These, then, are the general sociological references in Canada's understanding of Quebec. They include the failure to acknowledge the Conquest as a founding moment in Quebec political culture, and the clash between the individual rights model in the new Canadian political culture with the more communitarian Quebec model.

The only way to determine whether a new nation state should be created is to listen to the expression of identity itself. But Canadians have not yet listened, with understanding, to the plea of many Quebecers for independence. Since 1982 it has become very difficult to find pan-Canadian support for the recovery of something like the vision of two or three founding nations. After the collapse of the Meech Lake Agreement in 1991, the failure of the Charlottetown Accord in 1992 and the narrow loss of the 1995 Quebec referendum, the bridges between the two societies appear to be increasingly unstable.

Much of Quebec's political culture can be seen against this background. The institution that in many ways best demonstrates the cultural gap between Canada and Quebec is Radio-Canada. Its history is one that includes both federal collaboration and national separation. It is a distinctly Quebec cultural voice and yet it is officially a Canadian organization. For many, the institution of public broadcasting is the ideal model of what federalism should be. Yvon Deschamps, one of Quebec's most revered comedians, once defined the popular aspiration of the "average Québécois" as wanting to live "in an independent Quebec within a strong Canada." In many respects the vision applies to what Radio-Canada has become. But today, the Canadian Broadcasting Corporation (CBC) and Radio-Canada are slipping into deeper and deeper difficulties as a result of financial cutbacks. In the view of Quebec nationalists, the looming threats to the continued financial and even cultural viability of the CBC are a sign of the instability of the federal system. In this final section of the chapter we will consider how the debate over the communications sector in Canadian society reveals the growing urgency involved in Quebec's plea for the self-determination of its people.

QUEBEC'S CRITIQUE OF CANADA'S COMMUNICATION POLICY

For contemporary Quebec nationalists, the fight for jurisdiction over communications has become as urgent as the fight to save the French language has always been. In Section 9c of the 250-page Parti Québécois policy program in 1994, the politics of communications are seen as having arrived at an important crossroads: "Without complete control over the communications sector, Quebec is handicapped at the crucial moment of the advance of the information society and its technological innovations." Seventeen proposals were put forward regarding the transfer of the communications sector into a sovereign Quebec state apparatus. At the top of the list are proposals to replace the federal Canadian Radio-Television and Telecommunications Commission (CRTC) with a Quebec agency and to integrate the existing structures of Radio-Canada into Radio-Quebec. Third on the list of priorities is to move in quickly with a French language law for broadcasting that would redress the linguistic imbalance (too much English language content) created by previous licensing patterns of the CRTC.

The argument for Quebec's control over communications has a long history. Quebec interests have not been accommodated by the federal policy that has claimed to represent them. In the beginning, the technical capacity of the broadcasting signal was underdeveloped in Quebec compared to other provinces. In 1931 Quebec households had one-third the number of radio receivers compared to Ontario households. This meant that the original event of radio culture in Quebec was more of a collective experience than it was else-where.[6] It should also be remembered, as Michel Fillion shows in his history of the distinct origins of Quebec broadcasting, that early American radio and tele-vision became available at the same time that Quebec began broadcasting its own programmes. Unlike English-speaking Canadian audiences, the French-speaking majority in Quebec remained faithful to local programmes.

Quebec governments have challenged federal jurisdiction over broadcasting since 1929. In fact, Quebec tabled the first provincial legislation on broadcasting in that same year. In 1932, Quebec and the other the provinces lost a court bat-tle to retain jurisdiction over broadcasting. The decision that placed legislative control under the stewardship of the federal government was issued by the British Privy Council, and the federal government soon went ahead and created the Canadian Commission of Broadcasting. As Jean-Guy Lacroix and Benoit Levesque, two sociologists from the Université de Québec à Montréal, point out: "From this date on, the federal government exercised an absolute control over broadcasting regulation and only ever referred to the provinces in terms of geo-graphic divisions or regions."[7]

It is important to underscore this failure to recognize the special character of Quebec's demands and the collective concerns which gave rise to them. It is important to remember that Quebec does not see itself as a province or as region like the others. In his study of articles on mass communications that appeared between 1921 and 1947 in the Quebec nationalist review Action Nationale, Roger de la Guarde showed that Quebec nationalist intellectuals very early on presented analyses of the importance of the mass media for the transformation of Quebec into a fully "polycultural" society."[8]

By the 1940s French-Canadians outside Quebec clearly had unequal access to the national radio network. Less than three hours of programming a week were being aired in French out of a total of 115 available hours. In this same period English Montreal was well served by a CBC regional office. The prairie provinces banded together in 1942 to form a private network (Radio-Ouest-Française) that was an affiliate of the CBC. Still, most of southern Ontario, all the Maritimes and British Columbia had no French service until 1956. Toronto did not receive a French radio station until 1963, and only after highly controversial protests from anglophone groups against the bid to establish a French station.

---

[6] Elzéar Lavoie. "L'évolution de la radio au Canada français avant 1940." In *Recherches sociographiques* vol. 12, no 1, 1971, pp. 17-49.

[7] Jean-Guy Lacroix and Benoit Levesque. "L'Unification et la fragmentation des appareils idéologiques au Canada et au Québec: le cas de la radio-télévision", *Cahiers de socialisme*, no 5, 1980: 107-135, p.17.

[8] See Roger de la Guarde. "Y a-t-il un public dans la salle?" in Michel Beauchamp (editor). *Communication Public et société: Repères pour la réflexion et l'action*. Boucherville Québec: Gaëtan Morin Éditeur, 1991, pp. 245-284.

Despite the growth of French language services outside Quebec, few in Quebec view such services as a sign of French equality in the broadcasting system or as being in any way adequate to the task of preserving French culture. Among francophones outside Quebec, however, they are seen as crucial elements in maintaining some of Canada's most fragile communities. In the area of communications, as in many other areas, we see a gap developing between French Canada and Quebec political cultures which has been growing larger in recent years and is likely to increase as Quebec's drive to independence intensifies.

The Quebec government boycotted both the 1954 Massey-Lévesque and the 1956 and 1966 Fowler Commissions. In 1977, a Supreme Court judgement confirmed that the Quebec government had no jurisdiction over the cable industry and a 1993 judgement determined that the Quebec Commission of Telecommunications had to regulate its own long distance telephone industry through the CRTC, thus leaving the Quebec government without authority or jurisdiction over the development of the much-hyped electronic highway.

As we have seen, by the 1960s the development of the Quebec sovereignty argument had shifted from the old ethnic nationalism of the Duplessis era to a modern civic nationalism founded on territory and language rather than religion and race. The older confrontation that played out in committees and in backbench politics would soon come together under the umbrella of the constitutional crises and political disagreements that have haunted contemporary Canadian politics from the failure at the Victoria Conference in 1971 to Meech Lake and Charlottetown and the Quebec referendums. In the field of broadcasting communications, the conflict is rooted in Quebec's attempt to take control of the development of Québécois identity through the communications sector. As such, the political challenge is to recover jurisdiction over all communications policy presently under the control of the federal government. In recent decades, three key provincial-federal conflicts re-emerge and remain unresolved. Firstly, Quebec has sought to gain control over the full range of regulatory power of communications. Secondly, it has opposed the federal principal that has sought the transmission of Canadian culture to the largest number possible. In place of this principle the Quebec government has looked to provide a policy rationale that would permit the widest possible pedagogical distribution of Quebec programmes to its francophone audience. Finally, it has clashed with Ottawa over the financial development of educational television for Quebec versus the unified cultural policy for Canadian society.[9]

Part of the reasoning of the sovereignist argument for controlling the decision-making processes is to maintain the envious success of Quebec stations that have large television and radio audiences (averaging more than 25% of the population) and prevent them from meeting the same fate as the CBC (averaging as

---

[9] Alain Laramée. *La Communication mass-médiatique au Canada et au Québec : un cadre politique* Montréal: les Presses de l'Université du Québec, Télé-Université, 1989, p.24.

low as 9% of the audience). However, the existence of large audiences does not mean that Quebec broadcasting is working as it should. The number of radio stations doubled between 1961 and 1988 (100 radio stations, eight Radio-Canada stations, 26 community channels, 66 privately owned), yet French content has actually eroded despite the fact that quotas for French language music have existed for over 25 years.[10] The quotas set by the CRTC have never been strictly enforced, allowing English-language products to enter Quebec's linguistic territory in a disproportionate way. In this sense, it is not American products that directly threaten Quebec interests. Rather, it is federal policy-making and enforcement in Ottawa.

In the 1980s, Quebec television audiences were beginning to migrate to American channels brought in by the new cable industry. Sanctioned by the CRTC, a series of transformations occurred in the private Quebec television industry. Two new private networks emerged (Télémetropole and Quatre Saisons) largely organized by former Radio-Canada producers and administrators. An immediate consequence of the new networks was to stall the drift of viewers toward the American networks and to increase competition for advertizing revenue. Between 1982 and 1989 all four television networks achieved gains in advertizing revenues.[11] Before 1980, Radio-Canada financed its television operations with less than 25% from advertizing revenue. In contrast, private operations have remained entirely dependent on advertizing revenue from the beginning of radio to the present cable operations. With the cutbacks of the 1980s, Radio-Canada advanced its dependency on advertizing revenues significantly, increasing it as high as 30% in some years. Radio-Quebec (the Quebec government's public broadcasting network) has also depended on advertizing for about 2% of its budget.

Increased pressure on the public networks to find advertizing revenue means they have to compete directly with the private networks. Tremblay and Lacroix argue that the shift to privatization throughout the 1980s has produced a spiralling effect that: 1) is pushing program and editorial policies deeper into the area of entertainment; 2) is contributing to the weakening of public broadcasting both from Radio-Quebec and Radio-Canada, and 3) is generating a shift in the role of the state from that of public service broadcaster to a facilitator of the private industry.[12]

---

[10] Jean-Guy Lacroix. "La radio au Québec: un média en crise qui trahis son mandat social." In Alain Laramée (editor). *Les communications au Québec*. Montreal: Les Éditions coopératives Albert Saint-Martin de Montréal, 1993, p.57.

[11] Gaëtan Tremblay and Jean-Guy Lecroix in collaboration with Marc Ménard and Marie Josée Régnier. *Télévision: deuxième dynastie*.Montreal: Presses de l'Université du Québec, 1991, p.25.

[12] Ibid.

Compared to CBC English television, both Radio-Canada and private Quebec broadcasters, for the moment, have an envious record in producing successful world class drama for local audiences and export abroad. However, its service to local French-speaking cultures within the regions of its own society and those francophone milieux outside of Quebec remains problematic. French-language drama products are almost exclusively produced in Montreal. Part of the effect of producing programmes at the centre is that it leaves a folklorized image of the peripheral regions both outside and within the Quebec system itself. The resentment from the regions continues to fuel criticism against Radio-Canada. In the 1990 cuts, unlike the CBC, Radio-Canada didn't have to cut newsrooms in Quebec regions because they never existed. Radio-Canada journalists (not studio facilities) have only very recently been installed in regions like Lac St. Jean and the Gaspé. As Réale Casavant complains, "After more than 40 years of television, the SRC [Radio-Canada] has never had a news bureau in Mauricie, the Eastern Townships or in Abitibi-Témiscamingue."[13] On the other hand, there are relatively well equipped studios available for French broadcasting in Toronto, Sudbury, Windsor, Ottawa and even Vancouver. The French service of Radio-Canada maintains thirteen television stations across Canada. In Quebec, there is only one production outlet outside Montreal, CBVT in Quebec City. The overall system has 72 production outlets.

If we look at the history of policy and programming from a Québécois perspective, an obvious question arises. Has it been in the interests of Quebec society to have developed its communication policy over the last century on the front lines of the defense against American programming? Has American culture directly threatened Québécois identity in the same way as English-Canadian identity? Roger de la Guard asserts that the identity of Quebec society is "neither French nor English nor truly American" but rather "polycultural." He sees American products as a form of popular culture that is absorbed from the bottom of the society, not from the top. Quebec has always had access to American cultural products and they have always been in competition with Quebec's different popular, elite, religious and secular cultures. Nonetheless, Quebec has developed its own "*vision du monde*" or world perspective "which is largely based on mass-produced [and media-distributed] products, initially for and in an alien society (the United States)."

Canadian federalism is once again at a crossroads. Listening to claims of Québécois identity means thinking about the possibility of Quebec secession in a positive context. This does not mean negotiations between Canada and Quebec, between regions within Canada and between groups within Quebec will be resolved by Quebec's secession. Should Quebec go on to achieve a sovereign status somewhere in the near future, the organizational separation of its systems of

---

[13] Réale Casavant. "Ici Radio-Montréal." *Le Devoir*, April 13, 1994, A-9.

communication will depend on negotiations concerning the larger issues of the debt, the new monetary system, economic trade, citizenship, etc., all of which will have to be discussed by new stakeholders. Could the trade-offs following the move to sovereignty lead to some mutual recognition between Canada and Quebec? Could English-speaking Canada resist disintegration into the United States following Quebec separation? Could Quebec make new political covenants with its minority communities? When the dust settles, would Quebec and Canada recreate some version of a transnational public broadcasting service modelled on the skeleton of the old CBC? Would it not be better to maintain reciprocity concerning minority rights in both societies as a means of securing international recognition? These are some of the questions and trade-offs that should be carefully considered on both sides of the next referendum divide.

IMMIGRATION AND ETHNIC RELATIONS IN QUEBEC: PLURALISM IN THE MAKING

The limits of what is possible are set not only by the external requirements of institutions but also, and fundamentally, by the structure of the human mind (Berger et al, 1973:20).

INTRODUCTION

Questions of immigration, ethnic relations and ethnic pluralism are critical issues for contemporary Quebec society. The dynamics of intergroup relations occupy a central position in Quebec's social and political life, and will most definitely mould the face of Quebec in the future. Politicians, intellectuals, journalists, bureaucrats and community organizers regularly debate the merits of different ideologies, practices and policies concerning intergroup relations. Many of these discussions began during the late 1970s and early 1980s, at a time when Quebec's immigration rates were low compared to some other years (see Table 1). The debates continued and increasing immigration since 1986 has heightened reflection about Quebec's future and the forms of nationhood it should articulate.

Immigration, ethnic social relations and ethnic pluralism are, of course, all interrelated. Hence, the importance of immigration can be understood only by examining both the changes in ethnic boundaries as well as the transformations in ethnic social relations within the broad context of the entire society. This chapter demonstrates the centrality of ethnicity in Quebec by analysing the interplay of immigration policies and certain internal dynamics of Quebec as the host society. Such an analysis will explain why questions of immigration, ethnic social relations and ethnic pluralism are so salient today.

We begin with the evolution of immigration policies in Quebec by examining the nature of immigration over the past half century. Next, by studying the internal dynamics of the host society, we show how emerging forms of nationhood transformed ethnic dynamics in the province. This is illustrated with examples of the newly established system of social relations operating in the labour market, the family and the school system. We conclude by addressing the challenges facing Quebec at the end of the twentieth century.

THE PRODUCTION OF ETHNIC SOCIAL RELATIONS

Ethnic social relations unite, in a single material and symbolic universe, groups who share a cultural tradition and experience a subjective belief in a common heritage. Ethnic social relations are transversal, that is to say, they cut across all levels of society. Moreover, as part of a larger system of social relations encompassing human groups differentiated along the lines of 'race,' ethnicity and nationality (Juteau, 1993), ethnic social relations consist of a mode of social classification and hierarchical ordering in terms of cultural or national origin and belonging (Simon, 1983).

It is in the context of ethnic social relations that criteria are designated for defining ethnic groups and ethnic boundaries. These criteria (e.g. certain traits, attributes and/or labels) serve as a basis for creating a sense of belonging and constructing a community. Transforming ethnic social relations involves changing hierarchies based on ethnic differentiation, where such ethnic hierarchies entail an unequal distribution of power, privilege, prestige and possessions (Simon, 1983: 9).

Our theoretical approach to ethnicity and ethnic social relations seeks to avoid the pitfalls of economism and reductionism. Hence, ethnicity is defined as an aspect of consciousness, but not just that. Ethnicity is a label and a resource, but more than that as well. Ethnicity, however, is not a given: the production of ethnicity must be explained. To do this, we examine the material practices, relations and circumstances from which it emerges and the context in which it operates.

As a salient feature of Quebec society, ethnicity influences much of social space, including the division of labour, the distribution of economic and cultural capital, position in the social structure, and even the production of subjectivity. Ethnicity affects the definition of political issues, as well as the promotion of certain ideologies related to specific forms of pluralism. To address this issue of pluralism, we begin by examining immigration policies and practices in Quebec and in Canada as a whole.

IMMIGRATION POLICIES AND PRACTICES

Ethnic pluralism in Quebec is an ongoing dynamic, where ethnic social relations, Quebec's immigration history and Canadian immigration policies are intertwined. The province of Quebec had, in the past, abdicated its rights and responsibilities for immigration (secured in the British North America (BNA) Act) to the federal government. Modern Quebec society, however, has taken an increasingly active interest in the immigration issue.

While space precludes a detailed examination of the important history of Canadian immigration, some brief remarks deserve attention. Table 1 presents data on immigration to Quebec and Canada during the post-war period, specifically from 1946 until 1993. Observe that the number of immigrants who chose to settle in Quebec rarely corresponded to that province's allotted proportion of 25%[1]. In only two of the 47 years listed here, namely 1962 and 1963, was Quebec able to attract its share (25.7% and 25.0% respectively) of Canadian immigration.

---

[1] The proportion of 25% was chosen to mirror Quebec's approximate demographic weight within the Canadian confederation.

TABLE 1: Immigration by Year, Quebec and Canada, 1946 to 1993

Year	Quebec	Canada	% in Quebec
1946	9,712	71,719	13.5%
1947	8,272	64,127	12.9%
1948	24,687	125,414	19.7%
1949	18,005	95,217	18.9%
1950	13,575	73,912	18.4%
1951	46,033	194,391	23,7%
1952	35,318	164,498	21.5%
1953	34,294	168,868	20.3%
1954	28,419	154,227	18.4%
1955	22,117	109,946	20.1%
1956	32,284	164,857	19.6%
1957	55,073	282,164	19.5%
1958	28,443	124,851	22.8%
1959	24,816	106,928	23.2%
1960	23,774	104,111	22.8%
1961	16,920	71,689	23.6%
1962	19,132	74,586	25.7%
1963	23,264	93,151	25.0%
1964	25,973	112,606	23.1%
1965	30,346	146,758	20.7%
1966	39,198	194,743	20.1%
1967	45,717	222,876	20.5%
1968	35,506	183,974	19.3%
1969	28,477	161,531	17.6%
1970	23,228	147,713	15.7%
1971	19,221	121,900	15.8%
1972	18,583	122,006	15.2%
1973	26,871	184,200	14.6%
1974	33,458	218,465	15.3%
1975	28,042	187,881	14.9%
1976	28,282	149,429	19.6%
1977	19,248	114,914	16.7%
1978	13,899	86,313	16.1%
1979	19,522	112,096	17.4%
1980	22,538	143,117	15.7%
1981	21,063	128,618	16.4%
1982	21,331	121,147	17.6%
1983	16,374	89,157	18.4%
1984	14,641	88,239	16.6%
1985	14,884	84,302	17.7%
1986	19,459	99,219	19.6%
1987	26,822	152,098	17.6%
1988	25,789	161,929	15.9%
1989	33,602	189,956	17.7%
1990	40,842	214,230	19.1%
1991	51,707	230,834	22.4%
1992	48,377	252,842	19.1%
1993	44,385	254,675	17.4%
Total	**1,302,523**	**6,922,424**	**18.8%**

SOURCE: MCCI, "Le mouvement d'immigration d'hier à aujourd'hui", Montréal MAIICC, "Le Québec en mouvement", 1994.

The second table shows the continents from which peoples came when immigrating to Quebec in the years between 1968 and 1993. The data illustrate important changes in immigration patterns in the recent past. In 1968, for example, immigration from Europe represented more than 60% of the total immigration to Quebec, but by 1993 it had diminished, as Table 2 shows, to 19.4%. On the other hand, the share of Asian immigrants increased from 12% in 1968 to 48.8% in 1993. If we group together those from Africa, the Caribbean, and Central and South America, more than 70% of immigration now comes from countries traditionally considered part of the "Third World."

Table 3 provides more detailed information concerning immigration flow to Quebec. It is interesting to note that for the 20-year period from 1968 to 1988, Haiti remained the primary country of birth of immigrants admitted to Quebec. For the 1989—1993 period, Haiti fell to the third rank, surpassed by Lebanon in first place and Hong Kong in second place in terms of country of birth of Quebec immigrants.

TABLE 2: Immigration to Quebec, by Continent of Birth, 1968-1993

Year	Africa		Americas		Asia		Europe		Oceania		Total (100%)
	N	%	N	%	N	%	N	%	N	%	
1968	4,050	11.4%	4,960	14.0%	4,262	12.0%	21,987	61.9%	245	0.7%	35,504
1969	2,349	8.2%	6,414	22.5%	3,952	13.9%	15,525	54.5%	237	0.8%	28,477
1970	1,657	7.1%	5,929	25.5%	2,170	13.6%	12,242	52.7%	230	1.0%	23,228
1971	1,163	6.1%	5,676	29.5%	2,900	15.1%	9,340	48.6%	141	0.7%	19,220
1972	1,682	9.1%	5,385	29.0%	3,184	17.1%	8,197	44.1%	135	0.7%	18,583
1973	2,075	7.7%	9,068	33.7%	4,902	18.2%	10,693	39.8%	133	0.5%	26,871
1974	3,004	9.0%	12,641	37.8%	5,634	16.8%	12,054	36.0%	124	0.4%	33,457
1975	2,560	9.1%	8,941	31.9%	6,272	22.4%	10,159	36.2%	110	0.4%	28,042
1976	2,594	8.9%	9,034	30.9%	8,448	28.9%	9,079	31.0%	127	0.4%	29,282
1977	1,728	9.0%	6,037	31.4%	4,810	25.0%	6,600	34.3%	73	0.4%	19,248
1978	1,178	8.5%	4,831	34.8%	3,255	23.4%	4,583	33.0%	52	0.4%	13,899
1979	1,209	6.2%	4,099	21.0%	8,813	45.1%	5,353	27.4%	48	0.2%	19,522
1980	1,495	6.6%	4,127	18.3%	11,477	50.9%	5,398	24.0%	41	0.2%	22,538
1981	1,648	7.8%	6,123	29.1%	7,284	34.6%	5,960	28.3%	48	0.2%	21,063
1982	1,770	8.3%	6,768	31.7%	6,414	30.1%	6,338	29.7%	41	0.2%	21,331
1983	1,320	8.1%	6,191	37.8%	4,942	30.2%	3,901	23.8%	20	0.1%	16,374
1984	1,167	8.0%	4,584	31.3%	5,776	39.5%	3,091	21.1%	23	0.2%	14,641
1985	1,290	8.7%	4,194	28.2%	6,305	42.4%	3,063	20.6%	32	0.2%	14,884
1986	1,593	8.2%	5,965	30.7%	8,369	43.0%	3,495	18.0%	37	0.2%	19,459
1987	2,663	9.9%	6,897	25.7%	12,260	45.7%	4,960	18.5%	42	0.2%	26,822
1988	2,801	10.9%	5,104	19.8%	12,399	48.1%	5,456	21.2%	29	0.1%	25,789
1989	3,766	11.2%	5,968	17.8%	16,696	49.7%	7,098	21.1%	37	0.1%	33,565
1990	4,939	12.1%	7,143	17.5%	22,037	54.0%	6,691	16.4%	32	0.1%	40,842
1991	6,386	12.4%	1,237	23.9%	25,864	50.0%	7,028	16.6%	52	0.1%	51,707
1992	6,002	12.4%	10,509	21.7%	23,778	49.2%	7,983	16.5%	105	0.2%	48,377
1993	4,964	11.2%	9,072	20.4%	21,649	48.8%	8,605	19.4%	95	0.2%	44,385

SOURCE: MCCI, "Le mouvement d'immigration d'hier à aujourd'hui", Montrèal, 1990 & MAIICC, "Le Québec en mouvement," 1994.

Immigration to both Canada and Quebec, we must remember, is now an urban phenomenon. In 1989, for example, nearly 90% of the population immigrating to Quebec lived in the Montreal metropolitan area (GRES, 1992: 455). This region is currently facing serious new challenges in terms of ethnic social relations. The 1995 October referendum, for example, exposed more than the tip of the iceberg. When Montreal voted "no," the issue of ethnicity was brought to centre stage.

TABLE 3: Immigration to Quebec by Country of Birth, 1968-1988 and 1989-1993

1968-1988	Number	%
Haiti	42,088	8.8%
France	32,917	6.9%
U.S.	28,680	6.0%
Vietnam	23,386	4.9%
U.K.	23,064	4.8%
Portugal	19,864	4.2%
Italy	20,125	4.2%
Lebanon	15,959	3.3%
Greece	18,991	4.0%
India	13,643	2.9%
Morocco	11,394	2.4%
Egypt	11,300	2.4%
Peoples Republic of China	9,682	2.0%
Hong Kong	7,877	1.6%
Poland	8,137	1.7%
Philippines	8,221	1.7%
Kampuchea	7,997	1.7%
Other countries	174,344	36.5%
Total	**477,669**	**100.0%**

1989-1993	Number	%
Lebanon	25,973	11.8%
Hong Kong	13,073	6.0%
Haiti	12,260	5.6%
France	11,219	5.1%
China	9,752	4.4%
Vietnam	6,882	3.1%
El Salvador	6,028	2.7%
Morocco	5,639	2.6%
Sri Lanka	5,587	2.5%
Romania	5,286	2.4%
Other countries	117,783	53.7%
Total	**219,482**	**100.0%**

SOURCE: MCCI, "Le mouvement d'immigration d'hier à aujourd'hui", Montréal, 1990 % MAIICC, "Le Québec en mouvement", 1994.

Changes in the ethnic composition of immigrants is directly linked to the evolution of Canadian immigration policies and to Quebec's new role in these matters. Before 1967, it must be acknowledged that Canadian immigration policy had a distinctly discriminatory and racist character. Rooted in an ideology of dominant conformity (in this case, Anglo-conformity), the selection procedure was partial to certain ethnic groups over others (Juteau, 1986). In the 1956 regulation, for example, preference was given to immigrants, born of naturalized parents, from countries grouped in the following order of choice: 1) France, England, Ireland, the United States and the white dominions of the Commonwealth (Australia, South Africa, New Zealand); 2) other European countries west of the former Iron Curtain; 3) Eastern European countries, Egypt, Israel, Lebanon, Turkey, South and Central American countries; and finally 4) Asian countries (Corbet (1957: 46), cited in Labelle, Larose and Piché (1983: 7)).

Given such a hierarchy, Canadian boundaries were almost totally closed to black people or those of Asian origins, with the exception of a few limited programmes such as the hiring of Caribbean domestics in 1955 (Bled, 1965). As of 1962, however, the ethnic preference criteria were losing ground and by 1967 were completely eliminated. The selection process was replaced by the "point system," a new grid for "objective" selection based on professional and educational qualifications.[2]

Meanwhile, Quebec was awakening to the importance of the immigration issue, and at last began to take a serious interest in the immigration selection process. In 1965 a motion was presented to the National Assembly to create a provincial department of immigration. An immigration service was formed and linked to the Department of Cultural Affairs. In 1966 this service was transformed into the "Direction générale de l'immigration," and became the Department of Immigration in 1968.

The federal and provincial governments later signed four agreements extending Quebec's powers over the immigration process. The first step gave Quebec's immigration officers abroad a role in providing information about Quebec to potential immigrants (Cloutier-Lang agreement, 1971). A second agreement gave these immigration officers the power to voice their opinion regarding potential immigrants (Bienvenue-Andras agreement, 1975). The Couture-Cullen agreement of 1978 gave Quebec the right to choose its own candidates among those who wished to immigrate to Quebec (Juteau, 1986). And finally, the McDougall-Tremblay-Gagnon agreement of 1991 extended Quebec's rights, giving the province exclusive powers over the selection of independent immigrants. This more recent agreement also entails financial compensation by the federal government (that increased until 1995) for the reception and integration of immigrants in Quebec.

---

[2] Boyd's (1992) study, however, underscores the persistence of "ethnic criteria" in the selection of immigrants to Canada.

This brief overview of immigration policies and practices sets the scene for the analysis to follow. As we have shown, the ethnic composition of both Canada and Quebec has changed radically since the beginning of the 1970s. Since then, Quebec has experienced important internal transformations destined to affect the nature of ethnic social relations in the province. We will now take a look at these changes.

THE HOST SOCIETY: DEFINING NEW BOUNDARIES

The Quiet Revolution: The Impact of Political, Economic and Cultural Changes

The expansion of Anglo-American capitalism and the acceleration of industrialization and urbanization in Quebec after World War II transformed French Canada in a profound and lasting way. The loss of the Church's power as an apparatus of control and regulation of the nation, as well as the bureaucratization of the state (Juteau, 1986; McRoberts, 1988) increased the administrative and political power of the new technocrats. The creation of a Department of Education in 1964 heralded decisive changes for Quebec society. Furthermore, during the Quiet Revolution, state intervention in economic matters increased significantly. The nationalization of electricity in 1962 and the creation of state-owned companies such as the Société québécoise d'exploration minière and the Société générale de financement are telling examples. Moreover, ownership and management in many sectors passed from private anglophone hands to public francophone control.

While such changes are interesting in and of themselves, we shall concentrate on the impact of these transformations, namely, the construction of "la nation québécoise" by the state. By promoting the state as the only instrument controlled by the "communauté nationale," nationalist politicians and bureaucrats argued that it should therefore be a tool of national liberation. Thus, this "communauté nationale" became the foundation of the state, which in turn both protected the community and redefined it. The intelligentsia, sensitive to matters of national honour and pride, became its ally (Juteau, 1993).

The gradual emergence of the idea of a "nation québécoise" heightened the territorial basis of national identification and significantly altered the concrete and symbolic aspects of ethnic dynamics in Quebec. We shall examine the transformation of ethnic social relations in this context in terms of three interrelated issues, namely, the scission-division of French-Canadians inside and outside Quebec, the federal debate concerning Quebec's place in the Canadian nation, and finally, the process of defining who is a "Québécois."

While the reforms and interventions of the state in Quebec affected everyone living in the province, the Quebec government could not act on behalf of French-Canadians outside Quebec. A new community was constructed, "les Québécois," defining itself by excluding all French-Canadians living outside

Quebec (Juteau-Lee, 1980).[3] This process of scission-division created a boundary between French-Canadians in Canada: those living inside Quebec ("les Québécois"), and those living elsewhere in Canada, now known as francophones outside Quebec ("les francophones hors Québec"). From this particular point in history, the future of French-Canadians inside and outside Quebec was altered. The destiny of the Québécois and the future for francophones outside Quebec are now separate and different (Juteau-Lee, 1980).

While French-Canadians in Quebec were redefining insiders and outsiders, a second important transformation began as the federal government offered its own suggestions for new interpretations of Quebec's place within Canada. During the 1960s, the relationship between Quebec and Canada, the "two founding nations,"[4] was a source of continuing discussion and debate. Recognizing the need for constitutional changes, in 1963 the governing Liberal party of Canada headed by Lester Pearson set up the Royal Commission on Bilingualism and Biculturalism. Its mandate was:

> to recommend what steps should be taken to develop the Canadian Confederation on the basis of an equal partnership between the two founding races, taking into account the contribution made by the other ethnic groups to the cultural enrichment of Canada and the measures that should be taken to safeguard that contribution (Canada, 1965).

Quebec, in its turn, proposed different options for its place within Canada: "Egalité ou indépendance" proposed by Daniel Johnson Sr. in 1965; Paul Gérin-Lajoie's "Pour une société distincte" in 1966; and projects suggesting such arrangements as special status and associate states. All of these visions corresponded to a specific interpretation of Quebec's relationship with Canada, one known as the "compact theory." This theory defines the Canadian federation as a compact between two nations, one French, one English.

The question of equality between these two founding nations is, of course, critical. The Royal Commission on Bilingualism and Biculturalism redefined equality in terms of language. This reconstruction transformed the issue into equality between francophones and anglophones, rather than that of a French nation and an English one. Obviously, the difference between nations and linguistic groups is important. Recognizing equality between language groups did not entail the same political solutions as would have been required in recognizing equality between two nations. Excluding from the debate the compact theory and related propositions such as associate states or special status averted an extremely difficult discussion concerning major structural changes to the Canadian state (Juteau, 1986).

---

[3] The definition of anglophones and allophones (those whose mother tongue is neither English or French) living within Quebec's borders in terms of their "québécitude" was and remains a more problematic issue.

[4] This Eurocentric definition of Canada was not lost on the First Nations, as subsequent history has shown (Ponting and Gibbins, 1980, Ponting and Symons, 1996).

Thus, in this way the concept of equality between the French and English languages in Canada replaced the two-nation theory. The Official Languages Act of 1969 legally and officially recognized the existence of anglophones and francophones in Canada, as well as "official language minorities" (groups of either francophones or anglophones living in parts of Canada where they constitute a numerical minority). The Act ensured formal equality for the two official languages across the country and established "institutional bilingualism" at the federal level, which provided public services in either official language where sufficient numbers warranted.

The revamping of Canada undertaken at this time also recognized equality among cultures in the nation. In his speech to the House of Commons on October 8, 1971, Pierre Elliot Trudeau, then Prime Minister, declared that cultural pluralism constituted the essence of the Canadian identity. Although there were two official languages, there was no official culture, with the premise that no ethnic group should take precedence over any other.

> The government will support and encourage the various cultures and ethnic groups that give structure and vitality to our society. They will be encouraged to share their cultural expression and values with other Canadians and so contribute to a richer life for us all (House of Commons' Debate, (1971:8545), cited in Juteau (1986).

The importance of this new policy called "multiculturalism" should not be underestimated. It was tantamount to a new blueprint for Canada. Reaching beyond the official recognition of linguistic and cultural diversity, the multicultural policy marked the adoption of a normative pluralism for the Canadian nation. Furthermore, although very controversial in Quebec, multiculturalism greatly influenced the debate concerning appropriate ideologies, policies and practices regarding pluralism within Quebec society.

The question "Who is a Québécois?" constitutes the third issue concerning ethnic transformation in Quebec. Segments of Quebec society, including "l'Etat" have been involved in a seemingly endless process of redefining the national collectivity. Territory, culture, mother tongue, spoken languages, history and ancestry have all become competing, and sometimes overlapping criteria of inclusion. Defining who is Québécois depends on interpretations of matters of language, immigration and ethnic pluralism. The following sections take up these matters, all in an attempt to find an answer to this absorbing challenge.

Linguistic Policies

Since the late 1960s, linguistic accommodation has been at the centre of the confrontation between Quebec and Canada. In the past, anglophones and allophones in Quebec enjoyed linguistic freedom, and they more often chose to speak English than French. Moreover, they had come to accept French-English or English-French bilingualism, given the specificity of their workplace. Federal measures supporting bilingualism legitimized the right of Canadians to linguistic choice, in both legislative and legal terms.

Just when Canada began to endorse a new bilingualism, Quebec judged it best not to maintain nor encourage such a policy. Franco-Québécois public opinion favoured "francisation," a policy adopted in 1974 and in effect to this day in Quebec. A brief description of some salient events in the history of the development of linguistic policies allows us to better understand the different visions proposed by Quebec and Canada.

The first major attempt to regulate language in Quebec was provided by Bill 85, introduced into the National Assembly in December 1968 and withdrawn in March 1969. Aimed at preserving linguistic freedom of choice in education, the Bill was vigorously condemned by many francophones, who saw it as a threat to the future of their community. If immigrants were allowed to choose the language of education of their children, it was feared that they would choose English schools and in the long run anglophones would outnumber francophones in Quebec.

The first linguistic law, Bill 63, was passed in Quebec in November 1969. The law reinforced the status of French by requiring all school graduates to have a "working knowledge" of the language by encouraging immigrants to learn French, and by providing a mandate to the "Office de la langue française" to advise the government on linguistic matters and to monitor the status of French in Quebec. Bill 63 also restated the principle of linguistic freedom of choice in education. Once again, francophone nationalists wishing to reinforce French as the language of education criticized the bill.

In July 1974, "The Official Language Act" (Bill 22) was adopted in Quebec. Replacing Bill 63 and including a recognition of French as the official language of Quebec, Bill 22 was meant to be a compromise between conflicting views on the language issue in the province. Bill 22 targeted five main areas for promotion of French: public administration, professions, labour, business and schools. Linguistic freedom of choice in education was restricted by requiring that children entering English-language schools have a "sufficient knowledge" of English.[5] Contrary to legislators' expectations, Bill 22 met with fierce opposition from all sides, anglophones, francophone nationalists and allophones alike.

Finally, in August 1977, Bill 101, the Charter of the French Language was passed in the National Assembly. Radically changing the linguistic profile of Quebec, it stipulated that French was the official language and the province was

---

[5] This led to testing young children for language skills, producing a good deal of anxiety on the part of both children and parents alike. As an attempt to transform a political issue into a technical one, it failed miserably.

no longer to be considered officially bilingual. French was declared the "normal and usual language" of legislation and justice, public administration, parapublic organizations, labour, trade, business and education. Henceforth, public notices and billboards were to be in French only. Promotion of the use of French in companies with 50 employees or more became compulsory. Moreover, the "Quebec clause" stipulated that children could attend English schools only on the condition that at least one parent had received primary education in English in Quebec. Bill 101 also contributed to the expansion of the Quebec bureaucracy, as five new organizations were created to enforce the law. The "Conseil de la langue française," the "Office de la langue française," the "Commission d'appel," the "Commission de surveillance" and the "Commission de toponymie" were established to administer the new language laws.

Anglophone groups contested Bill 101 at both the provincial and federal levels, leading to a modification of parts of the Charter in favour of the English-speaking community. Bill 57, passed in 1983, recognized the contribution that anglophone institutions had made to Quebec's development. In 1984, the Supreme Court of Canada ruled that Article 73 of Bill 101, the "Quebec Clause," was unconstitutional. This was replaced by the "Canada Clause," stating that children could attend English schools if at least one of their parents had received primary education in English in Canada. In 1986 Bill 142 was passed in Quebec, guaranteeing anglophones the right to health and social services in English in regions where their numbers justified such services.

The battle continued and in December 1988 the Canadian Supreme Court ruled that the language bill's prescription for unilingual signs was illegal. Quebec's response was Bill 178 which, while maintaining the French-only ruling for signs on the streets, henceforth permitted bilingual signs inside buildings. In 1993 Bill 86 was passed in Quebec, giving primacy to French on public signs and in commercial advertising.

These details are sufficient to depict two opposing visions of linguistic relations, one by Quebec and the other by the federal government. The linguistic legislation adopted by Quebec accentuated the province's opposition to the central state. Both the Constitution, as amended in 1982, as well as the Canadian Charter of Rights agree on the principle of individual choice rather than territoriality, in linguistic matters. Quebec's laws, on the other hand, attempted to secure a certain unilingualism on a territorial basis. The federal state resorted to the judiciary, particularly the Supreme Court of Canada, to protect the rights of individuals, organizations and communities defined by place of residence as official language minorities.

The "made in Canada" debate over language (Symons, 1988) troubled many Quebecers, particularly those who feared the pressures of dominant conformity, this time in the guise of Franco-conformity. Would inclusion in Quebec society require complete cultural assimilation? Interestingly enough, soon after passing Bill 101, Quebec began to talk about pluralism.

From Immigrants to Cultural Communities

Historically speaking, the Quebec government had not given its immigrants the attention they deserved. Immigrants managed by participating in institutions established by their own community (Laferrière, 1985), and eventually they turned to English-speaking institutions and hence to Anglo-Canadian society. Meanwhile, immigrants and French-Canadians lived side by side, in different worlds.[6]

The language laws had a profound impact on Quebec society by modifying the boundaries between various ethnic groups. One of the effects of the legislation was increased interaction between immigrants and Québécois of French-Canadian ethnicity within institutions such as education, health and social services. Increased contact between immigrants and other Québécois made questions of ethnicity and ethnic relations more salient in everyday life.

Moreover, increased contact between immigrants and Quebec civil servants in various institutions led to new ideologies and practices concerning intergroup relations. Québécois of French-Canadian ethnicity, in addition to examining their relationship with Canada, now began to explore their relationship with other residents of "their" province. The search for a new model of society was afoot.

Although opposed to federal multiculturalism, Quebec developed a model that was necessarily influenced by it. Indeed, the province evolved towards a form of normative pluralism (Schermerhorn, 1970), as it affirmed measures aimed at respecting, and in some cases in the early years, reinforcing the rights of "non-francophone cultural communities" (Québec, 1981: 27). A certain genre of cultural pluralism was recognized as both legitimate and desirable. In 1975, for example, the Quebec Charter of Rights and Freedoms recognized the right of ethnic minorities to maintain and develop their own cultural life. Three years later the White Paper *La politique québécoise du développement culturel* (Québec, 1978:64) stipulated that all have the right to expect from the state those cultural tools and institutional apparatus necessary for their full development. Even though such a boundary redefinition might aim for greater inclusion of all groups in the national community, longitudinal analysis of this ideology and related practices reveals them to be exclusionary at the same time.

Out of the post-referendum political context of the 1980s came a new category of Québécois, the "cultural community." The term "communauté culturelle" was coined to designate all those who are not part of the "Québécois francophone majority." Attempting to win the loyalty of ethnic minorities, Quebec searched for ways to switch their allegiance from the federal cause. The Quebec-Ottawa competition over immigrants continues to this day.

Just prior to the April 1981 elections, the Parti Québécois government published its "Plan d'action des communautés culturelles," entitled *Autant de façons d'être Québécois*. The objectives were:

---

[6] Quebec's rich literary heritage in French, English and other languages gives interesting details of this mode of cohabitation.

To ensure the safekeeping and development of cultural communities and of their specificity, to sensitize the francophone Québécois to the contribution made by these communities to the common cultural heritage (patrimoine), and lastly to improve their integration within Quebec society, especially in areas in which they have, until now, been underrepresented, notably the civil service (MCCI, 1981:2. Our translation).

The Quebec government increased its efforts in intervention and extended the mandate of the Minister of Cultural Communities and Immigration to include responsibility for managing government policies concerning the development of cultural communities and their participation in national life.

What is occurring here? For some observers, the proposed measures set out in these documents express the recognition, albeit restricted, of cultural diversity and normative pluralism in Quebec (Juteau, 1986). Yet, as several analysts have noted (Fontaine, 1990; Juteau and McAndrew, 1992), the use of the category "cultural community" separates members of the "francophone Québécois majority" from other people living in Quebec. The issue at stake is no less than the social construction of the national community and its boundaries.

The National Community and its Boundaries

Addressing the question of the national community and its boundaries involves at least three concerns, namely, an operational definition of "cultural communities," Quebec society's choice of "interculturalism" over "multiculturalism" as a model of integration, and the matter of the increasing fragmentation of the bounded collectivity.

The ambiguities and problems that arise when searching for an operational definition of "cultural communities" are noted in the first report submitted by the Comité interculturel de la participation active des communautés culturelles. This committee (CIPACC, 1983: 10) defined a member of a cultural community as someone who meets any of the following criteria: a) place of birth outside of Canada, or place of birth of either parent outside of Canada and knowledge of the language of the original community, or knowledge of the language (other than French) of the original community; b) mother tongue other than French; c) membership in a visible community; d) membership in an ethnic or cultural group, defined as a group characterized by common ethnic or cultural traits. The difficulty of constructing the "other" is clearly evident here. Do anglophones constitute a cultural community? In attempting to make sense of "visible," a rather muddled notion of "race" is introduced to designate minority ethnic groups who differentiate themselves from the white majority by their skin colour or other distinctive physical traits (CIPACC, 1983:10).

Even senior officials at the Ministry of Cultural Communities and Immigration recognize the ambiguity and arbitrariness of such a notion as "cultural communities" as compared to the concept of "immigrants"[7] (Fontaine, 1990). "Cultural community" is a political category which constitutes an ideological compromise because it can include both anglophones and visible minorities. "Immigrant" is a category whose contours are clear. "Ethnic origin," when defined by country of birth is also comprehensible. But the difficulty of dealing with ethnicity is precisely its fuzziness. Its social construction is an ongoing process—one that is always open to transformations from many sides.

The second issue pertaining directly to a definition of the national community and its boundaries is the choice of "interculturalism" in Quebec over "multiculturalism" in the rest of Canada. The Quebec government rejected both monoculturalism (as illustrated by the American melting pot), and multiculturalism (the Canadian mosaic model). The argument runs as follows: in order for different cultural groups to flourish, the collective vitality of Quebec as a French society must first be guaranteed. In other words, cultural pluralism will be encouraged within the context of a French-speaking society. More to the point, accepting cultural pluralism does not preclude adopting measures to strengthen the French language in Quebec. For some critics, Quebec's interculturalism appears similar to the models adopted by the United States and Canada, in that, while the latter two countries look more like Anglo-conformity in practice, Quebec's interculturalism often translates into Franco-conformity in everyday life. Dominant-conformity triumphs once again.

For Quebec nationalists, multiculturalism is interpreted as "weak" ideology which separates immigrant and "ethnic" cultures from the majority. The policy is criticized for focusing on minority cultures as isolated and static entities and for ignoring the relationship of these cultures to that of the majority. Quebec rejects equal status for all cultural groups, as laid out in the Canadian multiculturalism policy. The Quebec government argues that such equality masks the political and historical differences between various ethnic groups, and favours the mobility of some groups at the expense of others. The idea of interculturalism, on the other hand, fosters a dynamic interaction between minorities and the (French-Canadian) majority. Interculturalism is seen as the desirable form of pluralism, since it allows societies and groups to achieve a greater "adaptive capacity" with respect to integration.

The third and final issue we examine in the context of the social construction of the national community is its increasing fragmentation. Some scholars argue that interculturalism fosters divisions in the collectivity, for it does not suggest full integration of individuals (the American "melting pot"), or the equal juxtaposition of groups, as suggested by the Canadian mosaic model. Rather, interculturalism constructs a structure of two categories of individuals: members of the "la nation québécoise francophone" and the Others, the "cultural communities."

---

[7] The Quebec government defines three categories of immigrants: 1) the "independent" category, constituted of people who are retired, businessmen, selected workers and helped parents; 2) the "family" category; and 3) the "refugee" category.

In December of 1990, *L'Enoncé de politique en matière d'immigration et d'intégration* was published by the Quebec government. In its proposal of a policy of intercultural rapprochement, the document introduced the expression "Québécois des communautés culturelles" (Québécois members of cultural communities). "Québécois" and "cultural community" would no longer designate mutually exclusive categories. The intention here was to make the category "Québécois" more inclusive. This policy of integration and the measures stemming from it were based on the three following principles: 1) Quebec is a society where French is the common language of public life; 2) Quebec is a democratic society where all are entitled to contribute and the participation of all is expected 3) Quebec is a pluralist society open to multiple expressions within, of course, the limits imposed by the respect for fundamental democratic values and the necessity of intercultural exchange (the centrality of French being iterated) (Québec, 1990: 15).

How should all of this be interpreted? It can be argued that recognizing historically diverse collectivities need not be equated with exclusion. The goal, on the contrary, is to reject a homogeneous nation and construct national boundaries in non-racist terms so as to include others, not isolate them. Nonetheless, the danger of exclusion remains ever present, as the comments of Jacques Parizeau on the night of the referendum of October 1995[8] strongly demonstrated. It is clear that embracing ethnic pluralism and developing policies aimed at assisting cultural communities to flourish is no guarantee of their *de facto* equality. The following section, which examines ethnic dynamics in present-day Quebec, provides evidence to support this hypothesis.

ETHNIC DYNAMICS IN CONTEMPORARY QUEBEC

Montreal, Quebec's great metropolis, provides the perfect setting for examining ethnic relations, since 90% of immigrants settle in this urban centre (Baillargeon, 1989:1). Immigrants now represent 9% of Quebec's total population and 17% of the population of Montreal. The city ranks third in Canada for its proportion of immigrants, preceded by Toronto (38%) and Vancouver (30%). The Montreal milieu is a fascinating place in many respects, and the presence of a "double majority" (Anctil, 1984) in the city has played an important role in shaping ethnic dynamics. The proximity of both anglophone and francophone communities has fostered a higher retention of ethnicity (measured by language, religion and endogamy, for example) in Montreal than in other Canadian cities.

Ethnic retention in Montreal is an interesting story, and one of the unintended consequences of the linguistic policies instituted in the past two decades. While the recent generation of immigrants are obliged to educate their children

---

[8] During his speech after the slim victory of the No forces on October 30, 1995, Premier Parizeau explained to the nation (and to the world) that the sovereignty side lost because of "money and the ethnic vote."

in French, the former generation learned English upon arrival in Quebec. Now, in order to communicate with grandparents who maintain the mother tongue, intergenerational communication takes place in that language. Painchaud and Poulin (1983) have suggested this explanation for the vitality of the Italian community in Montreal, and Meintel's (1991) research indicates a similar phenomenon for the Portuguese community. Certain groups, second-generation youth for example, are becoming more and more trilingual as their parents' mother tongue remains the common language of the group.

We have chosen three sites of ethnic social relations for discussion: the labour market, the family and the school system. The following three sections examine the articulation of relations between different ethnic groups in these fields of activity.

The Labour Market

Debates concerning ethnic dynamics in labour markets usually focus on discrimination and other types of exclusionary practices and measures. Census data are able to provide some descriptive information, but comparing broad categories must be done with caution, since such an approach can hide inequalities (Boyd, 1992:282).

Figure 1 presents information on the labour force classified according to occupation and immigrant status for Quebec in 1991. A first observation we can make is to note that immigrants in Quebec are spread out over various fields and do not cluster solely in a few categories. There are, however, significant gaps between the immigrant and non-immigrant population according to profession. A much higher percentage of immigrants than non-immigrants is found in product fabricating, assembling and repairing. Yet immigrants are much less numerous than non-immigrants among office clerks. Both groups are almost equally represented in managerial and administrative positions. This is also the case for two other areas which include the highest number of workers, namely sales and service. In areas with fewer workers, the most important differences are found in the natural sciences, engineering and mathematics, where immigrants outnumber the total population.

Table 4 reveals important differences between ethnic origin categories in terms of labour market participation. In the category of management and administration, persons of Egyptian (27.5%) and Lebanese (16.4%) origins are overrepresented compared to the general population (13.4%), whereas those of Greek (11.1%), Italian (12.9), Vietnamese (9.4%) and Haitian (4.9%) origins are underrepresented. In clerical and related occupations, the ethnic groups identified here are underrepresented compared to the total population. The proportions vary from 8.5% (Greeks) to 18.1% (Lebanese), compared to 18.5% of the total population. In sales, an occupational category accounting for 8.9% of the working population, we have found great differences among ethnic origin groups, with workers of Lebanese (16.2%) and Egyptian (11.9%) origins being overrepresented and the other groups identified here underrepresented. In the category

FIGURE 1: Percentage Distribution of the Labour Force, by Occupation and Immigrant Status, Quebec, 1991

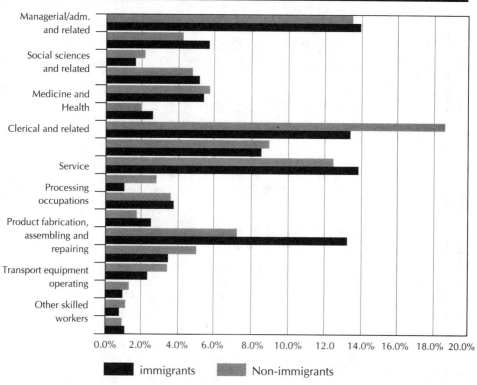

SOURCE: Census of Canada 1991, MAIICC data (unpublished).

of product fabricating, assembling and repairing, all groups except those of Egyptian origin (4.2%) are overrepresented, compared to 7.3% of the general population. Twenty percent of Greeks work in this field, 21.4% of Italians, 19.2% of Haitians, 19% of Vietnamese and 10.9% of Lebanese. Finally, in the field of medicine and health, which employs only 5.9% of the working population, 14.6% of workers of Haitian origin (mostly nurses) fall into this category.

Recent studies of immigrant women show a bimodal distribution of their participation in the labour force (Boyd, 1986). That is, for certain women, changing countries entails an improvement in both salary and legal status (Labelle et al, 1987). In general, immigrant women appear to participate more actively in the labour market than women born in Quebec. This observation does not take into account undeclared paid work done at home for industries such as the textile industry. In order to refine an analysis of immigrant women's labour it is necessary to study their activities in concrete situations and to specify the context (Boyd, 1992).

TABLE 4: Labour Force, by Occupation and Place of Birth, Quebec, 1991

Occupation	Total Pop.	Greece	Italy	Egypt	Lebanon	Haiti	Vietnam
Managerial/adm. and related	13.4%	11.1%	12.9%	27.5%	16.4%	4.9%	9.4%
Nat. sciences, engineering and mathematics	4.3%	2.4%	2.3%	9.1%	6.5%	2.4%	12.7%
Social sciences and related	2.1%	0.5%	0.6%	1.8%	0.9%	2.1%	1.2%
Teaching and related	4.7%	2.2%	2.4%	9.3%	3.2%	4.2%	2.5%
Medicine and health	5.9%	2.1%	1.5%	5.6%	3.5%	14.6%	8.1%
Artistic, literary, recreational and related	2.0%	1.0%	1.1%	2.4%	1.6%	1.1%	0.9%
Clerical and related	18.5%	8.5%	12.2%	16.3%	18.1%	13.1%	11.3%
Sales	8.9%	6.2%	8.6%	11.9%	16.2%	4.2%	6.4%
Service	12.5%	33.2%	11.3%	6.0%	11.7%	13.8%	14.5%
Agriculture, mining and fishing	2.7%	0.2%	1.8%	0.0%	0.4%	0.3%	0.3%
Processing occupations	3.6%	4.2%	5.1%	0.9%	2.4%	7.2%	4.8%
Machining and related	1.8%	1.2%	3.2%	1.3%	0.8%	2.3%	2.1%
Product fabricating, assembling and repairing	7.3%	20.2%	21.4%	4.2%	10.9%	19.2%	19.0%
Construction trades occupations	5.0%	2.3%	10.1%	0.8%	1.8%	1.2%	1.5%
Transport equipment operating occupation	3.5%	2.7%	2.6%	0.9%	3.2%	3.8%	0.8%
Materials handling and related	1.5%	0.5%	1.0%	0.4%	0.9%	2.8%	1.7%
Other skilled workers	1.2%	0.5%	0.8%	0.9%	0.7%	0.7%	1.3%
Not elsewhere classified	1.0%	1.0%	0.8%	0.5%	0.6%	1.9%	1.4%
Total	100%	100%	100%	100%	100%	100%	100%

SOURCE: Census of Canada, 1991, MAIICC data (unpublished).

Less educated immigrant women often find themselves in labour market ghettos structured according to ethnic criteria (e.g. the textile industry and house cleaning), where upward mobility is non-existent. Salaries are extremely low and working conditions are often unhealthy. Moreover, it is often the free labour of women, youths and older people that makes "ethnic" businesses profitable (Juteau, Moallem and Daviau, 1992; Anthias, 1983; Perez, 1986; Moallem, 1989). More highly educated immigrant women (and men) can experience longer- or shorter-term underemployment, resulting from lack of recognition of their credentials and/or their work experience outside Quebec.

A good number of these findings can be interpreted only in terms of systemic discrimination in various areas of economic activity (Omi and Wiunant, 1989; Moore, 1989; Bosset and Caron, 1987). The ghettoization of some immigrants and "visible minorities" in the secondary sector of the economy has induced both the federal and provincial governments to pass Employment Equity Acts. The federal government did so in 1986 (Boyd, 1992:280; Chicha-Pontbriand, 1989, 1990) followed by the Quebec government in 1987 (Quebec, 1992). The programmes aim to reduce poverty and unemployment among minority populations resulting from practices of economic exclusion. The so-called "visible" minorities are considered particularly vulnerable to this form of discrimination at work. Furthermore, the absence of professional networks (as in the case of educated refugees from Chile or Vietnam, for example) also fosters marginalization. Systemic discrimination consolidates various forms of socio-professional segregation and in the end limits access to different areas of economic activity.

Information on unemployment rates of young adults in Montreal gives us a disturbing picture of unequal access to jobs for different ethnic groups,[9] as well as an illustration of the dire economic situation in this city in 1991. As Table 5 shows, the lowest rates of unemployment are found among young adults aged 15-30 years who are of French origin. Of this group, 13.3% were unemployed in 1991 at the time of the census. This group is followed by young people of Italian (14.0%) and British (14.5%) origin in terms of unemployment. The highest rates of unemployment are found among black/Caribbean young adults, where 32.9% were without work in 1991, followed closely by those of Latin/Central American origin, with 31.0% of those between the ages of 15 and 30 years being unemployed in 1991 in Montreal. Moreover, in this same age category, 21.5% of immigrants and 23.5% of visible minorities were unemployed during this time. Is this what we can expect from federal and/or provincial legislation concerning equity in employment?

In Quebec, ethnic dynamics are further complicated by language and linguistic boundaries, which also structure economic activity. In the areas of manufacturing and financial services related to the private sector, English remains the

---

[9] We are aware of course, that other variables influence unemployment rates besides ethnicity—education, for example. But neither is access to education equally distributed among the population. The issue is complicated, but the reality for these young people is clear.

TABLE 5: Unemployment Rate of Young Adults (15-30 yrs), for Immigrants, Visible Minorities and Selected Ethnic Groups, Montreal, 1991

Group	%
Immigrants	21.5%
Visible Minorities	23.5%
French	13.3%
British	14.5%
Greek	15.7%
Italian	14.0%
Jewish	17.1%
Arab	26.1%
South Asian	25.3%
Latin/Central American	31.0%
Black/Caribbean	32.9%

SOURCE: Statistics Canada, 1991 Individual Public Use Sample Tape

language of work in both research and management (Béland, 1991). French, however, is predominant in the public and parapublic sectors (Bouchard, 1991) as well as most of the primary sector of the labour market.

It appears that the territorial organization of economic activity according to the use of French or English remains uncertain. As international markets develop, English increases its dominance, and this in turn affects national markets. Nevertheless, in Montreal a growing number of people speak mostly French in their work environment (Monnier, 1983; Béland, 1991). This does not change the predominance of English in places where language is the main working tool, as in management and research (Béland, 1991), although the increase in the spending power of francophones has entailed a significant rise in the use of French.

In general, economic activity in Quebec, particularly in Montreal, remains territorially organized—and complementary—according to the predominance of either French or English. The immigrant population is thus confronted with a series of socio-professional territories which are already structured along ethno-linguistic lines.

The Transformation of Family Relations

Migration is no easy endeavour, and it is rarely undertaken by individuals alone. Rather, it is more often a domestic strategy to improve the living conditions of the household (Labelle et al, 1987; Peressini, 1991). Greek and Portuguese men, for example, left their wives at home to run the peasant farmstead, and came alone to try their luck in Canada. Once established, they sent for their families.

Following the classic migration pattern (e.g. that of Italians, Portuguese and Colombians to Quebec), the decision to migrate is generally taken after consulting family members already established in Canada. Once the "family link" is made, new arrivals usually live with their predecessors in the migratory chain for shorter or longer periods of time. The newcomers count on established relatives to help them get oriented and find work (Labelle et al, 1987).

Refugees, on the other hand, experience a different migration process. They often leave their country of origin mainly for their children's safety. Unlike economic migrants, refugees rarely have a chance to plan their departure with other family or household members. With little choice in terms of destination, refugees go where they can in order to escape persecution at home. For these newcomers, the family network is often more severely fragmented, as lone individuals, couples, and parents with young children arrive with no family contacts in Canada. Fragmentation can be forestalled, however, even for refugees. In some cases, the creation of quasi-kin ties with other refugees (Gilad, 1990) and with ethnic associations involved in establishing new community ties can compensate for the absence of relatives. Salvadorians in Montreal, for example, have shown how this can be done (F. Juteau, 1991).

As is the case for couples' lives in general, migrant couples do not necessarily share the same migration experience. Differences are accentuated for refugees, where migration represents a rupture for the couple, rather than the unfolding of family projects (Meintel and Le Gall, 1995). Some refugee groups, Salvadorians, for example, experience considerable conjugal instability, while other groups, such as the Vietnamese, do not. Factors relating to the home milieu help, no doubt, to explain the differences. Despite the stresses inflicted on couples by the refugee experience, family collectivism, highly valued by the Vietnamese, appears to favour conjugal stability within this group.

Nevertheless, changes in family relations can and do occur. New economic conditions facing immigrant men and women, for example, oblige more of them to modify their traditional division of domestic labour. However, normative changes regarding sex status and sex roles seem less frequent and slower to materialize than do daily practical readjustments made either temporarily or permanently. Normative changes depend on a number of factors such as employment opportunities for women or men, and vary a great deal between groups (Meintel et al, 1984).

The changing status of migrant women, an interesting case of the transformation of ethnic social relations, cannot be analysed solely within the context of gender relations in the family. The situation of women must also be examined outside the home (Morokvasic, 1983), since gender relations permeate and structure society as a whole.

There remains much more work to be done to explore the complexities of family relations and ethnic social relations in Quebec. Our intention here is to provide the reader with some examples of the dynamics. We now turn to an examination of the school system and the process of ethnic social relations that occur in this site.

The School System

For the past twenty years, the field of education in Quebec has been dominated by the linguistic debate between francophones and anglophones (Plourde, 1991). These debates have projected Quebec schools into the forefront of exploring Quebec's future. The discussions have also acted to break the state of inertia which characterized the educational system since the '50s in the province. However, recent problems linked more precisely to questions of ethnicity have demonstrated that linguistic debates on the one hand, and the Catholic/Protestant division on the other, cannot account for all the value conflicts embedded in the educational system. In the early 1990s, with the arrival of new immigrant populations, Quebec schools were obliged to open up to the expression of cultural differences.

Discussions of ethnic identity in the educational system usually revolve around three issues, namely, academic performance, value conflict, and friction among ethnic groups in the schools. Regarding the first issue, various studies at different time periods show that academic performance of children of immigrant parents is as good as that of children of French-Canadian Québécois parents with comparable social origins (Tchoryck-Pelletier, 1989). Other studies have shown that Bill 101 has not altered this fact. Academic performance increases according to the number of years spent in an educational institution, regardless of whether it is French or English (St-Germain, 1988). This is not to deny the *a priori* insistence by some that Quebec schools generate discrimination. And while some argue that the existence of such discrimination has never been "proven" (Latif, 1988; McAndrew, 1993), the debate regarding the accusation of systemic racism often levied against Quebec's educational institutions remains an open one.

Schools confronted with diverse ethnic identities are placed at the centre of value conflicts, our second issue for discussion. The terms of such conflict have been manifested in collective demands for action. Such was the case, for instance, of the Brossard[10] school board when it was obliged to take a stand on the question of Islamic instruction, following official requests made by Muslim parents (Lemire, 1993). Elsewhere, students have been prohibited access to school while wearing the hidjab (head-covering worn by Muslim women), as was the case at Louis-Riel secondary school (Proulx, 1993). Such situations, while having been faced by other Western democracies for some time now, are relatively new to Quebec (CRISP, 1992). Value conflicts have taken on new importance, and the idea of pluralism espoused by school boards over the past 10 years is now being put to the test (McAndrew, 1993).

The debate over value conflicts also raises questions as to the content and future of cultural values traditionally diffused by the educational system, as well as the adaptation of schools to the dissemination of new identities in society. The status of women is a case in point. Having admitted that the feminist movement

---

[10] A south-shore suburb of Montreal.

has enabled considerable advances in terms of equality of access for men and women, how, in principle, can the pluralist school tolerate religious references that do not spontaneously advocate sexual equality?

The third issue of discussion concerning ethnic identity in schools focuses on the question of friction among ethnic groups. Research has focused on the conflictual aspect of interaction between a plurality of ethnic groups in schools. As Anne Laperrière (1991) notes, the school system in Quebec has been unable to create a situation of harmonious contact between different ethnic groups. More particularly, however, she demonstrates that adolescents of different cultural origins are capable of embracing new cultural values such as respect for individuals and the value of equality of access.

Schools today can no longer be considered simply as sites for the transmission and learning of knowledge and values. The socializing function of schools, which traditionally ensured certain privileges during the process of skill selection, has become blurred (Dubet, 1994). For immigrant parents, often in a less favourable position than French-Canadian Québécois parents in terms of social status, the educational system represents the only opportunity for their children to acquire social mobility. Thus are claims reinforced for recognition of respective identities, both social and cultural, as well as promotion of specific interests. It is at this juncture that the growing interest in the theme of ethnicity in the educational system becomes important.

Moreover, cases of conflicting cultural identities in the schools reveal the relative fragility of interculturalism, or at least the difficulties of its implementation. Lack of financial backing to undertake a project as ambitious as intercultural education puts the venture in serious jeopardy. Quebec schools have adapted reasonably well to the challenges of ethnic pluralism in the space of 15 years, and Bill 101 has not prevented the rapprochement of children of immigrants with those of the French-Canadian Québécois. Finally, the risk of misunderstanding between schools and society now extends beyond the traditional linguistic questions confronting francophones and anglophones, and concerns more directly the recognition of cultural values considered fundamental for all ethnic groups in Quebec.

QUEBEC AS A PLURALIST SOCIETY? PRESENT CHALLENGES AND FUTURE POSSIBILITIES

The present debates concerning ethnic social relations are often discussed in terms of the "new" immigration, furnishing the stuff of demographic politics (Piché, 1991). Indeed, the demographic issue is surely present when questions of immigration and integration surface. The nationalist discourse focusing on relations between anglophones and francophones (all others are labelled allophones) is based on demographic considerations. The argument relies primarily on the perceived effects of the decline of the birthrate, which could lead to a decrease in the overall population by the turn of the century. Even if, theoretically, immigration could play a major role in reviving Quebec's demographic weight, many doubt the province's capacity to welcome and integrate immigrants, on the one hand because of immigrants' preference to learn English,[11] and on the other because of the host society's resentment of this choice.

Beyond the linguistic issue, there is apprehension about an influx of immigratants who are perceived to be unfamiliar.

> there probably wouldn't be a reason for being so preoccupied with the future if we were in the presence of familiar immigrants to whom we were accustomed for the last fifty years (Rogel, 1989: 8. Our translation.)

This widespread concern can be found, interestingly enough, throughout history, with new immigrants always seeming less familiar than former ones (Ramirez, 1992). Interesting it may be, but such apprehension can lead to a position advocating restrictive immigration on the pretext that this "type" of immigrant is more difficult to integrate than previous cohorts. Realistically speaking, there are no data to confirm such a hypothesis. The challenges are indeed new and numerous, but there is no evidence that problems of integration will be greater than in the past.

Immigration remains a central question here and elsewhere, as the fiery debates of the European Economic Community attest. Quebec can still avoid creating conditions which favour right wing doctrines such as the budding "lepeniste" ideology in France, but to do so, immigration must be considered essential for the development of the national community.

The future possibilities for Quebec as a pluralist society are open. Looking back, we distinguish a twofold movement that has characterized the transformation of Quebec since the Quiet Revolution. First, there was the emergence of a "nation québécoise" comprised of the French-Canadians in Quebec ("Nous, les Québécois") and excluding French-Canadians outside Quebec. Now, efforts are continuing to try to broaden the boundaries of the national collectivity so as to include all those who live in Quebec. This form of "nation-ness" differs from the former ethnic type of nation represented by French Canada, and more closely resembles the territorial and civil model of the nation (Smith, 1986). As some scholars argue, members of the political and bureaucratic elites seem to be rejecting an assimilationist vision (Juteau and McAndrew, 1992) and are adhering to a pluralistic model. But this project remains fragile, as the political blunders of the sovereignty movement in the 1995 referendum campaign revealed. Anglophone and allophone communities in Quebec are very wary of the Parti Québécois' plans for pluralism in a future sovereign Quebec.

---

[11] It should be noted that immigrants learn both French and English and, along with their maternal tongue, are at least trilingual.

This chapter has outlined the challenges facing Quebec today. It remains to be seen if the political leaders in Quebec are willing and able to address the challenges now in evidence the world over. Will Quebec struggle against the vision of an ethnically homogeneous nation? Will it combat racist ideologies and racist practices? Will the government make a priority of reducing socioeconomic inequalities? Is Quebec capable of accepting the cultural diversity presented by history without making it a criterion for exclusion? Herein lie the challenges for Quebec as a pluralist society.

BIBLIOGRAPHY

Anctil, P. "Double majorité et multiplicité ethno-culturelle à Montréal," *Recherches sociographiques*, Vol. 25, No 3, 1984; pp. 441-450.

Anthias, F. "Sexual Divisions and Ethnic Adaptation: the Case of Greek-Cypriot Women," in A. Phizacklea (ed.): *One Way Ticket. Migration and Female Labor*, Londres, Routledge and Kegan Paul, 1983; pp. 73-94.

Baillargeon, M. *Population immigrée dans les régions métropolitaines du Québec et dans certaines municipalités du Grand Montréal, par pays de naissance*, recensement 1986: Document 5, Ministère des Communautés culturelles et de l'Immigration, Direction des études et de la recherche, Québec, 1989; 39.

Béland, P. *L'usage du français au travail: situation et tendances* (synthèse), Québec: Conseil de la langue française, 1991; 205.

Berger, P.L., Berger, B. Kellner, H. 1973. *The Homeless Mind. Modernization and Consciousness*. New York: Random House.

Bled, Y. *La condition des domestiques antillaises à Montréal*, mémoire de maîtrise anthropoloqie, Université de Montréal, 1965, 165 p.

Bosset, P., Caron, M. "Un nouvel outil de lutte contre la discrimination : les programmes d'accès à l'égalité," *Thémis*, Vol. 21, No. 1, 1987; pp. 71-124.

Bouchard, P. *Les enjeux de la francisation des entreprises au Québec (1977-1984)*, Québec: Conseil de la langue française, 1991; 321 pages.

Boyd, M. "Immigrant Women in Canada," in R.J. Simon and Brettell, C.B. (eds), *International Migration. The Female Experience*, Totowa, N.J., Rowman and Allanbeld, 1986.

Boyd, M. "Gender, Visible Minority, and Immigrant Earnings Inequality: Reassessing an Employment Equity Premise" *Deconstructing a Nation: Immigration, Multiculturalism and Racism in '90s Canada*, Fernwood Publishing, Halifax Nova Scotia and Social Research Unit, Department of Sociology, University of Saskatchewan, Saskatoon, Saskatchewan, 1992, pp. 279-321.

Canada, Government *Royal Commission on Bilingualism and Biculturalism.* Preliminary Report. Ottawa: Queen's Printer, 1965.

Chicha-Pontbriand, M.T. *Discrimination systémique: fondement et méthodologie des programmes d'accès à l'égalité*, Editions Yvon Blais, Cowansville, 1989; 197 pages.

Chicha-Pontbriand, M.T. *Les jeunes des minorités visibles et ethniques et le marché du travail: une situation doublement précaire*, Montréal: Commission des droits de la personne, 1990.

Cipacc: Comité d'implantation du plan à l'intention des communautés culturelles. *Rapport annuel 1981-1982*, Québec, 1983, 87.

Fontaine, L. *L'organisation étatique de l'inclusion et de l'exclusion: le cas du Québec (1976-1988)*, thèse de doctorat en science politique, Université Laval, Québec, 1990; 233 pages.

Gilad, L. *The Northern Route: An Ethnography of Refugee Experiences*, St. John's, Newfoundland, Memorial University, ISER, Social and Economic Studies, No. 39, 1990.

GRES. "Immigration et relations ethniques au Québec: Un pluralisme en devenir," in *Le Québec en jeu*, G. Daigle and G. Rocher (eds). Montréal, Presses de l'Université de Montreal, 1992, pp. 451-481.

Juteau, D. "L'Etat et les immigrés: de l'immigration aux communautés culturelles," *Minorités et Etat*, Pierre Guillaume, Réjean Pelletier, Jean-Michel Lacroix, Jacques Zylberberg (dir.), Centre d'études canadiennes de la Maison des Sciences de l'Homme d'Aquitaine, Laboratoire d'études politiques et administratives de l'Université Laval, P.U.B.P.U.L., 1986; pp. 35-50.

Juteau, D. "The production of the Québécois nation" *Humbolt Journal of Social Relations*, Vol. XIX, No. 2, 1993, pp. 79-108.

Juteau, D., McAndrew, M. *Projet national, immigration et intégration dans un Québec souverain*, mémoire présenté à la Commission d'Etude des questions afférentes à l'accession du Québec à la souveraineté, 19 février 1992; 29 pages.

Juteau, D., Moallem, M., Daviau, J. "Les entreprises ethniques à Montréal: une étude exploratoire," Communication présentée au colloque organisé par le Groupe de recherche ethnicité et société (GRES), Université de Montréal, 13 et 14 juin 1991; 12 pages.

Juteau, D. "Français d'Amérique, Canadiens, Canadiens-français, Franco-Ontariens, Ontarois: qui sommes-nous? *Pluriel-Débats*, Vol. V., No. 2, 1980, pp. 21-43.

Juteau, F. "Divorce and the Migration Process among Salvadorians in Montreal," S. P. Sharma, A.M. Ervin, D. Meintel (eds.), *Immigrants and Refugees in Canada: a National Perspective on Ethnicity, Multiculturalism and Cross-Cultural Adjustment*, University of Saskatchewan, Saskatoon and Université de Montréal, 1991.

Labelle, M., Larose, S., Piché, V. "Politiques d'immigration et immigration en provenance de la Caraïbe anglophone au Canada et au Québec, 1900-1979," *Canadian Ethnic Studies/Etudes ethniques au Canada*, Vol. 15, No. 2, 1983; pp. 1-24.

Labelle, M., Lemay, D., Painchaud, C. *Notes sur l'histoire et les conditions de vie des travailleurs immigrés au Québec*, Montréal: Centrale de l'enseignement du Québec, 1980; 63.

Labelle, M., Turcotte, G., Kempeneers, M., Meintel, D. *Histoires d'immigrées. Itinéraires d'ouvrières colombiennes, grecques, haïtiennes et portugaises de Montréal*, Montréal, Boréal, 1987; 275.

Laferriere, M. "L'éducation des enfants des groupes minoritaires au Québec: de la définition par les groupes eux-mêmes à l'intervention de l'Etat," *Education canadienne et internationale*, Vol. 14, No. 1, 1985; pp. 29-48.

Laperriere, A. "L'analyse sociologique des inégalités sociales et de l'ethnicité dans la formation des maîtres," in F. Ouellet (sous la direction de), *Pluriethnicité, éducation et société, construire un espace commun*, Institut québécois de recherche sur la culture, Québec, 1991; pp. 543-562.

Latif, G. *L'école québécoise et les communautés culturelles: Rapport déposé au Bureau du sous-ministre*. Québec, Ministère de l'éduction, 1988.

Lemire, F. *Les enjeux liés à l'insertion des jeunes immigrants dans les écoles françaises d'une commission scolaire de banlieue*. Thèse. Université de Montréal, 1993.

McRoberts, K. *Quebec: Social Change and Political Crisis*. Toronto, McClelland and Stewart, 3rd Edition, 1988.

Meintel, D. "Studying Immigrant and Refugee Groups in Quebec," in S. Ervin, D. Meintel S. Sharma (eds), *Immigrants and Refugees in Canada: a National Perspective on Ethnicity, Multiculturalism and Cross-cultural Adjustment*, University of Saskatchewan and Université de Montréal, Saskatoon, 1991.

Meintel, D., Le Gall, J. *Les jeunes d'origine immigrée: Rapports familiaux et transitions de vie*. Ministère des affaires internationales, de l'immigration et des Communautés culturelles, Québec, 1995.

Meintel, D., Labelle, M., Turcotte, G., Kempeneers, M. "Migration, Wage Labour and Domestic Relationships," *Anthropologica*, Vol. 26, No. 2, 1984; pp. 135-170. (Publié en 1988).

Moallem, M. *Pluralité des rapports sociaux: similarité et différence: le cas des Iraniens à Montréal*, thèse de doctorat en sociologie, Université de Montréal, 1989; 437 pages.

Monnier, D. *L'usage du français au travail*, Québec: Conseil de la langue française, 1983; 121 pages.

Moore, J. "Is there a Hispanic Underclass?," *Social Science Quarterly*, Vol. 70, No. 2, 1989; pp. 265-284.

Morokvasic, M. "Women in Migration: Beyond the Reductionist Outlook," In A. Phizacklea (ed.), *One Way ticket: Migration and Female Labour*, Routledge and Kegan Paul, London, 1983; pp. 13-32.

Omi, M., Winant, H. *Racial Formation in the United States, From the 1960s to the 1980s*, New York: Routledge & Kegan Paul, 1986, Londen: Routledge, 1989; 201 pages.

Painchaud, C., POULIN, R. "Conflit linguistique et structure de pouvoir dans la communauté italo-québécoise," *Sociologie et Sociétés*, Vol. 15, No. 2, 1983; pp. 89-104.

Peressini, M. *Sujets et identités: analyses des histoires de vie d'un groupe d'immigrants italiens à Montréal*, thèse de doctorat en anthropologie, Université de Montréal, 1991; 2 tomes, 886 pages.

Perez, L. "Immigrant Economic Adjustment and Family Organization: the Cuban Success Story Reexamined," *International Migration Review*, Vol. 20 , No. 1, 1986; pp. 4-20.

Piché, V. "La conception de l'intégration dans le discours démo- politique: inclusion ou exclusion?," communication présentée au colloque "Rapports conflictuels ethniques et nationaux" organisé par le Groupe de recherche ethnicité et société (GRES), Université de Montréal, 13 et 14 juin 1991; 12 pages.

Plourde, M. *La politique linguistique du Québec. 1977-1987,* Québec: Institut québécois de recherche sur la culture, Diagnostic 6, 1991.

Ponting, R.J., Gibbins, R. *Out of Irrelevance: A Socio-political Introduction to Indian Affairs in Canada.* Toronto: Butterworths, 1980, 360 p.

Ponting, R.J., Symons, G.L. "Environmental geo-politics and the new world order: Grande Baleine, the Crees and Hydro-Québec". Forthcoming in R.J. Ponting (Ed.) *First Nations in Canada: Perspectives on Opportunity, Empowerment, and Self-Determination* 1996.

Proulx, J. "Pour un accueil et un intégration réussis des élèves des communautés culturelles: Avis à la ministre de l'éducation et ministre de l'enseignement supérieur et de la sciences. Québec: Conseil supérieur de l'éducation 1993.

Québec, Gouvernement *La politique québécoise du développement culturel,* Éditeur officiel, Québec, 1978, 2 tomes; 472 pages.

Québec, Gouvernement *Autant de façons d'être Québécois,* plan d'action du gouvernement du Québec à l'intention des communautés culturelles, Ministère des Communautés culturelles et de l'Immigration, Bibliothèque nationale du Québec, 1981; 78 pages.

Québec, Gouvernement *L'Enoncé de politique en matière d'immigration et d'intégration.* Ministère des Communautés culturelles et de l'Immigration, Bibliothèque nationale du Québec, 1990.

Quebec, Gouvernement *Rapport d'évaluation sur le programme d'accès à l'égalité pour les femmes dans la fonction publique québécoise, 1987-1990.* Québec: Conseil du Trésor, 1992.

Quebec, Gouvernement *Le Québec en Mouvement.* Montréal, Ministère des Affaires Internationnelles, de l'Immigration et des Communautés Culturelles, 1994.

Ramirez, B. *Par monts et par vaux,* Boréal, Montréal, 1992; 206 pages.

Rogel, J.P. *Le défi de l'immigration,* Coll. Diagnostic, Institut québécois de recherche sur la culture, Québec, 1989; 123 pages.

Schermerhorn, R.A. *Comparative Ethnic Relations,* Random House, New York, 1970.

Simon, P.J., "Le sociologue et les minorités: connaissance et idéologie," *Sociologie et Sociétés,* Vol. 15, No. 2, octobre 1983; pp. 9-22.

Smith, A. *The Ethnic Origins of Nations.* Oxford U.K.: Blackwell, 1986, 312 p.

Symons, G.L. 1988. "Ideology and social change: Meech Lake and national identity," in H. Symonds and H.P. Oberlander (eds), *The Meech Lake Accord: From Centre for Periphery, The Impact of the 1987 Constitutional Accord on Canadian Settlements.* Vancouver: The University of British Columbia, Centre for Human Settlements, 1988, pp. 55-67.

Tchoryck-Pelletier, P. *"L'adaptation des minorités ethniques".* Saint-Laurent, Cegep de Saint-Laurent, 1989.

SCHOOL AND THE STATE
IN QUEBEC

As in so many other areas of social life, education presents a different face and plays a different role in Quebec society than that found elsewhere in North America. In part, this difference is structural, with unique features such as a two-year college (CEGEP) system that students are required to attend before entering a three-year undergraduate university program. But it is the cultural and political significance attached to education in Quebec which highlight its distinctiveness. Indeed, what we might call the "parapolitics" (Geertz, 1973) of education have been particularly contentious in Quebec because of the central symbolic role that education has played in the process of modernization which began with the Quiet Revolution of the 1960s. Since then, education has come to be seen as crucial to the collective project of transforming Quebec into a modern, francophone, distinctive — and for some, sovereign — society.

In this chapter we will examine the evolution of Quebec's education system over the past four decades, with particular attention to the cultural and political context in which this evolution has occurred. By documenting the interplay between the structural, cultural, and parapolitical components of Quebec's education system, we can identify the bases from which its schools and universities have developed, the structural changes that these institutions have undergone, and some of the problems they currently face.

EDUCATION IN QUEBEC BEFORE
THE QUIET REVOLUTION

The education system has always served as an index both of the state of group relations in Quebec and of the relations between the state and civil society. As a society divided along ethnic, linguistic, and religious lines, it is not surprising that the education system has often been a point of contention in Quebec. Prior to the Quiet Revolution of the 1960s, conflict over education among Quebec's diverse communities and interest groups usually focused on two issues: who would control education and who would pay for it. While everyone wanted to control it, no one really wanted to pay for it. The result was an underfunded education system divided along linguistic, confessional (Protestant and Catholic), and class lines. There were separate Protestant and Catholic schools, French and English schools, and public and private schools, along with various permutations and combinations of each. To a large extent the state stayed out of education, having no ministry of education to oversee the system, and not even initiating compulsory education until 1943.

Because of the absence of state coordination, the different educational institutions were highly autonomous, controlled by separate commissions, corporations, or committees, each of which largely ignored the other. So independent were these various segments of the education system from each other that a joint Protestant and Catholic coordinating committee that was to oversee the operations of all of the public schools failed to meet even once between 1908 and 1960. This institutional autonomy was reinforced by group preferences, by provisions of the British North America Act which prevented the state from altering the confessional character of public schooling, and by the fiscal weakness of the state, which for much of Quebec's history lacked the resources to devote to education (Jedwab, 1992). At no level, from kindergarten to university, did Quebec have anything approaching an integrated educational system.

The autonomy of educational institutions was further reinforced by the sheer complexity and fragmentation of the system. Within the public school system, for example, there were more than 1,500 school commissions in the Catholic sector alone. Most of these did not have a sufficient tax base to keep up with the new quantitative and qualitative demands placed on the system by the dramatic growth which began in the 1950s. In 1951, 70% of the schools in Quebec were still one room schoolhouses, and "60% had no electricity and 40% had no running water or indoor toilets" (Linteau, Durocher, Robert and Ricard, 1991: 244). Neither these schools nor the education system as a whole seemed able to meet the needs and desires of a new generation of Quebecers who were attending school in ever-increasing numbers. School attendance rose from about 729,000 students in 1945 to 1.3 million in 1959, while the total cost of public education rose from $69 million in 1951 to $213 million in 1959 (Linteau, Durocher, Robert and Ricard, 1991: 244).

The failure of the state to properly fund education had particularly severe consequences within the French Catholic sector with its multitude of school commissions. Limited to the resources available from the local population and inadequate government grants, most of these commissions lacked the funds to offer a high school education, maintaining only an elementary school. As a result, private schools played an especially crucial role in education, particularly in the French Catholic sector. Private schools were not merely an alternative to the public schools, they served as a sort of *de facto* public school system for the francophone Catholic middle class because they provided the only means of access to a higher education and a university degree; the public schools, as René Lévesque (Lévesque and Chaiton, 1977: 180) noted, usually "led nowhere."

With few students attending high school, even fewer attended university, and all universities in Quebec were elitist institutions accessible to only a small portion of the population. McGill University, the most prestigious educational institution in Quebec, for example, had quotas for groups such as Jews who were not a part of the dominant British community.

Francophone universities were limited not only in terms of students, but also in the type of education they provided. These universities, under clerical control, focused on a "classical" education in theology, medicine, or law. Slowly but surely, however, they began to include education in science, technology, and commerce. The establishment of l'Ecole des Hautes Etudes Commerciales, schools of surveying and forestry at Laval University, and the Faculty of Science at the University of Montreal were indications of this shift. The construction of a new, modern facility for the University of Montreal, completed in 1943, signalled the university's determination to participate in and even lead the modernization of Quebec education and society. Still, despite its large library, scientific laboratories, and university hospital, the University of Montreal remained a Catholic institution controlled by members of the clergy.

Criticism of the education system during the 1950s was an important part of the growing dissatisfaction with Quebec society which would culminate in the Quiet Revolution of the 1960s. The failure of the education system to properly educate more than a fraction of Quebec's student population was considered to be the main reason for the "backwardness" of Quebec society: its elitism, its failure to modernize, and the inability of the state to take its responsibility seriously regarding of leadership vis-à-vis civil society. Thus, reform of Quebec's education system was considered by almost all segments of Quebec society to be a central part of the process of social transformation and empowerment initiated by the Quiet Revolution. Education, together with the state itself, were expected to be the most powerful tools with which to remake Quebec society.

1960-1968: REFORM AND CENTRALIZATION

In 1960, the reform of the education system was a major priority of the new government which initiated the Quiet Revolution. Reform would be three-pronged: structural reforms which would reorganize the existing education system; the establishment of programs and mechanisms to ensure the accessibility of higher education to everyone; and pedagogical reforms which would give the education system a central role in building a new, modern and democratic Quebec society.

When it came to structural changes, the new government moved quickly, enacting a whole series of legislative reforms in 1961. Altogether, a dozen pieces of legislation were passed, ranging in scope from promoting the establishment of kindergartens to putting in place a system of loans and bursaries for university students. This, however, was only the beginning. A royal commission of inquiry on education, the Parent Commission, was established, which initiated a profound and comprehensive review of Quebec's education system and which led to the recommendation of a sweeping series of further reforms.

In addition to legislative changes, a broad series of regulatory reforms were initiated. These were primarily designed to rationalize and modernize the education system. For example, 55 regional corporations were set up to operate and administer regional secondary schools, eliminating the problem of 1,500 school commissions too small or too poor to operate secondary schools on their own.

The most significant change of all was the establishment of the Ministry of Education in 1964. The first volume of the Parent Commission's report recommended this step, arguing that given the fragmented and disorganized condition of Quebec's education system "only a strong and forthright authority can put the house in order" (Quebec, Commission of Inquiry on Education in the Province of Quebec, 1963: 82). This was not only an organizational issue, but also an ideological one. The Parent Commission viewed the extension of state control over educational institutions as the extension of democracy, an integral component of the ideology of the Quiet Revolution. "In a democratic society," the report asserted, "the government represents all those interested in education: families, religious groups, educational institutions, professional associations" (Quebec, Commission of Inquiry on Education in the Province of Quebec, 1963: 80).

Education, the Parent Commission stated, must be accessible to all, must be humanistic, and must be oriented towards the needs of the child. This was a tall order, but the Parent Report was imbued with a sense of optimism that anything was possible with careful research, rational planning and appropriate structures put into place. State action, it seemed, could accomplish anything.

That the Commission looked to the centralization of education under state control as the means of ensuring accessibility and democratization is typical of the period of the Quiet Revolution in which the Quebec state was perceived as the expression of the popular will. What the Commissioners did not appear to anticipate, however, was that the humanistic and democratic education system they were trying to implement might be incompatible with the centralized and bureaucratic structures they were recommending. For example, they recommended the establishment of the Superior Council of Education as an advisory body to the Ministry of Education (MEQ) to ensure that the MEQ would remain responsive to the views of a wide spectrum of concerned groups. However, this attempt to limit the powers of the MEQ proved unsuccessful. The MEQ began to treat the advice of the Council as a formality and tended to act very much as it pleased (Gallagher, 1972). The result was that educational policy, planning, administration, and funding soon became highly centralized and bureaucratized.

Local school commissions found their traditional autonomy eroded and the MEQ was able to impose its own policies, priorities and decisions in a variety of ways. The MEQ was able to control "local educational priorities through budgetary norms" and "inadmissible expenses" (Gallagher, 1972: 160). Another form of centralization evolved as the MEQ began to enact collective agreements with teachers and other workers in the education sector. These agreements standardized working conditions, pay scales, hiring practices and other matters previously under the control of the school commissions. As their authority and autonomy eroded, individual school commissions soon became "local or administrative units of the [MEQ] with almost no powers of any significance" (Gallagher, 1972: 162).

Critics of the MEQ charged that the ministry's zeal for rational planning failed to take into account the needs, abilities or concerns of teachers, students or the local community. For example, regional secondary schools became large impersonal centers to which thousands of students are now bused. Such a school, one former member of the Parent Commission complained, had become "a well-scheduled organization of lectures and movement with little or no consideration for human aspirations" (Sister Ghislaine Roquet, quoted in Buteau, 1972: 197).

After the MEQ consolidated its control over the public sector it turned its attention to the private sector. The Parent Commission had argued that private schools should come under the authority of the ministry: "Private institutions will continue to exist but their relations with the State, like those of the public bodies, must be channeled through a single authority, the Ministry of Education" (Quebec, Commission of Inquiry on Education in the Province of Quebec, 1963: 89). This was seen as a particularly serious issue because of the large proportion of students attending private schools and the high status and autonomy such schools had in Quebec.

The first step was to establish a comprehensive system of secondary schools to serve as a real alternative to the private classical colleges. This was followed by the establishment of a network of public colleges (CEGEPs) in 1967 which initiated a new era of accessible and inexpensive institutions of higher education. The creation of the CEGEP redefined the role of the private classical colleges, transforming most of them into CEGEPs that incorporated trade and technical programs, among others, into the existing institutions (Magnuson, 1981). This dramatic change served to subordinate the private colleges, which had played so important a role in Quebec's educational history, to the new public educational structures.

MEQ control over the private education sector was further extended and centralized in 1968 by requiring private schools to be certified by the ministry and to meet the same pedagogical and regulatory standards as public schools. Legislation also regularized and standardized public funding for private schools, some of which were made eligible for substantial government grants. Of course, the extension of state funding to these schools soon also led to the extension of state control over them. Indeed, one could argue that the state now exerts more control over some parts of the private sector than that over the public sector, since the public sector schools have certain constitutional as well as acquired rights with which the state has been unable to tamper but which do not exist for the private schools.

Structural change was occurring not only at the secondary and college level but at the university level as well. Indeed, the university was doubly associated with the Quiet Revolution, first by way of reflection and political debate, then as a new priority in itself. The university sector was subject to diverse forms of reorganization: a change in the method of financing; the establishment of a system of loans and grants for students; the development of teacher training programs; and the growth of continuing education programs. One of the most important recommendations of the Parent report was to entrust the responsibility for teacher training to the university institutions in order to upgrade the quality of teaching and teachers.

The creation of the multi-campus University of Quebec in 1968 dramatically expanded the accessibility of university education by establishing campuses in smaller communities. Also, the creation of the CEGEPs allowed francophone and anglophone university education to be aligned, with all universities shifting to a three-year undergraduate program.

Throughout the 1960s, the university system changed its method of internal functioning with the spread of the bureaucratic system of administration. The university landscape changed as these institutions moved in contradictory directions. The rise of the student movement, in particular, added a new and active player into the educational arena. Yet, at the same time, the continued efforts at "rationalization," the increasing complexity of communication, and the "professionalization" of both administration and faculty led to a depersonalization of relationships. New structures were put in place such as the Council Of Universities to advise the MEQ, and the Council of University Rectors was established to coordinate and integrate some of the functions of the universities as well as inter-university projects.

1968–1982: THE LINGUISTIC DEBATE

By 1968 Quebec's contemporary educational structure was largely in place, marking the end to major structural reforms of the province's education system. (An exception was the amalgamation of the 200 school boards on the island of Montreal into eight unified boards, six Catholic and two Protestant, in 1972.) Instead, interest in the education sector—as in Quebec society in general—was shifting from structural issues to cultural and political ones, with the role of language taking center stage. The demographic decline of the francophone population meant that the dramatic growth of the student population seen in the 1950s and early 60s had ended, and that schools now faced the prospect of declining enrolments. This posed a long-term threat to Quebec's cultural survival; it also posed a more immediate threat of job losses to Quebec's teachers and other workers in the education sector. Not surprisingly, many francophone teachers became among the most ardent of the linguistic nationalists.

The linguistic choice being made by new immigrants to Quebec was also having a significant impact on the school system. During the 1950s the majority of immigrants chose English as the language of education for their children. There were a number of reasons for this. One was that the anglophone Protestant system was willing to accept non-Protestant students such as Jews and Greeks. In contrast, the Catholic system of the time would accept only Catholic immigrants such as Poles and Italians. Moreover, even among Catholic immigrants there was a marked preference for anglophone schools, in part because the Catholic anglophone sector in the 1950s had established a network of high schools with a path that led to a university education. The francophone sector remained poorly organized with no clear path leading to acceptance at a university. Another factor was the perception on the part of immigrants that the use of the English afforded more opportunities and a higher status than did the use of French.

This "anglicization" of immigrants had, in the past, been seen as "normal" (Linteau, 1989: 191), but it was being redefined as an alarming trend by nationalists in the 1960s. What had changed was the scope of the new immigration, the impact it was likely to have on a declining francophone population, and the symbolic significance that preference for English had in the new Quebec.

Particularly significant in this respect was the new linguistic choice being made by Italian immigrants, the largest immigrant group arriving in the 1950s and 60s. Italian immigrants who had come to Montreal before World War II had largely integrated into the francophone milieu. As Catholics, Italians had been able to enter the Catholic school system with all their rights intact and had even been able to arrange to have Italian taught in a number of schools in addition to French and English. Also, Italians had tended to settle in largely francophone sections of Montreal and shared roughly the same socioeconomic status as their francophone neighbours, often resulting in intermarriage between Italians and French Quebecers (Linteau, 1989). Religion, residence and intermarriage, then, had all contributed to integrating the Italians into the francophone milieu.

The 60,000 Italian immigrants coming to Quebec after World War II, however, often made a different choice, tending to send their children to the English language sector of the Catholic school commissions. The residential concentration of the Italians in francophone districts allowed them to enrol in Anglo-Catholic or "bilingual" schools that were relatively monoethnic. In some schools, as high as 90% of the student population was of Italian descent. Altogether, 75% of Italian schoolchildren were attending English Catholic schools as opposed to French schools.

Linteau (1989) has suggested that this latter choice by Italian parents was particularly troubling and galling to Quebecois nationalists. Ironically, what made the linguistic choice of Italian parents so blatant was that most Italians were living in predominantly francophone neighbourhoods but their children were attending different schools from their francophone neighbours. This generated and exacerbated linguistic tensions between the two groups.

Under the circumstances, it is not surprising that conflict would erupt between the Italian and French communities over the language of education for immigrant schoolchildren. Nor, given the activist role of the state in Quebec society after 1960, is it surprising that this conflict led to a series of state interventions.

The Catholic school commission in St. Leonard (an area of Montreal) opened its first bilingual schools in 1962 to meet the demand for English-language instruction requested by Italian and other Catholic immigrant parents. Given the evolving nationalist climate in Quebec, however, opposition to these bilingual schools was soon organized and the decision was made by the commission in 1967 to switch to French as the primary language of instruction in all its schools, with English taught only as a second language.

This decision to francize the bilingual schools was fiercely opposed by the leadership of the Italian community, which organized the Saint Leonard English Catholic Association of Parents to oppose it. Francophone nationalists, too, organized to achieve their goals, forming the Mouvement pour l'integration scolaire (MIS). Given the numerical majority of the francophone population, the MIS won a majority of seats on the school commission in the 1968 commission election and reaffirmed a policy of French as the exclusive language of instruction in the commission's schools. This dispute became a highly emotional one, with public meetings mobilizing angry Italian parents, and a street demonstration led by MIS supporters in 1968 turning into a minor "riot." Many Italian parents refused to go along with the commission's action, some switching their children to English Protestant schools while the English Catholic Association of Parents organized private English classes in October of 1968 (Taddeo and Taras, 1987: 93).

This dispute soon had serious ramifications well beyond the area of St. Leonard. Widespread debate on the school issue increased public awareness of the role of language in Quebec society and hardened the views of both those who opposed and those who supported the right of parents to choose the language of instruction for their children. Clearly, the issue seemed too important to be left up to individual school commissions to decide or to end up as a source of further battles breaking out on the streets. Intervention by the provincial government seemed necessary to decide whether parents should have the right to choose the language of instruction, and if so, whether all parents, including immigrants, were to have this right.

The first of these interventions, Bill 63, passed by the National Assembly in 1969, was an attempt by the provincial government to establish an official language policy. The bill gave parents the right to educate their children in the language of their choice, a legislative decision which, far from settling the matter, provoked a storm of protest in the francophone community. At the same time, the government set up a commission to study the whole issue of language in detail, a sign that the government, too, had evolved no consistent policy on language and sought to tap public opinion.

Majority public opinion, however, seemed solidly against Bill 63, especially as reflected in the francophone media. The defeat of the Union Nationale government in the provincial election of 1970 meant that a new policy on the language of education would soon be in force. Although the new Liberal government did not act quickly, it took into account the recommendation by the Gendron Commission in 1972 that French be made the exclusive official language of Quebec. The Liberals were also influenced by the remarkable political strength shown by the newly formed Parti Québécois which obtained 24% of the popular vote in the 1970 provincial election,

The new linguistic policy, promulgated in Bill 22, stated that the French language "is a national heritage which the body politic is in duty bound to preserve, and it is incumbent upon the government ...to employ every means in its power to ensure the pre-eminence of that language and to promote its vigour and quality." Despite this straightforward claim, however, Bill 22 failed to establish a clear policy on the language of education. Instead, children seeking entry into an English school would now be tested on their proficiency in the English language prior to being allowed into such a school.

This policy, which was intended as a compromise among divergent groups, ended up being extremely unpopular with most segments of Quebec society. The requirement that pre-school children be tested led many immigrant families to obtain English instruction for their pre-school children in order for them to qualify for entry into English language schools. This posed a financial and emotional strain for many families not yet firmly established in their new country and generated massive resentment on the part of ethnocultural minority groups. Many members of these groups withdrew their support from the Liberal party in the provincial election of 1976.

As for francophone nationalists, they too were dissatisfied with Bill 22 which, despite its provision for testing, still left immigrants with a means of access to English language instruction. In any case, nationalists argued, how could one apply rigorous standards of "proficiency" in English to pre-school children? Such a policy would inevitably lead to simplistic tests which would make a mockery of the nationalists' desire to limit access to English education.

The election of a Parti Québécois government in 1976 put into power a party committed to building Quebec as a French society. Bill 101, passed by the National Assembly in 1977, presented a more emphatic vision of Quebec as a francophone society and the role of the government in promoting the language. The French language, the Bill asserts (Quebec, National Assembly, 1977: 8) is "the distinctive language of a people that is in the majority French-speaking [and] is the instrument by which that people has articulated its identity." As a consequence, "the Assemblée Nationale du Québec ...is resolved ...to make of French the language of Government and the Law, as well as the normal and everyday language of work, instruction, communication, commerce and business."

Bill 101 replaced the tests specified by Bill 22 with a clearcut definition of who is or is not eligible to attend English schools in Quebec. New immigrants were no longer allowed to send their children to English schools. Only those children with a parent who had attended English schools in Quebec or who had an older sibling in such a school would receive a certificate of eligibility for English language instruction. All others would be required to attend French schools.

The educational provisions of Bill 101 were not only intended to limit and control access to English language instruction, they were also seen as "destined to accelerate the integration of English-speaking institutions into the life and work of French-speaking Quebec society" (Quebec, Ministère de l'Éducation, 1982: 11)—a much more far-reaching objective. The assumption underlying Bill 101 and much of the educational policy over the next few years was that language and culture are equivalent; by learning French one was also learning the culture of the Québécois and being integrated into Quebec society.

This is an equation which is not made by anglophone Quebecers who, like other anglophone North Americans, do not assume that all those who speak English constitute one people with a common culture. Speaking English has not been a source of solidarity among blacks and whites in the United States, for example, nor among Jews, Italians, and British Protestants in Quebec. Public schools in the United States attempted to forge a "melting pot" out of immigrant ethnics not only by teaching their children English, but also by socializing them to a common set of values, sense of history, and feeling of identity. In any case, the American "melting pot," so far as it exists at all, has still failed to overcome such significant group differences as racial differences.

To the francophone Québécois, however, who, for most of their history have been a relatively homogeneous cultural group, the equation between language and culture seemed obvious. It is this which has made many Québécois view the teaching of English to francophone students as a cultural "threat" to such students unless they are of sufficient age and maturity to be firmly embedded in their own culture. English is therefore not taught to francophone students until after grade three, while anglophone schools are required to teach French from kindergarten on. Similarly, by requiring even anglophone school boards to function in French, these public institutions were believed to be set on a course towards integration into the francophone community (Quebec, Ministère de l'Éducation, 1982: 11).

1982–1993: RE-EVALUATION AND RESPONSE

The 1980s proved to be a period during which few substantive changes were made to the education system in Quebec. Instead, it was a time for fine-tuning, as the state's educational policies created new and unexpected problems both in the schools and in the relations among different groups in Quebec society. Throughout this period, ministerial regulations, interpretations, negotiations and court challenges served to define and limit both the state's legislative powers and the accommodations required on the part of the various public and private interest groups.

It was not the case that no more structural changes were needed or desired. Several attempts were made after 1968 to fundamentally alter the education system, by switching, for example, from confessional to linguistic school boards. Yet the educational system remained essentially the same as that of 1968, indeed, many components of the system such as confessional public schools date back to the 1840s. The inability to restructure Quebec's education system since 1968 is a sign of the continuing disagreements among Quebecers over the type of education system they wish to have. These disagreements occurred even within the Parti Québécois government which, by 1985, seemed to have lost both its sense of political direction and its ideological hold among Quebec's francophone population. The re-election of the Liberal Party to power in 1985 signalled a re-evaluation of Quebec's continuing development and an end to the dramatic pace of change initiated by the Quiet Revolution.

Nevertheless, while it moved cautiously in other areas of jurisdiction, the new Liberal administration did not give up on the issue of structural reforms to the education system. This was because the structural complexity that characterized Quebec's education system was preventing an administrative and cost-effective "rationalization" of the system. The existence of separate confessional and linguistic sectors, especially in the Montreal region, meant the maintenance of a high number of schools at a time when enrolments were dropping, and generated disagreements among interest groups seeking to control the schools and the school commissions. Indeed, the unexpected effect of government legislation restricting enrolment in English schools was the emergence of a new francophone school sector operated by the Protestant school boards which, together with "French-immersion" schools designed for anglophone students, further fragmented the school system and further increased the "duplication" of services. Regardless of whether one was motivated by nationalist ideology or bureaucratic expediency, it was becoming clear to many Quebecers that the constitutional guarantees placed in the BNA Act in the 1860s to preserve separate Protestant and Catholic schools had become an obstacle to reforms of the education system designed to meet the needs of contemporary Quebec society.

Bill 107, passed by the National Assembly in 1988, sought to replace the system of confessional public school boards with linguistic boards. This change, the MEQ asserted, "brings the legislative and administrative framework of the public elementary and secondary school system into line with the public consensus" (Quebec, Ministère de l'Éducation, 1989: 1). Given the failure of previous attempts, however, the decision was made not to implement the legislation until its "legal validity has been confirmed by the courts" (Quebec, Ministère de l'Éducation, 1989: 1).

Bill 107 was carefully designed to avoid the constitutional pitfalls which had killed previous bills. The key to the legislation was a literal compliance with constitutional provisions. Those confessional and "dissentient" boards in existence in 1867 would continue to exist in addition to linguistic boards, as constitutionally guaranteed. The MEQ reserved for itself, however, the power to redistribute educational facilities and resources from existing confessional boards to the new linguistic boards. The linguistic boards would thus be created using facilities taken from the existing confessional boards rather than being built from scratch. In addition, only Catholics and Protestants who so desired would have the right to attend confessional schools, as guaranteed in the constitution. All others would attend schools run by linguistic boards. Confessional schools would continue to exist, but would become only a small part of the education system.

Opposition to Bill 107, initially strong among anglophone groups and Catholics, began to diminish during the late 1980s. Anglophone opposition had centered on the perception that Protestant school boards were the most important protectors of English language rights, in part because the Protestant schools were the only anglophone institutions with a constitutional guarantee in Quebec. However, the Protestant school boards have been consistently moving towards more French language instruction as the effects of Bill 101 cause the anglophone student population to shrink. The Task Force on English Education (1992: 2) reported that English enrolment dropped by 48% between 1976 and 1986, and the total English enrolment, which had been at 250,000 in 1972, was down 56% to 108,000 by 1990. In contrast to the 1960s, when Protestant schools were almost exclusively English schools, in 1991 only 61% of students attending schools belonging to the Protestant School Board of Greater Montreal were attending English schools (Task Force on English Education, 1992).

In addition, as the anglophone leadership realized, current constitutional guarantees are confessional, not linguistic. In other words, the constitution guarantees Protestant denominational schools, not English language schools. This means that, realistically, the continuing existence of anglophone schools is a function of state policy, not constitutional guarantees. The question, then, is how best to ensure that such policy perpetuates English language instruction. The constitutional rights accorded the Protestant school boards has succeeded in preserving these boards for the moment, but given the drastic declines in enrolment their long-term future as anglophone institutions is in doubt. This is especially the case since more and more students who are registered at Protestant schools are attending French schools, causing conflicts to emerge between French and English groups within the Protestant system over the distribution of resources and facilities.

The issue of preserving English language instruction can now be separated from the issue of preserving the Protestant system. To some anglophones, state guarantees of anglophone rights are preferable to constitutional guarantees of Protestant rights. Moreover, having two separate anglophone schools in a community, one

Protestant and the other Catholic, often means that neither is viable, with the result that neighbourhood schools are being closed and students are being bused to schools in other areas. Combining anglophone Protestant and Catholic students in one board would make English language schools more viable in more areas. Finally, the composition of the anglophone community itself is changing, with increasing numbers of those identifying themselves as "anglophone" being neither British nor Protestant in origin, with no particular commitment to Protestant institutions. Thus, anglophone resistance to linguistic boards has diminished considerably, as was made evident in the report of the Task Force on English Education (1992) which came out in favour of linguistic boards.

As for the Catholic sector, here the situation was more complex. Numerous interest groups were active in the Catholic educational sector in the 1980s, contesting elections to school boards and acting as pressure groups. Henry Milner (1986: 45) argued that the end of the large-scale reform efforts of the 1960s meant that, "grand reform schemes gave way to conflicts over specific schools and the election campaigns of the commissioners who administered them." These conflicts arose because of the structural ambiguity inherent in having a Catholic school system serving as the *public* school system for the vast majority of Quebec's students.

Given the rapid secularization of Quebec society so noticeable in the 1960s, it might be supposed that the Catholic public school system, too, would be secularized, and to a large extent this has been the case, most dramatically in the virtual disappearance of clergy from the teaching profession. Certainly at the college and university level, clerical control over educational institutions evaporated. But at the public school level Catholic interest groups fought a relatively successful campaign to retain control over the Catholic school commissions.

Despite the *de facto* confessional status of Quebec's public schools, it was not until 1974 that the Catholic Committee of the Superior Council of Education declared all schools under its jurisdiction to be confessional (Milner, 1986: 45). This move reflected a growing concern among committed Catholics, particularly in Montreal, that they were losing control over the education system, on the one hand to the MEQ, which continued to grow in power and authority, and on the other hand to the many new groups entering the public schools.

This set the stage for broader-based competition for control over the schools and the emergence of parapolitical "parties" to contest school board elections. The first sign of this was the creation of two groups in 1973 to contest the first island-wide election of school commissioners. These were the Mouvement Scolaire Confessional (MSC), a coalition of Catholic groups, and the Mouvement Pour la Democratisation Scolaire, backed by trade unions and some local Parti Québécois committees. Numerous other groups and independent candidates ran in the election with a total of 106 candidates running for the 19 seats on the Commission des Ecoles Catholiques de Montreal (MCSC), the largest of the Catholic boards.

While there was a great deal of media interest in the elections, only 28% of the eligible voters turned out, with the MSC winning six of the 19 seats in the MCSC. The MSC was the best organized of the groups vying for election, a fact reaffirmed in 1977 when the MSC won all but one of the MCSC seats. Only 21% of eligible voters voted in 1977, and even fewer, 13.5%, in 1980 when MSC candidates were again largely successful. Milner argued that the MSC's organizational superiority was a consequence of close ties to the Catholic Church. The MSC, he claimed, had "official clerical support in most parishes and [the] unofficial endorsement at the archdiocese" (Milner, 1986: 50). This organization perpetuated what he called "traditionalist" Catholic control over the schools at the very time that the school's clientele was undergoing a dramatic change.

This change was in large measure a consequence of Bill 101 which caused the redirection of Quebec's immigrant schoolchildren into the francophone Catholic sector. Many of these children were neither francophone nor Catholic. Groups such as Russian Jews, Iranian Moslems, and Chinese Buddhists were attending supposedly public schools which asserted a particular confessional status. This issue was addressed by a White Paper (Quebec, Ministère de l'Éducation, 1982: 24) which noted that "We can hardly force immigrants into French schools if by doing so we relegate them to the status of second-class citizens."

This was not only a problem facing immigrants, however. Another change affecting the nature of the student body was the growing number of anglophones sending their children to francophone schools. These parents were not being "forced" to send their children to French Catholic schools, they did so voluntarily, yet some also found themselves culturally and ideologically uncomfortable with the religious content of the school programs. Wanting a high quality French language education for their children, they found their children were getting a religious education as well.

Finally, many francophone Québécois, too, sought a public school system which would be secular. A survey conducted by the MCSC in 1982 found that only 28% of 5,000 parents responding to the survey preferred a confessional school, while 55% preferred a "pluralist" school (Milner, 1986: 59). The new kinds of students in Quebec's public schools had difficulty fitting into the existing school structures, yet the provincial government found itself unable to change those structures.

This situation seemed to change with a positive ruling by the Supreme Court in 1993 on Bill 107. Yet, the new Parti Québécois government elected in 1994 decided to hold back on establishing linguistic boards, another sign of how contentious the issue of education is in Quebec. Given the lack of consensus on education and a new recognition that past reforms had led to unwanted consequences, the Parti Québécois government decided to move cautiously. An Estates General on Education was established to thoroughly investigate all aspects of education, consult the public, and make recommendations for change. At present the Estates General is continuing its work.

THE NEW SOCIAL CONTRACT

If the education system serves as an index to the state of relations among the groups in Quebec society and between the state and these groups, what does the current state of the education system tell us? The answer is that Quebecers have not yet made up their minds about what kind of education system they want because they have not made up their minds about what kind of society they want. The education system remains in limbo, the only significant changes coming in the form of budget cuts and staff reductions. If education once held out the promise of transforming Quebec society, much of that promise was never really fulfilled. The goals of the democratization of education and of equal access for all have not been met. As an example, the proportion of university students of working class origin increased only slightly between 1961 and 1978, from 31% to 37.5%. Rather than having opened up higher education to children of working class origin, we find today a very high drop-out rate among high school students.

On the other hand, access to a university education has become a reality for many women. Women made up 14% of university students in 1960; that increased to 45% by 1970 and has now risen to 55% of university graduates. Even here, though, women's access to an education is not spread equally among all programs. Women number only 44% of graduates in the pure sciences and 28% of graduates in the applied sciences.

Quebec society continues to evolve and change. To those living through it, the ongoing ebb and flow of events makes it difficult to identify precisely what is changing, how, or why. Confident analysis can only come from hindsight. Nevertheless we can identify a number of recent trends in Quebec society which are having a significant impact on both the education system and the relations between the state and Quebec's ethnocultural minorities.

One trend is the increasing attention being focused on ethnic groups and, in particular, ethnic conflicts in Quebec. In general, there has been a noticeable shift in the social position of ethnic minorities in Quebec which has become particularly evident since the Oka crisis of 1990. Concerned as they were with their own collective development, Quebec's francophone majority paid little attention to the needs or aspirations of the ethnic minorities. Insofar as minorities posed a "problem" in Quebec, it was largely seen as a linguistic one: the need to integrate the minorities into Quebec's linguistic majority.

This way of thinking has fundamentally changed, since many Québécois do, at present, perceive ethnic minorities as posing a problem. Integration, once assumed to be simply a matter of learning French, is now recognized to be a much more complicated and much more consequential issue, especially with regard to education. Given the diversity of students attending school in Quebec in the 1990s, it is not surprising that conflicts should arise within the schools. Some of these conflicts are predictable and by no means limited to Quebec, such as interethnic animosities and hostilities. Students who find themselves in a new country, learning a new language and new customs, quite naturally gravitate to others of their own background with whom they feel more comfortable. The resulting ethnic stratification and fragmentation within the schools provides a climate within which ethnic antagonisms can develop.

More telling, however, has been the development of ethnic antagonism towards students on the part of teachers, administrators, and school board officials. A short-lived but instructive debate arose in 1990 over whether non-francophone students should be allowed to speak to one another in their native tongues anywhere within the schools, such as corridors during recess or on school grounds. A proposal to limit such discussions in other languages was presented to the Montreal Catholic systems commissioners, but widespread opposition to what was seen as a "coercive" approach put an end to the proposal. Opponents included the Quebec Human Rights Commission which severely criticized the proposal.

This debate reflects the frustration of school personnel who had discovered that the teaching of French was not having the effect upon students that had been expected. As noted earlier, state cultural policy assumed that teaching the French language would suffice to integrate newcomers into Quebec culture. This was proving not to be the case, however, and frustrated teachers and principals, looking for some explanation for the failure of newcomers to integrate, focused again on language, coming to the conclusion that immigrant students fail to integrate into Quebec society because they continue to speak to one another in Chinese or Tagalog or Hindi. If they could prevent them from doing so, this last barrier to becoming a Québécois would be overcome.

This assumption ignores the circumstances in which the immigrants find themselves: their attachments to their relatives and friends both in Quebec and "back home;" their own motivations, desires and goals; the traditions and values they bring with them and to which they may remain attached; their perception of Quebec society and of their place within it; and the treatment accorded to them by the francophone majority. Immigrants do not come to a country in order to meet the objectives of some government agency; they come in response to their own needs and to improve their own lives. By 1990, it was clear that government policy on education would require an overhaul if it was to achieve its stated aims. Integration could not be a one-way process.

Many Québécois are now asking themselves how to open up Quebec society in such a way as to take advantage of what immigrants and minority groups have to offer (Langlais, Laplante and Levy, 1990). This was the government's own approach as expressed in *Vision*, a 1990 policy statement on immigration and integration (Quebec, Ministère des Communautés culturelles et de l'Immigration). This policy statement calls for the state to enter into a partnership with the various ethnic communities in establishing institutions to ensure that the integration of new immigrants is both effective and directed to the francophone milieu. This new partnership is referred to in the policy statement as a "social contract" between the state and the ethnic communities.

As articulated in the policy statement, ethnic community institutions are expected to help community members to "socialize" to and adapt to Quebec society. In return, the government will provide increased financial support for ethnic organizations, appoint community members to decision-making and advisory bodies, increase their representation in the public sector, and promote "the initiatives of organizations of the cultural communities to develop their partnership with public and parapublic institutions" (Quebec, Ministère des Communautés culturelles et de l'Immigration, 1990: 74). In this way, the ethnic community becomes a mediating agency which takes on the task of integration in exchange for obtaining state resources and being granted input on state policy. In terms of education, this makes the ethnic private schools primary vehicles for the integration of new immigrants—a change of focus which may reflect the failure of the public schools to work as expected.

Nevertheless, there are contradictory forces within the MEQ pushing in a very different direction. In a report made public in 1993, the Consultative Commission on Private Education suggested that the provincial government stop funding ethnic private schools. Ethnic schools, the report said, "risk favouring a form of ghettoization which can delay the integration of some communities into the common social fabric" (quoted in *The Gazette*, April 22, 1993: A1). This view is consistent with warnings by some that immigration threatens Montreal's "French face," with calls for immigration to be substantially reduced or halted.

At this point it is difficult to determine which point of view will prevail: the social contract called for by the *Vision* report or the restrictive approach of the Consultative Commission on Private Education. In a recent address, Premier Bouchard expressed his personal desire to see English education survive in Quebec, but given the continuing conflicts and disagreements over education in Quebec society, the future shape of education in the province is difficult to assess.

Universities today are not racked by the kind of political and cultural conflict which affects the public school sector, but university education seems to have entered a state of permanent crisis of its own since the end of the 1970s. A commission set up by the Quebec government to study university education in 1978 identified a wide range of problems which have persisted, such as: the absence of effective coordination and planning; the failure to systematically control or evaluate quality, productivity, or performance; inadequate financing; the overspecialization of programs; difficulties in hiring adequate staff; persisting difficulties in ensuring equal access to university education, and so on.

These problems have been aggravated by the "politics of contraction" practiced by the government during the 1980s and '90s. There has been a serious decline in the quality of libraries, laboratories, and scientific equipment; an increasing ratio of students to teachers; hiring freezes; a low completion rate and too lengthy a period of time for graduation; a growing indebtedness of universities; and delayed investment and development projects.

None of this is particular to Quebec. After the tremendous growth of the 1960s, education in general seems to have entered a period of contraction, and perhaps even crisis, all over North America. Yet in Quebec this contraction occurs in a context in which education remains a source of hope for some and a matter of contention for many. Anglophones, for example, have come to view the modification of Bill 101 to allow greater access to English schools as essential to the survival of their community. However, many francophones continue to believe that such access would threaten the survival of their own community. In such a climate of conflicting hopes and fears emotions remain high, and education continues to be an index of the cultural and political relations among Quebec's diverse communities and groups.

REFERENCES

Buteau, Magdelhayne F. 1972. 'Retrospective on the Parent Report'. *McGill Journal of Education,* 7: 189-204.

Gallagher, Paul 1972. 'Power and Participation in Educational Reform'. *McGill Journal of Education,* 7: 149-165.

Geertz, Clifford 1973. *The Interpretation of Cultures.* New York: Basic Books.

Jedwab, Jack 1992. *The Politics of Finance: A Comparative Analysis of Public Finance in the Provinces of Quebec and Ontario from 1867 to 1896.* Unpublished Phd Dissertation, Concordia University.

Langlais, Jacques, Laplante, P., Levy J. 1990. *Le Quebec de Demain et Les Communautes Culturelles.* Montreal: Meridien.

Levesque, Rene, Chaiton, A. 1977. 'Education in a Changing Society: A View From Quebec,' Pp. 176-183. in Alf Chaiton and Neil McDonald (eds.), *Canadian Schools and Canadian Identity.* Toronto: Gage.

Linteau, Paul-André 1989. 'The Italians of Quebec: Key Participants in Contemporary Linguistic and Political Debates,' Pp. 179-207. in Roberto Perin and Franc Sturino (eds.), *Arrangiarsi: The Italian Immigration Experience in Canada.* Montreal: Guernica Editions.

Linteau, Paul-André, Durocher, R., Robert, J.C., Ricard F. 1991. *Quebec Since 1930.* Toronto: James Lorimer.

Magnuson, Roger 1980. *A Brief History of Quebec Education: From New France to Parti Quebecois.* Montreal: Harvest House.

Milner, Henry 1986. *The Long Road To Reform: Restructuring Public Education in Quebec.* Kingston and Montreal: McGill-Queens' University Press.

Quebec, Commission of Inquiry on Education in the Province of Quebec 1963. *Report, Part One: The Structure of the Educational System at the Provincial Level.* Quebec: Editeur Officiel.

Quebec, Ministère des Communautés culturelles et de l'Immigration 1990. *Vision: A Policy Statement on Immigration and Integration*. Quebec: Ministère des Communautés culturelles et de l'Immigration.

Quebec, Minstere de l'Éducation 1982. *The Quebec School: A Responsible Force in the Community*. Quebec: Minstère de l'Éducation.

Quebec, Minstere de l'Éducation 1989. *Education Express*, 6: Special Issue, April.

Quebec, National Assembly 1977. *Bill 101*. Quebec: Editeur officiel du Quebec.

Taddeo, Donat J., Taras R.C., 1987. *Le Debat Linguistique au Quebec: La Communaute Italienne et la Langue d'Enseignement*. Montreal: Les Presses de L'Universite de Montreal.

Task Force on English Education 1992. *Report To The Minister of Education of Quebec*. Quebec: Minstère de l'Éducation.

CHAPTER 7

THE QUEBEC LABOUR MOVEMENT[1]

The Quebec labour movement, like such movements elsewhere, is in crisis. In the case of Quebec it might be more fitting, however, to speak in terms of a crisis regarding unionism. Indeed, when one considers how Quebec labour is used to defining itself in terms of its relations with the two other primary social players (the state and business), one can begin to imagine the extent of the problem by the fact that the current economic and political context has forced these two other players to redefine both themselves and the rules of the game they control. With regard to statistics on unionization rates, observers of Canadian labour (Murray, 1991) have pointed out that Quebec unions have apparently survived the turbulent 1980s better than those in Canada's predominantly English-speaking provinces. But one should be wary of purely quantitative assessments of labour's strength, since a sociopolitical analysis does not reveal any clear distinction between the labour movement in Quebec and those in the rest of Canada.

The labour crisis has affected all regions of Canada from coast to coast; in every area it has resulted from the same structural origins and manifests in the same phenomena. This crisis, however, should not be interpreted as a signal of the death of labour. More accurately, it represents a questioning of the sociopolitical role played by organized labour at all levels. This chapter will thus examine the current situation of the Quebec labour movement in terms of its membership, distinct character, ideological orientation, and action at the microsociological level (the firm) and the macrosociological level (society).

UNION MEMBERS AND LABOUR ORGANIZATIONS
The Declining Rate of Unionization

Since the 1970s, Canadian unions have watched with great concern as their American counterparts literally fall apart,[2] wondering if our borders are staunch enough to hold back this trend. The United States has a unionization rate of

---

[1] Several excerpts of this text were inspired by my other writings, particularly M.J. Gagnon, *Le syndicalisme au Québec : État des lieux et enjeux* (Québec: Institut québécois de recherche sur la culture, 1994); M.J. Gagnon, "La participation institutionelle du syndicalisme québécois : variations sur les formes du rapport de l'État," in J. Godbout (ed.), *Questions de culture*, 17 (Québec: Institut québécois de recherche sur la culture, 1991), pp. 173-204; M.J. Gagnon, "New Challenges Facing Trade-Unionism in Quebec," in C. Leys and M. Mendell (eds.) *Culture and Social Changes: The Genetic Matrix of Post-Capitalism* (Montréal: Black Rose Books, 1992), pp. 62-74.

[2] Nevertheless, a slight resurgence in unionization was observed in the United States in 1993. It is too early to tell whether this was only a temporary improvement or a trend reversal.

roughly 15%. This figure, however, conceals significant differences between states in the north and south, and east and west. For example, the unionization rate in the northeastern states is on par with the Canadian average. Conversely, South Carolina and New Mexico have rates similar to those in developing countries (Metz, 1989).

In comparison, the differences between the Canadian provinces are much less pronounced: the largest variation is a ratio of 2:1. In 1991,[3] the unionization rate in Quebec (40.6%) was second highest in the country behind Newfoundland (53.3%), and ahead of Ontario (31.9%). Since the 1960s, Quebec's rate has always been higher than the Canadian average. The unionization of the public sector, made possible through legislative amendments in 1961, has helped boost Quebec's unionization rate: from 30.5% in 1961,[4] to 41.1% in 1970, 36% in 1980, 44% in 1985, and 46.9% in 1990. The most recent figures, however, have given unions reason to be concerned: the rate fell from 49.7% in 1992 to 46.8% in 1993, and down to 41.9% in September 1995. Nevertheless, the Quebec labour movement has always claimed, and rightly so, to have coped better with the economic crisis and the collapse of traditionally unionized sectors than movements in other parts of Canada. In fact, Quebec unions have achieved spectacular gains in the services sector. But one may ask whether these successes have not reached a plateau, or if unions have become unable to fill the gaping cracks left behind by so many unemployed ex-union members.

One of the effects of the evolution of the labour market, in Quebec and elsewhere, has been a downsized workforce in traditionally unionized sectors (i.e. primary and secondary industries). Although the services sector accounts for close to three-quarters of all jobs, it has a unionization rate of only 41.5% (1993). However, it is important to note that in Quebec, 73.9% (1993) of all public-sector workers are unionized, compared with a mere 34.7% (1993) in the private sector (CRSMT, 1994). Furthermore, there is a strong tendency in traditionally unionized areas of the public and private sectors to minimize the regular workforce and hire temporary or part-time workers, with or without continuous employment ties. Although this does not necessarily mean a decrease in the unionization rate, it does have a negative impact on the real number of unionized workers. Finally, in certain industries (construction, clothing, etc.) the underground economy— clearly a non-unionized sector—is being discouraged less and less.

Faced with the difficulties of unionization in small businesses, Quebec labour has, for a long time, been calling for the right to implement multi-employer certification, without success. Quebec unions have also denounced the perpetuation of virulent anti-unionism by many employers, which the law does

---

[3] Statistics Canada. *Calura*. Catalogue 71-202, 1991.

[4] In contrast to the preceding figures, this figure and those immediately after it were obtained from Quebec sources. The method of calculating used in the Quebec sources is different and generates higher rates. See Centre de recherche et de statistique sur le marché du travail (CRSMT), *Le marché du travail*. (Gouvernement du Québec, January 1986 to January 1994).

not efficiently curtail. Employers shamelessly commit infractions (e.g. firing workers for union activities), preferring to pay fines and compensation than tolerate the presence of unions.[5] Thus, while it used to be that non-unionized companies were predominantly small businesses, since the 1970s many large businesses have succeeded in resisting all unionization drives. These businesses scrutinize anyone seeking employment and practice a high degree of "social engineering." This is why some researchers remain pessimistic regarding the possibility of increasing the unionization rate significantly within the current legal and economic context.

Four Labour Federations with Differentiated Memberships

Quebec's thousands of unions are, for the most part, organizationally linked to each other. In most cases, this link takes the form of affiliation with one of four Quebec-based multisectored labour federations (commonly referred to as the *centrales*). These are:

- the Quebec Federation of Labour (QFL), with 344,683 members in 1993;[6]
- the Confederation of National Trade Unions (CNTU), with 232,772 members in 1993;
- the Centrale de l'enseignement du Québec (CEQ), with 98,108 members in 1993;
- the Centrale des syndicats démocratiques (CSD), with 34,562 members in 1993.

The tendency of labour federations to be structured around legal regimes of union monopoly (one certified union per group) is unique to Quebec, and may be largely explained by its cultural and linguistic differences.

It is generally known that American-based unions were the first to organize labour in Canada, followed by domestic unions. The QFL represents workers who belong to these unions, and is the counterpart of other provincial federations affiliated with the Canadian Labour Congress. Quebec's other labour federations evolved from the tradition of Catholic trade unionism.

---

[5] A case in point is the Korean firm Hyundai, which took every legal recourse available to counter the unionization of its workers, before closing its doors in 1994.

[6] The data were obtained from a Quebec government publication, *Le marché du travail* (January, 1994: 28). This source is preferred to sources from labour federations in that the former helps eliminate factors caused by the federations' use of different methods to calculate dues-paying members. The data exclude the construction industry, in which the following labour federations (listed in decreasing order) have members: the QFL, the CNTU and the CSD. Furthermore, because the data exclude workers covered under the Canadian Labour Code, a category consisting almost entirely of QFL affiliates (federal civil servants, Canada Post Corporation, airline companies, Bell Canada, port authorities, railway companies, etc.), the size of the QFL is significantly reduced by as many as 60,000 to 80,000 members.

The birth of Catholic unionism in Quebec is largely attributable to the clergy's rejection of "foreign" trade unionism, presumed to be radical or even communist. The Quebec clergy had a significant influence on the creation of the first Catholic unions, which eventually came together to form a Catholic labour federation in 1921 (the CNTU's predecessor). In the eyes of the clergy, "French-Canadian" workers had to belong to "old-stock" (or *pure laine*) Catholic unions. In those days, the perils of socialist and athiest unionism were often preached from the pulpit. Though the clergy's influence was not as overt in the case of the CEQ, it was still present, in the sense that Catholic school teachers working in Catholic schools had to belong to a Catholic organization, which the CEQ was until 1967.

The CSD has quite a different history. It is a relatively young labour federation (begun in 1972) that sprung out of a rift within the CNTU. The official motives for the split were the overly "politicized" nature of CNTU rhetoric at the time, and the federation's insufficiently democratic functioning (hence the name of the CSD). Due to the circumstances surrounding its formation, the CSD was essentially ostracized by the other federations, and remains so today, though to a lesser extent.

Each labour federation has very distinct structures which are intimately related to its own history and origin. Thus, the QFL is structured along the lines of the North American union model, which in turn is fashioned after the British model. It is by far the most decentralized labour federation in Quebec. Receiving between only 2% to 5% of the dues of affiliated union-local members, the QFL provides each affiliate with representation and secondary services. In comparison, the other labour federations offer more direct services to their affiliate members.

Quebec's labour federations represent a fairly wide range of occupational categories. Only the QFL and the CNTU represent virtually all occupational categories in every sector. The CSD membership is less varied, and the CEQ's even less so.

Roughly 40% of QFL members are employed in the public sector (at the municipal, provincial or federal level). Despite the lack of any reliable statistics, it is still fairly safe to say that the QFL membership includes few professional-employee unions. The overwhelming majority of its membership consists of blue-collar workers, office workers, general service-sector workers and technicians.

The majority (64%) of CNTU members are employed in Quebec's public sector (teaching, municipalities, para-public institutions, etc.).[7] A significant number (between a fifth and a quarter of them) are professional workers.[8] Significantly,

---

[7] Centre de recherche et de statistique sur le marché du travail. *Le marché du travail*. Gouvernement du Québec, January, 1994.

[8] This estimate, more than merely an approximation, is based on the following reasoning: adding the membership (1994) of teachers', professional workers' and managers' unions, as well as the union members in the medical technologies sector (hypothetically all professionals) yields a percentage of 11.5%. Considering that the professional membership of other CNTU unions is large (e.g. the Fédération des affaires sociales), and in some cases even a majority (e.g. the Fédération nationale de communications), it is possible to suggest that the overall percentage of professionals is between 20% and 25%.

about a third of CNTU members belong to the health and social services sector. This characteristic is one of the keys to understanding the evolution of many of the CNTU's internal debates, as well as the recurring tensions between its private-sector and public-sector affiliates.

Until the 1970s the CEQ was a collective of teachers' unions, not a multisectored labour federation. Through its efforts to expand and increase its membership, the CEQ made a few breakthroughs in other occupational categories in the education sector, as well as in the communications, recreational, health and social services industries. But the CEQ is still characterized by homogeneity: 98% of its members are public-sector workers (CRSMT, 1994, op. cit.) and teachers (at all levels) make up 77% of the CEQ membership. Moreover, it is estimated that at least 85% of CEQ members are professionals.[9]

Lastly, 84% of CSD members work in the private sector. This factor, among others, explains why the overall membership of the federation levelled off in the early 1980s, as the net loss of union members has chiefly affected the private sector. Thus the hopes of the CSD founders proved to be too ambitious. Established in 1972 with 23,383 breakaway CNTU members, the CSD has only about 10,000 more members today.

This general survey shows that there are major differences between Quebec's labour federations, and that public-sector unionism accounts for almost half of overall union membership.[10]

The Rise of Women in the Labour Movement

Until the 1970s, women were generally absent from positions of union leadership. Even in the CEQ, where they had always been in the majority, women were generally represented by men. The CNTU and, to a greater extent, the QFL were male-dominated organizations from top to bottom. With some exceptions, the few unions that had a majority of women were headed by men. The unionization of the public sector (in the 1960s) and labour's subsequent expansion into the private sector (in the 1970s and 1980s) brought many women into the fold of unionism and, to a lesser degree, led to their hiring in subsectors of the manufacturing industry, from which they had been previously excluded. Today, the sexual distribution among Quebec's labour federations is as follows: those with the strongest female representation are the CNTU (roughly 46%) and the CEQ (roughly 66%), while the CSD estimates that women make up one-fifth of its membership and the QFL one-third.

Women now occupy federation leadership positions and hold other responsibilities. The QFL has even adopted the "quota" system, "reserving" three positions for women on its executive committee. In recent years, a number of

---

[9] Internal CEQ data (March, 1994).

[10] This figure is an approximation, due to the different methods of calculating used at the two levels of government, and the ensuing exclusion of a segment of the QFL membership.

labour federations and union locals have been in the throes of debates over name changes intended to recognize the presence of women.[11] The QFL feminized its name, the CEQ neutralized its name (the word *enseignants*, denoting male teachers, was substituted with the gender-neutral word for teaching, *enseignement*), while the CNTU could count its blessings for already possessing a gender-neutral name. Many unions and other labour organizations added a feminine noun to their title—it is safe to assume that those who did not already had a gender-neutral one. A perusal of official union documents strongly suggests that strict rules of feminization are now uniformly applied. Thus, the labour movement has, to a large extent, changed its face, but of course not without some gnashing of teeth.

During the 1970s, each labour federation set up committees to deal with the issue of the status of women, led by feminist union members concerned with achieving better recognition for women's place in general, their viewpoints and other issues.[12] A number of reports were produced—some better received than others. Meanwhile, union leaders recognized the political capital to be gained by displaying an openness to feminism. Their plans, however, were thwarted by the fact that union feminists had already built a political base of their own. Since then, profound changes have taken place. Today, feminists can afford to have divergent opinions on strategies and analyses, as women now constitute a political force in every labour federation. Though women do not wield power, those within the power structures can no longer neglect to take them into account. Nevertheless, this new force could become a weakness, since the rise of women in the labour movement is a reflection of the rise of the labour movement itself in Quebec society, including all of its contradictions. Thus, the presence of women in the backrooms of power could be the promise of a bright future, or of shaky times to come.

The Independent Labour Movement: The Achilles Heel of Quebec Labour

Let us, for a moment, look beyond the labour federations—after all, one out of four unionized workers belongs to a non-affiliated or independent union. This is indicative of a rapid change when we consider that in 1980 this figure was one out of five. Today, independent unionism has the wind in its sails, a trend which is mirrored in the growth of micro-identities and in the increasing tendency to retreat into familiar settings and to draw inward. Independent unionism is a

---

[11] The problem of overshadowing women in spoken language is more prevalent in French than in English, since most nouns and adjectives have a feminine and masculine form.

[12] For further details see M.J. Gagnon in Michael D. Behiels (ed.), *Quebec since 1845* (Toronto: Copp Clark Pitman Ltd, 1987), pp. 157-74; and J. White, *Sisters and Solidarity* (Toronto, Thompson Educational Publishing Inc., 1993).

composite reality which generally consists of an alliance of several groups whose only link is the employer they share. University professors, professionals working for the Quebec government, nurses, and aluminum workers are all organized as independent unions. While public-sector workers make up the bulk (68%) of the troops of independent labour, the vast majority of independent unions are former, disillusioned CNTU affiliates. The CNTU has thus experienced many large-scale defections other than the CSD-forming split.

In terms of membership, Quebec labour has become a multi-class movement. As a result, labour federations have great difficulty formulating any type of discourse that can accommodate all their affiliates—a situation that is all the more difficult given the federations' heterogeneous character. Thus, labour federations are discreetly trying their best to manage internal tensions, reconcile differences, emphasize common ground, and generally accommodate the concerns of deskilled workers with those of professionals worried about suddenly becoming deskilled themselves.

Inter-Federation Relations

In Quebec, inter-federation relations have historically fluctuated between love and hate, with long episodes of forced co-habitation. To begin with, the regime of the legal framework governing labour federations is riddled with problems, which ultimately play a significant role in all political debates. For example, a union local (the unit of certification) cannot be affiliated with two labour federations: it must choose between joining a federation or going it alone. Hence, the possibility of changing union allegiance or affiliation resurfaces with each round of negotiations. In some respects this facilitates union democracy as well as access to better services. But the characteristics of this framework are the cause of much inter-federation friction that is exacerbated by instances of "raiding" in the public sector or the construction industry, where labour relations are centralized.

Inter-federation relations are closely linked with political alliances, which in Quebec are in constant evolution depending on the economic circumstances. When government policies tend to the right, one can count on labour to mobilize into common fronts and to take united action. But when a government with social-democratic programmes or pretensions comes to power, as was the case with the Parti Québécois in 1976, labour federations tend to adopt widely different strategies. We can observe these trends by considering the example of the common fronts of unionized public-sector workers. In the 1970s, Quebec society was profoundly affected by the mobilization of inter-federation common fronts, which rallied around such demands as maternity leave and a $100/week minimum salary.[13] Then in the 1980s, although labour federations managed to voice a number of common demands, they were not able to coordinate their actions:

---

[13] See M.J. Gagnon in *Studies in Political Economy*, 31 (1990), pp. 169-79.

each one adopted their own strategy, concentrating their efforts on maintaining a minimum level of internal cohesion. A typical example this was the last round of public-sector negotiations, in 1983. Labour federations were once again divided on what strategy to follow: the QFL and the CEQ stood in one corner, the CNTU in another, and the nurses' union (the Fédération des infirmières et infirmiers du Québec) in a third. In practical terms, the fact is that there are no fundamental differences among the federations as to the basic issues. Ironically, however, the disagreements that arise between the federations also divide each one internally.

From time to time, the labour federations express their condemnation of recurring rivalries and their desire for an armistice. Some dream of permanent unity of action, maybe even unity of organization. Though this old fantasy almost became reality in the 1960s, it appears, now more than ever, to belong to the usual utopian visions of the left. More modestly, protocols were recently signed by the CSN and the QFL (in 1993) and between the CEQ and the QFL (in 1996) not to "raid" each other's memberships.

THE DISTINCT CHARACTER OF QUEBEC LABOUR

Union Pluralism

Now that we have an overall picture of the Quebec labour movement, it is possible to examine how it is distinct from the rest of the labour movement in Canada. There is a large body of sociological literature that emphasizes the role of cultural differences, in a broad sense, in explaining a host of legal and political variations between countries.[14] In recent years, culture is once again being used in Quebec to explain or assert differences between Quebec and the rest of Canada, particularly in relation to the labour movement and labour relations. These differences are invoked in industrial relations and sociological research to the same extent that they are held up in support of government discourse.[15] It is my contention, however, that such explanations are not justified by the existing body of research. To be more specific, before seeking to explain a difference, one must be sure that it exists.

The proof that such a difference exists in terms of the nature of labour relations, business policies and union policies has yet to be made.[16] Thus, while Quebec is obviously different culturally and linguistically, this does not mean that these differences can be brought to the fore to explain phenomena in every field of study.

Having said this, it is apparent that the Quebec labour landscape features one important structural difference with respect to that of English-speaking North America. Quebec stands alone in having experienced the development of Catholic trade unionism. Sectarian unionism, of course, is not unique to Quebec.

---

[14] A recent example concerning Canada and the United States can be found in S.M. Lipset, *Continental Divide: The Values and Institutions of the United States and Canada* (New York: Routledge, 1990).

Every country with a large Catholic population (France and Belgium, for example) has developed sectarian union structures since the Catholic Church did not
accept sectarian and non-sectarian mingling within the unions any more than it
did in the schools. Today, sectarian unionism is but a fading memory and, while
the Church has largely maintained a presence in schools, organized labour has
broken away from it. Nevertheless, there are remnants of this influence, the
most important being the pluralism that is unique to Quebec labour. The main
symbol of this pluralism is the vision which the QFL and the CNTU have always
shared, namely to represent workers from all sectors of industry.

As we have seen, union pluralism implies that several labour federations can
compete for the affiliation of any group. However, such competition necessarily
extends beyond the legal framework. Because labour federations are political
players, they must also compete in the political arena with the state, political
parties and special-interest groups, as well as with other players in the labour
relations domain, and with public opinion in general. Though this type of competition is not as conspicuous as that between political parties, for example, it is
nonetheless just as real. It is all the more fierce when inter-federation relations
are tense, or when a potentially legitimizing event turns labour federations into
rivals. This particular effect of union pluralism can lead to greater media interest
in the labour movement and, as a corollary, to a greater concern for the media
among unions in Quebec than in English Canada.

Another impact of sectarian unionism, one could argue, may be that its
highly centralized structures have led to different ways of engaging in union
action. Across North America, organized labour consists of decentralized federations, with resources remaining almost entirely in so-called "professional" structures, namely unions and federations. As the only labour federation in Quebec
with "North American" roots, the QFL is also the only one modeled in this fashion.[17] It could be argued that by adopting a centralized structure as a means of
providing affiliates with political representation and fostering solidarity, Quebec
labour is a movement that has stronger leanings towards political action and is
possibly more outspoken. The QFL itself has adapted to its environment, and

---

[15] See for example P.R. Bélanger and B. Lévesque in *Travail*, 24 (1992), pp. 71-90; O. Aktouf et al.,
in *Sociologie du travail*, XXXIV, 1 (1992), pp. 83-99; P. Gagné and M. Lefèvre (Montréal: Publi-Relais,
1993); P.A. Lapointe and P.R. Bélanger, in *Colloque international franco-québécois sur les perspectives de
recherche en relations industrielles*, (Québec: Université Laval, 1994), pp. 275-299.

[16] This judgment rests partly on an assessment of research material accumulated on Quebec which
seems to be either provisional, fragmentary, or insufficiently representative. The material is also relatively meagre compared with the large body of literature on Canada, and the even larger body on
the United States.

[17] During the course of acrimonious exchanges that have occasionally characterized inter-federation
relations in Quebec, the QFL has sometimes been described as the "federation of American unions."
Of course, QFL members are Quebecers just as much as other federation members, and the QFL and
its affiliates are headed by Quebecers.

consequently its operations are quite distinct from other provincial federations. In fact, it has secured a unique status within the Canadian Labour Congress (CLC), which differentiates it from other provincial federations and guarantees it greater powers.[18]

A Social-Democratic Party

Another major difference between labour in Quebec and the rest of Canada concerns union-related political action. There is no Quebec counterpart to the political representation of labour movements in English Canada by the New Democratic Party (NDP). The NDP is rooted in social democratic traditions, that is, it welcomes union-local membership to the party, with the result that organized labour exerts significant pressure on the federal NDP and each provincial party. Thus the NDP is, in some respects, the political "wing" of Canadian labour—that is, as long as it remains in the opposition. The recent New Democratic provincial governments have been marked by a deterioration in labour/NDP relations, as well as fratricidal quarrels. When a political party is organizationally linked to unions, labour tends to hold political discussions within that party's structures (but not exclusively, of course). To be sure, English-Canadian labour has its own political positions, and also engages in political action on its own. Nevertheless, there is a subtle difference, more sensed than seen, between the nature of political ties entertained by labour in Quebec and the rest of Canada.

As is well known, the New Democratic Party has made several attempts to establish a base in Quebec, often with the support of trade unionists. However, these efforts have all met with failure because of the party's inability to break away from its image as a centralized, Anglo-Saxon institution, because of its political blunders, such as refusing to grant its Quebec wing a strategic form of independence, and because of its lack of "high-profile" figures and popular support.[19] But to this list of reasons one must add the fact that Quebec's labour federations do not instinctively back political parties, an almost automatic custom among their Canadian and British counterparts.

Because of its Canada-wide ties, the QFL used to back the NDP. Indeed, a clause in the federation's charter declared its support, though in no concrete terms, for the NDP during federal elections. But the clause was removed in the 1970s and the QFL never actually supported the NDP's decision to participate in Quebec provincial elections. During the 1993 federal elections, the QFL supported the Bloc Québécois, not the NDP.

Quebec's other labour federations have never had a tradition of supporting any one party. Despite obvious signs of complicity, they have declared their intention to remain completely independent of political parties—something that

---

[18] This status is defined by various agreements, the most important of which were entrenched by the 1974 and 1994 CLC conventions. Along with greater powers, the QFL also receives part of CLC dues originating in Quebec, as well as a certain amount of financing from the federal government.

is rather difficult to confirm in reality. Even the QFL, which does not display such reserve, maintains that its support of any political party is always "critical." Quebec's labour federations, therefore, are distinct from Canadian unions in sharing a desire to remain autonomous from political machines. Having said this, one should not underestimate the impact of the "national" question on Quebec unions—which is not unrelated to the NDP's setbacks in Quebec, though it extends far beyond this matter.

The National Question

The Quebec labour movement is partly an offspring of Quebec nationalist sentiments. The history of the CNTU, which was born in the bosom of the Church and the agrarian ideology, is testimony to this. The lesser-known history of the QFL, which was mentioned earlier, provides another example. In the 1960s, the QFL[20] underwent a process of *"Québécization"* of its structures and operations, which turned it into a completely atypical federation in the Canadian and North American labour landscape. The result was a hybrid sprung from a desire to integrate into the continental labour system while remaining distinct.

The QFL's disagreements with the CLC are well known. Lesser known, however, are the disputes that drove many Quebec unions affiliated with Canadian or North American federations to assert their cultural and linguistic differences and in some cases, to disaffiliate, with the support of the QFL.[21] The problems encountered by Quebecers within these Quebec labour structures mirrored their experiences within the Anglo-Saxon-owned firms in which they worked. The fact that the QFL represented many unions that operated in these firms is not unrelated to its being the first federation to develop a sensitivity to language problems.

The increase in language-related demands and, more generally, of nationalist sentiments in Quebec coincided with the founding of Quebec's first separatist political groups, including a nationalist socialist party,[22] all of which disappeared in the late 1960s and early 1970s. It was about this time that the Parti Québécois (PQ) was created. Under the leadership of René Lévesque, a Liberal Party defector, the PQ was successful at tightly weaving the *souverainiste*[23] cause into the

---

[19] On the NDP's setbacks see E. Bernard in J. Jenson and R. Mahon, *The Challenge of Restructuring: North American Labor Movements Respond* (Philadelphia: Temple University Press, 1993), pp. 137-53.

[20] The QFL calls itself, and is called, a *"centrale"* (central union organization) in Quebec, contrary to other provincial federations.

[21] This was the case of several unions in the construction industry.

[22] The Parti socialiste du Québec was founded in 1963, through leftist labour and intellectual initiatives, to operate on the provincial political scene.

[23] The French terms *indépendantiste* and *souverainiste* have similar definitions, but convey different connotations. Since the emergence of the Parti Québécois, supporters of Quebec independence are called *souverainistes*.

fabric of Quebec politics. From that moment on, the national question influenced every debate concerning union-related political action. Nowhere was this more evident than within the QFL where, after many acrimonious debates between different nationalist and sovereignist factions, a decision was reached to support the Parti Québécois in the 1976 elections. Since then, the QFL has backed the PQ in all but one instance, the 1985 elections.

Following in the footsteps of the QFL, the other labour federations, with the exception of the CSD, have declared themselves in favour of sovereignty without going as far as backing the Parti Québécois. It is clear that the militant faction of Quebec labour is largely pro-*Péquiste*. In fact, the PQ's strength is manifest in ridings with the highest population of union members. Even though the Parti Québécois does not belong to the social democratic family, its programme is in many respects related. The government it formed was the driving force behind some *avant-garde* legislation, most notably anti-scab measures. The second Parti Québécois mandate (1980-85), however, was somewhat similar to the experience of the NDP governments in British Columbia, and more recently, in Ontario: a honeymoon, followed by a period of great tension between government and labour. Nevertheless, the Parti Québécois quickly managed to establish itself as the second political party in Quebec politics, and now shares the political stage alone with the provincial Liberal Party. The PQ constitutes the most socially progressive political option, thus being the most sympathetic to union demands.

As the preceding discussion has shown, the distinct character of Quebec labour is in many ways very real. Initially based on sectarianism, this distinctness has gradually centred around Quebec's linguistic and cultural differences, as well as the designation of Quebec as a distinct territory.

UNION ACTION IN THE WORKPLACE

Recent Developments in Labour/Business Relations

The current economic situation in Quebec is unlike any other in the past. The situation cannot be described merely as a typical recession, but as a lasting depression affecting the labour market. Even when economic indicators point in the right direction, unemployment figures do not necessarily follow. Moreover, many people with jobs are underemployed or do not have any form of job stability. There is sufficient reason, then, for workers to be concerned. What is more, workers stand opposite employers who face uncertainties of their own related to global competition, and public administrators who are themselves worried about deficits. As for union representatives, who assume and reflect everyone's fears, they must do their best to cope with all these factors, that is, develop a rationale for the union.

The uncertainty faced by many firms in relatively weak market positions has motivated a number of employers to search for common ground, instead of confrontation, with unions. This also explains the trend to negotiate long-term agreements prohibiting strikes and lockouts, which are viewed as a means of "stabilizing" labour relations for long periods of time. The creation of such conditions can be used as an argument by a subcontracting firm to secure a contract, or by a multinational subsidiary to justify its existence. Thus, a number of developments in labour relations practices can be observed, some of which are described below.

- Technical grievances are resolved among the parties concerned, without having to resort to the process of arbitration at all or to follow the procedure to its conclusion.

- Labour/business committees are set up with various mandates. It is worth mentioning that some committees are given a very general mandate, thus providing a framework for regular meetings between union representatives and key company managers.

- Unconventional collective agreements are negotiated more and more frequently. What is common to these agreements is their duration (over three years)[24]—which exceeds previous legal limits—and, as a corollary, their prohibition of strikes and lockouts during the same period of time. Salaries are generally renegotiated more frequently. In some cases, agreements provide for a degree of job security, or a minimum number of jobs that can be eliminated.

- Collective agreements are often renegotiated in part or in whole before they expire. These renegotiations, which are entered into of a common accord, are a means of modifying agreements before they create problems and, more generally, of adapting working conditions to the actual economic situation of the firm.

- According to statistics, the number of disputes (either strikes or lockouts) has continued to decline since 1993. The fact that the economic context has a strong influence on strike action is not a newly observed phenomenon. But the decrease in the number of recorded disputes has been accompanied by a proportional increase in the number of lockouts. In other words, while unions do not dare strike, employers (as a sign of the times) have not given up "their" pressure tactics, which are most effective during a period of economic restraint.

Old union wisdom holds that employers are more inclined to exhibit economic transparency when the going is bad than when the going is good. "Once the company is back making profits," militants may be asking, "will it close the books again?"

---

[24] Amendments to the Labour Code (1994) have changed the maximum duration of collective agreements from three to five years, against the wishes of labour federations.

The Organization of Work: Changes to Come

Despite modifications to machinery and technology, the way work is organized has not changed since the time of industrialization. The entire system of the division of labour and leadership has, so far, remained relatively inflexible. The need to modify the organization of work is probably the most debated issue in management studies. Taylorism and its inevitable damage in terms of workers' loss of responsibility, lack of concern for quality, loss of interest in work, etc. is increasingly perceived as the tawdry finery of days gone by and, more concretely, as a one-way ticket to bankruptcy. The list of top companies—which must be updated frequently—consists of those that invest in their workforce, delegate responsibilities to workers, and encourage them to work in semiautonomous teams.

Though these debates hardly ever translate into a willingness to effect real change, they do have a direct impact on labour relations. Indeed, in cases where workers are unionized, it is practically impossible to think of reorganizing work without not only the consent, but also the cooperation, of unions. This is partly because one could not reorganize work without touching important components of collective agreements such as job classifications, and also because within the legal framework that exists, employers cannot hope to accomplish fundamental change in the relationship between workers, the firm and their work without at least the tacit support of unions. Thus, employers are finding themselves making overtures to unions more and more frequently.

For unions, the willingness of employers to bring changes to the organization of work is perceived as a means of satisfying certain long-standing demands and of responding to the expectations and frustrations of members. In fact, in some workplaces, it is unions that are seeking and requesting changes to the way their work is organized. This is especially true of firms where management's failings are considered a threat to job security.

The issue of organization of work, however, also comes with its share of traps. Reorganizing work and improving efficiency can lead to the redundancy of a large number of workers, and can also mean increasing the work pace to an unsustainable rhythm, creating social pressure that may be unbearable for some workers, or the sudden delegation of responsibilities to workers without raising wages, etc.

The list of advantages of work reorganization can be long, but so can the list of drawbacks. Underlying the general concept of work reorganization (and the recent barrage of management schools of thought on the subject) is a hodgepodge of approaches. Furthermore, there are many workplaces where these ideas have not entered either the experience or the minds of those responsible for organizing work. Since each union is confronted with different situations, each one develops strategies to meet its own needs, which obviously cannot satisfy one and all. Workplaces that have adopted a dynamic approach to work organization are therefore the testing ground for new forms of labour relations. However, they also face a higher risk of destabilizing the unions which represent workers in diverse occupational categories, and whose support the unions must seek.

Precarious and Subcontract Work

There exists a large body of literature in economics dealing with the phenomenon of labour market segmentation, where the market is described as a two-, three-, or four-tiered system, with each segment characterized by differentiated working conditions, ranging from best to worst.

One cause of this segmentation is the current strategy of firms to create greater flexibility in all aspects of their operations. One tendency, for example, is to minimize the size of the workforce at all levels, including employees assigned to management and planning tasks as well as those directly involved in production. In case of an increase in demand, the firm's response is to have employees work overtime or to hire temporary workers. Thus, an entire grey zone of precarious jobs is created in the firm's periphery—jobs which are often filled by employees ejected from the core of the firm.

As a result, the protection of stable, unionized jobs is another area of great concern to unions. Here too, union representatives are faced with a difficult choice between two incompatible options: demanding job protection, which could threaten the firm's survival, or accepting some job cutbacks, which would ensure its survival. Unions are thus placed in a situation where they must develop strategies to help them navigate through rocky waters, sometimes in darkness when they have little knowledge about the firm's actual economic situation. In each case, the situation is potentially divisive and a threat to union cohesion.

The Private and Public Sectors

Analysis of the development of labour relations that has been carried out has been more focused on the private sector of the economy than on the public sector. In the latter case, labour relations are generally very traditional and often strained at the level of the workplace. Moreover, the lack of genuine, decentralized negotiations does nothing to guarantee the gains achieved. But since public-sector unions account for roughly half of Quebec's total union members, they do play a significant role in formulating union policy.

These are deeply uncertain times for public-sector labour relations. Budget cuts, privatization and job cutbacks coexist with new initiatives of labour/business cooperation aimed at improving productivity and reducing costs. The QFL and the CEQ, for example, signed a deal (fall of 1993) with the Quebec government in which all parties agreed to review work organization with a view to improving productivity. Although the other large labour federations are excluded from this agreement, they will nevertheless feel its effects. As a result, the focal point is the workplace, where management and labour must search for common ground.

On the whole, it is difficult to analyze the overall development of labour relations[25] since all observers lack perspective. There is a tendency to underestimate the impact of the economic situation, since its effects cannot be measured. In one sense, the cooperation between of business and labour is the result of gradual developments that have arisen out of labour/business committees set up to oversee newly negotiated spheres. In many workplaces, labour is a partner in discussions, and even in decision-making, about the firm's operations and work organization. While these developments can be seen as a step forward in the democratization of the firm, they are not without potential drawbacks.

First and foremost, it is difficult for labour to maintain, let alone define, a union rationale within the framework of talks focused on the firm and its development as an economic entity. There is also a danger of misrepresenting union members and of sending them wrong messages. Labour/business meetings can be so all-absorbing as to widen the gap (inevitable to some extent) between union representatives and their members. In such cases, union representatives can create the impression of being spokespersons for employers instead of workers.

It is important for union representatives to try to clear up these difficulties. In fact, they have no other choice, since their members will not re-elect representatives whom they feel do not adequately represent them. Creating and preserving a union identity is a never-ending task that is further complicated by the economic context and employers' appeals for company loyalty. Over and above the other difficulties encountered by union representatives, the question of union identity is a challenge that all unions, and by extension their members, must meet.

THE LABOUR MOVEMENT, IDEOLOGY AND SOCIETY

The Need for Pragmatism

Some observers of the labour movement feel, at times, that the ideological fervour of the past has died, or that there is no labour ideology left at all. The truth is that organized labour has always had an ideology. What has necessarily changed is the vanishing of utopian dreams, that is, dreams of a society which, as everyone knows, could only come about after a complete upheaval. Instead, the labour movement has become a player on the political scene, with a mission to formulate realistic demands in terms of both long- and short-term union needs. Labour was, and continues to be in the midst of ideological debates, which are all the more necessary today given labour's role in the polity. However, the labour movement must operate within a legal framework and, by obligation, a pragmatic and strategic framework; in short, labour is now guided by rationales other than

---

[25] There is a large body of literature on this issue in Quebec, including: Corporation des conseillers en relations industrielles, *Relations du travail : nouvelles tendances* (Montréal: Corporation des conseillers en relations industrielles, 1993); and R. Bourque, in *Colloque international franco-québécois sur les perspectives de recherche en relations industrielles* (Québec: Université Laval, 1994).

ideological ones, which is why the positions of labour federations may sometimes appear to be contradictory; for example, they may be tinged with corporatism or, inversely, with an apparently outdated radicalism. But certain situations, such as economic crises, necessarily call for union pragmatism.

Another important phenomenon that has prompted labour to adopt a reformist ideology is the modernization of the state. At different stages in its evolution, depending on the country, the state has come to play an important role in wealth redistribution and social security (yet, by repairing the damage caused by the economic system, the state, in so doing, ends up actually endorsing the system).

Unions have naturally turned to the state for assistance, and even forced it into taking on this role. Indeed, how can one separate the conditions negotiated with business from the general conditions engendered by government policies? Policies related to social security, regional development, taxation, health, etc. all have a direct impact on the economic conditions of unionized and non-unionized workers. It was therefore inevitable that unions would begin to participate in debates over government programmes, since much of their members' living conditions depend on them. In this context, it was inevitable also that union demands would become more and more "attainable."

From Divergent to Convergent Paths

After following different paths, Quebec's labour federations have all come to the fold of the social democratic family. In their early days, the two oldest federations, the QFL and the CNTU, were poles apart. The CNTU supported the social corporatist project of the Catholic Church, whereas the QFL's predecessors embraced a host of ideological strands, including a strong socialist strand. In the 1970s, the QFL, the CNTU and the CEQ began laying the foundations of a societal project known as "democratic socialism." In the early part of that decade the three federations underwent a Marxist period, and even published their own political manifestos: the QFL published *L'État, rouâge de notre exploitation* (The State, an Instrument of Our Exploitation); the CNTU, *Ne comptons que sur nos propres moyens* (Let Us Rely on Our Own Means); and the CEQ, *L'École au service de la classe dominante* (The School at the Service of the Dominant Class). These manifestos echoed many of the basic tenets of Marxist analysis: a bipolar and materialist view of the social classes, a vision of the state at the service of business, and the need for the working class, in its broadest sense, to cast off the various yokes weighing it down.

The QFL quickly abandoned this radicalism to embrace the social democratic model, influenced in particular by the Swedish experience. However, both the CEQ and the CNTU maintained their radical rhetoric until the early 1980s. These two federations were constantly at odds with the state—which in their case doubled as the employer—and the extreme tensions in public-sector labour relations played a significant role in the resilience of their Marxist discourse. In the case of the QFL, since it represents proportionally fewer Quebec government employees than the CEQ and the CNTU, it has had to contend with periodic tensions between its public-sector and private-sector affiliates.

Final resistance to the social democratic model faded when labour rallied around the cause which demanded a full-employment policy. As the centrepiece of the social democratic project, this policy is supported by an arsenal of Keynesian-style socioeconomic measures. The policy, as it was developed in Nordic social democratic countries, entails concerted action at several levels by the main protagonists (labour and business) and the state. Experience has shown that, for concerted action to succeed within such a framework, the parties involved must agree on a set of common objectives and make the necessary compromises regarding the means of achieving them.

However, today the Left is faced with a crisis that has caused more damage than merely rocking the foundations of communist parties and popular democracies. The crisis has also made it increasingly difficult to define a viable social democratic model, as indicated by increasing evidence of the failings of Keynesian policies. More and more so-called social democratic governments are adopting neo-liberalist measures. Even the social democratic models that inspired Quebec's labour movement are in the midst of their own crises. These social and political developments not only raise questions about the role of labour federations, but also force them to better define themselves ideologically. With the governments of Quebec and Canada reassessing various aspects of the welfare state, labour federations have no choice but to contribute to these debates and rethink the societal project they advocate. Thus, the federations themselves are debating how to modernize certain social democratic demands, and how to rekindle social solidarity in a highly constrictive economic environment. This is the context in which the emerging debate over job sharing is unfolding. Once again, we are reminded of the role of the labour movement as a political player. Indeed, from the moment labour begins defining itself in terms of political ideas, it has no choice but to become a political player.

THE EVOLUTION OF PARTICIPATORY PRACTICES

The mode of government greatly influences the type of political action taken by groups that are, like unions, essentially in a position of reaction to the state. Before the Quiet Revolution, there were few forums available where the voice of organized labour could be heard. This, of course, did not prevent labour from holding demonstrations or organizing press conferences to protest against the Duplessis government's anti-labour policies. Still, political action was carried out entirely within the framework of what is commonly called civil society.

During the 1960s, the labour movement developed a new form of relationship with the state, and thus radically changed the focal point of its political action. Labour was no longer merely an "external opponent" but had become an "internal participant" as well. Labour's new political status was reinforced by the expansion of the state, which led to the creation of many public agencies, as well as the development of diverse mechanisms, most notably a number of advisory boards, aimed at fostering the participation of collective groups in developing common goals.

For labour federations, the issue of whether to participate in consultative initiatives or public agencies was the subject of many internal debates. As early as 1973, the QFL adopted a set of guidelines and criteria concerning its participation, which it cautiously referred to as "presence." The issue resurfaced at its 1993 convention, when the federation reiterated that its participation in any public agencies should not be taken for granted, as each would be considered on the basis of merit. In reality, though, the QFL has always upheld a policy of "presence," unlike the CEQ and the CNTU.

Indeed, the CEQ stormed out of every public agency it attended in the early 1970s. It took the federation ten years to change its strategy and assess the merits of each opportunity. The CEQ, as well as the CNTU, occasionally walked out on the socioeconomic conferences held during the PQ government's first mandate. In another situation, the CNTU became locked in a bitter and divisive five-year-long debate over whether to sit on the board of directors of the Commission de la santé et de la sécurité du travail (CSST)—the board governing health and safety in the workplace. After much wavering, in 1984 the CNTU finally put an end to its internal squabbles on this issue with a decisive "yes."

The case of the CSST is particularly interesting. In many European countries, labour is intimately involved in the management of social security programmes (pension funds, insurance plans, etc.). While this tendency does not exist in North America, the CSST is one institution in which organized business and labour are equal partners. Established in 1979 during the PQ's first mandate, the CSST is headed by a board of directors composed exclusively of business and labour representatives, and presided over by a high-ranking civil servant named by the state. Both the direction and the very spirit of the law are based on the principle of parity. To this day, the CSST stands as the only direct incarnation of the social democratic model of representation in North America: the two major protagonists (labour and business) stand opposite each other in co-managing an institution with a significant operating budget.

The case of health and safety in the workplace is a good illustration of the flexibility of union action, which usually tends to "follow" the course set by specific cases and problems. In their desire to prevent workers from being subjected to local-level power struggles with different employers, unions have solicited the state's direct intervention in many areas, most notably pensions, and workplace health and safety. Direct state intervention thus ensures an entire population universal access to social security without excluding additional private plans.

The consequence of state intervention in areas of union activity is that certain spheres, once subject to negotiation, are thrust into the state's realm of influence. When labour is excluded from the administration of these spheres, its only means of intervention is in the form of an external pressure group. And when labour is party to the administration and application of government measures, as is the case with workplace health and safety, it functions within the state apparatus itself.

The PQ government stood out for implementing a new mode of consultation known as "concerted action." This approach took many different forms: socioeconomic conferences, industry conferences, thematic conferences and regional summits. The most highly publicized form of concerted action was a series of "grand summits" held in 1977, 1979 and 1982. The term "concerted action" is relatively new. It first appeared in political science literature to refer to consultative practices involving primarily the three main partners in the social democratic model: the state, organized business and organized labour. Concerted action is possibly one of the most engaging forms of consultation: it assumes agreement on a common problem and on the priority of consensus-building. In everyday language, concerted action has become a catch-all term to describe every kind of initiative at all levels.

In practical terms, concerted action is a term laden with symbolic overtones. It reflects the image of a society in which all social groups are stripped of effective and concrete means of economic and political power, only to be reinvested with the equal status of "representative group," "partner," or even "decision-maker." Refusing to be taken in by this concept, labour federations attended the first summits expressing their reservations regarding these initiatives.

After the Liberal Party's rise to power in 1985, "concerted action" initiatives came to a halt, at least in their systematic implementation as carefully planned, recurring events supported by a government agency.[26] In its place, other types of *ad hoc* and permanent consultative forums were set up, generally behind closed doors.

The ups and downs of the participatory practices of labour federations—and even more so of the related debates—testify to the political and symbolic significance of participation. Indeed, participation constitutes an endorsement of a process, which is why it cannot be considered an automatic step. The decision of labour federations to abstain from participating, on some occasions, can sometimes be construed as a challenge to the government's overall attitude, or sometimes even to an event or an agency.

It is apparent that the climate of public-sector labour relations has greatly influenced the internal debates of unions. It should not come as a surprise, then, that the QFL (which represents the smallest number of public-sector employees) has provided its members with the most stable representation among Quebec's labour federations.

---

[26] With the exception of "regional summits," which continued to be held until 1991.

CONCLUSION

Like labour movements everywhere, Quebec unionism is attempting to adapt to social and economic transformations. Despite the particular aspects of its history and traditions, Quebec labour faces essentially the same challenges as all other labour movements: to remain a primary sociopolitical player in the workplace, as well as in society as a whole.

At the level of the workplace, the current economic and political situation provides fertile ground for nurturing company loyalty and micro-identities, to the detriment of allegiances to larger union structures. Although union participation in labour/business joint-management initiatives aimed at reorganizing production and work can be seen in a positive light, it is futile to conceal the ambiguities therein. The increased recognition of labour by employers can result in the limiting of unions to a regulatory role—which they have always played, but in addition to a protest role. In this context, it is the complex sociological process by which workers identify with their union that could end up being challenged.

In society as a whole, it is apparent that the labour movement's ability to establish a unifying oppositional project has been undermined. The evolution of the labour market has led to such changes in its sociological make-up that organized labour has become a multiclass institution. It would be inaccurate, however, to portray organized labour as the defender of privileged workers: it has always upheld the political struggle against inequalities of all types. Furthermore, the labour movement, at least in Quebec, directly represents a large strata of workers in precarious jobs. Nevertheless, Quebec labour must strengthen its ties with organizations representing the interests of all the outcasts from what is still referred to as the "economic recovery." Indeed, this condition must be met to ensure the survival of labour's capacity to act as a large-scale social protest movement, a force that is bigger than the sum of its individual organizations. The labour movement must, therefore, be able to juggle its role as a major, naturally institutionalized, political player and its role as an instigator of social change.

Defined in these general terms, the dilemma facing organized labour is not unique to Quebec society. What is particular about this case is the weight labour commands due to Quebec's constitutional ambiguity. The outcome of this never-ending disagreement will have significant repercussions on the future of organized labour in Quebec. But, truth be told, for decades now Quebecers have been repeating what has become a trivial fact. Regardless of the outcome of the constitutional debate, Quebec labour will, for some time, be in the position of having to support an emancipatory project on both the social level and the national level. This dual role will not be easy to achieve. It is also a role that is not always well understood outside Quebec's borders.

REFERENCES

Amoroso, Bruno. 1992. "Industrial Relations in Europe in the 1990s: New Business Strategies and the Challenge to Organized Labour," in *The International Journal of Human Resource Management*, 3 (September), pp. 331-45.

Boucher, Jacques. "Les syndicats : de la lutte pour la reconnaissance à la concertation conflictuelle," in G. Daigle and G. Rocher (eds.), *Le Québec en jeu. Comprendre les grands défis*. Montréal: Presses de l'Université de Montréal, pp. 107-36.

Centre de recherche et de statistique sur le marché du travail (CRSMT), Le marché du travail. Gouvernement du Québec, January 1986-January 1994.

Jenson, Jane, Mahon, R. 1993. *The Challenges of Restructuring. North American Labor Movements Respond*. Philadelphia: Temple University Press.

Meltz, Noah M. 1989 "Interstate vs. Interprovincial Differences in Union Density," in *Industrial Relations*. 28: 2, pp. 142-58.

Murray, Gregor 1991. "Excetionalisme canadien? L'évolution récente du syndicalisme au Canada," in *Revue de l'IRES*. 7, pp. 1-25.

Rosanvallon, Pierre 1988. *La question syndicale*. Paris: Calmann-Lévy.

Rouillard, Jacques 1989. *Histoire du syndicalisme québécois*. Montréal: Éditions du Boréal.

Segretin, Denis 1981. *Les communautés pertinentes de l'action collective*. Paris: Laboratoire de sociologie et des relations professionnelles.

Statistics Canada, 1991. *Calura*, Catalogue 71-202.

QUEBEC FAMILIES

For decades, historians, sociologists, psychologists and demographers have, through diverse approaches, attempted to elucidate the inherent causes of the profound changes that have affected the Quebec family in recent years. Whereas in the late 1950s and early 1960s the family was considered a relatively concrete and stable phenomenon, a new sociological current, with feminist leanings, has challenged certain implicit assumptions that once provided the foundation for research on this institution. In an effort to distance themselves from functionalist perspectives, these recent studies have attempted to redefine the family. A number of researchers have focused on new family behaviour patterns, as well as new attitudes toward the family. Some studies looking into the various forms of the family unit have been based on morphological criteria alone, while others have also considered individuals' perceptions of the function of the family unit, marriage as an institution and, more generally, the integration of the family into the social environment.

This renewed interest in the family has also been manifested in the arena of Quebec politics. During the last ten years, the Quebec government has, through the process of public consultation, worked toward developing and implementing a policy on the family. However, segments of the policy sparked numerous debates over the responsibilities of the state and the family and the transformation that has occurred with respect to relations between men and women. At the heart of these discussions was the definition of the family. Indeed, no other issue addressed during the consultation fuelled more controversy. This is partly due to the fact that a variety of subjects dealing with distinct social representations have been addressed under the guise of the family.

The primary goal of this chapter is to highlight the ideological origins of the diverse definitions of the family used in Quebec today. But first, to place the subject within a broader context, I will begin with a brief history of the Quebec family over the course of the last century. At the same time, I will discuss the myths surrounding the family and then explore the main sociodemographic characteristics of today's families. I will then present the results of an analysis of the definitions of the family submitted by 35 national organizations during the 1985 consultation on family policy in Quebec. I will examine four theoretical perspectives from which the family is typically viewed. This study will attempt to shed new light on the concept of family by emphasizing not only the many diverse forms of the family unit, but also the ways in which individuals and groups define the family and perceive its place and role in Quebec society. It is hoped that this analysis will, to some extent, contribute to the understanding of the relationship between the social upheaval affecting Quebec society today and the new issues being considered in the field of the sociology of the family. I will finish with an overview of the major themes and debates in this field so as to help orient the current sociological research on the family in Quebec within a broader perspective.

QUEBEC FAMILIES: A CENTURY OF HISTORY

It would be futile to think that the history of family life styles during the last century could be told in a few lines. Without claiming to provide a comprehensive account of all the transformations that have occurred to the Quebec family, I will attempt to outline the main stages of development that have played a significant role in the evolution of this institution in Quebec. I will begin by looking at the family in preindustrial society, the first known form of the family in the province. Using this as a reference point, it will then be possible to examine the main effects of industrialization on the family as Quebec evolved from an agrarian to an urban society. I will show that this evolution had significant repercussions on the assignment of roles both in the family and society as a whole. I will then turn to the period between 1940 and 1960, analyzing the results of the effects of World War II, and the important institutional reforms that eventually influenced family living conditions.

After this period came another stage in Quebec's history that had a significant impact on the family: the appropriately named "Quiet Revolution" which occurred between 1960 and 1970. During this period, Quebecers were forced to confront major challenges to traditional morals and values. Finally, in the last part of this historical review, I will examine the changes that have occurred over the last 25 years. As we will see, the Quebec family—like families in other Western countries—survived this period of turmoil, but has developed different forms, to the point where we should no longer speak of the family, but rather of families.

The Family at the Turn of the Century

Despite the earlier existence of commerce-based urban centres, the rural family is often invoked as the first family form to have existed in French Canada. The rural family—the most common type of family up until the turn of the century—was essentially a unit of production, as its existence was based on a self-sufficient mode of farming. At a time when agriculture was the primary economic activity and farming techniques were still rudimentary, running a farm entailed a large labour force and thus required the participation of all family members. The land was the mainstay of the survival of family life, since ownership provided the family inheritance that was passed on to the sons, the dowry of those daughters who married, and a source of funds to educate those children who wished to enter a religious order. Women and children were an important economic resource since they represented the principal source of labour. Until 1931, only 10% of Quebec's labour force, on average, were hired workers (Clio, 1982: 303).

The function of the family as an agricultural unit of production, which was dependent on seasonal variations, required that the family's interests take precedence over those of the individual (Roussel, 1989). This trait of the preindustrial family was nurtured by a patriarchal system, which in Quebec was sanctioned by the Catholic Church and the Civil Code. Prior to industrialization, the sexual division of labour was based on the separation and complementarity of female and male roles and spheres of activities. In spite of the many responsibilities of married women and their leadership role on a legal level (wrongly called matriarchy by numerous authors), these women were forced to submit to the husband's authority, since upon entering into marriage they were stripped of their legal capacity and relegated to the status of minor.

Looking to the past and to tradition for solutions to everyday problems, the family found support in the teachings of the Church. During the first half of the century, the Church controlled various aspects of family life through moralizing sermons during mass, the confessional and counselling functions assumed by priests, and its exclusive control over education and population registration. The teachings of the Catholic Church left an indelible mark on Quebec culture. As the most fundamental institution of catholicism, the family served as a privileged means though which the Church nurtured and reinforced its positions. The Church had a different influence on the population of Quebec than it had on other nations because, in Quebec, the Church and the state exercised total power in distinct spheres. This division of power, which allowed the Church to impose its hegemony over education, medicine and welfare, removed the family from the state's sphere of influence (Fahmy-Eid, Laurin-Frenette, 1983: 345).

Until the middle of the twentieth century, young people of marrying age were forced to choose between entering a religious order or getting married. Remaining single was not an alternative, with the exception of those women who took care of the dependent members of the family (Clio, 1982: 243). In 1866, a law was passed recognizing only church weddings as legal. By virtue of this law, ministers of religion were given exclusive control over marriage registration. The following year was marked by the adoption of the British North America Act, including Section 91, which placed marriage and divorce under the exclusive jurisdiction of the federal parliament (Bohémier, 1966). Nevertheless, at the turn of the century, marriages contracted in Quebec's countryside still sometimes resembled a utilitarian exchange between partners. The religious commitment often coincided with the couple moving into a distinct dwelling, from where it was necessary to find a means of subsistence and carry out the chores of domestic labour. Marriage, work and founding a family were intimately related in both time and space (Dandurand, 1988).

Quebec has long been perceived as a society with a highly fertile population consisting of large families of ten or more children. But as certain demographers have shown (Henripin, 1981; Lavigne, 1983), this perception is more myth than reality. First of all, it should be noted that in the mid-1800s the fertility of Quebec women was inferior to that of women not only in Ontario but in Canada as a whole (Bouchard and Lalou, 1993: 31). Many demographers have rejected the nationalist hypothesis at the root of the "revanche des berceaux" (revenge of the cradle) movement, especially because fertility levels in other regions of Canada were the same as in Quebec. Thus, while 45% of women born in Quebec between 1886 and 1895 gave birth to six or more children, many women either gave birth to one or two children only, or had no children at all (Lapierre-Adamcyk, Péron, 1983: 31). Moreover, in 1917 only 20.5% of married women in Quebec had an average of ten children (Clio, 1982). Also, before World War I, lifetime fertility fell considerably and remained stable at around four children until 1950. This rapid drop in the number of large families began in the middle of the nineteenth century among urban families. That the reproduction level remained high until the turn of the century was mainly due to large families in rural areas. Contraception, though forbidden by the Church, was practiced perhaps more than we tend to think, especially in urban communities. Until World War II, birth control, which was still not widespread nor efficient, continued to be practiced secretly, either through prolonged abstinence or periodic continence (Lapierre-Adamcyk, Péron, 1983: 32). Finally, we should not underestimate the impact of infant mortality on the reduction in the number of children, especially in Quebec's urban communities where the percentage of deaths were among the highest levels in the Western World.

> Between 1901 and 1929, infant mortality was responsible for between 12.6% to 17% of all deaths in Quebec. This type of mortality more directly affected poor districts of urban centres. In the six years between 1910 and 1915, 78,000 children less than one year of age died in Quebec. (Clio, 1982: 256). (Our translation.)

Without denying the fact that large families have always existed in Quebec, it is important to note that this mythical image of the Quebec family perhaps has more to do with the vivacious and convivial character of familial ties among French Canadians than it does with fertility.

The Family in Urban Communities Before the Second World War

In comparison to previous decades, the composition of Quebec society began to change during the last few decades of the nineteenth century. Although the settling and clearing of remote areas was being carried out in earnest, the process of urbanization was about to upset the dominance of rural areas which had characterized the province up to this point. Indeed, statistics show that in 1940, as many as 60% of Quebecers lived in towns, while at the turn of the century the same proportion lived in the countryside (Clio, 1982: 239).

As early as the beginning of this century, industrialization and the ensuing migration toward the city brought about a redefinition of sexual roles. As several researchers have shown, this phenomenon had an enormous impact on parent-child relations as well as marital relations. Thus, a marked division between domestic work and work outside the home began to emerge whereby men and women were assigned to separate workplaces and clearly distinct spheres of activities: the housewife in the domestic sphere and the breadwinner on the labour market (Dandurand, 1988).

Contrary to the family model found in rural areas, love had become a requirement of urban marriages. In the city, the family also gradually abandoned its authority over the selection of spouses, leaving this decision to the individuals concerned (Goode, 1963). With this change, conjugal union increasingly came to be viewed as a private matter (Dandurand, 1988: 15). From this point on, affection became the leitmotif of the democratization of relations not only between spouses, but also between parents and their children. With the reinforcement of the distinction between male and female attributes, marriage took on a greater significance in the lives of women than ever before. As Dandurand explains:

> In this type of society, integration into the paid labour market was the primordial rite of passage of men into adulthood and the main referent of their social identity, while for women integration into married life served an equivalent function, given the central role it played in their lives. Despite notions to the contrary, there was no sexual symmetry in marriage (a fact which is confirmed by the very rite of the Catholic wedding), since the institution increasingly—and more exclusively—dictated the fate of women. (Dandurand, 1988: 15). (Our translation.)

Until the second half of this century, the marriage rate in Quebec was both stable and high, varying between 89% and 95%. There were, however, significant variations in the age at which people married, which, as elsewhere, were primarily related to the state of the economy. Indeed, such a variation was first observed during the Great Depression, when the number of marriages dropped and the age at marriage increased; another occurred during and immediately after World War II (1940-50), when the increase in the number of weddings was matched with a concurrent drop in the age at marriage (Péron, Lapierre-Adamcyk, Morrissette, 1987).

Regarding aid to the family, in comparison with other Canadian provinces, Quebec was slow to adopt a law enabling the implementation of social assistance programmes for needy mothers. In 1937, in response to the demands of doctors, feminists and social workers, Quebec finally passed this legislation, hoping it would lower the rates of delinquency and infant mortality, as well as safeguard the cohesion of the family in the absence of a father.

The legislation had a major impact on the conception of child welfare in Quebec. It marked the first step toward the recognition of the family as being more dependent on parenthood than conjugality by giving precedence to kinship ties over orphanages or other adoption institutions in crisis situations (Deleury, Cloutier, Binet, 1985: 197). By elevating the family to the status of most "natural" and appropriate environment for a child to grow up in, successful child development was increasingly seen to be dependent on the family's success (Clio, 1982: 263).

From World War II to the Quiet Revolution

During World War II, one of the federal government's responses to the labour shortage was to establish day-care services as a means of encouraging women's integration into the armament industries. In contrast to Ontario, these services enjoyed little success in Quebec because they were denounced by the Church as an intrusion on the part of the state into the affairs of the family, reminiscent of communism (Clio, 1982: 372). After the war, despite government efforts to entice women to return to the household, the proportion of married women with jobs outside the home doubled in less than ten years, jumping from 8% in 1941 to 17% in 1951 (Clio, 1982: 391).

As Quebec was becoming a modern society the discourse of the Church became increasingly disconnected from the realities of the family (Clio, 1982: 242). By the end of the 1930s it was apparent that the Church, which controlled numerous sectors (education, health, culture, etc.), could no longer meet the needs of the population. While the Church's glory days in education occurred in the 1940s, it was, paradoxically, during those years that its hold over this sector came under great criticism.

The 1940s were marked by important school reforms, but also by large-scale public morality campaigns (Desjardins, 1990: 393). The discourse claiming that women were naturally destined to serve the family was still widely believed, as the proliferation of schools teaching home economics in the late 1930s showed. At the same time the focus of young girls' education switched from domestic and agricultural subjects to topics closer to the needs of the city dweller. "Female education," as it was called, became centred on family life to the point where it, as well as femininity, was accorded cult status (Clio, 1982: 391). Nevertheless, while the feminine mystique was occupying an important place in the public sphere, the trend toward the democratization of interpersonal relations was gaining ground. Women won the right to vote in the 1940s. Also, legislative amendments led to changes that increased women's access to education. Teachers' colleges were established where women, in particular, could be trained, and liberal arts postgraduate programmes, previously open only to men, began to admit women (Clio, 1982: 392).

As was the case across North America, Quebec was in the midst of a population explosion combined with high marriage rates. The baby boom, however, was less pronounced in Quebec than in Ontario (Dumont, 1995). In Quebec, many people who were hoping to establish a sense of normalcy and stability after the war reverted to the old sexual division of roles which had survived the challenges of the previous two decades.

The Quiet Revolution: 1960-1970

The period between 1960 and 1970, commonly referred to as the "Quiet Revolution," was a critical turning point in Quebec's history, as illustrated by demographic statistics and the profound changes that occurred in the province's social, political and economic structures. The Church, whose influence had already diminished, ceded some of its power to the state. Indeed, during the Quiet Revolution the Church's declining influence was further accelerated as the number of practicing Catholics fell substantially and the process of secularization began to undermine the Church hierarchy. For example, the proliferation of professionals in a variety of disciplines (medicine, education, social work, psychology, etc.) were providing secular alternatives to the traditional religious values (Dandurand, 1988). According to Dandurand:

> These new experts, in their roles of policy makers, confessors and counsellors, took over from the Church in its decline, and in so doing helped to define a more individualistic and secular culture (Dandurand, 1988: 32). (Our translation.)

The discourse that once revolved around the duties of individuals and the family became centred on personal rights and freedoms. Despite the decline and inadequacy of ecclesiastic powers in the area of social security, the people of Quebec had to wait until the end of the 1960s before structured social programmes were established. A series of social measures were inplemented that were intended to help families, and particularly women, including the Public Health Protection Act in 1960, the Quebec Pension Plan in 1965, and the provincial family allowance programme in 1967. According to Dandurand (1988), in alleviating much of the burden shouldered by the family and especially women, who had traditionally dispensed care to dependent family members (the sick, the aged and the handicapped), these measures likely had a significant impact on the family, especially the aspect of kinship.

Finally, in 1970, the provincial government established a comprehensive welfare assistance programme that not only embraced a series of existing policies (programmes to aid invalids, handicapped, needy mothers, etc.), but also extended their coverage to a broader segment of the population by relaxing certain regulations. For the state, adopting a welfare plan signified that it accepted to offset the "risks" of marriage break-ups, which it had refused to do until then (Dandurand, 1988).

With regard to the condition of women in society, the women's liberation movement, which had been less outspoken in previous years, experienced a resurgence in the mid-1960s. This renewed feminism had repercussions on the lives of Quebec women, as well as society as a whole and, by extension, the family. Indeed, by promoting the rights of all women regardless of social standing, this large-scale movement addressed issues such as contraception, abortion, matrimonial regimes, women's place in the family, sexual stereotypes, and the socialization of children in the school (e.g., textbook reforms). Tackling all these issues eventually led to a profound rethinking of relations between men and women, and initiated a complete realignment of parental roles within the family. For example, during the period between 1965 and 1970 a major shift took place in society as women, including wives and mothers, joined the ranks of salaried workers. This phenomenon, which grew over time, coincided with a major educational reform that put an end to the clergy's reign over this domain and men's predominance in graduate school. The elimination of tuition fees, the opening of schools to both sexes, and the reforms to elementary schools, colleges and universities gave women, both young and old, access to the training required for careers in areas that had previously been the reserve of men.

There were also numerous reforms to sections of the Civil Code dealing with matrimonial bonds. The willingness to democratize these bonds set the tone for several new laws and measures adopted by the government. Thus, as of 1964 married women were no longer considered minors. Also, in 1970, the legal regime was changed in order to give women the right to manage property.

In 1968 the Canadian state authorized the provincial courts to legislate in the area of divorce. Quebec subsequently adopted divorce legislation that radically changed Quebecers' attitudes about marriage, as the continually increasing number of break-ups shows. In 1969, the year after the divorce legislation was implemented, the divorce rate was 8.7%, compared with 49.6% in 1991 (Valois, 1993). Although this latter figure shows that one out of every two marriages ends in divorce, we should add that the number of contracted marriages also decreased during the same period, as we will soon see (Lapierre-Adamcyk, Péron, 1983: 36).

During the Quiet Revolution, Quebec society also underwent a revolution in the area of birth control and, more generally, in people's attitudes about sexuality. During the 1960s,[1] birth control became essential almost overnight for the purpose of delaying pregnancies, and for limiting the number of children, as was shown in the practices of young, newly married couples (Lapierre-Adamcyk, Péron, 1983: 33). Another development in the quest for greater control over fertility occurred in the 1970s, when a growing number of couples resorted to sterilization after attaining a desired family size.

---

[1] Though the birth-control pill became available toward the middle of the 1960s, it was only after the Omnibus Bill was passed in 1969 that therapeutic abortions and the sale of contraceptives became legal.

A Quarter Century later

The Quiet Revolution was not only a period of major change to social, political and economic institutions, it was also a catalyst for the emergence of new family life styles that continued to evolve into the 1990s. In response to all these changes the government implemented various social policies in the 1970s. However, the state's ability to reduce social inequalities began to be called into question in Quebec, as in all Western countries (Lesemann and Chaume, 1989). Indeed, a series of economic reforms in the period between 1975 and 1990 due to the combined action of the federal and provincial governments actually reduced the redistribution of public wealth, to the detriment of the poorest families (Dandurand, 1988: 89).

In the 1980s two important events left their mark on the Quebec family: the reform to the sections of the Civil Code dealing with the family, and the implementation of a family policy. In 1977, a few years before the above-mentioned reform, the Civil Code changed the concept of paternal authority to that of parental authority. This amendment was significant in that it brought about a complete redefinition of the family. As Joyal (1987) points out, the amendment reflected the transition from the primacy of paternal authority over children to that of parental responsibility for children. The same year also saw the passing of the Youth Protection Act which, according to Dandurand (1988), gave the state the power to judge parental competence: not only did the state take on the role of watchdog over child protection, but it also reserved the right to intervene in families considered to be dysfunctional.

In adopting Book Two, The Family, in the Civil Code in 1980, Quebec hoped to legally ensure the equality of the sexes in the household and of all children regardless of filial relation (i.e. legitimate, out of wedlock, or adopted). Thus, for example, since both spouses were now equal in the eyes of the law, the Civil Code of Quebec ordered that they should each retain their surnames for their entire lives. The changes to the Code even recognized, at least theoretically, the economic contribution of domestic labour. Although this concept was generally well received, it also came under some criticism due to the difficulty of applying it (Dandurand, 1988; Gauthier, 1985). In 1989, the Quebec government added yet another section dealing with the family to the Civil Code: the Act respecting Family Patrimony. The Act was adopted to rectify the inequities between men and women vis-à-vis divorce, separation and marriage annulment. Based on the principle of equal partition between the spouses, the Act respecting Family Patrimony stipulated that all property acquired during a marriage should be equally divided among the parties, regardless of the matrimonial regime. In so doing, the Act recognized the economic contribution of women working in the home. In addition to these major changes that were specifically aimed at couples united in marriage, the new Civil Code also attempted to reduce the discrepancies between married and common-law couples. However, by refusing to give a precise definition of the family, the Code came short of formally recognizing common-law unions.

Finally, as we will see in the next section, in 1985 the Quebec government began a long consultation process that led to the implementation of a comprehensive family policy. The policy, in addressing the issue of parents' responsibilities over their children, encouraged families to become more autonomous. It affirmed that the family belonged to the private sphere and that the state should not interfere in its affairs. Thus, the state's involvement in the area of the family could no longer be viewed within the framework of the welfare state; instead, the state's role was changed to that of educator. During the consultation held in 1985, participants repeatedly suggested the "developing and perfecting of the means best suited to educating parents and the public at large" such as courses on "parent effectiveness" (i.e. parent-child and parent-teenager relations), as well as psychology courses on early childhood years and adolescence (Secrétariat au développement social, 1985: 119).

After perceiving marriage as the only acceptable family model for more than a century, it took less than 20 years for Quebec society to remove all social sanctions against common-law unions. Thus, while divorce rates have continued to climb since the end of the 1960s, marriage rates have experienced a downward trend since 1973. The marriage index fell from over 92% in 1972 to under 40% in 1992 (Péron, Lapierre-Adamcyk and Morrissette, 1987; Motard and Desrochers, 1995: 17). In comparison, in the early 1990s, the index was approximately 60% for the whole of Canada. During the last few years, the trend away from legal marriages has been accompanied by a reduction in remarriages. According to demographers, the number of common-law unions has steadily increased, which would seem to indicate that marriage has become less popular. Although cohabitation is viewed by some couples as a prelude to marriage, many others see it as a permanent substitute. In 1991, the proportion of common-law couples in Quebec was 19% compared with only 11.3% for all of Canada (Valois, 1993). Finally, not only single people but also, to a lesser extent, people who have already experienced a divorce or separation choose cohabitation as a life style.

On the issue of birth rate, it appears that even though couples are giving birth to fewer children, young people are still expressing a desire to have children (Dandurand et al., 1994). The tendency toward fewer births, which began near the end of the last century, persisted after the period known as the baby boom and attained its lowest level in 1987 when the birth index measured 1.35 (Secrétariat à la famille, 1989: 11). Since then, the index has risen to 1.67 in 1992, bringing it closer to national values, which have been above normal for several years (Motard, Desrochers, 1995: 21). It should be noted that in Quebec the number of out-of-wedlock births has jumped from 8% in 1971 to 40.8% in 1991 (Valois, 1993: 102). The number of children born to common-law parents to those of single mothers was difficult to assess prior to the 1981 census since this was the first time a census included a category for common-law unions (Péron, Lapierre-Adamcyk, Morrissette, 1987). While the increase in the number of out-of-wedlock births is mainly due to the increase in common-law unions, it is also true that the proportion of single-parent families has risen dramatically in just a few decades. As Renée Dandurand clearly states in her book *Le mariage en question:*

> ...between 1971 and 1981, the number of single-parent families grew by 54%, while the number of two-parent families rose by only 11%. In the mid-eighties, single-parent families accounted for one family in five in Quebec (Dandurand, 1988: 67). (Our translation.)

The growth in the number of single-parent families has been slightly more pronounced in Quebec than in the rest of Canada. Between 1971 and 1991, the proportion of single-parent families grew from 13.2% to 20% in Canada and from 13.4% to 21.6% in Quebec (Valois, 1993: 219).

As in other Western societies, what characterizes the Quebec family in the 1990s is the widely diverse forms it may assume. Along with the "typical" family of the 1950s, where cohabitation coincided with marriage and children were necessarily included in marital plans, other forms of individual and family life courses have emerged (Ravanera, Rajulton and Burch, 1994), as well as many diverse life styles: men and women cohabitating or living alone, single-parent families, blended families, common-law unions, etc. While families in Quebec and other Canadian provinces have similar histories, the former stand out for having experienced greater and quicker changes to marital relations, intergenerational relations and kinship in general. As Pitrou pointed out:

> ...the radical nature and suddenness of changes to behaviour and values concerning the family are striking to observers from other countries, who are used to more gradual historical changes. Quebec is like a shortened version of history, especially with regard to social interaction (Pitrou, 1992: 226). (Our translation.)

In a context where a multiplicity of familial arrangements prevails, it seems justified to examine the different ways in which the family is perceived, since this could lead to a greater understanding of the nature of changes affecting the family. The next section will therefore examine the debate surrounding the definition of the family that took place during the development of the family policy in Quebec.

RELATIONS BETWEEN THE INDIVIDUAL, THE FAMILY AND THE STATE IN TERMS OF PARENTAL TIES

In recent years, a growing number of articles in the sociology of the family have attempted to bring a certain coherence to new phenomena observed in family demographics. Both Jean Kellerhals et al (1984) and more recently Bawin-Legros and Sommer (1987) examined classification systems of various family structures with the aim of isolating shared characteristics. What these authors explained, first of all, is that the family types they looked at were all theoretical in nature, that is, they did not claim to catalog concrete types of family models. Instead they sought to establish broad categories based on a limited number of variables. In this sense, their work can be used as a tool for developing more detailed analyses. The authors of the family types used both macrosociological indicators (divorce rate, fertility, marriage rate, etc.) and microsociological indicators (affectivity, socialization, development of the psychoemotional identity, etc.). Finally, the types were often based on the hypothesis that family structures are closely related to the social environment. Indeed, almost all types of family organization tended to be classified in terms of their integration into, or relationship with, exogenous factors. For example, some types emphasized the economy (Menahem, 1979); others related to family exchanges or the guiding principle of integration (Roussel, 1979); while others focused on the types of relations that prevail between members of the family unit (Faber, 1962) (Bawin-Legros, Sommer, 1987).

Although the aim of these typological essays has been to deepen our understanding of the transformations of the family institution, it appears that the various ways of perceiving the family still has not been the subject of an in-depth analysis. This chapter is therefore a first attempt to fill this gap. As we will see, when discussing the family, we are in fact addressing a variety of subjects. The complex nature of discussions surrounding the definition of the family is essentially due to shifts in meaning which may create the illusion of consensus based on the definition of parental ties. Unlike the previous research, the ideas developed here are not based on family models, but instead on ways of conceptualizing the family. This study, it is hoped, will elucidate these concepts by uncovering the ideological bases of the various definitions of the family and, more specifically, the ways in which individuals and groups perceive the relationship between the state and the family, between the state and civil society, between the individual and the family, and finally between men and women.

In order to underscore the importance of the issues involved in defining the family, I will discuss some of the results of an analysis based on a sample of 35 papers submitted by national organizations during the 1985 consultation process on the development of Quebec's family policy. Despite efforts made to reach a consensus on a government strategy in this area, the policy has come under much criticism. The definition of the family lies at the heart of these debates. Using this observation as a point of departure, I propose that the difficulty in reaching a consensus on a family policy is due to the fact that there are many different ways of perceiving the family. Thus, I have looked at definitions proposed by various national organizations in the above-mentioned papers in order to uncover the perceptions organizations have of the family's role and place in society.

After reviewing these concepts of family, I will then briefly analyze the political and social context of the debates over conflicting definitions and the arguments supporting them. This will hopefully contribute to a better understanding of the debates surrounding the implementation of Quebec's family policy and, more globally, of the issues involved in this type of state intervention. Before proceeding, however, it is necessary to address a few methodological considerations.

Given the scope of Quebec's family policy and the wide diversity of the sectors represented at the consultation, I began my analysis by selecting those papers submitted by national organizations that included a definition or discussion of the family. It should be noted that the term "national organization" includes associations, professional groups and unions, as well as government and parapublic agencies. For the purpose of this study, I identified seven categories for classifying organizations according to their ideology and/or particular sphere of activity. Each organization was assigned to one of the following: 1) religious organizations; 2) family and related organizations; 3) organizations dealing with the status of women or feminism; 4) unions; 5) social work professionals; 6) rural organizations; and 7) miscellaneous organizations.

It then became apparent that the majority of the themes addressed in the organizations' arguments could be grouped into four parameters, as I have called them here: the morphology of the family; the functions of the family; the temporal context; and the ways of understanding the private/public dichotomy. The aim here was not to define the axes of the classification *a priori*, but instead to get a better grasp of the various aspects covered in the papers through an inductive method. The four parameters examined here are very broad and there is, in many respects, some overlap between them. I first proceeded by analyzing the parameters independently of one another, and then by examining the relationship between them. For the sake of clarity, morphology was used as a reference point for the analysis of the other three parameters. Finally, using this classification, I compared the definitions provided by each organization, and ultimately was able to identify four theoretical perspectives from which to view the family, each based on a distinct rationale.

What follows is a synthesis of this analysis presented in the form of a classification of the main elements of the different ways of viewing the family. I have grouped these different approaches into four perspectives. It should be noted that there is no perfect match between the way in which the national organizations view the family and any one of the perspectives examined here. Indeed, some organizations' viewpoints are based on different concepts, but are still related on an ideological level.

WAYS OF VIEWING THE FAMILY: A CLASSIFICATION

First Perspective: The Family as an Extension of Society

According to this first perspective, the family is viewed as an extension of society and is defined as a conjugal union, that is, it is based on the existence of the couple. Proponents of this perspective emphasize the fact that the family is a universal and natural phenomenon. They perceive the family institution as the guarantor of the social order, since it both engenders and determines society, and thus represents an essential component of social evolution. The ties between family members are governed by the institution of marriage, which, whether civil or religious, is seen as a virtually indissoluble social contract that plays an essential regulating role in social life. Thus, marriage and the family are intimately related. Some proponents even argue that since children are born of both a father and a mother, this means that matrimony is more important than parenthood.

According to this line of thinking, relationships between family members are emotional in nature and reflect a set of duties, rights and responsibilities largely dictated by the Catholic Church. Of all the functions served by the family, procreation is the most important, whether it is understood as the primary purpose of marriage or as a natural and unifying component of the conjugal union. Reproduction is also seen as functioning to rejuvenate society and is thus an aspect to be encouraged to ensure the survival of society. In addition, the education and socialization of children is considered one of the family's primary functions, since both can be used to teach family values and develop future citizens. Regarding the roles of family members, it is also worth noting the importance attached to women's role as wife, mother and child educator, despite claims that sharing domestic chores is essential to the well-being of families.

Finally, the state, whose mandate is apparently to maintain social order, is assigned the primary role of protecting the institution of the family, which is the foundation of the social structure. Though it should not interfere in the private affairs of the family, the state is expected to ensure that a degree of conformity is maintained (through laws and regulations such as a family charter) with respect to both the family structure (by promoting a single family model) and family responsibilities (by emphasizing its essential values). The consequence of the state's failure to fulfil this role would be the jeopardization of the whole of society. Thus, while this perspective seems to recognize that society has some influence on the family, it emphasizes the inverse relationship, namely, that the family shapes society.

Second Perspective: The Family as Guarantor of Social Solidarity

According to this second perspective, the family is founded on the union of parent(s) and child(ren). Based on emotional ties and mutual support that may extend beyond the nuclear family, some say the family serves an important integrating function. By socializing its members, the family is perceived as the bridge between the private and public spheres, and thus represents a community of its own. The family is society's most fundamental element, since its primary characteristic is to nurture solidarity and union within the family, as well as between its members and the larger community. While its structure may take different, and continually evolving, forms, the family is defined as the "nucleus" of society.

Because the emphasis here is on parental responsibilities and child welfare, socialization and education are considered the family's most important functions. Procreation, and for that matter the type of ties uniting family members, is up to the couple's discretion. The sharing of roles within the family—which according to proponents of this approach must grow more egalitarian—is dependent on the state's adoption of a comprehensive set of social and collective measures. State intervention should therefore focus on education; in fact, as an educator the state is responsible for ensuring the smooth running of families. Proponents of this perspective advocate the state's implementation of courses in parent training, psychology and interpersonal relations between family members. The ultimate goal of this form of state intervention is to firmly establish cultural conformity, especially in terms of parenting and relations between men and women.

While this approach recognizes that families have an effect a determining impact on society and vice versa, more emphasis is placed on the fact that a healthy and caring society is the necessary condition for the development of families. The state's role should be to support and improve the material and social environment of families in order to strengthen the bonds of solidarity between families and encourage their autonomy. The state should therefore not interfere in the lives of families, but instead should ensure that family members and families, on the whole, become more autonomous, and that families support one another with the help of organizations and through community involvement. In short, from this perspective, the family belongs to the private sphere, and has the right not to be interfered with by the state as long as it adequately assumes its responsibilities.

Third Perspective: The Family Oriented Toward Individual Autonomy

Here the family is viewed as a unit based on parent-child relations. As a conglomerate of individuals, the family has no essence in and of itself, although its functions seem to have a bearing on the collective whole. According to this perspective, the types of ties between parents, as well as those between parents and their children, are a matter of individual choice. While relationships between family members are founded on love proper to blood relations, the relationship between partners (married or not) is based on the complete autonomy of individuals. In other words, the relationship between adults may constitute a form of partnership between a man and a woman. In this case, parental responsibility requires the mutual commitment of both partners, even in the case of a break-up.

This way of conceptualizing the family appears to be rooted in the respect for individual choice and the protection of the rights and freedoms of the person, but even more so in the autonomy of individuals. It is in this sense that, according to this approach, the family's role is to train individuals to become autonomous beings. The family here is thus an open-ended entity, and is not the only element ensuring the development and well-being of its members.

Finally, according to proponents of this approach, state measures should not only target families, but should also include social programmes focusing on the individual. They see the state's diminishing role in the affairs of the family as an attempt to reprivatize the family, thus constituting a serious impediment to the autonomy of family members, especially women. Like those organizations advocating a definition of the family based on a parental union in the broad sense of the term, respect for the plurality of family forms is highly regarded by the organizations who adhere to this third perspective. What is different in this case, however, is that the emphasis is on the autonomy of individual family members, not the family. Thus, these groups support a number of government measures intended to reinforce the autonomy of individuals (e.g. the sharing of family income and the elimination of sexual inequalities). In short, this individualistic perspective regards the autonomy of family members as the precondition to the family's well-being.

Fourth Perspective: Individual Autonomy as Guarantor of Solidarity

What distinguishes this fourth perspective from the others is that it defines the family as a fraternal union, that is, a group of people united by emotional ties. The family in this case is defined as a unit based on parent-child relations or the presence of emotional ties and the willingness of autonomous and non-autonomous individuals to mutually support one another. Since love and the institution of the family are not seen as easily reconcilable, the view is that the concept of family should be as flexible as possible to accommodate individual needs. The main function of the family here is to ensure the solidarity and cohesion of individuals, families and groups through mutual support and the social recognition of individuals.

The emphasis is thus placed on the autonomy of individuals and on individual choice. It is in this sense that shared parental responsibilities and the right to individual parenthood, for both men and women, are underscored. From this perspective, the family is not necessarily viewed as the basic element of society; in fact, the family is one of many institutions and social groups that help to structure society. Moreover, this approach emphasizes the fact that families are not homogeneous and should be considered on the basis of the human relations which constitute them, since they may be different in nature and intensity. Each individual is seen as belonging to more than one social group and as having ties with more than one community. Thus, the state is assigned the task of making sure that all individuals are autonomous and accounted for socially (through such measures as job guarantees, universal income, etc.) so that they can mutually support one another and make personal contributions to society through their involvement in the community. Finally, as in the second perspective outlined above, there appears to be a split between the functioning of the state and the community, in contrast to the continuity flowing between the individual, the family and the community in the other two perspectives.

AN ANALYSIS

It is clear from this comparative analysis that there are distinct rationales for each of the above concepts of the family. Focusing on parent-child relations as the common denominator of every family, as is recommended by the Quebec state, appears to group together a series of antagonistic political objectives by creating a sort of superficial consensus. Although the majority of the organizations agree that a family policy must first and foremost take into account the plurality of family forms existing in society, they have been unable to agree on a definition of the family. With regard to the parameter of family functions, there are again significant differences in the way each organization views the family. While every group considers education and socialization as the primary functions of the family, proponents of the conjugal-union definition also see procreation as one of its primary functions. For these organizations, procreation is perceived as serving the function of regenerating society and thus of ensuring its survival; in fact, these groups view family and birth control policies as going hand in hand.

Differences among the four perspectives also become apparent when taking into account the temporal parameter. In cases where the family is seen as an extension of society, the duration of conjugal ties is perceived as a precondition of social stability. The more one moves away from the concept of parental union to that of fraternal union as the common denominator of Quebec families, the less duration is seen as a defining element of the family. As Roussel points out, it seems that time is perceived "as a juxtaposition of equivalent moments, but which become less and less probable the further one moves away from the present" (Roussel, 1989: 243). Indeed, those organizations who define the family on the basis of parent-child relations consider the permanent status of matrimonial and parental ties as a priority, although they recognize the transformations which are affecting family life styles and the emergence of new constraints that may limit reciprocal support (for instance, the greater geographical mobility of young people). Conversely, according to those organizations who regard parent-child relations as a priority, only parenthood can be viewed in relation to a continuous temporal dimension. In fact, a number of organizations limit parental responsibility to the age of majority of the child. Moreover, these organizations tend to reject all references to the past, particularly to the traditional family, since this amounts to an idealization of living conditions of days gone by.

The problem with constructing a definition of the family results not only from the diversity of life styles, resources and objectives of participants in the 1985 consultation, but also from the eminently political nature of the issue. To be sure, each organization sought to make its interests known to the government. Consider, for example, the concept of the right to non-interference, which took on a different meaning from one group to the next. To those organizations for whom daily life and future existence are both seen as precarious, such as single-parent organizations, unions and anti-poverty groups, the autonomy of all family members is considered very important. In this case, the private sphere is viewed from an individualistic perspective and the family is depicted as an organization of people whose common goal is the development of individual family members. Proponents of this position favour the implementation of measures that are primarily geared toward developing the autonomy of family members, without which the well-being of families would be undermined.

In contrast, those organizations whose position is in keeping with that of the Catholic Church see the family and society as intertwined to such an extent that the development and well-being of one is necessarily dependent on the other. Since from this perspective the family is viewed as an institution in crisis, some organizations feel that measures are urgently needed to guarantee the reversal of the tendency toward the disintegration of the family. It is apparent, however, that so-called "private" matters often become a reflection of the self-centred interests of these organizations. For example, most of them cannot envisage a family policy that does not include measures aimed at increasing the birth rate. The declining influence of the Church on families, especially with regard to the respect of some of its values and norms, is not unrelated to the fact that, according to these groups, the government's primary role should be to promote a unique family model based on marriage.

Finally, as I have noted in the analysis above, several groups of health and social service professionals argue that the state should help families become more autonomous. It seems that the interests these groups seek to promote have an influence on their way of viewing the family as well. Indeed, they favour the implementation of a series of preventive measures such as educational and support programmes aimed at strengthening the bonds of solidarity among families. Given the fact that in recent years the state has become less involved in social programmes, these organizations have adopted a compromise position between their own interests and those of the state. By defining the rapid changes in Quebec families as social problems, these experts can emphasize the importance of their services. While they appear to have given up, as the government has, on the idea of maintaining the welfare state, they nevertheless advocate the establishment of the "education state," in which they would have a central role. In the end, the variety of positions taken by different groups regarding the definition of the family and, more generally, family policy seems to result from a power struggle, and continues to contribute to the establishment of the family as an independent field of research.

Indeed, hidden behind the diversity of definitions examined above, there lies general consensus. Despite the disparate points of view on the family, these definitions all share a number of fundamental elements. This analysis has revealed that, although kinship is still an important variable, the notions of individual will and choice are becoming increasingly important in defining the family (Belleau, 1994). Indeed, blood lines are no longer considered to be the main point of reference (Ouellette, 1994). Links of solidarity increasingly consist of unrelated individuals, and ties uniting family members are becoming more elective or, perhaps more accurately, selective in nature. Nevertheless, relations between individuals and their family members are still important for the teaching of values.

The process of individualization, which characterizes modernity, points to another aspect of consensus underscored in this study. The various ways of viewing the family each assume *a priori* the notion that the family is the ideal environment for individual development. The rights, duties, and autonomy of the individual are central components of each definition. In fact, every organization speaks of the importance of implementing measures aimed at addressing sexual inequalities and at facilitating task-sharing among family members. These measures are presented as preconditions for the application of any family policy, since the well-being of families, according to many, depends upon it. What is most striking, however, is that the vast majority of the organizations examined here recommended that the state recognize the financial contribution of domestic labour. A great number of papers suggested the implementation of measures aimed at redistributing total family income among both spouses. Other papers proposed that spouses working at home be paid a salary and have access to the same social benefits as other workers. This is especially significant, given that almost all the organizations who participated in the consultation agreed on this point despite having fundamentally opposed interests and perceptions concerning the roles and place of the family in society.

In recent decades, the values, ideologies and behaviour of individuals have undergone radical changes. In Quebec, the feminist movement has greatly influenced the ways of perceiving the family and of perceiving the role of women and men in society. But the greatest change affecting Quebec families has probably been the integration of women into the labour market: first married women, then mothers of young children. The family used to be perceived as distinct from the sphere of work because of the sexual division of labour among spouses. Today, the breakdown of this dichotomy has become clearly evident as both spouses are forced to combine the two realities of work and family. In this context of fundamental change, the sociology of the family has had to gradually modify its analytical frameworks to better accommodate emerging social phenomena. In the next section, I will attempt to outline some of these modifications.

THE SOCIOLOGY OF THE FAMILY IN QUEBEC

During the 1960s and 1970s, sociological analysis of the family in Quebec, as elsewhere, was still greatly influenced by major theoretical currents such as functionalism and Marxism. These classic perspectives essentially offered macrosociological conceptual frameworks. The family, then considered as a relatively homogeneous category, was viewed as almost entirely determined by its social environment. Over the years, however, it became apparent that these theories were insufficient to explain its complexity and subjective dimensions. As was mentioned earlier, this realization resulted in no small part from the work of feminist researchers who revealed the biases and *a priori* assumptions of classic sociological theories (Dandurand, 1994). For example, they challenged the idea put forth by numerous scholars that the family constituted a group of unified individuals who all shared the same interests (Pitrou, 1987). Other researchers have stressed the importance of studying the family as an open-ended entity, that is, with ties to various external networks and institutions. During the 1980s, then, old theoretical frameworks were criticized in numerous studies, mainly those dealing with the family and its relation to the state, the educational system, the judiciary, and the labour market.

Given the profound sociodemographic and cultural changes that occurred in the years following the Quiet Revolution, a renewal of theoretical approaches to the sociology of the family became necessary. New research and the finetuning of empirical methods were motivated by the emergence of numerous unexplained phenomena, such as divorce rate increases, cohabitation, which young couples considered as an alternative to marriage, and the simultaneous increase in births out of wedlock and decline in fertility (Pitrou, 1994). Motivated by their own interests, but also by the government's concern with finding solutions to these new social "problems," most scholars in the social sciences used the individual family member and his or her subjectivity as the starting point of their research, thereby rebuffing the abstract determinism of traditional analytical frameworks. This more "individualistic" approach to the family brought about studies of such subjects as the couple or parental relations, which were examined most often from the perspective of a single socioeconomic variable such as age, gender or genealogical position. Some examples of studies in this new current of thought included research conducted on the family from several perspectives: that of the life courses of women in the family and the professional world (Kempeneers, St-Pierre, 1992; Le Bourdais, Desrosiers, 1988); from the point of view of the role of maternity and new reproductive technologies (Gauvreau, 1991; Lavigne, 1983; Ouellette, 1988); and from the point of view of the absence of children (Carmel, 1990; Guilbert, 1992). Numerous studies have looked at parental relations, including those of single-parent families, bi-parent families and multi-parent families (Le Bourdais, Rose, 1986; Dandurand, St-Jean, 1988), as well as marital relations (i.e. marriage, divorce, separation and free unions) with regard to task-sharing (Mercier, 1992; Vandelac et al., 1985) or love relations (Hurtubise, 1992).

The concepts of "children," "the young," and "the aged" have also attracted researchers' attention. Some studies have looked at the aged and the issues of autonomy and of family care-taking (Légaré, Marcil-Gratton, 1988); and others have analyzed the young and their aspirations (Bernier, 1986; 1990) and poverty (Gauthier, 1988). Thus, the decompartmentalization of the family as a research field occurred through a proliferation of studies on a wide range of topics.

These studies have had repercussions on our way of examining the family. There can be no denying that the results of the many analyses undertaken in recent years have provided us with greater and more accurate knowledge of the realities of Quebec families. This theoretical resurgence has also engendered a number of developments with regard to methodological issues. Many sociologists have revived the used of qualitative methods such as diaries, while demographers have emphasized the importance of longitudinal analyses and of more detailed studies.

By concentrating on individual family members instead of looking at the family as a series of complex interrelationships, these studies (which have often been incomplete) have had a tendency to favour the emergence of independent fields of research (Kempeneers, 1995). However, certain domains have been neglected more than others, as Agnès Pitrou has pointed out, citing the example of the lack of attention paid to paternity in research on the family, and the biases that result from it:

> Approaches have a tendency to consider men's individual and collective strate-
> gies as if they were static, or a constant point of reference, whereas women's
> strategies are viewed as flexible and mobile. (Pitrou, 1994: 7). (Our translation.)

Current trends in the sociology of the family seem to be heading in a different direction. Numerous studies position themselves at the crossroads of the subjectivity of individuals and families, which are viewed as social agents. Families are thus examined in terms of the relations among nuclear and extended family members in a more general context, taking into account spacial and temporal dimensions. Research dealing with the collective memory of the family, intergenerational relations and the transmission of material and symbolic values are particularly noteworthy, as they allow one to study the family while taking into account not only the ties between individual family members and the subjectivity of agents involved (through material and symbolic dimensions), but also the continuity of family units with respect to both time and space. Relationships among family members are central to all these questions. It should be noted that, in recent years, researchers have shown renewed interest in the study of Quebec's social networks. These developments have led to a reworking of theoretical frameworks in which new models have been developed to explain the cooperation between families and their network structures on the one hand, and the state on the other (Lesemann, Chaume, 1989). In this context, families are considered to be groups of social agents belonging to large informal support networks that differ from one social class to the next and function on the basis of their economic interests and objectives (Dandurand, Ouellette, 1992). Consequently, the state is expected to take the specific and pluralistic traits of these networks into consideration in the management and organization of assistance programmes.

The decompartmentalization of this field of research has provided new insights into the relationship between the family, work, various institutions (especially education) and social policies. Moreover, there appears to be a certain openness on the part of researchers toward disciplines other than those which have traditionally informed our knowledge of the sociology of the family, namely demography, anthropology, psychology, social work, history and feminist studies. Indeed, a number of new disciplines have recently been added to this list. In particular, there are a growing number of studies being conducted in family law, as well as in the field of urban studies, where the family is examined from a geographical point of view (Teasdale and Wexler, 1992). The contribution of these disciplines will no doubt open up new areas of exploration in the sociology of the family. However, it still remains to be seen what directions these will take.

BIBLIOGRAPHY

Bawin-Legros, B., Sommer M., "Famille/familles : difficiles et mouvantes typologies," in *Revue internationale d'action communautaire,* 18/58, 1987, pp. 47-55.

Belleau, H., "L'articulation des rapports individu/famille/État dans les représentations du lien parental," in F.R. Ouellette and C. Bariteau (eds.), *Entre tradition et universalisme.* *Québec:* Institut québécois de recherche sur la culture, 1994, pp. 273-283.

Bernier, L. "Les jeunes, les conditions de leur devenir et la place de la famille," in *L'action nationale,* 18: 4, 1990.

Bernier, L. "Tant qu'ils choisiront de vieillir... Point de vue sur les aspirations des jeunes," in F. Dumont (ed.), *Une société de jeunes?* Québec: Institut québécois de recherche sur la culture, 1986, pp. 29-44.

Bohémier, A. "Le droit de la famille au Québec," in *Relations,* 305, 1966, pp. 32-136.

Bouchard, G., Lalou, R. "La surfécondité des couples québécois depuis le XVIIe siécle, essai de mesure d'interprétation," in *Recherches sociographiques,* 34: 1, 1993, pp. 9-44.

Carmel, M. *Ces femmes qui n'en veulent pas. Enquête sur la non-maternité volontaire au Québec.* Montréal: Saint-Martin, 1990.

Clio (ed.) *L'Histoire des femmes au Québec depuis quatre siècles.* Montréal: Ed. Quinze, 1982, p. 521.

Comité ministériel permanent du développement social, *Livre Vert : Pour les familles québécoises : document de consultation sur la politique familiale.* Québec: Gouvernement du Québec, 1984.

Conseil des affaires sociales et de la famille. *Inventaire des principales mesures et actions du gouvernement du Québec à l'égard des familles.* Québec: Gouvernement du Québec, CASF, 1982.

Dandurand, R.B. "Femmes et familles : sous le signe du paradoxe," in *Recherches féministes : familles,* 7: 1, 1994, pp. 1-21.

Dandurand, R.B. "Le couple : les transformations de la conjugalité," in D. Lemieux (ed.) *Familles d'aujourd'hui.* Québec: IQRC, 1990, pp. 23-41.

Dandurand, R.B. *Le mariage en question.* Québec: IQRC, 1988, pp. 188.

Dandurand, R.B. "Une politique familiale, enjeux et débats," in *Recherches sociographiques,* 28: 2-3, 1987, pp. 349-70.

Dandurand, R.B., Bernier, L., Lemieux, D., Dulac, G. *Le désir d'enfant : Du projet à la réalisation*. Québec: Institut québécois de recherche sur la culture, 1994.

Dandurand, R.B., Ouellette, F.R. "Famille, Etat et structuration d'un champ familial," in *Sociologie et sociétés*, 27: 2, 1995, pp. 103-19.

Dandurand, R.B., Ouellette, F.R. *Entre autonomie et solidarité. Parenté et soutien dans la vie de jeunes familles montréalaises*. Québec: Institut québécois de recherche sur la culture, 1992.

Dandurand R.B., St-Jean, L. *Des mères sans alliance. Monoparentalité et désunions conjugales*. Québec: Institut québécois de recherche sur la culture, 1988.

Dandurand R.B., St-Jean, L. "La nouvelle monoparentalité comme révélateur des contradictions familiales," in *La morphologie sociale en mutation au Québec*. Québec: Presses de l'Université du Québec, 1986, pp. 125-39.

Deleury, E., Cloutier, A., Binet, L. *Grandir à l'ombre de la famille et de l'Etat : rapport de recherche*. Ste-Foy: Centre de recherche sur les droits et libertés, Faculté de droit, Université Laval, 1985.

Desjardins, G. "La pédagogie du sexe: un aspect du discours catholique sur la sexualité au Québec (1930-1960)," in *Revue d'histoire de l'Amérique Française*, 43: 3, 1990, pp. 381-401.

Dumont, F., Langlois, S., and Martin, Y. *Traité des problèmes sociaux*. Québec: Institut québécois de recherche sur la culture, 1995.

Fahmy-Eid, N., Laurin-Frenette, N. "Théories de la famille et rapports famille/pouvoirs dans le secteur éducatif au Québec et en France, 1850-1960," in N. Fahmy-Eid and M. Dumont (eds.), *Maîtresses de maison, maîtresses d'écoles*. Montréal: Boréal Express, 1983, pp. 339-62.

Gauthier, M. *Les jeunes chômeurs*. Une enquête. Québec: Institut québécois de recherche sur la culture, 1988.

Gauvreau, D. "Destins de femmes, destins de mères: images et réalités historiques de la maternité au Québec," in *Recherches sociographiques*, 32: 3, 1991, pp. 321-46.

Goode, W.J. *World Revolution and Family Patterns*. New York: The Free Press, 1963.

Guberman, N. "Discours de responsabilisation de la famille et retrait de l'Etat-providence," in R.B. Dandurand (ed.), *Couples et parents des années quatre-vingt*. Québec: IQRC, Question de Culture, 1987, pp. 193-208.

Henripin, J. *Naître ou ne pas être*. Québec: Institut québécois de recherche sur la culture, 1989.

Henripin, J. *Les enfants qu'on n'a plus au Québec*. Montréal: Presses de l'Université de Montréal, 1981.

Hurtubise, R. "Être amoureux et le dire : à propos des rapports amoureux," in *Revue internationale d'action communautaire*, 27/67, 1992, pp. 39-49.

Joyal, R. "La famille entre l'éclatement et le renouveau : la réponse du législateur," in R.B. Dandurand (ed.), *Couples et parents des années quatre-vingt.* Québec: Institut québécois de la recherche sur la culture, 1987.

Kellerhals, J. "Diversité et diversification des types de familles dans les pays industrialisés," in *Les Familles d'aujourd'hui,* Colloquium held in Geneva Sept. 17-20, 1984. Association internationale des démographes de langue française, AIDELF, 1984, pp. 91-128.

Kellerhals, J., Troutot, P.Y., Lazega, E. *Microsociologie de la famille.* Paris: Presses Universitaires de France, 1984.

Kempeneers, M. "Présentation," in *Sociologie et sociétés,* 27: 2, 1995, pp. 3-8.

Kempeneers, M., St-Pierre, M.H. "Discontinuité profesionnelle et charges familiales : le poids de la famille en question," in R.B. Dandurand and F. Descarries (eds.), *Mères et travailleuses. De l'exception à la règle.* Québec: Institut québécois de recherche sur la culture, 1992, pp. 45-76.

Lapierre-Adamcyk E., Péron, Y. "Familles et enfants au Québec : La toile de fond démographique," in *Santé mentale au Québec,* 8: 2, 1983, pp. 27-42.

Lavigne, M. "Réflexions autour de la fertilité des Québécoises," in M. Dumont and N. Fahmy-Eid (eds.), *Maîtresses de maison, maîtresses d'école.* Montréal: Boréal Express, 1983, pp. 319-38.

Le Bourdais, C., Hamel, P.J., Bernard, P. "Le travail et l'ouvrage. Charge et partage des tâches domestiques chex les couples québécois," in *Sociologie et sociétés,* 19: 1, 1987, pp. 37-56.

Le Bourdais, C., Desrosiers, H. *Trajectoire démographiques et professionnelles : une analyse longitudinale des processus et des déterminants.* Montréal: INRS-Urbanisation, 1988.

Le Bourdais, C., Rose, D. "Les familles monoparentales et la pauvreté," in *Revue internationale d'action communautaire,* 16/56. 1986, pp. 181-89.

Légaré, J., Marcil-Gratton, N. *Les réseaux de soutien pour les personnes âgées de demain: ce qu'onpeut attendre du réseau familial.* Montréal: Université de Montréal, 1988.

Lesemann, F., Chaume, C. *Familles-providence : La part de l'État.* Montréal: Eds. Saint-Martin, 1989.

Menahem, G. "Les mutations de la famille et les modes de reproduction de la force de travail," in *L'homme et la société,* 51-54, 1979, pp. 63-101.

Mercier, L. "Le quotidien et le partage tâches," in D. Lemieux (ed.), *Familles d'aujourd'hui.* Québec: Institut québecois de recherche sur la culture, 1992, pp. 143-55.

Motard, L., Desrochers, L. *Les Québécoises déchiffrées. Portrait statistique.* Québec: Conseil du statut de la femme, Les publications du Québec, 1995.

Ouellette, F.R., "Modernité, filiation et pratiques d'adoption," in F.R. Ouellette and C. Bariteau (eds.), *Entre tradition et universalisme* (Québec: Institut Québécois de recherche sur la culture, 1994), pp. 259-72.

Ouellette, F.R., Bariteau, C. "L'expérience de l'infertilité féminine vécue sous expérience médicale," in *Sociologie et sociétés,* 20: 1, 1988, pp. 13-52.

Péron, Y., Lapierre-Adamcyk E., Morissette, D. "Le changement familial: aspects démographiques," in *Recherches sociographiques,* 28: 2-3, 1987, pp. 317-39.

Pitrou, A. "Introduction," in G. Pronovost (ed.), *Comprendre la famille,* Acts of the 2nd Symposium québécois de recherche sur la famille. Québec: Presses de l'Université du Québec, 1994, pp. 1-11.

Pitrou, A. "Conclusion," in D. Lemieux (ed.), *Familles d'aujourd'hui.* Québec: Institut québecois de recherche sur la culture, 1992, pp. 225-31.

Pitrou, A. "La notion de projet familial : conditions de vie et stratégies familiales à court et à long terme," in B. Bawin-Legros (ed.), *La dynamique familiale et les constructions sociales du temps.* Liège: Université de Liège, 1987.

Ravanera, Z.R., Rajulton F., Burch, T.K. "Tracing the Life Courses of Canadians," in *Canadian Studies in Population,* 21: 1, 1994, p. 21-34.

Roussel, L. *La famille incertaine.* Paris: Editions Odile Jacob, 1989.

Roussel, L. "Mariages and divorces. Contribution à une analyse systématique des modèles matrimoniaux," in *Population,* 35: 6, 1980, pp. 1025-40.

Secrétariat à la famille. *Familles en tête : Plan d'action en matière de politique familiale 1989-1991.* Québec: Editeur officiel du Québec, 1989.

Secrétariat à la politique familiale. *La politique familiale. Énoncé des orientations et de la dynamique administrative.* Québec: Ministère de la Santé et des Services Sociaux, Gouvernement du Québec, 1987.

Secrétariat à la politique familiale. *Le soutien collectif recommandé pour les parents québécois: rapport de consultation sur la politique familiale, deuxième partie.* Québec: Comité de consultation sur la politique familiale, 1986.

Secrétariat à la politique familiale. *Le soutien collectif réclamé pour les familles québécoises: rapport de consultation sur la politique familiale, première partie.* Québec: Gouvernement du Québec, 1985.

Teasdale, P., Wexler, M. "Dynamique de la famille, ajustements résidentiels et souplesse du logement," in D. Lemieux (ed.), *Familles d'aujourd'hui.* Québec: Institut québecois de recherche sur la culture, 1992, pp. 117-42.

Valois, J. *Sociologie de la famille au Québec.* Montréal: Centre Educatif et Culturel Inc, 1993.

Vandelac, L., Delisle, D., Gauthier A., Pinard Y. (eds.), *Du travail et de l'amour.* Montréal: Editions Saint-Martin, 1985.

TODAY'S WOMEN

To assess the situation of women in Quebec today one needs to focus attention on the transformations that have occurred in family life, the workplace and in politics. These three parameters indicate the course of this evolution over the past three decades and provide a basis for discussion that is supported by statistical data. They testify to transformations that may be perceived as positive if one considers that the path of women's emancipation has brought about women's release from familial confinement and inclusion in the male-dominated spheres of work and politics. But beyond this perspective of "catching up" or alignment (still relatively uneven) of the situation of women with respect to that of men, it is obvious that certain issues (still too difficult to define) continue to arise. A particular case in point is the family, which has long been dismissed as a sub-political issue. However, without wishing to give new life to the 1970s slogan that "the personal is political," one wonders today whether the family is not the barometer of social relations, given the transformations that it is undergoing.

THE CONTEXT

Serge Moscovici (1994: 389-90) recently noted that the ongoing metamorphosis of the family

> "heralds the complete dilution of paternity in contemporary society.... The social pact of paternity is rejected, the rituals and rules that consecrate filiation are ignored. In reality, all the evidence seems to point to a rebirth of societies based on affiliation, which can better satisfy the desire for freedom and individuality in our culture." (Our translation.)

The challenge to the traditional representation of paternity as the cornerstone of the family has more than merely sociological implications. Above all, it is a manifestation of the link between filiation and politics, which could be concealed as long as the assimilation of women into the sphere of motherhood resulted in women's exclusion from the public sphere.

We submit that the fact that women's access to full citizenship—in civic terms (right to vote and eligibility) as well as civil terms (abolition of laws and regulations hindering women's civil equality, establishing, for example, equality in the face of divorce and parental authority in lieu of authority of the father)—coincided with the recognition of their right to control their fertility shows the need to theoretically reconsider the relationship between the public and private spheres, between the political and the family. We will not attempt to prove this hypothesis in this, a chapter intended as a survey of the situation of women. However, the mere fact that women are examined as a separate theme, in a chapter of their own, shows that we have not yet broken free of the model that views women as a distinct group.

To make matters more complicated, this chapter is part of a volume that, among other things, is attempt to explain Quebec's distinct character. But, from whom, we may ask, are women distinct? And Quebec is distinct with respect to what? Paradoxically, this double marginalization of women probably does not strengthen their situation. In the 1970s, Quebec women had the historic "opportunity" of mobilizing around an international movement of women's liberation—an opportunity that women involved in the decolonization movements of the 1950s and 1960s did not have. The internationalization of the feminist movement helped Quebec women carve out an identity above all as "women," whereas Quebec's "national liberation movement" grew out of old ethnic nationalism. Moreover, the emergence of Quebec's feminist movement has no doubt contributed significantly to the shift, during the 1980s, from a representation of Quebec in terms of a "global society" founded in the Quiet Revolution to that of a "society of individuals" (Thériault, 1994).

But Quebec women, like women elsewhere, did not wait until the 1970s to demand access to the public sphere. As early as the beginning of the century, women attempted to use French-Canadian nationalism to improve their situation (Cohen, 1992). Because the nationalists needed women to succeed in their crusade, women were portrayed as guardians of the faith and language, and were given the role of preserving and promoting the national heritage threatened by industrialization and urbanization, marked by Anglo-Protestantism. This alliance, however, did not extend to the political promotion of women. For example, the diatribes of Henri Bourassa, founder of the Montreal daily *Le Devoir*, against women's right to vote are well known. Nonetheless, women contributed to establishing a new public stance within "civil society" in which the French-Canadian identity was no longer defined in terms of the Catholic Church alone. This paved the way for the secularization of Quebec, a process which did not happen overnight but in the years before the Quiet Revolution. At this time, in addition to being vested with the role of protector of values, women constituted a secular centre of attraction which helped to move Quebec society toward modernity. To observe how this occurred, one must look at what was going on behind the scenes, beyond the issue of the right to vote.

The 1970s marked a turning point for the feminist movement, not only because the movement unfolded within a more "modern" nationalism, but also because, as in other Western countries, it emerged in the tide of the 1960s protest movements and in a period of economic prosperity that was supported by the welfare state and an expanding services sector which required an increasingly educated female workforce liberated from some of its household chores. As in other Western countries, the feminist movement's principal cause revolved around the right to contraception and free choice concerning abortion. In Quebec, the amendments to the Civil Code and the opening of the "Lazure" abortion clinics date back to the same year, 1980.

These various points demonstrate that women, and their movements, do not merely absorb the effects of social and political transformations; rather, not only do they support these transformations, but they are also actively involved in bringing them about. If Quebec ever succeeds in formulating the identity question from a perspective of "constitutional patriotism" as defined by Habermas, it would certainly owe it in part to Quebec women, who have had to face the never-ending dilemmas between "equality" and "difference." Although women have not yet resolved these dilemmas, it is they who have put the question that transcends social relations between the sexes in the forefront of social debate. To support this hypothesis, let us now provide an overview of the situation of women in Quebec society today.

WOMEN INSIDE AND OUTSIDE THE FAMILY

Today, fewer and fewer Quebec women are entering into the bonds of marriage. Moreover, since the adoption of the Quebec Charter of Human Rights and Freedoms and the successive amendments to the Civil Code of Quebec beginning in the early 1980s, all the legal conditions are fulfilled for the application of section 47 of the Charter, which states that: "Husband and wife have, in the marriage, the same rights, obligations and responsibilities. Together they provide the moral guidance and material support of the family and the education of their common offspring." For example, the provisions pertaining to married names are a form of legal recognition of women's identity. Also, the provisions concerning children, who may take the mother's name, have put an end to patrilineal monopoly. Joint material support of the family is not an empty term, given the latest statistics which reveal that 70% of mothers whose children are less than 16 years old have a job (compared with only 48% in 1981).

Even if marriage is no longer a tether, compared with other Canadian provinces, Quebec has by far the smallest proportion of families structured around the married couple, at only 69.4% of Quebec families. The province with the next closest proportion is Nova Scotia with 78.2%; Newfoundland and Saskatchewan are both in first place with 81.4%. When looking only at families with children, two-parent married families account for 67.6% of all families in Quebec. We recall that civil marriage ceremonies alone became legal in the province only in 1968. Although the vast majority of ceremonies are still religious, the rate of civil ceremonies is rising: from 4% in 1970, to 19% in 1980, and 28% in 1990.

"Common-law"[1] families are therefore more numerous in Quebec than in any other Canadian province: in Quebec, they constitute 16.3% of "husband-wife families;" British Columbia holds second place with only 9.6%; and Prince Edward Island comes last with 6.0%. Common-law families with children represent 10.8% of all families with children in Quebec.

With regard to the proportion of "lone-parent families," Quebec does not stand out as much, though it still occupies first place with 14.3%; Nova Scotia is in second place with 13.5%; and Saskatchewan is last with 11.7%. However, if we consider only those families with single children of all ages, the proportion of lone-parent families in 1971 was 13.2% in Canada and 13.4% in Quebec. Since then, the gap has tended to widen: 16.6% in Canada and 17.6% in Quebec in 1981; 20% in Canada and 21.6% in Quebec in 1991 (see Valois, 1993: 219). It is estimated that over 80% of lone-parent families are headed by women, but this figure rises to over 90% when the children are less than 13 years old. In 1991, "matricentric" lone-parent families represented 17.7% of all families with children and "patricentric" lone-parent families 3.9% of families.

Women, as well as mothers, are therefore becoming more "free" of all formal ties of male appropriation. Concurrent with the demise of marriage, the birth rate has remained below the population replacement level since the end of the 1960s: the measure of fertility has dropped from 3.07 in 1965, to 1.58 in 1989. The measure reached its lowest level in 1987, when it dipped to 1.41. At that time, the decreases in first and second children were responsible for much of this decline. The number of "single-child" families has risen constantly: from 29% in 1971, to 38% in 1981, and to 44% in 1991. Thus fewer women are marrying and they are having fewer children. Since 1981 the Civil Code no longer distinguishes between legitimate and "natural" children. From this moment on, a net growth in the number of births out of wedlock has been recorded. In 1961 these births accounted for only 3.6% of all births; from 15.6% in 1981, this figure went up to 27.2% in 1986, and reached 40.8% in 1991.

Thus, without even mentioning divorce, it seems that the "traditional" foundations of the Quebec family—union symbolized by marriage, rituals characterizing the eruption of the social sphere into the private sphere, and patrilineal filiation (i.e. "the father is the wife's husband")—are clearly being challenged. And while most Quebecers who choose to marry do so in church, this does not prevent them from disobeying the Pope and divorcing in large numbers: one out of every two marriages ends in divorce (the measure of divorce was 49.6 in 1991).

Concurrent with these indications of the demise of the fundamental principles of "the traditional family" is the fact that women are becoming more educated. Today women make up 55% of all high school graduates and 57% of college graduates. At the university level, the female population has climbed

---

[1] This is the term used by Statistics Canada (document 89-523E) to refer to unmarried couples. It should be used with greater caution to the extent that this type of union is itself becoming increasingly regulated, e.g., partition of the patrimony in the event of separation.

from 20% in 1960 to 57% in the early 1990s. Women represent 54% of the undergraduate student body and, while they are still a minority at the graduate levels, they nevertheless account for 45% of master's students and 36% of doctoral students. As a general rule, girls seem to be clearly less affected than boys by the "drop-out" problem. Yet, for all these changes, the tendency still exists for gender differentiation in terms of programme of studies. At the CEGEP level, although we see a male/female ratio in the sciences of 54: 46, the gap is much wider in three-year career programmes: 86:14 in physical science technologies; 29: 71 in social science technologies. At the university level, female students clearly form a majority in the health sciences (74%), in education (71%), and in the social sciences (62%). While they are a minority in the applied sciences (24%), their integration into the pure sciences is noteworthy (44%).

In terms of employment, 55% of Quebec women have an occupation and, as was said earlier, 70% of mothers with children less than 16 years of age have a job (compared with 48% in 1981). In 1992, women formed a majority (51.3%) of the membership of professional corporations. This fact can be explained by the presence of the nurse's corporation which has by far the largest membership (27% of all professional corporations) and a strong female representation (91.6%). Statistics also show that women have made noticeable breakthroughs in some of the more prestigious and historically male-dominated professional corporations: between 1986 and 1992, the percentage of women rose from 10.3% to 17% among architects; from 24.2% to 36.7% among notaries; from 24.2% to 33.1% among lawyers; from 3.1% to 10.2% among certified managers; from 11.8% to 21.4% among chartered accountants; and even from 2.8% to 5.4% among engineers.

All of these factors, i.e. the loosening of legal constraints on the family and improvements in education and employment, the latter of which could stand to be qualified,[2] point to a serious trend: the individuation of Quebec women. But, for all these changes, do women have the same status as citizens as men do? The answer to this question must be put in context.

First, with respect to the family, it must be noted that the observed transformations all point in one direction: that women are assigned greater, and graver, responsibilities. Women who live in two-parent families not only assume much of the moral-guidance function and, in most cases, much of the material-support function of household labour, but they are also obliged to work outside the home. Their financial contribution to the family is not compensated by a proportional relief of household labour, even if access to domestic appliances and modifications to the nature of labour power[3] have altered the

---

[2] For example, the proportion of part-time employment for women—see Desrosiers and Le Bourdais (1991)—without mentioning persistent pay inequities between men and women.

[3] From the evolution of labour power for industry, which ultimately required the presence of a third force because of its more "physical" nature, to the evolution of labour power for the more individualized tertiary sector, e.g. night courses, remedial courses, etc. (see Tahon, 1994).

volume of household labour. The assignment of women to employment and to domestic responsibilities has diverse repercussions, including a less visible presence in managing the affairs of society in general.

Moreover, a large proportion of women who are confronted with the role of sole guardianship of children are condemned to poverty. In 1990, two-parent families in Quebec had an income of $53,148, compared with an average income of $35,648 for patricentric families, and an average income of only $22,015 for matricentric families. Furthermore, lone-parent families constitute 70% of all families with children receiving welfare assistance. Beyond their extremely precarious financial state, these women are subjected to social-state control of their "private lives" which encroaches on their status as "independent" individuals.

WOMEN AND POLITICS

To address this issue it is necessary to look into the conditions that have made women's exclusion from politics possible. This investigation gives rise to slightly different interpretations on the part of political scientists (see Gingras, Maillé and Tardy, 1989; Cohen, 1994, 1987, 1981). Ever since women received the right to vote, three criteria have been used to measure their representation in politics: women's nomination to elective positions, women's participation in elections, and the development of programmes taking into account (or not) feminist demands. These criteria—established by critical feminist theory of the 1970s to challenge the pretensions of universality and neutrality of the political system— make it possible to assess the state of women's participation in electoral life.

An analysis of women's nomination to elective positions (Maillé, 1990) provides an overall statistical picture of female candidacies (elected and non-elected) and of women's participation in parties, as well as a profile of female political personnel (Drouilly, Dorion, 1988; Drouilly, 1990). Based on the regular integration model, these analyses show that women follow the same avenue as men to gain access to the elective process, but that women advance more slowly along the road to power in terms of their elected numbers.

The quantitative data conceal the fact that women must adapt to a political world that claims to be asexual. The progress achieved (which has been slow, cyclical and not necessarily unrelated to the number of female candidates and elected members) shows that women have made breakthroughs in achieving political office. While participation in the process itself is still characterized by glaring differences between men and women, a number of important transformations have occurred during the past 20 years.

Until the 1968 elections, women's participation was only symbolic: the number of candidates never exceeded the low teens (less than 3%); only Claire Kirkland-Casgrain managed to get elected to the National Assembly in 1961. Lise Bacon, President of the Liberal Party of Quebec between 1970 and 1973 (Lévesque, 1993), was still the only woman to sit in the National Assembly between 1973 and 1976. However, women represented 19.8% of all candidates in the 1985 provincial elections, and 14.8% in the 1984 federal elections. During these elections the proportion of newly elected women (20.6%) surpassed that of men elected for the first time (15.6%). Thus, the 1980s marked a turning point defined in the numerous women who became involved in the elective process, which was a direct result of the dissemination of feminism among women. But it was also due to an opening of political parties to women, who viewed this move as a commitment to renewal.

Female candidates had, until then, been confined to third parties, and therefore had little chance of being elected: less than one in three to Quebec City, and less than one in four to Ottawa (the probability for men was twice as high). The situation changed dramatically in 1984 and in 1985.

The two Liberal parties welcomed female candidates to run in ridings where they had good chances of winning. Although the rate of female candidacies remained clearly low, their chances of being elected were more than proportional to it. Fourteen female candidates were elected to the House of Commons in 1984, and eighteen to the National Assembly in 1985. This first group of female elected representatives can no doubt be seen as a "caution to a male political system that requires legitimacy and legitimation on the issue of women" (Drouilly, Dorion, 1988: 27). (Our translation.) But it also indicates that the parties themselves had become aware of the necessity to revise their partisan structures.

In any case, it was clear that the major parties had begun to consider female candidacies more seriously. As a result, the feminization process of Parliament took root more rapidly in Quebec than in the other Canadian provinces, and Quebec had a relatively greater female representation than the other provinces in the federal Parliament. One wonders whether Quebec feminists do not tend to rally more around political parties to have their demands met, while English-Canadian feminists rely more on the Canadian Charter of Rights and Freedoms. Are the ties between feminists and provincial political institutions stronger in Quebec than in other provinces? If so, is this due to the province's particular context? Is it an indication of a shift away from the identity question to "constitutional patriotism"?

These questions cannot be met with a simple answer. Neither can they be tackled without reference to the political context in which the Quebec feminist movement and its different tendencies evolved (Lanctôt, 1980; Lamoureux, 1986). Here we will emphasize only a few elements with direct political implications.

Feminism began to integrate into Quebec political life when the Parti Québécois government, elected in 1976, created a Ministry of the Status of Women, headed by Lise Payette. There were, of course, precedents to such an alliance between women's social movements and political parties: the suffrage movement with the Liberal Party, and Thérèse Casgrain with the Cooperative Commonwealth Federation (CCF) (Trofimenkoff, 1985).

The alliances between militant suffragettes and the Liberal Party, and between the feminist movement and the Parti Québécois have shaped the political culture of Quebec women (Bashevkin, 1983). In contrast to the politically ambivalent attitude of English-Canadian women (Bashevkin, 1985) who waver between adherence to an autonomous, independent social movement and integration into the workings of a political party, the attitude of Quebec feminists seems to be characterized by attachment to partisan politics. The cohesion of the community in Quebec around specific values still seems prevalent enough for feminists to remain hopeful that their aspirations can be embraced by political parties.

The "Yvette affair"[4] of 1980 clearly illustrates women's attachment to political parties. For feminist supporters of the Parti Québécois, the project of equality between men and women went hand in hand with the proposition of independence submitted to a referendum in 1980. Lise Payette's blunder was to reject women who did not adopt this vision of Quebec or this societal project, pushing them into the pre-feminist folds of the Liberal Party. The Liberal Party and its female supporters managed to capitalize on the incident, thereby renewing its ties with women's groups.

Even though Quebec and English-Canadian women draw their inspiration from the same sources of North American feminism, it seems that the difference in their political practices is based on factors related to culture or community. This would explain, for example, the opposition or indifference of Quebec feminists to the enshrinement of their legal equality in the Canadian Charter of Rights and Freedoms, which was firmly demanded by English-Canadian women (Les Cahiers de la femme, 1992). Quebec feminists could not join their ranks without renouncing their adherence to Quebec's emerging political community. Thus, by strongly supporting the Quebec Charter of Human Rights and Freedoms, Quebec women expressed a twofold aspiration for sexual equality and independence.

The 1980s saw Quebec women make breakthroughs in the political arena as a result of the mobilization of the feminist movement. This would seem to confirm that a social movement can efficiently exert pressure on political parties (even traditional and refractory ones) as well as support the integration of those individuals it represents. But should this still be viewed as a major or profound transformation? Should this conquest of political power be understood, as Chantal Maillé (1991) suggests, as a concrete reversal of women's exclusion from positions of power? The last federal elections, held in 1993, should dampen all optimism. These elections were characterized by silence regarding women's problems and issues. The concerns of women were ignored by most (but especially female) candidates. Indeed, female candidates, including Kim Campbell, who was briefly Canada's prime minister, wanted to be treated like "everybody else," least of all like women. Feminist demands such as universal daycare services, social security for the underprivileged, job sharing, etc. were

---

[4] Lise Payette, then Minister of the Status of Women, derogatively referred to some female federalist supporters as "Yvette," a name once used in readers to refer to a well-behaved, traditional girl who worked in the home.

dismissed as the utopian dreams of a rich country that has henceforth convert-
ed to the "debt culture" (Martin, Savidan, 1994). Only the New Democrats,
already in a tailspin, continued to address women's concerns.

Should this be seen as a political setback for women and their concerns? The
electorate, however, displayed a great deal of political maturity during the 1993
elections. The Bloc Québécois's landslide victory in Quebec clearly demonstrated
that the paths of the national question, feminism and politics had once again
converged. However, the Quebec elections of September 1994, which brought
the current Parti Québécois government to power, did not send a larger number
of women to Parliament. Not only that, but several ridings gave themselves the
luxury of pitting two top-rate women candidates against each other. All the
same, it should be noted that women are responsible for key portfolios for
Quebec's immediate future.

Is this a signal that female candidacies are already being trivialized? Have
political parties already begun retaining candidates only on the basis of competence and of their chances of success in elections, regardless of gender? This
would be an indisputable victory for the principle of democratic universalism. To
be sure, we have not yet reached that stage. But the tendency can no longer be
ignored.

THE ISSUE OF RIGHTS AND CIVIL SOCIETY

Quebec women's rights are safeguarded by the Quebec Charter of Human Rights
and Freedoms, as well as the Canadian Charter of Rights and Freedoms. The
Quebec Charter came into effect in 1976 and was modified in 1982, most
notably to include equal access programmes. The Charter lays down the basic
principles pertaining to women's right to equality: prohibition of harassment
and discrimination based on sex, pregnancy, marital status and sexual orientation with respect to employment, working conditions, salary, housing, and
access to goods and services; prohibition of discriminatory clauses in contracts;
obligation to harmonize legislation with the right to equality; creation of a programme for the protection of rights and freedoms. As a rule, Quebec women
place their trust in their own legal instruments, particularly the Quebec Charter,
and are uninterested in the Canadian Charter. This divergence between
Canadian and Quebec feminists came to light during discussions on the Meech
Lake Accord. As Thérèse Mailloux (1991: 33) noted:

> behind the divergent strategies of Quebec feminists and English-Canadian femi-
> nists are two different perceptions of the state. For the latter, the provincial
> state has often been something to be wary of. They are more likely to address
> their concerns to the federal state and to rely on national strategies, such as the
> Canadian Charter. For Quebec women, their concerns lie primarily with the
> government of Quebec, and it is this government they solicit the most and from
> which they expect the most. They make use of all the legal instruments and

programmes the Quebec state has acquired to make equality a reality, and attach more importance to the positive action taken by their government to improve their social and economic rights. (Our translation.)

According to Hélène Tessier (1991, 18):

the Charter has had considerably more influence on women's rights than nature, as the number of judgments on discrimination will attest. The Charter has contributed to create a sociopsychological environment that has fostered important attitude changes about work, culture, advertizement and education. (Our translation.)

In general terms, one could say there are clearly fewer institutional difficulties limiting Quebec women's access to certain spheres of activity. However, and this does not apply to Quebec alone, it is legitimate to wonder whether it is well founded to rely on the courts to consecrate equality. What is more, and again this limit is not unique to Quebec, women's reliance on the judiciary in itself implies that they must establish themselves as victims of men's discrimination, which tends to foster assimilation into "male values" and to stifle the recognition of "female values" that would enable women to live more comfortably in a mixed society. It would be an exaggeration to claim that these issues are now being debated.

With regard to what is called "civil society," some Quebec women have made remarkable breakthroughs during the 1980s. For example, the current president of the Chambre de Commerce de la Province du Québec and the head of the Centrale de l'Enseignement du Québec (The Quebec Teachers' Federation) are women, and for many years the Montreal Urban Community Transit Commission was headed by a woman. Women have generally made significant progress in terms of representation in union and corporate leadership structures, and are traditionally well represented in "popular movements." They are less underrepresented on the boards of administration of the health and social services network (42.2%[5] in 1992) than on the boards of administration of CEGEPs (26.7% in 1992). In research fields, the arts and the media, women are not in a less favourable position than their colleagues in the rest of the Western world. For example, the directors of the Montreal daily *Le Devoir* and the most prestigious theatre company in Montreal, the TNM, are both women. Nevertheless, feminist intellectuals are clearly less vocal today than a decade ago, and many have grown more silent. One factor probably related to this situation is the tragedy at the Polytechnique where 14 women were killed (December 6, 1989) and the emotional outpouring it engendered, which has been little analyzed, if, indeed, such an analysis were possible.

The proportion of women in senior executive positions in the Quebec civil service is still extremely low despite having risen from 6.5% in March 1986, to 12% in March 1992. These figures are similar in upper-management and senior-executive job categories of the Quebec government: 6.6% in March 1986, and 11.5% in March 1992. Lastly, the proportion of women sitting on the bench has grown from 3.6% in 1983, to 5.7% in 1986, and to 9.1% in 1992 (Desrochers, 1993).

---

[5] It is interesting to note that the proportion of elected women is sigificantly higher (43.3%) than that of appointed women (35.8%).

CONCLUSION

This brief survey of the situation of Quebec women today underscores the fact that while equality between men and women does not yet prevail in the public sphere, significant progress has been achieved, especially in the past ten years. The improvement in the status of women has less to do with the "organized" feminist movement than with a combination of sociopolitical factors (e.g. higher level of education of girls, the need for a second income to maintain the family's standard of living in time of economic crisis) that exist against a background of "popular" feminism. This, however, is not to say that the social and political action of women's groups has not been a powerful catalyst in having their demands recognized by the state and political parties. Indeed, thanks to the feminist movement, today these types of action are also taken by women who do not identify themselves as feminists.

Although Lise Payette left active politics, she maintained a daily television presence as director of a soap opera that ran for several seasons until the spring of 1995. The programme's storyline revolved around a housekeeper, with the fated name of Marilyn, who became municipal counsellor and then City Mayor. In the last episode, Marilyn was offered the position of prime minister. She accepted the offer on the condition that the party not enthrone her like another Kim Campbell. Like Lise Payette's previous programmes, the show emphasized (sometimes in no uncertain terms) traditional female qualities serving a more humane society. Moreover, Marilyn portrayed a street-wise "woman of the people," and some of the male characters personified traditional macho types, whose conduct was ridiculed in contrast with other men who were allies with women. Although the Payette serials will not be remembered for having advanced Quebec culture, their contents are a reflection of a widely shared state of mind.

Must we conclude, then, that the situation of Quebec women is to be envied? We will not go that far. Indeed, we must consider a few sobering points, most notably the growing problem regarding the consideration of women as a single entity (twenty years ago some women even used the term "women's class"). Even after decades of noticeable progress, there can be no denying the clear-cut social distance that exists among women, i.e. between poor women who are generally excluded from the social sphere and women who, somehow or other, have managed to hoist themselves up to similar social levels as men. Parallel to this distance among women is another, in some respects more insidious, distance among men. Indeed, the much-needed public service campaigns against spousal abuse have shed light on a new sociological category, "violent men." If we consider the public's overexposure to media content emphasizing "social work" approaches to the problem (which tend to submerge all sociological debate) and the crusade of certain "sensitive men," it becomes clear that the emergence of this new category is indicative of a deep social fragmentation.

Moreover, one of the most important problems facing Quebec society today has to do with the foundations of the family. For the moment, the general tendency is to denounce everything, from family violence (and rightly so) to men's lack of haste in assuming their share of family responsibilities, to fathers' lack of haste in becoming "good mothers." But certainly the solution has less to do with changing women into men and fathers into mothers, than it does with the imagination required to make room for one and all. It is clear that "traditional" structures have broken down, and that it is not appropriate to rebuild them. However, Quebec's democratic fabric will continue to grow only if it manages to reinforce the necessary separation between the public and private spheres. It will also have to oversee the coexistence of "old-stock" (*pure laine*) Quebecers with other groups without resorting to the sterile concept of multiculturalism. The two themes are intimately related, and are being played out even now. But we must face the ongoing transformations, especially those affecting citizenship guidelines. There will be no avoiding these issues in the debates that will surely arise during the next referendum. In light of women's recent history, Quebec women of all ethnic origins should play a central role in achieving the difficult balance between the recognition of identity and the promotion of a sovereign state liberated from old nationalist demons. In this respect, the path taken by women during the past two decades is promising. Building on their experience, women can stand up and testify to the conditions that must be met to foster a more democratic community.

REFERENCES

Bashevkin, S. 1983. "Social Change and Political Partisanship. The Development of Women's Attitudes in Quebec, 1965-1979," *Comparative Political Studies*, 16: 2, pp. 147-172.

Bashevkin, S. 1985. *Toeing the Lines: Women and Party Politics in English Canada*. Toronto: University of Toronto Press.

Cahiers de la femme, 1992. *Gender equity and institutional change*, 12: 3.

Cohen, Y. (ed.), 1981. *Femmes et politique*. Montréal: Le Jour.

Cohen, Y. (ed.), 1987. *Femmes et contre-pouvoirs*. Montréal: Éditions Boréal.

Cohen, Y., 1992. "Du féminin au féminisme : l'exemple québécois," in *Histoires de femmes*, G. Duby, M. Perrot (eds.), V. Paris: Plon. pp. 521-538.

Cohen, Y. 1994. "Le rôle des mouvements de femmes dans l'élargissement de la citoyenneté au Québec," in *Québec : État et société*, A. Gagnon (ed.). Montréal : Québec-Amérique. pp. 181-202.

Desrochers, L. 1993. *Femmes et pouvoir, La révolution tranquille*. Québec : Les publications du Québec.

Desrosiers, H., Le Bourdais 1991. "La montée du travail à temps partiel féminin : une aide aux mères ou à l'emploi?," in *Femmes et questions démographiques*. Québec: Les publications du Québec. pp. 27-51.

Drouilly, P., Dorion, J. *Candidates, députées et ministres. Les femmes et les élections.* Québec: Bibliothèque de l'Assemblée nationale.

Drouilly, P. 1990. *Répertoire du personnel politique québécois féminin,* 2nd ed.. Québec: Bibliothèque de l'Assemblée nationale.

Gingras, A.M., Maillé, C., Tardy, E. 1989. *Sexe et militantisme.* Montréal: Editions du CIDHICA.

Lamoureux, D. 1986. *Fragments et collages. Essai sur le féminisme québécois des années 70.* Montréal: Editions du Remue-ménage.

Lanctôt, M. 1980. *Le mouvement des femmes.* Master's thesis, Université du Québec à Montréal.

Lévesque, M. "Vingt ans d'action politique féminine : la Fédération des femmes libérales du Québec (1950-1970)," in A. Caron, L. Archambault (eds.), *Thérèse Casgrain, Une femme tenace et engagée.* Sainte-Foy: Presses de l'Université du Québec. pp. 335-53.

Maillé, C. 1990. "Le vote des Québécoises aux élections fédérales et provinciales depuis 1921 : une assiduité insoupçonnée," in *Recherches féministes,* 3: 1, pp. 83-95.

Maillé, C. 1991. *Les Québécoises et la conquête du pouvoir politique.* Montréal: Editions Saint-Martin.

Mailloux, T. 1991. "Le droit à l'égalité de la Charte canadienne des droits et libertés : les perceptions féministes du Canada anglais et du Québec," in *L'égalité : les moyens pour y arriver.* Québec: Les publications du Québec, pp. 25-35.

Martin, P., Savidan, P. 1994. *La culture de la dette.* Montréal: Éditions Boréal.

Moscovici, S. 1994. *La scociété contre nature,* revised and corrected ed. Paris: Le Seuil.

Tahon, M.B. 1994. "La démocratie et le menu du dîner," in *Conjonctures,* 20-21, pp. 163-87.

Thériault, J.Y. 1994. "L'individualisme démocratique et le projet souverainiste," in *Sociologie et sociétés,* XXVI: 2, pp. 191-204.

Trofimenkoff, S.M. 1995. "Thérèse Casgrain and the CCF in Quebec," in *Canadian Historical Review,* 66: 2.

Valois, J. 1993. *Sociologie de la famille au Québec.* Anjou: Centre éducatif et culturel Inc.

MORE HEALTH FOR QUEBECERS MAY MEAN LESS AND DIFFERENT CARE

INTRODUCTION

In the last two decades the standard of health of the Quebec population has improved tremendously. Only thirty years ago, it was among the lowest of the Canadian provinces and other industrialized countries. At present, Quebecers enjoy a high health status which, on several accounts, is comparable to that of other Canadian provinces, superior to that in the United States, and among the best of the industrialized countries.

Most of this improvement has been attributed to Quebec's spectacular development and originality of its health care system. One key feature was to make health care accessible to all Quebecers according to their needs rather than their ability to pay. Its financial investment in health care is, at present, among the highest in the world although reasonable in comparison to that of other Canadian provinces and the United States. However, this investment is still growing faster than that of the province's collective wealth.

Even with such a level of financial support and universal accessibility, the Quebec health care system is facing increasing problems, criticisms and questions. Two questions are becoming predominant: how to deal with the rising costs of health care and determining the extent to which continued increasing investment in health care will contribute to the further improvement of the health of the population. The answers to these questions are changing substantially and are likely to change the Quebec health care system even further in the years to come.

This chapter provides an insight to the development, function, questioning and future trends of the Quebec health care system. The seven sections focus respectively on: (1) recent trends in the health status of Quebecers; (2) development of the Quebec health care system; (3) its main characteristics; (4) the problems it is now facing; (5) their causes; (6) the main thrusts adopted to solve them; and finally, (7) a future perspective.

HEALTH STATUS OF QUEBECERS[1]

Quebec's performance on major health indicators has now reached the Canadian average.

Since 1960, Quebecers' life expectancy has increased by 8.1 years for women (from 72.8 to 80.9) and 6.5 years for men (from 67.3 to 73.8). This compares with the Canadian averages of 6.8 years for women (from 74.2 to 81.0) and 6.2 years for men (from 68.4 to 74.6), and the American averages of 4.2 years (from 73.6 to 78.8) and 4.9 years (from 67.1 to 72.0).

The percentage of life that Quebecers are expected to live free from morbidity and disability is also among the highest in Canada. It is certainly higher than that of the United States. In Quebec, 86% of women's lives and 89% of men's lives are expected to be free from disability and morbidity. This is in comparison to 81% for women and 84% for men in Canada, and 78% and 79% respectively in the United States.

In 1960, the infant mortality rate, at 30 deaths per 1,000 live births, was also high in Quebec in comparison to North American standards. However, by 1991 it had become among the lowest on the continent, at 5.9. It is lower than the Canadian average, 6.4, and substantially lower than that of the United States, at 8.9.

Quebec has achieved major improvements with respect to maternal mortality as well. In 1960, Quebec's performance was one of the worst in Canada. Its maternal mortality rate was 6.2 deaths per 10,000 births, in comparison to 4.5 in Canada. Its rate was more than two times higher than that of the United States, at 2.8. By 1991, Quebec had reached the Canadian average, 0.2, almost four times lower than that of the United States at 0.8.

THE DEVELOPMENT OF THE QUEBEC HEALTH CARE SYSTEM

The development of the Quebec health care system has been rooted in the public recognition and acceptance that health and health care are above all, collective responsibilities and that the state holds a legitimate position to assume these responsibilities. Before 1960, the Quebec health care system was very similar to what exists in the United States. Health and health care were essentially within the realm of individual and family responsibilities. Quebecers paid out of their pocket or through their own health insurance for the care they received. The possible financial burden and catastrophy which could result from a serious disease posed a threat to many Quebecers. The collective responsibility for the population's health was limited to communicable diseases, and that for financing health care was limited to the needy population. Most of the care was provided

---

[1] Health data of this section are from Statistique Canada (1986, 1990, 1991), Pampalon (1994), OCDE (1993c) and Nations-Unis (1992, 1987, 1977).

through community and religious groups, and most health facilities were operated on a private, non-profit, basis. Never, in Quebec history, were health and health care considered a domain for commercial venture.

It was under the impetus of the Canadian government that the Quebec public health care system began its development. The first action of the federal government involved the development of health care resources. It instituted, in 1948, a grant programme to provide provincial governments with funds for health care, of which a considerable share was reserved for the building of hospitals and the development of faculties of medicine at universities (Bergeron and Gagnon, 1994).

Although Quebec objected to these federal initiatives on the grounds that health and health care were, according to the Canadian constitution, provincial jurisdictions, it used the federal financial support to upgrade and develop its obsolete health care infrastructure.

The second federal government action was aimed at increasing health care accessibility to all Canadians. It proposed, in 1957, a fifty-fifty cost-sharing programme to the provinces that would introduce a hospital-based public insurance programme. This federal initiative was not immediately put into practice in Quebec (Bergeron and Gagnon, 1994).

The year 1960 was certainly a benchmark in the evolution of Quebec society as a whole and of its health care system in particular. It was marked by the election of a political party which promoted the idea that Quebecers be "Masters at home." To achieve this self-determination, it promoted the necessity, appropriateness and legitimacy of the government to take collective action to ensure the economic and social development of Quebec. The year 1960 is often referred to as the beginning of the "Quiet Revolution" of Quebec.

The coming to power of this political party greatly influenced the development of the Quebec health care system. This period was marked by the increasing presence of the state in health care resource development, in the introduction of public health care insurance programmes and in the regulation of the health care system.

Quebec adhered, in 1961, to the federal government hospital insurance programme. The number of health care personnel almost tripled in 10 years: from 18,000 in 1960 to 50,000 in 1969 (Turgeon and Anctil, 1994).

A Study Commission (Commission Castonguay-Nepveu (1970), named after the two persons who successively chaired it, was instituted in 1966 to formulate recommendations on how to improve the health of the Quebec population. This commission had tremendous impact on the evolution of the Quebec health care system. Also, it reaffirmed the deep-rooted notion of collective responsibility for both improving the health of the population and ensuring equitable access to health care for all Quebecers. The commission provided the impetus for continuing to develop the publicly financed health care insurance programmes as a condition for improving the population's health. In addition, it proposed the adherence of Quebec to the federal cost-sharing medical insurance programme, which was carried out in 1970. But above all, it reinforced and enlarged the role of the state in the regulation and the organization of the health care system (Bergeron and Gagnon, 1994).

As a result, Quebec undertook a completed restructuring of its health care system whereby most health facilities became public or were required to conform to the same publicly defined rules and regulations (Loi sur les services de santé et les services sociaux, 1971). During the following decades several changes were made to the Quebec health care system (Loi sur les services de santé et les services sociaux, 1991). However, its basic structure and function still follow the fundamental principles originally outlined by the 1970 Study Commission.

MAIN CHARACTERISTICS OF THE QUEBEC HEALTH CARE SYSTEM

Quebec has almost complete autonomy in health and health care matters, since these areas are, according to the Canadian constitution, a provincial matter. Thus, it is the provinces which define which services will be publicly insured and how they will be delivered. But Quebec, as with the other provinces, has had to respect five national principles of the Canada Health Act (1984) to be eligible for its federal share of the financing of health care. These five principles are:

- universality, which means that virtually every person who has residency in Canada is covered;

- comprehensiveness, meaning that every citizen is insured for at least medical and hospital care that is medically needed;

- accessibility, meaning that there should be no direct or indirect financial obstacles to the use of medical and hospital services such as a deductible fee, co-payment, overbilling or user fees;

- portability, which means that, even though people are covered by their own provincial health care insurance program, the coverage is extendable to all provinces; and

- publicly managed, meaning that the insurance programs are managed by public and non-profit organizations.

These five principles have made the 10 provincial health care systems more fundamentally similar than different. However, the contribution of the federal government to the financing of health care has decreased substantially over the last decade, placing a greater share of the burden of paying for health care on the provinces. But, more importantly, it has weakened the federal government's ability to maintain the five basic national principles of the Canadian health care system.

The practice of these principles by Quebec has resulted in the development of a health care system in which 73% of the total costs of health care is paid for through public funding. All residents of Quebec are insured for medical and hospital care without co-payment, deductible, any limit or overbilling. The main source of public funding is through income taxes from both individuals and industry. Private financing is mostly for dental care, drugs and non-medical health services provided in private offices by specialists such as occupational therapists, nutritionists, psychologists, etc.

Medical care is provided mostly by physicians who operate as private entrepreneurs and by non-profit community hospitals which are managed by local boards of trustees. Physicians are mostly paid on a fee-for-services basis, even in hospitals. This mode of remuneration is perceived as providing incentives for the provision of more and more, and sometimes unecessary, care. The provision of care in Quebec is based heavily on hospitals. Hospitals are run on global budgets based essentially on historical reasons and on individual discussions between each hospital and the ministry. The consequences of this type of hospital budgeting has been reasonably good control over cost increases of hospital care but through a rationing of services. This rationing is subject to major criticisms on the part of both the public and the medical profession.

Quebec has succeeded in integrating within a single delivery system, the provision of both health care and social services. It is quite unique in this respect in Canada as well as in industrialized countries. The main reasons for this integration are twofold: first, several emerging or growing problems are considered to be at the junction of both health and social domains, such as AIDS and mental health problems; and second, several health problems require the intervention of both health and social services (for the elderly, handicapped persons, etc.).

The net result is that Canada in general, and Quebec in particular, have developed health care systems which are considered to be among the best in the world. A recent analysis by the Organization for Economic Cooperation and Development (OECD) on the Canadian health care system concluded that Canada occupies, with the nordic countries and Japan, the first ranks among the OECD countries regarding equal accessibilty to health care (OCDE 1993a: 77-78). It also stated that Canada is an example of a country which combines universal health care coverage, cost containment and good health outcomes.

PROBLEMS FACING THE QUEBEC HEALTH CARE SYSTEM

Although the Quebec health care system is part of one of the best health care systems in the world, it is facing major problems. Four of them are of particular importance. The first is its cost. The Quebec health care system is considered to be costly, possibly too costly. Although its cost is relatively low in comparison to other Canadian provinces and the United States, it is very high in comparison to other industrialized countries, particularly the Group of Seven (G7) countries. This is true both in terms of amount of dollars per capita and percentage of gross domestic product (GDP) spent on health care.

In 1991, Quebec was spending $2,174[2] per capita on health care. This was $186 less than the Canadian average ($2,360). These expenditures represented 9.9% of Quebec collective wealth (GDP). The national average (9.9%) was the same. Of these expenditures, 73.1% is assumed through public financing. This is also at the same level as the national average (Santé Canada, 1994a and MSSS, 1994).

Canada has the second most expensive health care system of the G7 countries, after the United States. In 1991, Canada spent $1,915[3] per capita on health care. This is close to $1,000 per capita less than the United States, at $2,876, and more than the United Kingdom, at $1,035. These expenditures represented 10.0%[4] of Canada's collective wealth (GDP). This is substantially lower than the United States (13.4%) but higher than Japan (6.6%) and the United Kingdom (6.6%) (OCDE, 1993c).

If Quebec were to spend on health care at a level comparable to that of the third most expensive G7 countries (Germany in terms of dollars per capita ($1,659) or France in terms of percentage of GDP (9.1%)), its total health care expenditures would have to be reduced by $800 million to $1.2 billion in Canadian dollars. This represents a reduction of between 6% to 9% of its 1991 total expenditures.

The second problem is the inflationary nature of the province's health care system. The internal dynamic of the Quebec health care system leads to the provision of more and more services which are increasingly sophisticated and costly. Between 1987 and 1991, the per capita total health care cost increased by an annual rate of 8.2%. This is higher than the Canadian average (7.7%)(Santé Canada, 1994b).

Canada had the second highest annual rate of net increase of health care costs (4.4% after adjustment for inflation) of the G7 countries, after the United States (4.5%). This is substantially higher than the G7 average (3.5%)(OCDE, 1993c). The net effect for Quebec is that the cost of health care has increased during the last few years at a rate which is four to five times faster than that of its collective wealth. Quebec can afford this rate of increase for a while, but not very long.

The third problem is the difficulty with which the Quebec health care system adapts its services to the changing needs of the population. It had difficulties in adapting its services to emerging and growing problems such as AIDS and mental health and to the needs of growing segments of the population such as

---

[2] Expenditures of Quebec and Canada are in Canadian dollars.

[3] For the G7 countries, expenditures are in $US PPPs (Purchasing Power Parities) (OCDE, 1993c).

[4] In this case, data from OCDE (1993c) for Canada are different from the data of Santé Canada (1994b).

elderly people and ethnic minorities. It also had difficulties in providing services closer to where people live and work, such as remote geographic areas and poor neighbourhoods of city centres. Finally, it had difficulties in providing immediate care, even if delays were only a reasonably short amount of time, to people who present themselves to obtain services.

The fourth and final problem concerns the effectiveness of health care. More and more, health care practitioners are being challenged as to their real contribution to the improvement of the health of the population. There is a growing feeling that if Quebec really wanted to improve the health of its population, the priority should not be on investing more collective resources on health care, at least not on the type of care and the manner in which it is provided at present. Certain indicators are used in support of these challenges. However, it is difficult to show any relationship between the amount of resources countries invest in health care and the health of their population. There seems to be an absence of relationship over time between the improvement in health status of the population of a given country and its investment in health care. There are tremendous variations in the amount of care provided to different segments of a given population which cannot be explained by the health and socio-economic characteristics of the population receiving them. The factors which seem to contribute most to these variations are related to the supply side of health care rather than the consumer side. Finally, there is a growing literature revealing that a great percentage of the care provided is either inappropriate or unnecessary.

This questioning of the health care system in Quebec is quite fundamental. But it is not limited to Quebec or even to Canada. Rather, it is a deep and important problem in a number of industrialized countries.

THE IDENTIFIED CAUSES OF THE PROBLEMS

The Rochon Commission (Commission Rochon, 1988), which studied the functioning of the Quebec health care system between 1985 and 1988, summarized the main cause of these problems. It said:

> Everything in the Quebec health care system operates as if the system had become a prisoner or hostage of the numerous interest groups which evolved in the health care system, and as if the interests of the individuals and the population to be served, the needs to be met, the problems to be solved, in short the common well-being, had been forgotten in lieu of the benefits of these interest groups (Commission Rochon, 1988: 407, translation from the original French test).

Although the Rochon Commission was alone in the way it expressed the main cause of the problems facing the Quebec health care system, several other reports and analyses pointed in the same direction (Gouvernement du Québec, 1989, 1990, 1991, 1992).

Very few reports or analyses considered a lack of money as the main cause of the problems. On the contrary, many of them explicitly mentioned that providing more money to do more of exactly what was being done would not solve the problems being faced, and would be completely ineffective in terms of improving the health of the population, and inefficient in terms of using collective resources. Likewise, few reports or analyses considered the attitude or the behavior of consumers to be the main culprit, including the report concerning the rapidly growing costs of health care, even though abuses by consumers are often mentioned. It has been estimated that consumers' decisions influence directly, at most, 10% of the health care cost. The remaining 90% are decided by health care providers (Stoddart et al., 1993).

Most reports and analyses identified the causes of these problems as being within, not outside, the health care system (Lamarche et al., 1995). Particularly problematic areas include: the ways in which health care systems have been managed over the last 20 years, that is, overcentralized, bureaucratic, rigid, overregulated and inefficient management systems; the overemphasis on curative and institutional care as compared to preventive and ambulatory care; the physicians' mode of practice. In Quebec, the number of physicians is still growing faster than that of the population; their mode of remuneration, fee for service, is perceived as an incentive for providing more and more costly services; and their monopoly over the provision of health care is perceived as being an obstacle for using effective but less costly alternatives such as clinical nurses, assistant-physicians and midwives.

Also pointed out is the overuse of hospitals in the provision of care which could be carried out outside hospitals, and the overuse of technological industries, including drug companies. Although the health benefits of some technological developments are recognized, critics are often in agreement regarding commercial or marketing practices that are believed to lead to overuse or improper use of technologies. Corporations' pricing practices are perceived to cover a lot more than the costs of developing the technologies, and their claims about the relative efficiency of new types of technology are perceived as not always being supported by valid scientific evidence.

In Quebec, as in many other provinces and countries, it is the production side of the health care system which is thought to be the main cause of the problems. It is not the lack of financing and not the consumer. Thus, it is the reform of the production side of its health care system to which Quebec is devoting most of its efforts to solve the problems it is facing.

PRESENT THRUSTS OF THE QUEBEC HEALTH CARE SYSTEM

Major debates are emerging in Quebec as to the extent to which the production side of its health care system can be effectively reformed while respecting the same principles used for developing it. Some argue that the state should continue to use its regulatory power to take the necessary actions while others strongly believe that only a shift to a market-like system would provide the necessary mechanisms and incentives. This debate is intensified by the cutbacks of the federal government in the financing of health care and the loosening of its power in maintaining the five national principles, particularly that regarding accessibility.

So far, Quebec has adhered closely to the fundamental principles in developing its health care system. The province is now attempting to reform the production side of its health care system while maintaining the collective responsibility for improving the health of the population, ensuring equal access to health care to all Quebecers, and by regulating the health care system accordingly. To achieve these goals, a major reform of the Quebec health care system was initiated in 1992. The major thrusts of the changes introduced through this reform are aimed at establishing outcome-oriented goals for the health care system; decentralizing and democratizing its decision-making; shifting the provision of services toward community care; and allocating resources according to the population rather than being producer-based (Gouvernement du Québec, 1990, 1992).

Outcome-oriented Goals

Since the early seventies the Quebec health care system was pursuing only one main objective: ensuring accessibility of quality care to the whole population. As noble as this objective may be, its pursuit so permeated the health care system during the last decades that the "raison d'être" of providing this care was virtually forgotten: that is, solving health problems facing the population.

The pursuit of this objective alone has had three main consequences in terms of the function, development and financing of the Quebec health care system. To begin with, there was no limit to the development of services. Accessibility to quality health care could always be improved, especially when the impact on the health of the population did not have to be proven. The individual, the family and the community were perceived as beneficiaries of services that the health care system magnanimously decided to provide them, instead of being seen as real contributors with a key role in solving the problems affecting their own health. The health care system came to be thought of as the sole contributor to the improvement of the health of the population. Thus, the important contribution of all other sectors of society in improving health had been completely forgotten in the process.

The objective of accessibility to quality services is now being replaced by outcome-oriented objectives, that is, objectives aimed at reducing the incidence and prevalence of concrete, specific health problems facing Quebec's population. This shift from accessibility to outcome-oriented objectives has been initiated through "The Policy on Health and Well-being." This policy was formally adopted by the Quebec government in June 1992 (Gouvernement du Québec, 1992). It formulates 19 specific outcome-oriented objectives that the health care system should aim for. The main purpose of this policy is to urge the health care system to look at problems to be solved rather than only services to be provided.

To further strengthen the emphasis on health, Quebec has created a distinction between the concepts of health and health care. This distinction is based on the premise that health is a domain broader than health care. It encompasses all factors which influence people's physical, psychological and social capabilities to lead socially and economically productive lives. These factors include but extend beyond health care. Given the scope of the factors involved in health, its improvement requires the contribution of many diverse areas.

The concrete manifestation of this differentiation was the creation, in 1994, of two distinct authorities: one for health and one for health care. The health authority is assumed by the Quebec Health and Well-being Council while the health care authority continues to be assumed by the Ministry of Health and Social Services.

Decentralization and Democratization of Decision-making

It became obvious that a main cause of the problems facing the health care system in Quebec was the overcentralization of decision-making in the hands of the Ministry of Health and Social Services. The ministry could not know the needs and preferences of the people better than the people themselves. Similarly, it could not judge the performance of health resources better than the people who are closer to these resources and who see the results.

A major thrust is to bring the decision-making closer to where the "action" is (Gouvernement du Québec, 1990). To do this, Quebec has been divided into 18 health and social services regions. Each region is headed by a Regional Health and Social Services Board. These boards have the power to adopt their own health and well-being priorities, to organize the delivery of health care and the allocation of resources within their region, and to obtain the collaboration of sectors other than health and social services whose action could have an impact on health (environment, education, labor, etc.).

The decision-making within the health care system is not only being decentralized but also democratized. It had become evident that a main reason for the difficulties facing the Quebec health care system was, as diagnosed by the Rochon Commission (1988), the absence of democratic forums for debating and selecting among the multitude of requests, often contradictory, which were coming from the numerous interest groups involved in health care. Through the participation of the public, the Quebec health care reform intended to create a democratic basis for deciding among the requests of these interest groups. Thus, the democratization of decision-making could constitute a counterinfluence to the pressure exerted by these groups.

There are other reasons for increasing the involvement of citizens in decision-making. It is the citizens for whom health care is provided, and they who pay for the costs of care no matter what the form. Therefore, why should they not decide on the orientation of the system? It was also felt necessary to open to the public the debates that were being held and the choices that were being made in health and health care. For the decisions to be credible, legitimate and understood, the choices have to be made public where they can be discussed and debated.

This concept is being put into practice by reorganizing the boards of trustees of health institutions and regional boards to give the majority of seats, and an increasing role, to citizens. These boards are elected by the people themselves. These debates and choices have to be made by people selected by and coming from the specific regions. This is the basis of the legitimacy of boards of trustees and also the likely basis of their influence. Furthermore, all meetings of boards of trustees of all health institutions and regional boards are open to the public, with a period of time specifically devoted to questions from the public (Gouvernement du Québec, 1990).

A Shift Toward Community Care

If there is one single thrust of the Quebec health care reform for which there is unanimity, is the necessity to develop better community health care. Community health care encompasses all care which can be provided where people live and work, and which does not require the technological and specialized professional infrastructure of institutions. Community care is perceived as a major component of the solution in solving the problems facing the Quebec health care system. This is especially true during times of financial constraint, which is the case at present in Quebec. To make this shift from institutional to community care, the thrust is not on investing new money but on reallocating already available resources from health institutions, particularly hospitals. The new direction is towards the development of alternatives to institutionalisation, the reduction of the number of acute hospitals and beds, and the better use and management of hospital resources.

Quebec ranks first, among the Canadian provinces, regarding both per capita expenditures on hospitals and health institutions and the percentage of total health care expenditures spent on hospitals and health institutions. In 1991, the Quebec per capita expenditures on hospitals and all health institutions were, respectively, $971 and $1,238 in comparison to $923 and $1,166 in Canada, $921 and $1,149 in Ontario and $827 and $1,077 in British Columbia (Santé Canada, 1994b).

In addition, Canada is the G7 country which relies most on hospitals for the provision of medical care. In Canada, in 1990, 56.3% of medical encounters and procedures were performed in hospitals in comparison to 53.8% in the United States, 40.1% in Germany and 33.2% in Japan. Moreover, Canada is the G7 country which spends the greatest proportion of its health care dollar on hospitals. In Canada, 49.1% of each health care dollar is spent in hospitals in comparison to 46.2 in the US, 36.6% in Germany and 30.2% in Japan (OCDE, 1993b).

This shift toward community health care is also being achieved through a repositioning of medical practice in the provision of health care. The measures involve: the reduction in the rate of increase of the number of physicians, at least to bring it in line with that of the population; the training of an increasing number of primary specialists through a decrease in the training of subspecialists; the use of modes of remuneration which do not provide incentives (or give the impression of providing incentives) to the production of more and more costly services as the fee for service lets one believe; a better geographic redistribution of physicians; and the revision of the organization of professional practices so as to allow the use of alternatives to physicians in the provision of health care such as midwifes and clinical nurses (Lamarche et al., 1995).

Better community-based care is also being achieved through better control of technological development, particularly pharmaceutical drugs. In Quebec, pharmaceutical drugs are the health item for which costs are increasing the fastest (RAMQ, 1994). To control this cost increase, the province is developing an information system (smart-card) which allows the monitoring of pharmaceuticals used by consumers (Papillon M.J. et al., 1994).

Allocation of Resources Based on Population

Quebec is shifting to a mode of allocation of resources that does not provide incentives to produce more and more costly services. Until now, resources were allocated based on the number of institutions and health professionals in a region. The more providers a region had, the more services they provided, the more costly the services were, and the more money they got.

There are at least three perverse consequences of this way of allocating resources. It gives no incentives to provide the most effective and least costly services. On the contrary, the more costly the services, the more money a region gets. In addition, a region which has no provider has no money. Thus, it requires the presence of providers to obtain financial support, not population needs. Finally, it obliges the population to travel to where the resources are and not the resources to go where the population is. To alleviate these perverse effects, resources are being allocated increasingly on the basis of the population of the regions and their socio-demographic characteristics rather than on the number of providers in a region and the services already being provided (Gouvernement du Québec, 1990).

FUTURE TRENDS

These changes are in the process of being implemented. However, pressures are being exerted on the health care system to accelerate its transformation and to go even beyond what was foreseen only a few years ago. This pressure is coming from the rising costs of health care and the increasing concern about the contribution of health care to the improvement of the health of the population.

To curtail these rising costs, the government of Quebec has frozen, at the 1994 level, the financial resources allocated to the health care system up to 1997. If these financial constraints are respected, and if the forecast for the Quebec economy holds true for this period, the net effect will be a reduction in the percentage of Quebec collective wealth (% of GDP) spent on health care to below the 9% level, closer to the 8.5% mark. This should bring Quebec spending on health care more in line with what is observed in other industrialized countries.

The concern about the impact of health care on the improvement of the health of the population is based on rapidly growing evidence that spending more collective resources for the provision of more health care, at least the type of health care provided at present and in the way it is now provided, may not be contributing to the further improvement of the health of the population.

Thus, it is not only the cost of health care *per se* but the issue of health value for money which is increasingly being questioned and opened for public debate. Investing 10% or even 14% of a country's collective wealth to improve the health of the population may not be too high. But investing 14%, 10% or even 6% of the collective wealth in a domain in which the health return is questioned may, in fact, be too high. Health value for money seems to have become the crucial issue in health care for the decades ahead. This may be the real issue behind the cost issue.

The main health challenges for Quebec in the years to come appear to be twofold: to operate its health care system within unprecedented and severe financial constraints while maintaining its public characteristics, particularly universal accessibility; and to orient the provision of care and stimulate action from non-health sectors of society so as to further improve the health of the population.

To meet these challenges, the Quebec health care system will have to rechannel financial resources from health institutions to community care. This need for rechanneling is acquiring consensus in Quebec. There is also increasing agreement regarding the extent of this shift in resources, which will likely represent close to 25% of the resources allocated to health institutions. What is very much still open for debate are the conditions under which and the speed with which this shift should be done.

At least two conditions need to be met if such a radical change is to be made with the agreement of the population and the people involved in the provision of care. The first concerns the maintenance of care to the people. This consists of a proper balance and sequence between reducing financial resources to health institutions and strengthening community resources so that they become substitute institutions in the provision of care. The extent to which the population will continue to obtain the care needed, no matter what the source, is likely to determine the level of acceptance and support of this shift.

The second condition concerns the people involved in the provision of care. Close to 80% of health care spending goes towards remuneration of health care personnel. Such a major change from institutional to community-based care cannot be done without affecting a sustantial number of health care providers. Some are very likely to lose their jobs while others are likely to be transferred to other positions. The extent to which the changes affecting health care personnel are managed in a civilized and humane way will determine the extent of support or resistance of health care providers.

The meeting of both these conditions seems to be related to the timespan taken for introducing these changes. Some argue that it is impossible to introduce these changes properly within a three-year period as requested by the government. They argue that if this time period is maintained, the changes are likely to be detrimental to the population. Others argue that this time period should be maintained. Their opinion is based on the fact that these measures are needed urgently to reduce the government deficit, that health care has been using collective resources that are desperately needed in other sectors, and that similar major shifts have already occurred in other provinces within similar time periods with no negative impact on the services to the population. However, the extent to which the time frame will allow these conditions to be met in Quebec remains to be seen.

Quebec will also have to strengthen its capacity to assess the efficacy of the care provided and the effectiveness in the use of health resources. This assessment would allow decisions on resource allocation and reallocation to be based on these criteria rather than on historical bases or political pressure exerted by some interest groups. It would also allow consumers to be more knowledgeable about the efficacy of treatments prescribed to them by health professionals and the best place to obtain them. Experiences with consumer involvement in clinical decision-making have shown that it is profoundly changing the care provided.

Finally, Quebec will have to rechannel a proportion of the resources made available from the transformation of its health care system to other sectors whose influence on health is likely to be important. More and more evidence is accumulating to the effect that the health of the population is determined more by socioeconomic conditions than by the health care it uses. Debates are ongoing in Quebec as to the extent to which the resources made available from health institutions should be used to reduce the government deficit or to improve the conditions in which Quebecers live. This debate is fuelled by the fact that, although Quebec's wealth has increased over the last decades, the proportion of the population benefiting from it has been rather limited. The net result is an increasing proportion of the Quebec population who may be living in conditions less conducive to health. To improve the health of Quebecers this issue will have to be seriously addressed.

CONCLUSION

The health status of the Quebec population has improved in great strides over the last decades. Part of this improvement can be attributed to the spectacular development of its health care system which has been rooted in the public recognition and acceptance that health and health care are, above all, collective responsibilities. It has also been based on the public recognition of the legitimacy of the state to assume these responsibilities. Ever since, the state has maintained a rather strong presence in the development of health care resources, in the financing of health care insurance programmes, and in the regulation of the health care system.

The Quebec health care system is now facing serious problems, criticisms and questions. What seems to be at the root of these questions are the high costs of health care and, more importantly, the increasing evidence that the further improvement of the health of the Quebec population depends more on action outside the health care system than on the provision of more health care.

The tackling of both of these issues requires a profound transformation in the type of care and the way it is provided. It requires, at least, the rechannelling of care from health institutions to community care. These changes are needed to reduce the cost of health care, to respond to the evolution of health care technology and the needs of the people, and to free up collective resources for other sectors whose impact on health is likely to be more important than traditional health care. Better health for Quebecers may, in fact, imply different and perhaps also less care.

Important changes are now being introduced. Quebec decided to introduce these changes by using the regulatory power of the government while maintaining the main public characteristics of its health care system. Their introduction is facing tremendous resistance on the part of those most affected by them, mainly health care providers. Thus, means need to be developed to deal appropriately with this problem.

The extent to which the public characteristics of the Quebec health care system is maintained depends heavily on the successful introduction of these changes. Either Quebec succeeds and the fundamental public characteristics of its health care is maintained or Quebec does not succeed and consumers will gradually have to pay more for the health care they use in order to absorb the costs that the governement cannot or does not want to absorb anymore.

REFERENCES

Bergeron P., Gagnon F. 1994. "La prise en charge étatique de la santé au Québec," in Lemieux V., Bergeron P., Bégin C. and Bélanger G. (eds.), *Le système de santé au Québec: organisations, acteurs et enjeux*. Les Presses de l'Université Laval, Sainte-foy.

Canada Health Act. (1984) c.6, s.1.

Commission d'enquête sur les services de santé et les services sociaux (Commission Castonguay-Nepveu) 1970. *Rapport de la Commission d'enquête sur les services de santé et les services sociaux*. Québec, les publications du Québec.

Commission d'enquête sur les services de santé et les services sociaux (Commission Rochon) 1988. *Rapport de la Commission d'enquête sur les services de santé et les services sociaux*. Québec, les publications du Québec.

Gouvernement du Québec 1992. *La politique de la santé et du bien- être.* Ministère de la Santé et des Services sociaux (MSSS) Québec.

Gouvernement du Québec 1989. *Pour améliorer la santé et le bien-être au Québec: orientations.* Ministère de la Santé et des Services sociaux (MSSS), Québec.

Gouvernement du Québec 1990. *Une réforme axée sur le citoyen.* Ministère de la Santé et des Services sociaux (MSSS), Québec.

Gouvernement du Québec 1991. *Un financement équitable à la mesure de nos moyens.* Ministère de la Santé et des Services sociaux (MSSS) Québec.

Lamarche P.A., and Rossi C. 1995. "Les systèmes de services de santé en mutation," in *Médecine préventive et santé publique au Canada* (In press: Presses de l'Université Laval).

Loi sur les services de santé et les services sociaux 1971. L.R.Q. chapitre S-5

Loi sur les services de santé et les services sociaux 1991. L.R.Q. chapitre S-4.2

Ministère de la Santé et des Services sociaux du Québec (MSSS) 1994. *Les dépenses de santé au Québec, en Ontario et au Canada,* Comparaison particulière avec l'Ontario, 1987 à 1992, document de travail. Service des études opérationnelles, Direction des études et indicateurs.

Nations-Unis 1992, 1987, 1977. *Annuaire démographique des Nations-Unis.*

Organisation de coopération et de développement économique (OCDE) 1993a. *Études économiques de l'OCDE: Canada.*

Organisation de coopération et de développement économique (OCDE) 1993b. *Les système de santé des pays de l'OCDE: Faits et tendances 1960-1991,* Vol. 1, Paris.

Organisation de coopération et de développement économique (OCDE) 1993c. *Programme ECO SANTE OCDE du CREDES,* version 1,5.

Pampalon R. 1994. "La santé des Québécois et des Québécoises," in Lemieux V., Bergeron P., Bégin C. et Bélanger G.(eds.), *Le système de santé au Québec: organisations, acteurs et enjeux.* Les Presses de l'Université Laval, Sainte-foy.

Papillon, M.J., Bérubé, J., Comeau, M., Lavoie, G., Kirouac, S., Fortin, J.P. 1994. "Futuristic Microchip Health Card Experiment in Québec", in *Canadian Medical Informatics,* Vol. 1, No 1.

Régie de l'assurance-maladie du Québec (RAMQ) 1994. *Statistiques annuelles 1993,* Québec.

Santé Canada 1994a. *Dépenses nationales de santé au Canada 1975-1993.* Direction de l'information et de la politique de la santé, Direction générale de la politique et de la consultation.

Santé Canada 1994b. *Estimations préliminaires des dépenses de santé au Canada.* Rapport sommaire provincial\territorial 1987-1991. Division de l'information sur la santé, Direction générale de la politique et de la consultation.

Statistique Canada 1986. *Longévité et tables de mortalité chronologiques* (abrégées) 1921-1981, Canada et provinces.

Statistique Canada 1991. *Statistiques choisies sur la mortalité infantile et statistiques connexes, 1921-1990.* Centre canadien d'information sur la santé.

Statistique Canada 1990. *Projections démographiques pour le Canada, les provinces et les territoires: 1984-2006.* By J. Perreault.

Stoddart, G.L., Barrer, M.L., Evans, R.G., Bhatia, V. 1993. *Pourquoi ne pas imposer le ticket modérateur? les véritables enjeux.* Conseil du premier ministre sur la santé, le bien-être et la justice sociale, Ontario.

Turgeon J., Anctil H. 1994. "Le Ministère et le réseau public," in Lemieux, V., Bergeron, P., Bégin, C., Bélanger, G. (eds.), *Le système de santé au Québec: organisations, acteurs et enjeux.* Les Presses de l'Université Laval, Sainte-foy.

SOCIAL MOVEMENTS IN QUEBEC: ENVIRONMENTAL GROUPS AS A CULTURAL CHALLENGE TO THE NEO-CORPORATIST ORDER

Before the 1960s, the progressive social sphere in Quebec was occupied mainly by older social movements, such as the trade-union and workers' movements and the cooperative and credit-union movements. These social actors were primarily involved in negotiating for better working and living conditions, and in supporting new types of economic activities and production processes. From their point of view, these changes required the removal of the traditional elites or a change in direction of the state (Babin, Vaillancourt, 1995: 173). Other social movements, such as the nationalist and religious movements, were quite strong but relatively conservative, while feminism and pacifism were quite progressive but relatively underdeveloped.

With the end of the 1960s and the blossoming of the Quiet Revolution, the unfolding of social change took a different turn. The major characteristic of the period was the rise of the new middle classes in the political arena and in the ranks of the state bureaucracy. In calling for a progressive type of nationalism, which was more open to the needs of the economy and the need for modernizing both state and civil society, and in making their political, cultural and linguistic demands (Guindon, 1988), the agents of these new middle classes played leading roles in the social and political arenas. The nationalist and student movements, and especially trade-unionism, supported the rise of the middle classes through the state and the political field because it promoted social development and technical expertise. During this period, Quebec society was displaying characteristics similar to those that have occurred in the evolution of dependent societies elsewhere, characterized by the call to nationalism, manifestations of evolving technical and social expertise, and demands for the modernization of the social fabric (Maheu, 1979).

During the 1970s and 1980s, as neo-fordism was strengthened in Quebec, social relations were further transformed (Bélanger, Lévesque, 1992).[1] Forces opposed to the modernizing political class and the new technocracy allied themselves with trade unions operating in the public and private sectors. A further link was created with various popular citizens' movements, whose members included users and consumers of state services, especially in urban areas, demanding better socioeconomic and living conditions, as well as a more lively local democracy (Hamel, 1991).

Recent phenomena are pointing to another important transformation of social relations. These include the crisis of fordism, the questioning of the role of the welfare state, severe constraints on public finances, as well as the growing opposition to the current mode of socioeconomic development and its aggression toward nature, as well as human beings. There has also been a distinct rise of the "culture of authenticity" (to use Taylor's expression (1989, 1991)) on the social fabric of all societies of radical modernity (Giddens, 1990, 1991). Consequently, several new forces are now invading the field of social change. Their social demands tend to be based on subjectivity and individualism, on control of technology, on the affirmation of identities and differences, and on the right to choose and to experiment.

Quebec society has not been different from others in this respect. Like many other societies of radical modernity, it is affected by a growing gap between trade-unionism and its causes and social agents on the one hand, and on the other, newer social struggles which have succeeded in transforming urban movements, women's movements and environmental and green movements. In recent years, these movements, which can be more accurately called new social movements (Melucci, 1995; Maheu, 1995 c; Maheu, Descent, 1990), have emerged in Quebec. Others in this same category include the peace movement, the international solidarity movement, and movements based on cultural, ethnic or sexual identity.

These new social movements work for social change not only at the political level but also at the cultural and social levels, in the struggles of everyday life. The loose networks of people and organizations associated with new social movements are striving to orient the society towards distributive justice, social equity, peace, sustainable development, environmental protection, the democratization of choice and the intimate experience of global environments. Separate from the traditional trade-union movement, and sometimes even in opposition to certain of its official positions, new social movements now tend to occupy their own social, cultural and political space.

It is still too early to speculate on the extent, duration and consequence of this new social space. We can nevertheless try to understand its significance and characteristics through an analysis of the collective actions that constitute it. In taking

---

[1] Fordism refers to the provision of high salaries and social benefits to workers in order to help maintain the economy and ensure social peace.

an inductive, grass-roots approach, we shall look at one social movement, namely the environmental movement, and more particularly, at those groups involved in waste issues, to see how they function as networks of groups that cooperate and struggle with various other actors, both inside and outside the green movement.

Our studies have focused specifically on the links between grassroots environmental groups and a provincial organization called the Quebec Common Front for an Ecological Management of Waste (Front commun québécois pour une gestion écologique des déchets: FCQGED). Founded in 1991, this coalition is made up of individual members as well as more than 30 environmental groups located in various regions of Quebec. The majority of these groups include people mobilized against the locating of incinerators in their vicinity, and against projects aimed at establishing or expanding landfill sites for mixed solid waste. (Solid waste is a general term used here to describe domestic, municipal, commercial and industrial waste, excluding dangerous waste and special waste such as used cars.) The Common Front supports a selective treatment of waste rather than a mixed type of waste disposal. It is also involved in the promotion of new ways of managing waste that are more respectful of the environment and of democratic decision-making.

The study of the networks emerging from within the green movement allows us to describe the ongoing struggles for a cleaner environment in communities affected by waste disposal projects. This type of mobilization has been observed in numerous other regions (Bullard, Wright, 1992; Cans, 1990; Freudenburg, Steinsapir, 1992; Hofrichter, 1993; Walsh, Warland, Smith, 1993).

In this chapter, we shall describe the various dimensions of these networks. We will show that environmental groups have created links with groups involved in other social movements, such as the civil rights and labour movements. These kinds of links have also been observed in activities organized by other social movements. We will then analyze the social and institutional conditions that facilitate the emergence of controversies over the question of waste management. These conditions lead to the institutionalization of collective protest activities and movements. We shall then examine if and how waste management, as well as more global environmental issues, may produce a more democratic community at the local level, and a major cultural and political reorientation at the societal level. In the second part of this chapter, we will broaden the perspective by discussing the theory of new social movements within late modernity. But first of all, we will present a brief history of the environmental movement in Quebec.

THE QUEBEC ENVIRONMENTAL MOVEMENT AND WASTE MANAGEMENT CONTROVERSIES

A Brief History of the Quebec Environmental Movement

Before the 1970s, the green groups that flourished in Quebec were mostly conservationist in orientation. The Young Naturalists (Cercle des Jeunes Naturalistes), the 4-H Clubs, and the Linnean Society are good examples of groups founded in the first part of the century (Lord, 1994). These conservationist groups, like the more numerous and more powerful equivalent groups in the United States (Dunlap, Mertig, 1992) were generally oriented towards the dissemination of knowledge concerning nature, and towards the preservation of various types of green spaces, particularly parks and other wilderness sites. Some conservationist groups were founded during the 1970s, but many of the green groups that emerged during this period were considered to be environmentalist or political and social ecology groups, rather than conservationist groups.

The environmentalists, according to Vaillancourt (1982, 1985, 1992), are mostly preoccupied with pollution and the protection of the urban environment, whereas the political and social ecologists are aiming, through a global perspective, to promote a new type of society, an ecosociety based on the respect of humans and nature. Many types of groups flourished during the 1970s and 1980s, such as local citizens' committees struggling to protect the urban environment, promoters of ecological agriculture and forestry, and provincial groups involved in environmental education. Questions of energy, transport, water and air pollution are just a few of the myriad topics that were addressed by these environmentalist groups.

Like everywhere else, an important economic crisis hit Quebec in the 1980s. Many environmental activists switched their interest to other new social struggles like the international solidarity movement and the disarmament and peace movements, but this did not impede the formation of other green groups interested in more global issues. When the 1990s came along, because of a renewed interest in the environment, due in good part to the publication of the Brundtland report, the end of the Cold War, and the discovery of global environmental problems, the green movement in Quebec remained strongly rooted and diversified, as was the case in many other places. The goals of the newer groups are focused on issues such as sustainable development, climate change, ozone depletion, the restoration and protection of lakes and rivers, acid rain, biodiversity, green spaces and waste management.

From Local and Interregional Solidarity to the Creation of the Quebec Common Front

Local Struggles and Their Links with Other Battles and Groups Dedicated to the Defense of the Environment.

The stories of local struggles bear many similarities. Small communities like Senneterre and Valleyfield had intentionally been chosen for the establishment of incineration projects. In Mercier, the small local community had to cope with a dangerous waste incinerator, while in the case of Blainville, it had to deal with a company that utilized a process for the "stabilization" of dangerous waste. Similarly, in small-town Joliette, a cement factory was planning to use dangerous waste, particularly PCB-laden oil, as fuel in its cement-making process.

In these communities, local groups were mobilized to fight against the waste disposal facilities. Some Greenpeace representatives had been individually solicited by the local groups to help them obtain information on the waste treatment processes utilized or proposed in their communities. According to some members of these groups, the Greenpeace representatives offered advice on ways to organize and distribute information, and presented public lectures on the environmental impact of incineration or the "stabilization" of dangerous waste.

Greenpeace is an international organization with a strong membership base in many countries. Its international campaign aimed at countering the proliferation of incinerators, using the slogan "Ban don't burn," and its campaign against toxic materials and dangerous waste made it possible for these representatives to provide the names of experts working on these issues in various regions of Canada, and even the United States and Europe. Thus, certain groups were able to obtain information from people living near waste incinerators already in operation, or from experts on the question of waste disposal facilities. The people who mobilized against the dangerous waste incinerator in Senneterre were able, through such channels, to communicate directly with others knowledgeable about this issue in other countries. They obtained numerous documents, including press clippings, describing the problems which occurred in the vicinity of incinerators already in operation elsewhere.

A representative of the Société pour Vaincre la Pollution (SVP), a Montreal-based provincial organization dedicated to environmental protection, also offered public lectures in Valleyfield and Senneterre, thus helping local groups raise the issue of holding private companies responsible for their production of various types of waste. An expert in chemistry, Dr. Paul Connett from St. Lawrence University in the state of New York, also offered much valuable information which challenged the need for incineration as a technology for the treatment of waste.

The establishment of these links between grass-roots groups and provincial and international organizations was coupled with mobilization among local people and organizations, such as trade unions, native people, and municipalities.

The Creation of a Provincial Coalition

In 1991, one of the Greenpeace representatives thought it would be a strategy to bring the different groups together at a provincial level, so that they could help each other and exchange information that would be pertinent and useful in their action vis-à-vis the provincial government. A few meetings were organized in 1991 to create what was to become the Quebec Common Front for an Ecological Management of Waste (FCQGED). The organization consisted at that time of about 15 member groups. Thus, solidarity and cooperation were established not only within the various localities and regions, but also between the local groups and certain provincial groups, and between the local groups from different regions and municipalities. With the creation of the FCQGED, the sharing of information and of mobilization efforts were formalized, and increased solidarity and cooperation were encouraged.

The founding members of FCQGED expressed their desire for interregional solidarity and cooperation at their very first meetings, when they created decision-making structures and forged the orientation of the organization. In fact, the first meetings of the Common Front were held in two different towns where companies were already operating waste management facilities. These meetings were accompanied by demonstrations in the streets of the towns. At the same time, many members of the FCQGED also participated in a demonstration in Valleyfield against the incineration project in that municipality.

Once the main foundations of the organization were in place, a key meeting of groups that had mobilized in communities near private solid waste landfill sites was organized, with the help of the FCQGED. This meeting was aimed, in part, to pursue discussions with the Common Front on principles for guiding the management of solid wastes in ways respectful of both the environment and the local communities.

The most important moments of this meeting were undoubtedly when the representatives of the various local groups described, one after another, the waste management situation in each region. Many people realized then that what they were going through in their own milieu was similar to situations experienced by many other people in other regions. For example, many private landfill sites dedicated mainly to the garbage disposal needs of a particular region had gradually begun accommodating considerable quantities of waste originating from other regions. This resulted in an increase in the negative environmental impact due to the growth in the volume of wastes treated on the site, and in a considerable reduction in longevity of the sites, and consequently of the space available for such sites. Moreover, in many regions, people noticed increasing problems related to the lack of control by the Quebec Ministry of the Environment (now called the Ministry of the Environment and Wildlife) over the activities of the site owners and operators, as well as to difficulties accessing information concerning the waste landfill sites. Anomalies were also noted regarding adherence to emission procedures specified for obtaining certificates of conformity to municipal zoning and regional planning.

The meetings of the Common Front also helped the participants share their strategies and develop personal links amongst each other. These new social relationships not only led to common action at the local level, but also served to help put pressure on the government at the provincial level. Furthermore, following these meetings, more than 30 local groups joined the ranks of the FCQGED, thus widening considerably the networking capacity of the organization.

Many other activities were organized to put more pressure on the government, with the aim of implementing a real provincial policy for waste management which would set as its priorities the reduction, reuse and recycling-composting of waste. Thus, in February 1992, for example, demonstrations were held simultaneously in many municipalities to emphasize the links between the various local waste management controversies. This series of demonstrations was followed by a national press conference where representatives of the Common Front launched a "manifesto for an ecological management of solid waste," which presented a summary of local waste management issues, as well as principles to be followed when planning waste management projects in an ecological and democratic manner. This document has since been extensively revised and published in book form by Michel Séguin under the title *Le scandale des déchets au Québec* (1994).

Collaboration was also established with the Quebec Teachers' Central (Centrale de l'Enseignement du Québec; CEQ), the trade-union organization representing most of Quebec's schoolteachers, which reproduced the above-mentioned manifesto. The Quebec Environmental Law Center (Centre québécois du droit de l'environnement; CQDE), a group of jurists interested in the promotion of environmental law in Quebec, also offered its collaboration by participating in the press conference. In its declaration during that press conference, the coalition of groups requested from the government a moratorium on the establishment and extension of landfill sites, and on the construction of new incinerators. It also asked that this moratorium be maintained until the end of public hearings and a public inquiry into Quebec's waste management policies. During the last few years, most of the groups united under the banner of the Common Front have concentrated their efforts mainly on pressing for these demands and on promoting a more ecological and democratic form of waste management.

Broadening of Support for the Common Front

To promote their views, representatives of local groups and the members of the board of directors of the Common Front initiated steps to obtain the widest support possible. For example, numerous local and provincial environmental groups, some trade-union organizations, as well as more than twenty municipalities (municipalités régionales de comté; MRC) have declared their support for the resolutions demanding public hearings on solid waste management. This support on the part of the MRCs is important because these sub-regional groupings are decision-making structures made up of mayors, responsible for managing local territorial planning. Other groups have also given their support for public hearings on Quebec waste management policies. These include the Union of Regional and Local Municipalities of Quebec (UMRCQ), which includes the various Quebec MRCs; the Union of Quebec Municipalities (UMQ), which includes the most important Quebec municipalities; plus certain organizations dedicated to the development of programs for the selective collection, reduction, reuse and recycling-composting of resources. Thus, the backing received has gone much beyond the initial network of grass-roots groups involved in the defense of environmental issues and better waste management.

To give a more complete picture of the different links that developed among the environmental groups, and between them and other social organizations, it is interesting to look at the facts concerning a police investigation undertaken by the Sûreté du Québec, the provincial police force in charge of public security at the supra-municipal level. The operation was directed mainly against the people involved in the citizens' groups mobilized around waste management issues. As the emerging network of groups became larger and larger, it attracted the attention of the Sûreté du Québec, which in turn encouraged additional links between these groups and others, especially watch-dog groups that keep an eye on police violations of civil rights. Thus, a link was created between the environmental movement and the movement for the defense of civil rights. Futhermore, this episode opened up strategic structural opportunities for media coverage of the struggle over waste management.

The daily newspaper *Le Devoir* mentioned on November 26, 1992 that the Sûreté du Québec had begun "a vast information-gathering operation on certain environmental and citizens' groups involved in about twenty environmental controversies concerning mainly the issue of waste management." Quoting the person in charge of communication at the Sûreté du Québec, the journalist indicated that the investigation had been instituted because there had been numerous cases of "highly emotional responses and sometimes even of violence." A few cases of acts of violence were cited as examples in the article. The information was given further publicity that same morning by other journalists and radio commentators.

This whole episode immediately put the Common Front in a delicate position. These events could have been very costly for all the people involved in the organization. This type of publicity threatened to undermine trust amongst members and to lead certain activists to withdraw.

To cope with this situation, the Common Front had to use a variety of strategies to counter the bad publicity and re-establish the facts. They showed that the acts of violence referred to in the article were, in every case, acts perpetrated against, not by the people who had mobilized to put an end to waste management practices deemed to be environmentally, financially, and/or ethically inadequate. The FCQGED also began proceedings with the Quebec Human Rights Commission, the Civil Liberties Union, the Quebec minister in charge of public security, and those persons and groups involved in investigating police officers responsible for security investigations. Following these actions undertaken by the Common Front, the unwarranted visits by agents of the Sûreté du Québec were discontinued. Finally, the Common Front, with the help of the Civil Liberties Union, organized workshops for its members to inform them of the situation, and to present the various options they had when police investigators asked to meet them.

These events made it possible to identify new types of relationships that could be developed with other organizations, such as those dedicated to the defense of rights and liberties. Furthermore, it allowed for the establishment of links between these police investigations and similar activities perpetrated by the Sûreté du Québec against workers' groups, feminist, peace and nationalist movements, and groups created to defend gay rights. This type of social control by the police is only one form of interference from above that influenced the development of these groups. Thus, it can be seen that groups mobilized in the area of waste management challenge many levels of the institutional framework.

INSTITUTIONALIZATION OF COLLECTIVE ACTION AND THE ENVIRONMENTAL MOVEMENT

One point in particular emerges from the tendencies that we have observed in the environmental struggles of grass-roots groups and their national coalition: these struggles penetrate deeper and deeper within the social fabric and make use of numerous and varied sociopolitical and cultural opportunities to put forward their social claims and arguments. We have come a long way since the early 1960's in terms of expanding our repertory of social movements. Movements have left their distinct mark, as well as their collective memories on the social fabric of late modernity. Through their wide range of conflicts and struggles, their organizational resources, strategies, formal structures of leadership and diverse networks of activists and sympathizers, they enlarge and institutionalize their repertory of collective action as they network with the society's existing structures.

If we want to give some meaning to collective environmental action, and to better comprehend its impact on our societies, we must think theoretically about the process of institutionalization that the green movement has undergone. Analyses of the building of large coalitions, and of the articulation of social movements through networks, resources and institutional opportunities, generally tend to overestimate the extent to which "accommodative institutionalization" occurs. Accommodation is said to characterize the politics of mediation between interest groups and regulatory bodies. Within modern societies, new social movements, according to Neidhardt and Rucht, are vehicles for claims related to life and world issues. They emerge alongside the official political agenda. Social movements and green movements in particular complement the processes of interest group mediation by voicing particular social demands that might not otherwise be heard if left up to political parties or interest groups (Neidhardt, Rucht, 1991: 448-449).

As Melucci has argued, new social movements make visible the unknown, systemic and impersonal forces of our complex informational society. Once visible, these powers become routine targets of dispute and are maintained as such (Melucci, 1985; 1989). Dalton and Kuechler also focus on how social movements challenge the political order. They have hypothesized that new social movements "as an unintended consequence, may be securing the political order" (Kuechler, Dalton, 1990: 298).

Should the institutionalization of collective action be understood only through an "accommodative integration" hypothesis? Should this process be reduced to collective action that ultimately seems totally embedded within the existing political system? The ambivalence within the green movements toward their own institutionalization should bring us to a clearer understanding of the tendencies of social movements in late modernity. Two dimensions of these struggles, which are illustrated by the observations concerning Quebec environmental groups, warrant further discussion.

Institutionalization of Collective Action and the Alternative Normative Order

One of the main demands of citizens' groups and individuals active in the controversies related to waste management is for the implementation of institutional conditions favourable to the 3Rs, namely, the reduction, reuse and recycling-composting of waste. These demands propose a new social paradigm involving all the major social systems that generate and distribute resources within modern societies. In this sense, we could say that the green movement is in the process of developing a counter-discourse, insofar as it is leading a critical cultural struggle against the established order (Kuechler and Dalton, 1990). It can also be portrayed as a new social movement sustained by a progressive ideological bond.

These critical demands and struggles imply, more specifically, deep transformations at the level of personal life style, as well as at the level of production and consumption (for example, reducing consumption and modifying production processes to generate less waste). In fact, the very modes of production and lifestyles that encourage accumulation and growth should be organized so as to create less waste. Demands to reduce the volume of waste are based, on the one hand, on the need to curtail the quantity of garbage that has to be treated, and on the other hand, on the need to conserve resources to meet the needs of future generations. These demands and struggles are highly controversial, inasmuch as established decision-making processes are ill-suited for dealing with demands that imply far-reaching global societal changes.

Quite often, the contemporary literature on green and social movements rightly places much emphasis on institutional forms of action that are basically normative. We are dealing here with the very production of meaning within a context of conflictual collective action, through reference to knowledge, values, representations and norms. As producers of an alternative discourse regarding the orientation of public interest, social movements have become partially institutionalized. This is particularly true of green movements, according to Klaus Eder. This happens as they build on self-produced institutional pathways around issues of collective action, developing their discourse in such a way as to establish legitimacy (Eder, 1993 a, 1993 b).

This perspective underscores important characteristics in the institutionalization of green and social movements. The accent is rightly placed on the conflictual dimension of the re-embedding of social representations. But Eder's way of looking at institutional innovation as discursive self-production ultimately makes social movements indistinguishable from social movement organizations (Eder, 1993b: 19). This may raise more problems than it solves, as it blurs the distinction between the struggle for autonomy and the struggle for emancipation, both of which are embedded within, as well as opposed to exisiting institutions. These struggles are part of the social construction of collective identity. They create categories of meaning for the disenfranchised, which social movements can then use against the established social order.

The normative dimension of collective action is thus intrinsically conflictual. In fact, it belongs to the culture of authenticity, to those cultural conflicts that are characteristic of modernity, according to Charles Taylor (1989, 1991). This cultural field is made up precisely of struggles and conflicts that, through alternative categories developed to "name" the world, seek a more universal, as well as a more democratic process through which we might interact with nature and constitute the social fabric.

Ecological and other new social movements thus have a moral impetus (Pakulski, 1991) and an ideological bond (Kuechler, Dalton, 1990) which distinguish them from interest groups and political parties. The moral foundation of their action is what distinguishes their presence in a society. It also leads us to look beyond analyses that point to conformism and integration as the only ways to frame the institutionalization of collective action pertaining to nature and the environment.

Institutionalization of Collective Action and Cultural Challenges to the Neo-corporatist Order

Among the institutional structures that lead to collective action and that support green movements and their social struggles, sociopolitical relationships between leaders of government, private enterprise and local communities merit consideration. These relationships, complex and problematical as they are, influence many controversies regarding the location of waste treatment facilities. Thus, for example, the public processes of environmental evaluation are generally judged to be inadequate. When certain projects are submitted to public scrutiny, various noxious elements are often confirmed to be unavoidable, or worse still, the options have not even been studied.

Access to information is one of the key elements that distinguishes the different people who are involved in waste disposal issues. Improving access to information for local communities is tantamount to giving them more power over the activities that take place within their territories, and that have an impact on their quality of life. The lack of guarantees concerning access to information about the nature, source and quantities of garbage treated in existing facilities can encourage popular resistance. Without this type of information, it becomes extremely difficult for the population to evaluate the risk incurred during the transportation and treatment of waste. This information is also essential for evaluating the actual and potential use of various types of facilities.

The nature and results of governmental controls to verify the environmental impact of waste disposal are also part of the information that is often difficult or even impossible for the population to obtain. Thus, access to information becomes, at many levels, a basic tool for increasing a local community's control over facilities planned for its region, or already established on its territory.

Demands regarding the nature of public consultations, access to information and decisional roles of various institutional players, challenge the existing decision-making processes. They imply a need for a new sharing of power between the various levels of government, private companies, and communities. All this constitutes an important issue for democratic processes.

Beyond political processes, other issues are raised by these social struggles. For example, they highlight the organizational and institutional problems of harmonizing the views of those who act at various levels and in distinct ways on the issues of waste management. Some projects require the establishment of links between municipal, regional and agricultural zoning on the one hand, and on the other, regional and national economic development, transportation facilities and technological development. The roles involved in these different fields are themselves numerous and varied. Quebec, as we have already mentioned, is not a special case in this area: the demands and the social struggles challenge the agencies responsible for municipal zoning, regional planning, and the protection of agricultural land. All of these institutions are concerned with the implementation of waste disposal projects, since the choice of sites for the treatment of waste must not contravene the different sets of rules managed by these authorities. Because environmental issues are not necessarily considered in each of these areas, projects can cause important environmental problems.

The boundaries between the different processes and players, whose actions and decisions are necessarily dependent on each other, create a barrier between the supposedly public decision-making processes and the various local, regional and national communities. The invisibility of the real powers-that-be underlie some of the demands and struggles over the environment, including the question of waste disposal.

The same type of argument can be applied to deficient legislation, insufficient environmental controls over facilities, and the absence of guarantees of legal proceedings in cases where norms are violated. These problem areas are targets of discontent, of demands and struggles that question the representativeness, the visibility, and the democratic quality of political decision-making processes, as well as the transparency of political-institutional models of waste management.

A fact remains: green and other new social movements in Quebec and other modern societies generally not only make use of cultural and symbolic opportunity structures, they also penetrate the institutional levels of political action that allow for the best access to the ruling elites. Gaining access to these institutional levels of political action also extends the influence of these movements, for example, as an authorized political mediator. This status may even lead to participation in processes of political regulation. But it has often been noted too that green and social movements maintain, on and off, a certain autonomy with respect to these political processes and structural opportunities. Through complex and dynamic relations between institutional and non-institutional politics (Lustiger-Thaler, Maheu, 1995), green and social movements embrace sociopolitical mechanisms which take the form of arbitration, and often go beyond the state and its traditional political structures (Eder, 1993b). These movements are simultaneously at a distance from the political order and also near it. The moral foundations of their actions lie in the alternative normative order they are seeking, in which respect for both nature and humankind, and dignity and social justice for all would be paramount.

Insofar as political regulation processes are concerned, we might say that green and other social movements are challenging the corporatist and the neo-corporatist political order. They encourage the extension of public forums and commissions with the intent of politicizing decision-making processes within the society regarding, for example, environmental and ecological issues. New representatives who are selected according to the norms of modern political society and new interest mediation mechanisms are a part of this neo-corporatist political market (Offe, 1985). Availing themselves of emergent political processes, new social movements also challenge them at the cultural level.

Through such cultural challenges to the neo-corporatist order, green and other social movements are involved in the social construction of a community, as part of the process of building their own sense of meaning and identity. Indeed, social movements are often the symbols of an engaged community in times of heightened fragmentation. They are part of a dialogue and conflictual relationship with known and unknown "others" who demand a place in the construction of the *sensus communis*. These multidimensional relations are not without their tensions and breaks, as well as social innovations that are confrontational and emancipatory at their very root.

The social direction of a community is obviously grounded in a series of links to diverse institutional networks. Through these networks, relations with "others" are established, engendering different ways of giving voice and naming the world, and opening up areas where issues of risk and relations with nature are discussed. The social construction of community therefore extends itself into alliance-building. Social networks affirm themselves through different coalitions of interests. It is by taking part in the give-and-take of institutions, by developing dialogue and creating alliances against opposing forces and established forms of rationality and subjectivity that a politically conscious and territorially grounded community emerges. Through this community-building process, issues of authenticity, dignity and human rights, as well as struggles for more democratic decision-making regarding environmental and ecological issues, become the new bases for a rationality and a subjectivity that challenge older benchmarks of community-building and democracy.

Such a political understanding of the social construct of community allows us to appreciate the radical institutionalization of green and other new social movements within late modernity. It is important not to focus too narrowly on the accommodative institutionalization of social movements. It is more useful to see how, and if, the building of community, via the multiple institutional strands that compose it, is integral to a form of contemporary collective action that retains the potential to rebuild the social fabric in a more autonomous and egalitarian way.

CONCLUSION

The analysis of networks of environmental groups mobilized around waste management issues has shown links between grass-roots environmental groups involved in local controversies, and provincial and international environmental organizations. These networks are also involved in mobilizing local people, trade unions, native people, municipalities and other social movements such as the civil rights movement. Large coalitions have also been observed in other domains. For example, in 1988, the government wanted to implement a bill (Bill 37) that would reduce social security. Around 100 organizations, including women's groups, labour movement organizations and groups of young people mobilized on this issue. Five thousand people took to the streets to support the coalition on October 15, 1988 (Hamel, 1989, p. 163-164).

In the spring of 1995, the Women's Federation of Quebec (Fédération des femmes du Québec), with the participation of a coalition of 40 different organizations working on different issues such as poverty and intergenerational justice, was able to mobilize over 15,000 people in the streets of Quebec City around the theme "Bread and Roses." Their purpose was mostly to obtain better social and economic conditions for women but also for people in other disavantaged social categories.

These different links between various social movements may exist on a regular basis or in connection with specific issues, or they may be activated at strategic moments. Networks of groups facilitate the exchange of key information needed to understand these issues, and offer important technical and moral support in the struggles against projects and models of development imposed on communities.

In Quebec, these networks are not only involved in the struggle against certain policies and projects, but in addition, are working towards the creation of projects to improve the quality of life, for example, by reducing the production of waste or by increasing recycling. Examples of specific projects taken on by various groups are demonstration sites for domestic composting, centres for educating people to reuse and recycle (called *ressourceries*), and projects for collecting used clothing or dangerous domestic waste.

The institutionalization of collective action and of green and other social movements that we have described entails, above all, a strong normative and cultural component. We would argue that the struggles over waste management contribute to the development of a new social paradigm (Kuechler, Dalton, 1990) belonging to the culture of authenticity (Taylor, 1989, 1990). In the midst of this cultural arena, conflictual issues pertaining, on the one hand, to the use of technocratic and instrumental rationalities, and, on the other hand, to the relationship between the sphere of human nature and the global characteristics of material nature itself, occupy a central place. Struggles over the social management of waste entail yet another component; they constitute a process of community-building which is based on challenges to the neo-corporatist social order. This path towards institutionalization can be extended to many other conflictual social processes and protest actions besides those described here (Maheu, 1995 a, 1995 b; Lustiger-Thaler, Maheu, 1995). The dimensions that we have just summarized also allow us to better understand certain characteristics of the social, cultural and political space that new social movements have been developing within Quebec society. Inasmuch as certain sectors of the trade-union movement or certain older social movements are part of the neo-corporatist order, they will become, potentially, social adversaries of the new social movements, somewhat like the established socioeconomic powers that be. These tendencies confirm our earlier observations: this new sociopolitical space separates itself off from older social struggles and from their major social actors.

But, as the social struggles around the issue of waste have demonstrated, the space for contestation that the new social movements develop is inseparable from the symbolic struggles through which the culture of authenticity, typical of radical modernity, is constituted. The future of democracy and of radical politics is linked to these social struggles that articulate natural and planetary issues, the opposition to a neo-corporatist order, and the tensions of community-building. In this sense, the social struggles around waste issues and ecological questions in general turn out to be a good case study for helping to identify the characteristics of new social movements, and their impact on Quebec society as well as other societies of late modernity.

In sum, as Maheu and Descent (1990) note, new social movements try to defend forms of self and collective identity, as well as personal autonomy, and to oppose manipulation, control, dependence and bureaucratization processes that are too often characteristic of late modernity. They also try to break down the boundaries, rigidity and mismanagement of governments and bureaucratic systems. Consequently, environmental social movements in the area of waste management could be said to constitute, alongside many other new social movements, a definite cultural challenge to the neo-corporatist order that is pervasive in contemporary society.

REFERENCES

Babin, Ronald, Vaillancourt, Jean-Guy. "Développement durable, sécurité globale et reconversion économique: points de convergence pour le mouvement vert et le mouvement pour la paix", *Sociologie et sociétés,* vol. XXVII, no 1, printemps 1995, p. 171-181.

Bélanger Paul, Lévesque, Benoit. "Le mouvement populaire et communautaire, de la revendication au partenariat (1963-1992)", in Gérald Daigle (sous la direction de), *Le Québec en jeu. Comprendre les grands défis,* Montréal: Presses de l'Université de Montréal, 1992, pp. 713-747.

Bullard, Robert D., Wright, Beverly H. "The Quest for Environmental Equity. Mobilizing the African-American Community for Social Change", in Dunlap, Riley E., Mertig, Angela G. (Eds), *American Environmentalism, The U.S. Environmental Movement 1970-1990,* Philadelphia: Taylor and Francis, 1992, p. 39-49.

Cans, Roger. *Le monde poubelle,* Paris: First, 1990.

Cotnoir, Liliane, Maheu, Louis, Vaillancourt, Jean-Guy, "Démocratie, écodécision et implantation des projets d'élimination de déchets dangereux", dans Pradès, José A., Tessier, Robert, Vaillancourt, Jean-Guy, *Instituer le développement durable: éthique de l'écodécision et sociologie de l'environnement,* Montréal: Fides, 1994.

Descent, David, Maheu, Louis, Robitaille, Martin, Simard, Gilles, *Classes sociales et mouvements sociaux au Québec et au Canada,* Montréal: Les Editions St-Martin, 1989.

Dunlap, Riley E., Mertig, Angela G. "The Evolution of The U.S. Environmental Movement from 1970 to 1990: An Overview", in Dunlap, Riley E., Mertig, Angela G., (Eds), *American Environmentalism, The U.S. Environmental Movement 1970-1990,* Philadelphia: Taylor and Francis, 1992, pp. 1-10.

Eder, K. "Negotiating a Postcorporatist Order in Advanced Societies. An Institutional Analysis of Environmentalism". Florence: European University Institute, Project n° 42, Research paper n° 8, 1993 a.

Eder, K. "The Institutionalization of Social Movements. Towards a New Theoretical Problematic in Social Movement Analysis?", Florence: European University Institute, Project no. 42, 1993 b.

Freudenberg, Nicholas, Steinsapir, Carol. "Not in Our Backyards: The Grassroots Environmental Movement", In Dunlap, Riley E., Mertig, Angela G., (Eds), *American Environmentalism, The U.S. Environmental Movement 1970-1990,* Philadelphia: Taylor and Francis, 1992, pp. 27-36.

Giddens, Anthony. *The Consequences of Modernity,* Stanford: Stanford University Press, 1990.

Giddens, Anthony. *Modernity and Self Identity. Self and Society in the Late Modern Age,* Cambridge: Polity Press, 1991.

Gouvernement du Québec. Bureau d'audiences publiques sur l'environnement, *Les déchets dangereux au Québec: une gestion environnementale,* Commission d'enquête sur les déchets dangereux, Les publications du Québec, 1990.

Guindon, Hubert. *Quebec Society, Tradition, Modernity, and Nationhood*, Toronto: University of Toronto Press, 1988.

Hamel, Pierre. "Les mouvements sociaux", in Monière, Denis, (sous la direction de), *L'année politique au Québec 88-89*, Montréal: Québec/Amérique, 1989, 161-169.

Hamel, Pierre. *Action collective et démocratie locale: les mouvements urbains montréalais*, Montréal: Presses de l'Université du Montréal, 1991.

Hofrichter, Richard. *Toxic Struggles: The Theory and Practice of Environmental Justice*, Philadelphia: New Society Publishers, 1993.

Krauss, Celene. "Grass-Root Consumer Protest and Toxic Wastes: Developing a Critical Polical View", *Community Development Journal*, vol. 23, no 4, 1988, pp. 258-265.

Kuechler, Manfred, Dalton, Russel J. "New Social Movements and the Political Order: Inducing Change for Long-term Stability?", in Dalton, Russell J., Kuechler, Manfred (Eds), *Challenging the Political Order: New Social and Political Movements in Western Democracies*, New York: Oxford University Press, 1990.

La Ligue des Droits de l'Homme, "L'escalade de la répression: signification et importance du phénomène au Québec et au Canada", in La Ligue des Droits de l'Homme, *On vous a à l'oeil; police et liberté*", 1978, p.15-16.

Lord, René. *Les précurseurs du mouvement écologiste québécois*, mémoire de maîtrise, département de sociologie, Faculté des Arts et des Sciences, Université de Montréal, 1994.

Lustiger-Thaler, Henri, Maheu, Louis. "Social Movements and the Challenge of Urban Politics", in Maheu, L., (Ed.), *Social Movements and Social Classes. The Future of Collective Action*, London: Sage, 1995.

Maheu, Louis. "La conjoncture des luttes nationales au Québec: mode d'intervention étatique des classes moyennes et enjeux d'un mouvement social de rupture", *Sociologie et sociétés*, vol. 11, no 2, 1979, pp. 125-144.

Maheu, Louis. "Les nouveaux mouvements sociaux entre les voies de l'identité et les enjeux du public", dans Maheu, Louis, Sales, Arnaud (sous la direction de), *La recomposition du politique*, Montréal, PUM, Paris: Editions l'Harmattan, 1991, pp. 163-192.

Maheu, Louis. "Les mouvements sociaux: plaidoyer pour une sociologie de l'ambivalence", in Dubet, F., Wieviorka, M., *Penser le sujet; autour d'Alain Touraine*, Paris: Fayard, 1995 a.

Maheu, L. " The Sociology of Alain Touraine: A Modernist Look at Post-industrialization and the Ambivalence of Collective Action," in Clark, J., (Ed.), *Alain Touraine: Falmer Sociology Series*, London: Falmer Press, 1995 b.

Maheu, Louis. "General Introduction", in Maheu L. (ed), *Social Movements and Social Classes: the Future of Collective Action*, London: Sage, 1995 c, pp. 1-20.

Maheu, Louis, Descent, David. "Les mouvements sociaux: un terrain mouvant", *Nouvelles pratiques sociales*, vol. 3, no 1, 1990, pp. 41-45.

Matheney, Albert R., Williams, Bruce A. "Knowledge vs Nimby: Assessing Florida's Strategy for Siting Hazardous Waste Disposal Facilities", *Policy Studies Journal*, vol. 14, no 1, 1985, pp. 70-80.

Melucci, Alberto. "The Symbolic Challenge of Contemporary Movements", *Social Research*, Vol. 52, no. 4, 1985.

Melucci, Alberto. *Nomads of the Present; Social Movements and Individuals' Needs in Contemporary Society*, London: Keane, Mier (Eds), Hutchinson Radius, 1989, 288 pages.

Melucci, Alberto. "New Social Movements Revisited: Reflections and Sociological Misunderstanding", in Maheu L. (Ed.), *Social Movements and Social Classes. The Future of Collective Action*, London: Sage, 1995.

Neidhardt, Friedhelm, Rucht, Dieter. "The State of the Art and Some Perspectives of Further Research", in Rucht, D., (Ed.), *Research on Social Movements: The State of the Art in Western Europe and the USA*, Boulder: Westview Press, 1991.

Offe, Claus. "New Social Movements Challenging the Boundaries of Institutional Politics", *Social Research*, vol. 52, no 4, 1985, pp. 817-868.

Pakulski, Jan. "Mass Social Movements and Social Class", University of Tasmania, Australia, 1991, 38 pages.

Séguin, Michel. *Le scandale des déchets au Québec*, Montréal: Écosociété, 1994.

Taylor, Charles. *Sources of the Self, the Making of the Modern Identity*, Cambridge Mass.: Harvard University Press, 1989.

Taylor, Charles. *The Malaise of Modernity*, Concord, Ontario: Anansi Press, 1991.

Vaillancourt, Jean-Guy. "Deux mouvements sociaux québécois: le mouvement pour la paix et le mouvement vert", in Daigle, Gérard (sous la direction de), *Le Québec en jeu. Comprendre les grands défis*, Montréal, Les Presses de l'Université de Montréal: 1992, pp. 791-807.

Vaillancourt, Jean-Guy. "Le mouvement vert québécois: entre l'écologie et l'écologisme", *Possibles*, vol. 9, no 3, printemps 1985.

Vaillancourt, Jean-Guy. *Mouvement écologiste énergie et environnement: Essais d'écosociologie*, Montréal: Éditions coopératives Albert Saint-Martin, 1982.

Walsh, Edward, Warland, Rex, Smith, D. Clayton. "Backyards, NIMBYs, and Incinerator Sitings: Implications for Social Movement Theory", *Social Problems*, vol. 40, no 1, February 1993.

Appendices

INTRODUCTION TO THE APPENDICES

Since most readers of this work are unlikely to be familiar with Quebec society, these appendices to *Quebec Society: Critical Issues* have been prepared with two objectives.

The first is to provide some substance to the pieces of legislation often referred to in the text, the Charter of the French Language (Bill 101), the Quebec Charter of Human Rights and Freedoms, and the Canadian Charter of Rights and Freedoms. These pieces of legislation have taken on enormous symbolic significance in Quebec society and an examination of them helps us to understand the kinds of issues of concern to Quebecers and how they choose to deal with these issues.

The second objective is to provide some basic demographic, social and socio-economic information to complement the analytical approach taken in most of the book's chapters. Presented in tables and graphs, this data becomes a resource and gives us a picture of how Quebec compares to the rest of Canada, and, in some cases, the world.

On Bill 101 (Appendix A)

We have included in this appendix a substantial part of Quebec's highly controversial Charter of the French Language, informally known as Bill 101. This was the first major legislation to be adopted by the Parti Québécois, in 1977, one year after they came to power. It was followed by a second piece of major legislation in the same year, the Charter of Human Rights and Freedoms, which we have also included in this appendix and will discuss further on. The excerpts from the Charter of the French Language included here comprise all of Title I, which deals with language rights and obligations.[1] It is interesting to note much of the law refers to rights rather than obligations, and to the rights of minority languages as well as the majority language. Yet it is the obligations regarding the use of

---

[1] Those parts of Bill 101 not included are the sections pertaining to the Office de la langue française (established to monitor the implementation of Bill 101 and to promote the French language in Quebec), the Conseil de la langue française (established to advise the government on language policies), as well as the Commission de toponymie (established to choose and regulate place names); and the sections on the francisization of business firms (significantly revised since the Bill's first adoption) as well as of the civil service.

French, particularly in the workplace, the restriction of access to English educa-tion, and restrictions to the public use of written English, that have naturally cre-ated the most controversy and captured the attention of the Anglophone media.

Language legislation in Quebec is often interpreted in the light of "nationalist intolerence." In their efforts to protect and promote the French language in the only North American territory where it continues to thrive, Quebec's legislators are often accused of defining Anglophones as second-class citizens. For example, Anglophones cannot place public signs advertising any aspect of their business in English, except under specific conditions which sometimes take on an almost ludicrous air—for example, in the case of the relative size of the lettering for the French and English sections of an indoor poster indicating the price of goods (see Bill 101, chapter VII). The "sign issue" has become symbolic of Anglophones' resentment of Bill 101. It is typically perceived as an effort to muzzle the English language, and to wipe out all evidence of the historical Anglophone presence in the province, and the role of English-speakers in building the province. It is also perceived as a civil rights issue, an attack on the personal liberty to put up one's shingle, or to represent oneself publicly, in whatever language one chooses. On the other hand, the "sign issue" is particularly significant for Francophones because of its relevance for the "public face" of Quebec.

Restricting the use of English in public signs has been used as a real and a symbolic means for the Francophone majority to re-appropriate the public face of Quebec—and of the cosmopolitan city of Montreal in particular, where most of the downtown area had once been prominently dominated by English commercial signs and billboards. The restriction of English signs represented an effort to wipe out the most visible and "humiliating" remnants of those times when English busi-ness dominated the city, and Francophones were forced to work, and in some cases, even to shop in the language of the small minority. The strong desire to make Francophones feel at home when wandering the streets of Montreal and Quebec in general is expressed in Chapter II of Bill 101, which simply states that no Quebecer can be denied the right to work, shop, be educated, receive public services and generally carry out their everyday lives in French. The infamous sign laws have been somewhat softened since the first adoption of Bill 101 in 1977, as can been seen from the various sections of Chapter VII that have been repealed or abrogated, but there are those who now wish to see them reinstated.

If this bill has been seen as problematic by many Anglophones and immi-grants, it has also created certain problems for some Francophones. In particular, while Anglophones and immigrants have been encouraged, helped or coerced to become functionally bilingual—and almost all of the younger generations, who have entered school since 1975, are bilingual—Francophone youth remain largely unilingual. Many middle class and better off francophone families opt to send their children to English language private schools, or French language pri-vate schools with a strong English program in order to ensure that their chil-dren have the same bilingual advantage. This means, however, that unilingual Francophone youths, mainly from less well off families, remain at a disadvan-tage when trying to break into the labour market.

Quebec, of course, is not the only society to have language laws. Indeed, Canada's own language law declares French and English the two official languages. Some U.S. states have enacted legislation making English the only official language, in order to pre-empt any effort on the part of the growing Hispanic population to call for the provision of public services in Spanish in regions where it is in the majority. The Canadian language law could ostensibly be used by future generations to similar, exclusionary purposes. The reason that Quebec's language law appears exceptionally exclusionary is because, in contrast to the Canadian law reigning in other provinces, it does not accord English the status of an official language.

Now, Quebec's language law was enacted several years later than Ottawa's, and was in many ways a response to it—an official "dissenting opinion." In the place of the bilingual and bicultural view of Canada, it was meant to affirm a "two nations" view, with Quebec representing the homeland of Francophone Canadians, and having the particular role of protecting, promoting and developing French language and French Canadian culture. This role was considered critical for several reasons. First, a policy of bilingualism and biculturalism from sea to sea would forever cast French as the minority language across Canada, and there was concern that this would extend the process of assimilation that was already well advanced in all provinces but Quebec. Assimilation was looming as a problem in Quebec as well, insofar as the rising numbers of immigrants to the province continued to choose English over French, and English continued to be the language of work and public life in many areas of Montreal.

But such defensive strategies were not the only motives for Bill 101. The promotion of a uniquely Francophone society in Quebec, especially in the workplace and the public sphere, was seen as an important occupational and economic facilitator for Francophone workers and business people, and as a means of managing more smoothly the social and occupational integration of immigrants.

On the Charters of Human Rights (Appendices B and C)

We have reproduced excerpts of both the Quebec Charter of Human Rights and Freedoms (1977)[2] and the Canadian Charter of Rights and Freedoms (1982)[3]. The Canadian Charter is significantly shorter than the Quebec, yet deals with some issues not touched upon by the Quebec Charter. For example, language rights form the largest single section of the Canadian Charter. They were intended not only to affirm the language rights of both language groups throughout Canada, but also, in so doing, to limit the legality of Quebec's Charter of the

---

[2] We have left out substantial sections of the Quebec Charter, dealing with its interpretation, with the Human Rights Commission and the Human Rights Tribunal, with procedures for making complaints, on issues of confidentiality, as well as the lengthy part of the Charter that details the regulations for its application.

[3] The Canadian Charter is presented in its near entirety, with only a brief section on its application left out.

French Language (Bill 101) that had been adopted five years earlier. Since provincial legislation normally cannot contravene Canadian law, the Quebec legislature was required to invoke the "notwithstanding clause" in order to keep in force certain sections of Bill 101 related to the language of education, which after 1982, contravened the new Canadian Charter (Quebec has not been the only province to use the "notwithstanding clause" to override language provisions of the Constitution.)

The structure of the Quebec Charter reflects the province's unique tradition of civil law, which in certain areas retains the characteristics of the old Napoleonic Code. The main difference between the Napoleonic and British legal traditions is that Napoleonic law is basically a set of axiomatic principles from which decisions in specific cases are to be deduced. In contrast, the British tradition relies far more on "precedent" and is more susceptible to reinterpretation and social change. The difference does not necessarily mean that the Quebec legal system is more rigid, since juries ultimately play the decisive role in both systems. Thus, for example, three consecutive Quebec juries acquitted a man, charged three times with performing illegal abortions. The abortion law thus became inapplicable. Yet this tradition of "deduction from principles" explains why we find that the Quebec Charter of Rights and Freedoms begins with a long preamble stating the principles by which it is justified, in contrast to the Canadian Charter which has almost no preamble at all. The principles stated in the Quebec preamble are reminiscent of the the American Constitution, in that they make reference, for example, to the intrinsic rights, freedoms and equality of every human being.

More significantly, these initial principles state that the "rights and freedoms of the human person are inseparable from the rights and freedoms of others and from the common well-being." This balancing between the rights of the individual and those of the collectivity, or between visions of the society as an aggregate of individuals and as a community, is a central feature of the Quebec Charter. The distinction between a society in which individual rights are paramount, and one in which "the common well-being" is considered equally important are highlighted by comparing the U.S. and Quebec cases. For example, in the U.S., citizens are within their rights to refuse to help someone in peril, on the grounds that if they unintentionally caused harm in the process, they could be prosecuted. In Quebec, the Charter of Rights includes the right to assistance for every human being whose life is in peril, and this right is further reinforced by an obligation on the part of others to come to the aid of a person in peril, unless this would endanger the "helper." The interest in collective or community rights expressed in the Charter helps us to understand the basis for a language law such as Bill 101, which is perceived to protect and serve the Francophone community.

Individual rights are not given less attention than community rights, however. In fact, the community is expected to play an important role in upholding individual rights. The Quebec Charter not only recognizes the equality of all without discrimination before the law, but unlike the Canadian Charter, also holds all ordinary citizens to non-discriminatory behaviour. (Some similar provisions exist in Canadian law, such as the prohibition of hate-mongering, but were not included in the Canadian Charter of Rights). The human characteristics expressly noted as potential sources of illegal discrimination include several not mentioned in the Canadian Charter: sexual orientation, pregnancy, civil status, political convictions, and most significantly, language and "social condition."

Finally, amongst the important distinctions between the two Charters is the inclusion, in the Quebec Charter, of a series of economic and social rights. In the Canadian context, the call for a social charter has fallen on deaf ears ever since the enactment of the Charter in 1982.

The mere existence of a Charter of Rights of Freedoms does not say much about the extent to which, or the ways in which it is applied, nor about its accessibility in practice to the ordinary citizen. However, it does tell us quite a bit about the way in which a society sees itself, and about the ideals that it sets for itself. In this context, it is clear that the Canadian Charter is a minimalist charter, a difficult consensus reached by the representatives of 9 out of 10 provinces (Quebec is not a signatory to the Canadian Charter, enacted at the time that the Constitution was "repatriated" in 1982 without Quebec's assent). In contrast, the Quebec Charter of Human Rights and Freedoms is clearly a proud statement of collective identity, along with the province's other emblematic piece of legislation, the Charter of the French Language.

The Tables

The tables that are presented in this appendix all originate from government documents. In some cases, chapter authors may have provided somewhat different statistics that either emanate from their own research, or that they may have identified as coming from some other source. Discrepencies in the actual figures presented must not be taken to suggest that one statistic is correct and the other wrong. They may simply be due to the precise time period in which the statistics were collected, and to which they refer. Often, they result from the definition given to the phenomenon being measured. For example, the official, government definition of "unemployed" does not include people on welfare, since they are considered to have abandoned the labour market. An author, however, may consider it important to include these people when talking about the unemployed. Finally, discrepencies between figures provided in chapters and those found in the appendix may be due to the way in which an author has classified the information, so that the categories (for example, the age intervals they refer to) reflect their own analytical framework rather than that of the government statisticians.

Appendix A

CHARTER OF THE FRENCH LANGUAGE

Preamble

Preamble. WHEREAS the French language, the distinctive language of a people that is in the majority French-speaking, is the instrument by which that people has articulated its identity;

Whereas the National Assembly of Québec recognizes that Quebecers wish to see the quality and influence of the French language assured, and is resolved therefore to make of French the language of Government and the Law, as well as the normal and everyday language of work, instruction, communication, commerce and business;

Whereas the National Assembly intends to pursue this objective in a spirit of fairness and open-mindedness, respectful of the institutions of the English-speaking community of Québec, and respectful of the ethnic minorities, whose valuable contribution to the development of Québec it readily acknowledges;

Whereas the National Assembly of Québec recognizes the right of the Amerinds and the Inuit of Québec, the first inhabitants of this land, to preserve and develop their original language and culture;

Whereas these observations and intentions are in keeping with a new perception of the worth of national cultures in all parts of the earth, and of the obligation of every people to contribute in its special way to the international community;

Therefore, Her Majesty, with the advice and consent of the National Assembly of Québec, enacts as follows:

TITLE I

STATUS OF THE FRENCH LANGUAGE

CHAPTER I

THE OFFICIAL LANGUAGE OF QUEBEC

Official language. **1.** French is the official language of Québec.

CHAPTER II

FUNDAMENTAL LANGUAGE RIGHTS

Communications with public and private sectors.

2. Every person has a right to have the civil administration, the health services and social services, the public utility firms, the professional corporations, the associations of employees and all business firms doing business in Québec communicate with him in French.

In deliberative assembly.

3. In deliberative assembly, every person has a right to speak in French.

Workers.

4. Workers have a right to carry on their activities in French.

Consumers.

5. Consumers of goods and services have a right to be informed and served in French.

Instruction.

6. Every person eligible for instruction in Québec has a right to receive that instruction in French.

CHAPTER III

THE LANGUAGE OF THE LEGISLATURE AND THE COURTS

7. French is the language of the legislature and the courts in Québec, subject to the following:

(1) legislative bills shall be printed, published, passed and assented to in French and in English, and the statutes shall be printed and published in both languages;

(2) the regulations and other similar acts to which section 133 of the Constitution Act, 1867 applies shall be made, passed or issued, and printed and published in French and in English;

(3) the French and English versions of the texts referred to in paragraphs 1 and 2 are equally authoritative;

(4) either French or English may be used by any person in, or in any pleading in or process issuing from, any court of Québec.

8. Where an English version exists of a regulation or other similar act to which section 133 of the Constitution Act, 1867 does not apply, the French text shall prevail in case of discrepancy.

9. Every judgment rendered by the court of justice and every decision rendered by a body discharging quasi-judicial functions shall, at the request of one of the parties, be translated into French or English, as the case may be, by the civil administration bound to bear the cost of operating such court or body.

10.–13. *(Replaced).*

CHAPTER IV

THE LANGUAGE OF THE CIVIL ADMINISTRATION

Designation.

14.   The Government, the government departments, the other agencies of the civil administration and the services thereof shall be designated by their French names alone.

Texts and documents.

Exceptions.

15.   The civil administration shall draw up and publish its texts and documents in the official language.

This section does not apply to relations with persons outside Québec, to publicity and communiqués carried by news media that publish in a language other than French or to correspondence between the civil administration and natural persons when the latter address it in a language other than French.

Communication with other governments and artificial persons.

16.   The civil administration shall use the official language in its written communications with other governments and with artificial persons established in Québec.

Interdepartmental communications.

17.   The Government, the government departments and the other agencies of the civil administration shall use only the official language in their written communications with each other.

Internal communications.

18.   French is the language of written internal communications in the Government, the government departments, and the other agencies of the civil administration.

Notices of meetings.

19.   The notices of meeting, agendas and minutes of all deliberative assemblies in the civil administration shall be drawn up in the official language.

Knowledge of French for appointment or promotion.

Criteria and procedures.

20.   In order to be appointed, transferred or promoted to an office in the civil administration, a knowledge of the official language appropriate to the office applied for is required.

For the application of the preceding paragraph, each agency of the civil administration shall establish criteria and procedures of verification and submit them to the Office de la langue française for approval, failing which the Office may establish them itself. If the Office considers the criteria and procedures unsatisfactory, it may either request the agency concerned to modify them or establish them itself.

Applicability.

This section does not apply to bodies, services and departments recognized under the first paragraph of section 29.1 which implement the measures approved by the Office according to the third paragraph of section 23.

Contracts.

21. Contracts entered into by the civil administration, including the related sub-contracts, shall be drawn up in the official language. Such contracts and the related documents may be drawn up in another language when the civil administration enters into a contract with a party outside Québec.

Signs and posters.

22. The civil administration shall use only French in signs and posters, except where reasons of health or public safety require the use of another language as well.

In the case of traffic signs, the French inscription may be complemented or replaced by symbols or pictographs, and another language may be used where no symbol or pictograph exists that satisfies the requirements of health or public safety.

The Government may, however, determine by regulation the cases, conditions or circumstances in which the civil administration may use French and another language in signs and posters.

Designation of thoroughfares.

22.1. In a municipality, a specific term other than a French term may be used in conjunction with a generic French term to designate a thoroughfare if the term is sanctioned by usage or if its use has unquestionable merit owing to its cultural or historical interest.

Services to the public.

23. The bodies, services and departments recognized under the first paragraph section 29.1 must ensure that their services to the public are available in the official language.

Notices.

They must draw up their notices, communications and printed matter intended for the public in the official language.

Approval.

They must devise the necessary measures to make their services to the public available in the official language, and criteria and procedures for verifying knowledge of the official language for the purposes of application of this section. These measures, criteria and procedures are subject to approval by the Office.

Recognized bodies and services; bilingual signs and posters.

24. The municipal and school bodies, the health services and social services and the other services recognized under the first paragraph of section 29.1 may erect signs and posters in both French and another language, the French text predominating.

25. *(Repealed).*

Bilingual names and internal communications.

26. The bodies, services and departments recognized under the first paragraph of section 29.1 may use both the official language and another language in their names, their internal communications and their communications with each other.

French version. In the recognized bodies, services and departments, two persons may use what language they choose in written communications to one another. However, a body, service or department shall, at the request of a person required to consult such a communication in the course of his duties, prepare a French version of it.

Clinical records in health services and social services.

27. In the health services and the social services, the documents filed in the clinical records shall be drafted in French or in English, as the person drafting them sees fit. However, each health service or social service may require such documents to be drafted in French alone. Resumés of clinical records must be furnished in French on demand to any person authorized to obtain them.

Communications in the language of instruction.

28. Notwithstanding sections 23 and 26, school bodies recognized under the first paragraph of section 29.1, as well as departments recognized under the same provision which, in the school bodies, are entrusted with giving instruction in a language other than French may use the language of instruction in their communications connected with teaching without having to use the official language at the same time.

29. *(Abrogated).*

29.1. The Office shall, for the purposes of the provisions of the third paragraph of section 20 and sections 23, 24, 26 and 28, recognize, at their request, the municipal or school bodies within the meaning of the Schedule, or the health and social services institutions referred to in the Schedule, that provide services to persons who, in the majority, speak a language other than French. It shall also recognize, for the purposes of those provisions and at the request of a school body, the departments of such a body that have charge of organizing or giving instruction in a language other than French.

The Government may, at the request of a body or institution that no longer satisfies the condition which enabled it to obtain recognition under the first paragraph, withdraw such recognition if it considers it appropriate in the circumstances and after having consulted the Office. Such a request shall be made to the Office, which shall transmit it to the Government with a copy of the record. The Government shall inform the Office and the body or institution of its decision.

CHAPTER V

THE LANGUAGE OF THE SEMIPUBLIC AGENCIES

Public utilities and professional corporations: services.

Notices, tickets.

30. The public utility firms, the professional corporations and the members of the professional corporations must arrange to make their services available in the official language.

They must draw up their notices, communications and printed matter intended for the public, including public transportation tickets, in the official language.

Members of professional corporations.

30.1. When, before a member of a professional corporation draws up a notice, opinion, report, expertise or other document concerning a person who calls upon his services, the person asks to have it in French, the member shall furnish it in French without requiring a charge for translation.

Written communications.

31. The public utility firms and the professional corporations shall use the official language in their written communications with the civil administration and with artificial persons.

With general membership.

Option: with individual member.

32. The professional corporations shall use the official language in their written communications with their general membership.

They may, however, in communicating with an individual member, reply in his language.

Exceptions.

33. Sections 30 and 31 do not apply to communiqués or publicity intended for news media that publish in a language other than French.

Professional corporations: designation.

34. The professional corporations shall be designated by their French names alone.

Appropriate knowledge of French.

Presumption.

35. The professional corporations shall not issue permits except to persons whose knowledge of the official language is appropriate to the practice of their profession.

A person is deemed to have the appropriate knowledge if

(1) he has received, full time, no less than three years of secondary or post-secondary instruction provided in French;

(2) he has passed to fourth or fifth year secondary level examinations in French as the first language;

(3) from and after the school year 1985–86, he obtains a secondary school certificate in Québec.

Certificate.

In all other cases, a person must obtain a certificate issued by the Office de la langue française or hold a certificate defined as equivalent by regulation of the Government.

The Government, by regulation, may determine the procedures and conditions of issue of certificates by the Office, establish the rules governing composition of an examining committee to be formed by the Office, provide for the mode of operation of that committee, and determine criteria for evaluating the appropriate knowledge of French for the practice of a profession or a category of professions and a mode of evaluating such knowledge.

Proof before diploma is obtained. **36.**   Within the last two years before obtaining a qualifying diploma for a permit to practise, every person enrolled in an educational institution that issues such diploma may give proof that his knowledge of the official language meets the requirements of section 35.

Temporary permit for outsiders. **37.**   The professional corporations may issue temporary permits valid for not more than one year to persons from outside Québec who are declared qualified to practise their profession but whose knowledge of the official language does not meet the requirements of section 35.

Renewal. **38.**   The permits envisaged in section 37 may be renewed, only three times, with the authorization of the Office de la langue française and if the public interest warrants it. For each renewal, the persons concerned must sit for examinations held according to the regulations of the Government.

In its annual report of activities, the Office shall indicate the number of permits for which it has given authorization for renewal pursuant to this section.

Temporary permit for Québec graduates. **39.**   Persons having obtained, in Québec, a diploma referred to in section 36 may, until the end of 1980, avail themselves of sections 37 and 38.

Restricted permit. **40.**   Where it is in the public interest, a professional corporation, with the prior authorization of the Office de la langue française, may issue a restricted permit to a person already authorized under the laws of another province or another country to practise his profession. This restricted permit authorizes its holder to practise his profession for the exclusive account of a single employer, in a position that does not involve his dealing with the public.

Spouse. In the case of this section, a permit may be issued to the spouse as well.

CHAPTER VI

THE LANGUAGE OF LABOUR RELATIONS

Employer's notices, offers.

41. Every employer shall draw up his written communications to his staff in the official language. He shall draw up and publish his offers of employment or promotion in French.

Offer of employment in newspaper.

42. Where an offer of employment regards employment in the civil administration, a semipublic agency or a firm required to establish a francization committee, have an attestation of implementation of a francization programme or hold a francization certificate, as the case may be, the employer publishing this offer of employment in a daily newspaper published in a language other than French must publish it simultaneously in a daily newspaper published in French, with at least equivalent display.

Collective agreements.

43. Collective agreements and the schedules to them must be drafted in the official language, including those which must be filed pursuant to section 72 of the Labour Code (chapter C–27).

44. An arbitration award made following arbitration of a grievance or dispute regarding the negotiation, renewal or review of a collective agreement shall, at the request of one of the parties, be translated into French or English, as the case may be, at the parties' expense.

Prohibition: dismissal, or demote for ignorance of other language.

45. An employer is prohibited from dismissing, laying off, demoting or transferring a member of his staff for the sole reason that he is exclusively French-speaking or that he has insufficient knowledge of a particular language other than French.

Prohibition: knowledge of other language as condition of employment.

Onus.

46. An employer is prohibited from making the obtaining of an employment or office dependent upon the knowledge of a language other than the official language, unless the nature of the duties requires the knowledge of that other language.

The burden of proof that the knowledge of the other language is necessary is on the employer, at the demand of the person or the association of employees concerned or, as the case may be, the Office de la langue française. The Office de la langue française has the power to decide any dispute.

Vindication of worker's rights under Labour code.

47. Any contravention of section 45 or 46, in addition to being an offence against this act, gives a worker not governed by a collective agreement the same entitlement to vindicate his rights through a labour commissioner appointed under the Labour Code as if he were dismissed for union activities. Sections 15 to 20 of the Labour Code then apply, *mutatis mutandis.*

Arbitration of grievance.

If the worker is governed by a collective agreement, he has the same entitlement to submit his grievance for arbitration as his association, if the latter fails to act. Section 16 of the Labour Code applies *mutatis mutandis*, for the arbitration of this grievance.

Juridical acts null.

48.   Except as they regard the vested rights of employees and their associations, juridical acts, decisions and other documents not in conformity to this chapter are null. The use of a language other than that prescribed in this chapter shall not be considered a defect of form within the meaning of section 151 of the Labour Code.

Associations of employee's written communications.

49.   Every association of employees shall use the official language in written communications with its members. It may use the language of an individual member in its correspondence with him.

Ss. 41 to 49 integral to all collective agreements.

50.   Sections 41 to 49 of this act are deemed an integral part of every collective agreement. Any stipulation in the agreement contrary to any provision of this act is void.

CHAPTER VII

THE LANGUAGE OF COMMERCE AND BUSINESS

Labels, directions, warranties, menus: in French.

51.   Every inscription on a product, on its container or on its wrapping, or on a leaflet, brochure or card supplied with it, including the directions for use and the warranty certificates, must be drafted in French. This rule applies also to menus and wine lists.

Other languages.

The French inscription may be accompanied with a translation or translations, but no inscription in another language may be given greater prominence than that in French.

Catalogues, brochures.

52.   Catalogues, brochures, folders, commercial directories and any similar publications must be drawn up in French.

Exceptions.

53.   The Government may, by regulation, provide, on such conditions as it may fix, for exceptions to the application of section 51 or section 52.

Toys and games.

54.   Except as provided by regulation of the Government, it is forbidden to offer toys or games to the public which require the use of a non-French vocabulary for their operation, unless a French version of the toy or game is available on no less favourable terms on the Québec market.

Contracts
pre-determined by
one party.

55.   Contracts pre-determined by one party, contracts containing printed standard clauses, and the related documents, must be drawn up in French. They may be drawn up in another language as well at the express wish of the parties.

Exception.

56.   If the documents referred to in section 51 are required by any act, order in council or government regulation, they may be excepted from the rule enunciated in that section, provided that the languages in which they are drafted are the subject of a federal-provincial, interprovincial or international agreement.

Application forms
for employment.

57.   Application forms for employment, order forms, invoices, receipts and quittances shall be drawn up in French.

58.   Public signs and posters and commercial advertising must be in French.

They may also be both in French and in another language provided that French is markedly predominant.

However, the Government may determine, by regulation, the places cases, conditions or circumstances where public signs and posters and commercial advertising must be in French only, where French need not be predominant or where such signs, posters and advertising may be in another language only.

58.1.–58.2.   *(Replaced).*

Exceptions.

59.   Section 58 does not apply to advertising carried in news media that publish in a language other than French, or to messages of a religious, political, ideological or humanitarian nature if not for a profit motive.

60.   *(Repealed).*

61.   *(Abrogated).*

62.   *(Abrogated).*

Firm names.

63.   Firms names must be in French.

Juridical
personality.

64.   To obtain juridical personality, it is necessary to have a firm name in French.

Delay to comply.

65.   Every firm name that is not in French must be changed before 31 December 1980, unless the act under which the firm is incorporated does not allow it.

66.   Sections 63, 64 and 65 also apply to firm names entered by way of declaration in the register instituted in accordance with the Act respecting the legal publicity of sole proprietorships, partnerships and legal persons (1993, chapter 48).

Family names in firm names.

67. Family names, place names, expressions formed by the artificial combination of letters, syllables or figures, and expressions taken from other languages may appear in firm names to specify them, in accordance with the other acts and with the regulations of the Government.

68. A firm name may be accompanied with a version in a language other than French provided that, when it is used, the French version of the firm name appears at least as prominently.

However, in public signs and posters and commercial advertising, the use of a version of a firm name in a language other than French is permitted to the extent that the other language may be used in such signs and posters or in such advertising pursuant to section 58 and the regulations enacted under that section.

In addition, in texts or documents drafted only in a language other than French, a firm name may appear in the other language only.

69. *(Repealed).*

Health services and social services.

70. Health services and social services the firm names of which, adopted before 26 August 1977, are in a language other than French may continue to use such names provided they add a French version.

Non-profit organizations.

71. A non-profit organization devoted exclusively to the cultural development or to the defense of the peculiar interests of a particular ethnic group may adopt a firm name in the language of the group, provided that it adds a French version.

CHAPTER VIII

THE LANGUAGE OF INSTRUCTION

Language of instruction.

72. Instruction in the kindergarten classes and in the elementary and secondary schools shall be in French, except where this chapter allows otherwise.

Scope.

This rule obtains in school bodies within the meaning of the Schedule and in private educational institutions accredited for purposes of subsidies under the Act respecting private education (1992, chapter 68) with respect to the educational services covered by an accreditation.

Nothing in this section shall preclude instruction in English to foster the learning thereof, in accordance with the formalities and on the conditions prescribed in the basic school regulations established by the Government under section 447 of the Education Act (R.S.Q., chapter I–13.3).

73.   The following children, at the request of one of their parents, may receive instruction in English:

(1) a child whose father or mother is a Canadian citizen and received elementary instruction in English in Canada, provided that that instruction constitutes the major part of the elementary instruction he or she received in Canada;

(2)   a child whose father or mother is a Canadian citizen and who has received or is receiving elementary or secondary instruction in English in Canada, and the brothers and sisters of that child, provided that that instruction constitutes the major part of the elementary or secondary instruction received by the child in Canada;

(3) a child whose father and mother are not Canadian citizens, but whose father or mother received elementary instruction in English in Québec, provided that that instruction constitutes the major part of the elementary instruction he or she received in Québec;

(4) a child who, in his last year in school in Québec before 26 August 1977 was receiving instruction in English in a public kindergarten class or in an elementary or secondary school, and the brothers and sisters of that child;

(5) a child whose father or mother was residing in Québec on 26 August 1977 and had received elementary instruction in English outside Québec, provided that that instruction constitutes the major part of the elementary instruction her or she received outside Québec.

74.   The parent who may make the requests provided for in this chapter must be the holder of parental authority. However, the person who has *de facto* custody of the child and who is not the holder of parental authority may also make such a request provided the holder of parental authority does not object.

Verification of eligibility.

75.   The Minister of Education may empower such persons as he may designate to verify and decide on children's eligibility for instruction in English under any of sections 73, 81, 85 and 86.1.

Verification of eligibility.

76.   The persons designated by the Minister of Education under section 75 may verify the eligibility of children to receive their instruction in English even if they are already receiving or are about to receive their instruction in French.

Such persons may also declare a child eligible to receive instruction in English where his father or mother attended school after 26 August 1977 and would have been eligible to receive such instruction under any of paragraphs 1 to 5 of section 73, even if he or she did not receive such instruction. However, where the father or mother attended school before 17 April 1982, his or her eligibility shall be determined in accordance with section 73 as it read before that date, by adding, at the end of paragraphs *a* and *b* of that section, the words "provided that that instruction constitutes the major part of the elementary instruction he or she received in Québec."

76.1.   The persons declared eligible to receive instruction in English under any of sections 73, 76, 81, 85.1 and 86.1 are deemed to have received or be receiving instruction in English for the purposes of section 73.

Fraud.   **77.**   A certificate of eligibility obtained fraudulently or on the basis of a false representation is void.

Revocation of certificate.   **78.**   The Minister of Education may revoke a certificate of eligibility issued in error.

Prohibition.   **78.1.**   No person may permit or tolerate a child's receiving instruction in English if he is ineligible therefor.

Authorization to introduce instruction in English.   **79.**   A school body not already giving instruction in English in its schools is not required to introduce it and shall not introduce it without express and prior authorization of the Minister of Education.

Instruction in English.   However, every school body shall, where necessary, avail itself of section 213 of the Education Act (chapter I–13.3) to arrange for the instruction in English of any child declared eligible therefor.

Authorization at Minister's discretion.   The Minister of Education shall grant the authorization referred to in the first paragraph if, in his opinion, it is warranted by the number of pupils in the jurisdiction of the school body who are eligible for instruction in English under this chapter.

Procedure and proof.   **80.**   The Government may, by regulation, prescribe the procedure to be followed where parents invoke section 73 or section 86.1, and the elements of proof they must furnish in support of their request.

81.   Children having serious learning disabilities may, at the request of one of their parents, receive instruction in English. The brothers and sisters of children thus exempted from the application of the first paragraph of section 72 may also be exempted.

Regulation: exemption.

The Government, by regulation, may define the classes of children envisaged in the preceding paragraph and determine the procedure to be followed in view of obtaining such an exemption.

82. An appeal lies from every decision rendered by the persons designated by the Minister of Education under section 75.

Time limit.

An appeal is brought within 60 days after communication of a decision.

Appeals committee.

83. An appeals committee is established to hear appeals provided for in section 82. This committee consists of three members appointed by the Government after consultation with the most representative associations or organizations of parents, teachers, school boards, school administrators and socio-economic groups. The decisions of this committee are final.

Powers of the committee.

83.1. The committee has all the necessary powers for the exercise of its jurisdiction; it may make such orders as it sees fit to safeguard the rights of the parties and rule on any question of fact or of law.

Procedure.

83.2. Appeals are brought and heard according to the procedure and rules of proof prescribed by regulation of the Government.

Immunities.

83.3. For the exercise of their functions under this Act, the members of the committee are vested with the immunities provided in sections 16 and 17 of the Act respecting public inquiry commissions (chapter C–37).

Secondary school leaving certificate.

84. No secondary school leaving certificate may be issued to a student who does not have the speaking and writing knowledge of French required by the curricula of the Ministère de l'Éducation.

85. Children staying in Québec temporarily may, at the request of one of their parents, be exempted from the application of the first paragraph of section 72 and receive instruction in English in the cases of circumstances and on the conditions determined by regulation of the Government. The regulation shall also prescribe the period for which such an exemption may be granted and the procedure to be followed in order to obtain or renew it.

File transmitted to the Minister.

85.1. Where the appeals committee cannot allow an appeal pertaining to an application relating to the eligibility of a child for instruction in English but deems that proof of the existence of a serious situation has been made on family or humanitarian grounds, it shall make a report to the Minister of Education and transmit the child's file to him.

Certification.   The Minister may certify eligible for instruction in English a child whose file is transmitted to him by the appeals committee under the first paragraph.

Report.   The Minister of Education shall indicate, in the report referred to in section 4 of the Act respecting the Ministère de l'Éducation (chapter M–15), the number of children certified eligible for instruction in English under the second paragraph and the grounds on which he certified them eligible.

Reciprocity agreement.   **86.**   The Government may make regulations extending the scope of section 73 to include such persons as may be contemplated in any reciprocity agreement that may be concluded between the Gouvernement du Québec and another province.

Instruction in English.   **86.1.**   In addition to the cases provided for in section 73, the Government, by order, may, at the request of one of the parents authorize generally the following children to receive their instruction in English:

(*a*) a child whose father or mother received the greater part of his or her elementary instruction in English elsewhere in Canada and, before establishing domicile in Québec, was domiciled in a province or territory that it indicates in the order and where it considers that the services of instruction in French offered to French-speaking persons are comparable to those offered in English to English-speaking persons in Québec;

(*b*) a child whose father or mother establishes domicile in Québec and who, during his last school year or from the beginning of the current school year, has received primary or secondary instruction in English in the province or territory indicated in the order;

(*c*) the younger brothers and sisters of children described in subparagraphs *a* and *b*.

Applicability.   Sections 76 to 79 apply to the persons contemplated in this section.

Amerindic languages and Inuktitut.   **87.**   Nothing in this Act prevents the use of an Amerindic language in providing instruction to the Amerinds, or of Inuktitut in providing instruction to the Inuit.

Languages of instruction.   **88.**   Notwithstanding sections 72 to 86, in the schools under the jurisdiction of the Cree School Board or the Kativik School

Board, according to the Education Act for Cree, Inuit and Naskapi Native Persons (chapter I–14), the languages of instruction shall be Cree and Inuktitut, respectively, and the other languages of instruction in use in the Cree and Inuit communities in Québec on the date of the signing of the Agreement indicated in section 1 of the Act approving the Agreement concerning James Bay and Northern Québec (chapter C–67), namely, 11 November 1975.

Cree School Board and the Kativik School Board.

The Cree School Board and the Kativik School Board shall pursue as an objective the use of French as a language of instruction so that pupils graduating from their school will in future be capable of continuing their studies in a French school, college or university elsewhere in Québec, if they so desire.

Rate of introduction of French and English.

After consultation with the school committees, in the case of the Crees, and with the parents' committees, in the case of the Inuit, the commissioners shall determine the rate of introduction of French and English as languages of instruction.

Non-qualifying Crees or Inuit.

With the assistance of the Ministère de l'Éducation, the Cree School Board and the Kativik School Board shall take the necessary measures to have sections 72 to 86 apply to children whose parents are not Crees or Inuit. For the purposes of the second paragraph of section 79, a reference to the Education Act is a reference to section 450 of the Education Act for Cree, Inuit and Naskapi Native Persons.

Naskapi of Schefferville.

This section, with the necessary changes, applies to the Naskapi of Schefferville.

CHAPTER IX

MISCELLANEOUS

French use exclusive only if specified.

89. Where this Act does not require the use of the official language exclusively, the official language and another language may be used together.

Statutory publication may be in French only.

90. Subject to section 7, anything that, by prescription of an act of Québec or an act of the British Parliament having application to Québec in a field of provincial jurisdiction, or of a regulation or an order, must be published in French and English may be published in French alone.

Publication in French newspaper.

Similarly, anything that, by prescription of an act, a regulation or an order, must be published in a French newspaper and in an English newspaper, may be published in a French newspaper alone.

Prominence of French version.

91. Where this act authorizes the drafting of texts or documents both in French and in one or more other languages, the French version must be displayed at least as prominently as every other language.

International organizations.

92. Nothing prevents the use of a language in derogation of this act by international organizations designated by the Government or where international usage requires it.

Regulations.

93. In addition to its other regulation-making powers under this act, the Government may make regulations to facilitate the administration of the act, including regulations defining the terms and expressions used in the act or defining the scope.

94. *(Abrogated).*

Right to use Cree and Inuktitut.

95. The following persons and bodies have the right to use Cree and Inuktitut and are exempt from the application of this act, except sections 87, 88 and 96;

(*a*) persons qualified for benefit under the Agreement indicated in section 1 of the Act approving the Agreement concerning James Bay and Northern Québec (chapter C–67), in the territories envisaged by the said Agreement;

(*b*) bodies to be created under the said Agreement, within the territories envisaged by the Agreement;

(*c*) bodies of which the members are in the majority persons referred to in subparagraph a, within the territories envisaged by the Agreement.

Naskapi of Schefferville.

This section, with the necessary changes, applies to the Naskapi of Schefferville.

Introduction of French.

96. The bodies envisaged in section 95 must introduce the use of French into their administration, both to communicate in French with the rest of Québec and with those persons under their administration who are not contemplated in subparagraph *a* of that section, and to provide their services in French to those persons.

Transitional period.

During a transitional period of such duration as the Government may fix after consultation with the persons concerned, sections 16 and 17 of this act do not apply to communications of the civil administration with the bodies envisaged in section 95.

Naskapi of Schefferville.

This section, with the necessary changes, applies to the Naskapi of Schefferville.

Indians reserves.   **97.**   The Indian reserves are not subject to this act.

Exception.   The Government, by regulation, shall determine the cases, conditions and circumstances where or whereunder an agency or body contemplated in the Schedule is authorized to make an exception to the application of one or several provisions of this Act in respect of a person who resides or has resided on a reserve, a settlement in which a native community lives or on Category I and Category I–N lands within the meaning of the Act respecting the land regime in the James Bay and New Québec territories (R.S.Q., chapter R–13.1).

Agencies contemplated.   **98.**   The various agencies of the civil administration, and the health services and social services, the public utility firms and the professional corporations referred to in this act are listed in the Schedule.

Appendix B

CHARTER OF HUMAN RIGHTS AND FREEDOMS

Preamble.   WHEREAS every human being possesses intrinsic rights and freedoms designed to ensure his protection and development;

Whereas all human beings are equal in worth and dignity, and are entitled to equal protection of the law;

Whereas respect for the dignity of the human being and recognition of his rights and freedoms constitute the foundation of justice and peace;

Whereas the rights and freedoms of the human person are inseparable from the rights and freedoms of others and from the common well-being;

Whereas it is expedient to solemnly declare the fundamental human rights and freedoms in a Charter, so that they may be guaranteed by the collective will and better protected against any violation;

Therefore, Her Majesty, with the advice and consent of the National Assembly of Québec, enacts as follows:

PART I
HUMAN RIGHTS AND FREEDOMS

CHAPTER I
FUNDAMENTAL FREEDOMS AND RIGHTS

Right to life.   **1.** Every human being has a right to life, and to personal security, inviolability and freedom.

Juridical personality.   He also posses juridical personality.

Right to assistance.   **2.** Every human being whose life is in peril has a right to assistance.

Aiding persons whose life is in peril.   Every person must come to the aid of anyone whose life is in peril, either personally or calling for aid, by giving him the necessary and immediate physical assistance, unless it involves danger to himself or a third person, or he has another valid reason.

Fundamental freedoms.

3. Every person is the possessor of the fundamental freedoms, including freedom of conscience, freedom of religion, freedom of opinion, freedom of expression, freedom of peaceful assembly and freedom of association.

Safeguard of dignity.

4. Every person has a right to the safeguard of his dignity, honour and reputation.

Respect for private life.

5. Every person has a right to respect for his private life.

Peaceful enjoyment of property.

6. Every person has a right to the peaceful enjoyment and free disposition of his property, except to the extent provided by law.

Home inviolable.

7. A person's home is inviolable.

Respect for private property.

8. No one may enter upon the property of another or take anything therefrom without his express or implied consent.

Right to security.

9. Every person has a right to non-disclosure of confidential information.

Disclosure of confidential information.

No person bound to professional secrecy by law and no priest or other minister of religion may, even in judicial proceedings, disclose confidential information revealed to him by reason of his position or profession, unless he is authorized to do so by the person who confided such information to him or by an express provision of law.

Duty of tribunal.

The tribunal must, *ex officio*, ensure that professional secrecy is respected.

Exercise of rights and freedoms.

9.1. In exercising his fundamental freedoms and rights, a person shall maintain a proper regard for democratic values, public order and the general well-being of the citizens of Québec.

Scope fixed by law.

In this respect, the scope of the freedoms and rights, and limits to their exercise, may be fixed by law.

CHAPTER I.1

RIGHT TO EQUAL RECOGNITION AND EXERCISE OF RIGHTS AND FREEDOMS

Discrimination forbidden.

10. Every person has a right to full and equal recognition and exercise of his human rights and freedoms, without distinction, exclusion or preference based on race, colour, sex, pregnancy, sexual orientation, civil status, age except as provided by law, religion, political convictions, language, ethnic or national origin, social condition, a handicap or the use of any means to palliate a handicap.

Discrimination defined.

Discrimination exists where such a distinction, exclusion or preference has the effect of nullifying or impairing such right.

Harassment.

10.1. No one may harass a person on the basis of any ground mentioned in section 10.

Discriminatory notice forbidden.

11. No one may distribute, publish or publicly exhibit a notice, symbol or sign involving discrimination, or authorize anyone to do so.

Discrimination in juridical acts.

12. No one may, through discrimination, refuse to make a juridical act concerning goods or services ordinarily offered to the public.

Clause forbidden.

13. No one may in a juridical act stipulate a clause involving discrimination.

Nullity.

Such a clause is deemed without effect.

Lease of a room in a dwelling.

14. The prohibitions contemplated in sections 12 and 13 do not apply to the person who leases a room situated in a dwelling if the lessor or his family resides in such dwelling, leases only one room and does not advertise the room for lease by a notice or any other public means of solicitation.

Public places available to everyone.

15. No one may, through discrimination, inhibit the access of another to public transportation or a public place, such as a commercial establishment, hotel, restaurant, theatre, cinema, park, camping ground or trailer park, or his obtaining the goods and services available there.

Non-discrimination in employment.

16. No one may practise discrimination in respect of the hiring, apprenticeship, duration of the probationary period, vocational training, promotion, transfer, displacement, laying-off, suspension, dismissal or conditions of employment of a person or in the establishment of categories or classes of employment.

Discrimination by association or professional corporation forbidden.

17. No one may practise discrimination in respect of the admission, enjoyment of benefits, suspension or expulsion of a person to, of or from an association of employers or employees or any professional corporation or association of persons carrying on the same occupation.

Discrimination by employment bureau.

18. No employment bureau may practise discrimination in respect of the reception, classification or processing of a job application or in any document intended for submitting an application to a prospective employer.

Information on job application.

18.1. No one may, in an employment application form or employment interview, require a person to give information regarding any ground mentioned in section 10 unless the information is useful for the application of section 20 or the implementation of an affirmative action program in existence at the time of the application.

Penal or criminal offence.

18.2. No one may dismiss, refuse to hire or otherwise penalize a person in his employment owing to the mere fact that he was convicted of a penal or criminal offence, if the offence was in no way connected with the employment or if the person has obtained a pardon for the offence.

Equal salary for equivalent work.

19. Every employer must, without discrimination, grant equal salary or wages to the members of his personnel who perform equivalent work at the same place.

Difference based on experience, non-discriminatory.

A difference in salary or wages based on experience, seniority, years of service, merit, productivity or overtime is not considered discriminatory if such criteria are common to all members of the personnel.

Distinction based on aptitudes, non-discriminatory.

20. A distinction, exclusion or preference based on the aptitudes or qualifications required for an employment, or justified by the charitable, philanthropic, religious, political or educational nature of a non-profit institution or of an institution devoted exclusively to the well-being of an ethnic group, is deemed non-discriminatory.

not in force

Non-discriminatory data.

Similarly, under an insurance or pension contract, a social benefits plan or a retirement, pension or insurance plan, or under a public pension or public insurance plan, a distinction, exclusion or preference based on risk determining factors or actuarial data fixed by regulation is deemed non-discriminatory.

CHAPTER II

POLITICAL RIGHTS

Petition to Assembly.

21. Every person has a right of petition to the National Assembly for the redress of grievances.

Right to be candidate and to vote.

22. Every person legally capable and qualified has the right to be a candidate and to vote at an election.

CHAPTER III

JUDICIAL RIGHTS

Impartial hearing before independent tribunal.

23. Every person has a right to a full and equal, public and fair hearing by an independent and impartial tribunal, for the determination of his rights and obligations or of the merits of any charge brought against him.

Sittings *in camera*. The tribunal may decide to sit *in camera*, however, in the interests of morality or public order.

Grounds for deprivation of liberty. **24.** No one may be deprived of his liberty or of his rights except on grounds provided by law and in accordance with prescribed procedure.

Search and seizure. **24.1.** No one may be subjected to unreasonable search or seizure.

Treatment of person arrested. **25.** Every person arrested or detained must be treated with humanity and with the respect due to the human person.

Right to separate treatment. **26.** Every person confined to a house of detention has the right to separate treatment appropriate to his sex, his age and his physical or mental condition.

Person awaiting outcome of his trial to be kept apart. **27.** Every person confined to a house of detention while awaiting the outcome of his trial has the right to be kept apart, until final judgment, from prisoners serving sentence.

Information on grounds of arrest. **28.** Every person arrested or detained has a right to be promptly informed, in a language he understands, of the grounds of his arrest or detention.

Rights of accused person. **28.1.** Every accused person has a right to be promptly informed of the special offence with which he is charged.

Right to advise next of kin. **29.** Every person arrested or detained has a right to immediately advise his next of kin thereof and to have recourse to the assistance of an advocate. He has a right to be informed promptly of those rights.

Right to be brought before tribunal. **30.** Every person arrested or detained must be brought promptly before the competent tribunal or released.

Right to be released on undertaking. **31.** No person arrested or detained may be deprived without just cause of the right to be released on undertaking, with or without deposit of surety, to appear before the tribunal at the appointed time.

Habeas corpus. **32.** Every person deprived of his liberty has a right of recourse to *habeas corpus*.

Right to trial. **32.1.** Every accused person has a right to be tried within a reasonable time.

Presumption of innocence. **33.** Every accused person is presumed innocent until proven guilty according to law.

Self-incrimination.

33.1. No accused person may be compelled to testify against himself at his trial.

Right to advocate.

34. Every person has a right to be represented by an advocate or to be assisted by one before any tribunal.

Full and complete defence.

35. Every accused person has a right to a full and complete defense and has the right to examine and cross-examine witnesses.

Interpreter.

36. Every accused person has a right to be assisted free of charge by an interpreter if he does not understand the language used at the hearing or if he is deaf.

Non-retroactivity of law.

37. No accused person may be held guilty on account of any act or omission which, at the time when it was committed, did not constitute a violation of the law.

Res judicata.

37.1. No person may be tried again for an offence of which he has been acquitted or of which he has been found guilty by a judgment that has acquired status as *res judicata.*

Lesser punishment.

37.2. Where the punishment for an offence has been varied between the time of commission and the time of sentencing, the accused person has a right to the lesser punishment.

Self-incrimination.

38. No testimony before a tribunal may be used to incriminate the person who gives it, except in a prosecution for perjury or for the giving of contradictory evidence.

CHAPTER IV
ECONOMIC AND SOCIAL RIGHTS

Protection.

39. Every child has a right to the protection, security and attention that his parents or the persons acting in their stead are capable of providing.

Free public education.

40. Every person has a right, to the extent and according to the standards provided for by law, to free public education.

Religious or moral education.

41. Parents or the persons acting in their stead have a right to require that, in the public educational establishments, their children receive a religious or moral education in conformity with their convictions, within the framework of the curricula provided for by law.

Private educational establishments.

42. Parents or the persons acting in their stead have a right to choose private educational establishments for their children, provided such establishments comply with the standards prescribed or approved by virtue of the law.

Cultural interests of minorities.

43. Persons belonging to ethnic minorities have a right to maintain and develop their own cultural interests with the other members of their group.

Right to information.

44. Every person has a right to information to the extent provided by law.

Financial assistance.

45. Every person in need has a right, for himself and his family, to measures of financial assistance and to social measures provided for by law, susceptible of ensuring such person an acceptable standard of living.

Conditions of employment.

46. Every person who works has a right, in accordance with the law, to fair and reasonable conditions of employment which have proper regard for his health, safety and physical well-being.

Equal rights of spouses.
Moral guidance of family.

47. Husband and wife have, in the marriage, the same rights, obligations and responsibilities.

Together they provide the moral guidance and material support of the family and the education of their common offspring.

Protection of aged and handicapped persons.
Family protection.

48. Every aged person and every handicapped person has a right to protection against any form of exploitation.

Such a person also has a right to the protection and security that must be provided to him by his family or the persons acting their stead.

PART III

AFFIRMATIVE ACTION PROGRAMS

Affirmative action program.

86. The object of an affirmative action program is to remedy the situation of persons belonging to groups discriminated against in employment, or in the sector of education or of health services and other services generally available to the public.

Non discriminatory.

An affirmative action program is deemed non-discriminatory if it is established in conformity with the Charter.

not in force
Approval.
Assistance.

87. Every affirmative action program must be approved by the Commission, unless it is imposed by order of a tribunal.

The Commission shall, on request, lend assistance for the devising of an affirmative action program.

Proposal.

88. If, after investigation, the Commission confirms the existence of a situation involving discrimination referred to in section 86, it may propose the implementation of an affirmative action program within such time as it may fix.

Application to the
court.

Where its proposal has not been followed, the Commission may apply to a tribunal and, on proof of the existence of a situation contemplated in section 86, obtain, within the time fixed by the tribunal, an order to devise and implement a program. The program thus devised is filed with the tribunal which may, in accordance with the Charter, make the modifications it considers appropriate.

Administration.

89. The Commission shall supervise the administration of the affirmative action programs. It may make investigations and require reports.

Withdrawal of
approval.

90. Where the Commission becomes aware that an affirmative action program has not been implemented within the allotted time or is not being complied with, it may, in the case of a program it has approved, withdraw its approval or, if it proposed implementation of the program, it may apply to a tribunal in accordance with the second paragraph of section 88.

Modifications.

91. A program contemplated in section 88 may be modified, postponed or cancelled if new facts warrant it.

Agreement.

If the Commission and the person required or having consented to implement the affirmative action program agree on its modification, postponement or cancellation, the agreement shall be evidenced in writing.

Application to the
tribunal.

Failing agreement, either party may request the tribunal to which the commission has applied pursuant to the second paragraph of section 88 to decide whether the new facts warrant the modification, postponement or cancellation of the program.

Modifications.

All modifications must conform to the Charter.

Implementation.

92. The Government must require its departments and agencies to implement affirmative action programs within such time as it may fix.

Inapplicable
provisions.

Sections 87 to 91 do not apply to the programs contemplated in this section. The programs must, however, be the object of a consultation with the Commission before being implemented.

Appendix C

CANADIAN CHARTER OF RIGHTS AND FREEDOMS

Whereas Canada is found upon principles that recognize the supremacy of God and the role of Law:

Guarantee of Rights and Freedoms

1. The *Canadian Charter of Rights and Freedoms* guarantees the rights and freedoms set out in it subject only to such reasonable limits prescribed law as can be demonstrably justified in a free and democratic society.

Fundamental Freedoms

2. Everyone has the following fundamental freedoms:
    (a) freedom of conscience and religion;
    (b) freedom of thought, belief, opinion and expression, including freedom of the press and other media of communication;
    (c) freedom of peaceful assembly; and
    (d) freedom of association.

Democratic Rights

3. Every citizen of Canada has the right to vote in an election of members of the House of Commons or of a legislative assembly and to be qualified for membership therein.

4. (1) No House of Commons and no legislative assembly shall continue for longer than five years from the date fixed for the return of the writs at a general election of its members.

(2) In time of real or apprehended war, invasion or insurrection, a House of Commons may be continued by Parliament and a legislative assembly may be continued by the legislature beyond five years if such continuation is not opposed by the votes of more than one-third of the members of the House of Commons or the legislative assembly, as the case may be.

5. There shall be a sitting of Parliament and of each legislature at least once every twelve months.

Mobility Rights

6. (1) Every citizen of Canada has the right to enter, remain in and leave Canada
   (2) Every citizen of Canada and every person who has the status of a permanent resident of Canada has the right
      (a) to move to and take up residence in any province; and
      (b) to pursue the gaining of a livelihood in any province.
   (3) The rights specified in subsection (2) are subject to
      (a) any laws or practices of general application in force in a province other than those that discriminate among persons primarily on the basis of province of present or previous residence; and
      (b) any laws providing for reasonable residency requirements as a qualification for the receipt of publicly provided social services
   (4) Subsections (2) and (3) do not preclude any law, program or activity that has as its object the amelioration in a province of conditions of individuals in that province who are socially or economically disadvantaged if the rate of employment in that province is below the rate of employment in Canada.

Legal Rights

7. Everyone has the right to life, liberty and security of the person and the right not to be deprived thereof except in accordance with the principles of fundamental justice.

8. Everyone has the right to be secure against unreasonable search or seizure.

9. Everyone has the right not to be arbitrarily detained or imprisoned.

10. Everyone has the right on arrest or detention
    (a) to be informed promptly of the reasons therefor;
    (b) to retain and instruct counsel without delay and to be informed of that right; and
    (c) to have the validity of the detention determined by way of *habeas corpus* and to be released if the detention is not lawful.

11. Any person charged with an offence has the right
    (a) to be informed without unreasonable delay of the specific offence;
    (b) to be tried within a reasonable time;
    (c) not to be compelled to be a witness in proceedings against that person in respect of the offence;
    (d) to be presumed innocent until proven guilty according to law in a fair and public hearing by an independent and impartial tribunal;
    (e) not to be denied reasonable bail without just cause;
    (f) except in the case of an offence under military law tried before a military tribunal, to the benefit of trial by jury where the maximum punishment for the offence is imprisonment for five years or a more severe punishment;
    (g) not to be found guilty on account of any act or omission unless, at the time of the act or omission, it constituted an offence under Canadian or international law or was criminal according to the general principles of law recognized by the community of nations;
    (h) if finally acquitted of the offence, not to be tried for it again and, if finally found guilty and punishment for the offence, not to be tried or punished for it again; and
    (i) if found guilty of the offence and if the punishment for the offence has been varied between the time of commission and the time of sentencing, to the benefit of the lesser punishment.

12. Everyone has the right not to be subjected to any cruel and unusual treatment or punishment.

13. A witness who testifies in any proceedings has the right not to have any incriminating evidence so given used to

incriminate that witness in any other proceedings, except in a prosecution for perjury or for the giving of contradictory evidence.

14. A party or witness in any proceedings who does not understand or speak the language in which the proceedings are conducted or who is deaf has the right to the assistance of an interpreter.

Equality Rights

15. (1) Every individual is equal before and under the law and has the right to the equal protection and equal benefit of the law without discrimination and, in particular, without discrimination based on race, national or ethnic origin, colour, religion, sex, age or mental or physical disability.
    (2) Subsection (1) does not preclude any law, program or activity that has as its object the amelioration of conditions of disadvantaged because of raced, national or ethnic origin, colour, religion, sex, age or mental or physical disability.

Official Languages of Canada

16. (1) English and French are the official languages of Canada and have equality of status and equal rights and privileges as to their use in all institutions of the Parliament and government of Canada.
    (2) English and French are the official languages of New Brunswick and have equality of status and equal rights and privileges as to their use in all institutions of the legislature and government of New Brunswick.
    (3) Nothing in this Charter limits the authority of Parliament or a legislature to advance the equality of status or use of English and French.

17. (1) Everyone has the right to use English or French in any debates and other proceedings of Parliament.
    (2) Everyone has the right to use English or French in any debates and other proceedings of the legislature of New Brunswick.

18. (1) The statutes, records and journals of Parliament shall be printed and published in English and French and both language versions are equally authoritative.

    (2) The statutes, records and journals of legislature of New Brunswick shall be printed and published in English and French and both language versions are equally authoritative.

19. (1) Either English or French may be used by any person in, or in any pleading in or process issuing from, any court established by Parliament.

    (2) Either English or French may be used by any person in, or in any pleading in or process issuing from, any court of New Brunswick.

20. (1) Any member of the public in Canada has the right to communicate with, and to receive available services from, any head or central office of an institution of the Parliament or government of Canada in English or French, and has the same right with respect to any other office of any such institution where

    (a) there is a significant demand for communications with and services from that office in which language; or

    (b) due to the nature of the office, it is reasonable that communications with and services from that office be available in both English and French.

    (2) Any member of the public in New Brunswick has the right to communicate with, and to receive available services from, any office of an institution of the legislature or government of New Brunswick in English or French.

21. Nothing in sections 16 to 20 abrogates or derogates from any right, privilege or obligation with respect to the English and French languages, or either of them, that exists or is continued by virtue of any other provision of the Constitution of Canada.

22. Nothing in sections 16 to 20 abrogates or derogates from any legal or customary right or privilege acquired or enjoyed either before or after the coming into force of this Charter with respect to any language that is not English or French.

Minority Language Educational Rights

23. (1) Citizens of Canada
  (a) whose first language learned and still understood is that of the English or French linguistic minority population of the province in which they reside, or
  (b) who have received their primary school instruction in Canada in English or French and reside in a province where the language in which they received that instruction is the language of the English or French linguistic minority population of the province,
  have the right to have their children receive primary and secondary school instruction in that language in that province.

  (2) Citizens of Canada of whom any child has received or is receiving primary or secondary school instruction in English or French in Canada, have the right to have all their children receive primary and secondary school instruction in the same language.

  (3) The right of citizens of Canada under subsections (1) and (2) to have their children receive primary and secondary school instruction in the language of the English or French linguistic minority population of a province
  (a) applies wherever in the province the number of children of citizens who have such a right is sufficient to warrant the provision to them out of public funds of minority language instructions; and
  (b) includes, where the number of children so warrants, the right to have them receive that instruction in minority language educational facilities provided out of public funds.

Enforcement

24. (1) Anyone whose rights or freedoms, as guaranteed by this Charter, have been infringed or denied may apply to a court of competent jurisdiction to obtain such remedy as the court considers appropriate and just in the circumstances.

(2) Where, in proceedings under subsection (1), a court concludes that evidence was obtained in a manner that infringed or denied any rights or freedoms guaranteed by this Charter, the evidence shall be excluded if it is established that, having regard to all the circumstances, the admission of it in the proceedings would being the administration of justice into disrepute.

General

25. The guarantee in this Charter of certain rights and freedoms shall not be construed so as to abrogate or derogate from any aboriginal, treaty or other rights or freedoms that pertain to the aboriginal peoples of Canada including
  (a) any rights or freedoms that have ben recognized by the Royal Proclamation of October 7, 1763; and
  (b) any rights or freedoms that now exist by way of land claims agreements or may be so acquired.

26. The guarantee in this Charter of certain rights and freedoms shall not be construed as denying the existence of any other rights or freedoms that exist in Canada.

27. This Charter shall be interpreted in a manner consistent with the preservation and enhancement of the multicultural heritage of Canadians.

28. Notwithstanding anything in this Charter, the rights and freedoms referred to in it are guaranteed equally to male and female persons.

29. Nothing in this Charter abrogates or derogates from any rights or privileges guaranteed by or under the Constitution of Canada in respect of denominational, separate or dissentient schools.

30. A reference in this Charter to a province or to the legislative assembly or legislature of a province shall be deemed to include a reference to the Yukon Territory and the Northwest Territories, or to the appropriate legislative authority thereof, as the case may be.

31. Nothing in this Charter extends the legislative powers of any body or authority.

TABLE 1 **Population Change**
Québec, Ontario, Canada, 1971–1993

Date	Population			Growth[1]			Distribution		
	Québec	Ontario	Canada	Québec	Ontario	Canada	Québec	Ontario	Canada
		000				%			
1971–07–01	6 155.6	7 868.4	22 026.4	4.3	7.2	6.8	27.9	35.7	100.0
1976–07–01	6 420.5	8 432.1	23 517.5	2.3	4.8	5.9	27.3	35.9	100.0
1981–07–01	6 568.0	8 837.8	24 900.0	2.5	7.2	5.2	26.4	35.5	100.0
1986–07–01	6 733.8	9 477.2	26 203.8	5.2	10.5	7.3	25.7	36.2	100.0
1991–07–01	7 081.2	10 471.2	28 117.6	1.0	1.3	1.1	25.2	37.2	100.0
1992–07–01	7 150.7	10 609.8	28 435.6	0.8	1.3	1.1	25.1	37.3	100.0
1993–07–01	7 208.8	10 746.3	28 753.0	...	...	...	25.1	37.4	100.0

[1] Five-year growth until 1991, then annual. Rate calculated on population at the start of the period.

Taken from: *Le Québec statistique*, 60th edition (1995), Bureau de la statistique du Québec, Les publications du Québec, pg. 55.

FIGURE 1 **Per capita GNP by Regions or by Provinces in Canada,**
1976–1992

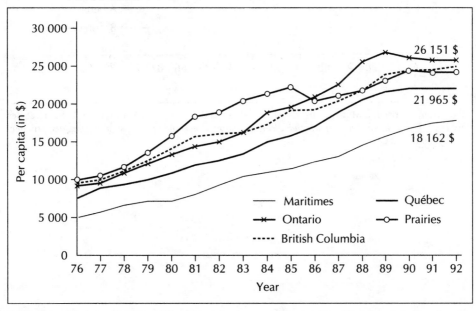

Taken from: Christiane Morin, "PIB, niveau de vie et endettement" in Ministère de la Santé et des Services sociaux, *Le Québec comparé: Indicateurs sanitaires, démographiques et socio-economiques*, Québec, 1995, pg. 92.

FIGURE 2 Gross Debt of Government as a Percentage of GNP, Québec, Ontario, Alberta and British Columbia, 1976 to 1992

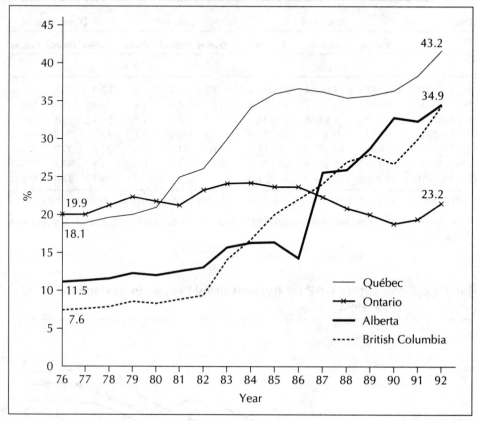

Taken from: Christiane Morin, "PIB, niveau de vie et endettement" in Ministère de la Santé et des Services sociaux, *Le Québec comparé: Indicateurs sanitaires, démographiques et socio-economiques*, Québec, 1995, pg. 93.

FIGURE 3 Unemployment Rate by Region of Canada, 1976 to 1993

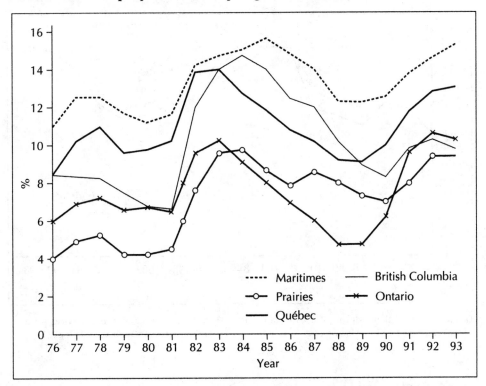

Taken from: Christiane Morin, "Taux de chômage" in Ministère de la Santé et des Services sociaux, *Le Québec comparé: Indicateurs sanitaires, démographiques et socio-economiques*, Québec, 1995, pg. 83.

FIGURE 4 Unemployment Rate by Gender, Québec, 1976 to 1993

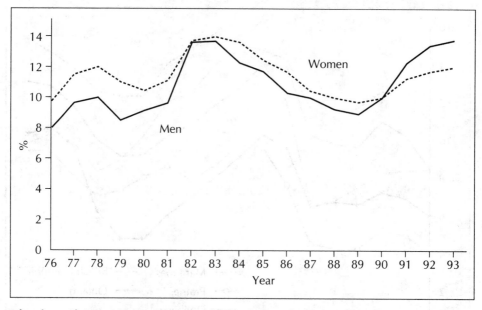

Taken from: Christiane Morin, "Taux de chômage" in Ministère de la Santé et des Services sociaux, *Le Québec comparé: Indicateurs sanitaires, démographiques et socio-economiques*, Québec, 1995, pg. 81.

TABLE 2 Labour Force Activity of Population 15 Years and Over, Québec, Ontario and Canada, 1986–1993

	Population 15 Years and Over			Active Population			Rate of Activity		
	Québec	Ontario	Canada	Québec	Ontario	Canada	Québec	Ontario	Canada
	000						%		
1986	5 090	7 098	19 397	3 174	4 862	12 746	62.4	68.5	65.7
1987	5 137	7 231	19 642	3 253	4 992	13 011	63.3	69.0	66.2
1988	5 178	7 357	19 890	3 311	5 118	13 275	64.0	69.6	66.7
1989	5 222	7 469	20 141	3 343	5 214	13 503	64.0	69.8	67.0
1990	5 284	7 591	20 430	3 399	5 268	13 681	64.3	69.4	67.0
1991	5 350	7 723	20 746	3 392	5 276	13 757	63.4	68.3	66.3
1992	5 418	7 857	21 058	3 385	5 286	13 797	62.5	67.3	65.5
1993	5 476	8 013	21 392	3 404	5 362	13 946	62.2	66.9	65.2

Taken from: *Le Québec statistique*, 60th edition (1995), Bureau de la statistique du Québec, Les publications du Québec, pg. 209.

TABLE 3 **Rate of Labour Force Activity by Gender**
Québec, 1986–1993

	1986	1987	1988	1989	1990	1991	1992	1993
				%				
Men	74.6	75.0	75.5	75.3	74.7	73.0	71.9	71.1
Women	50.9	52.4	53.1	53.4	54.6	54.3	53.6	53.7

Taken from: *Le Québec statistique*, 60th edition (1995), Bureau de la statistique du Québec, Les publications du Québec, pg. 211.

TABLE 4 **Rate of Labour Force Activity for Women**
by Presence of Children in the Home
Québec, 1976–1993

	All Women	Women 25–44	Women With a Family		
			All Women	With Children Under 3 Yrs.	With Children Under 16 Yrs.	Without Children[1]
			%			
1976	41.1	48.5	37.3	28.5	35.4	39.6
1977	42.2	51.0	39.1	30.2	38.1	40.4
1978	44.1	53.8	41.6	34.7	41.3	42.1
1979	44.6	54.8	42.9	37.2	42.7	43.2
1980	46.2	57.0	44.8	39.7	45.2	44.2
1981	47.3	60.3	46.0	43.2	48.1	43.9
1982	46.3	59.0	45.9	42.7	47.9	43.8
1983	47.6	61.2	47.3	48.5	50.2	44.6
1984	49.0	64.6	49.0	51.1	52.5	45.9
1985	50.2	66.6	50.8	53.5	55.5	46.7
1986	50.9	68.8	52.4	54.7	58.1	47.6
1987	52.4	70.6	53.8	56.7	60.8	48.1
1988	53.1	71.1	54.7	56.4	61.9	48.9
1989	53.4	72.6	55.4	57.9	64.2	48.2
1990	54.6	75.6	57.8	60.3	67.0	50.5
1991	54.3	74.5	57.8	60.6	67.0	50.3
1992	53.6	73.8	57.6	61.3	66.9	50.4
1993	53.7	74.4	57.9	62.1	67.3	50.6

[1] No children under 17 yrs.

Taken from: *Le Québec statistique*, 60th edition (1995), Bureau de la statistique du Québec, Les publications du Québec, pg. 299.

**TABLE 5 Part-Time Employment and Relative Distribution
of Total Employment by Age and Gender
Québec, 1987–1993**

Age Group	1987		1989		1991		1993	
	000	%	000	%	000	%	000	%
15–19 years	99	52.9	108	56.0	112	65.1	109	71.2
20–24 years	64	17.2	58	16.5	65	22.1	74	27.0
25–34 years	86	9.8	83	9.1	85	9.7	93	11.2
35–44 years	69	9.3	71	8.9	83	10.0	86	10.1
45–54 years	36	7.8	48	9.5	59	10.7	63	10.7
55–64 years	29	12.0	28	11.8	31	13.2	31	13.7
65 years and over	11	34.4	14	36.8	9	31.0	10	33.3
Total	**395**	**13.5**	**410**	**13.5**	**445**	**14.9**	**465**	**15.7**
Men	114	6.8	119	6.9	141	8.5	149	9.1
Women	281	22.6	291	22.4	304	22.9	316	23.8

Taken from: *Le Québec statistique*, 60th edition (1995), Bureau de la statistique du Québec, Les publications du Québec, pg. 211.

**TABLE 6 Distribution of Workers by Reason for
Part-Time Employment and by Gender
Québec, 1978–1993**

	By Choice		Unsuccessful Search for Full-Time Work		Personal or Family Obligations		Studies and Other Reasons		Total	
	Men	Women	Men	Women	Men	Women	Men	Women	Men	Women
	%								000	
1978	17.2	37.2	26.6	21.3	—	22.0	54.7	19.5	64	164
1981	12.0	36.6	31.5	25.8	—	18.8	56.5	18.8	92	213
1984	12.1	33.6	42.1	35.7	—	11.9	45.8	18.4	107	244
1987	14.9	33.8	34.2	34.5	—	10.3	50.0	21.4	114	281
1990	14.6	34.6	30.1	34.2	—	9.1	51.2	22.1	123	298
1993	12.8	28.8	43.0	41.5	—	7.3	43.6	21.5	149	316

Taken from: *Le Québec statistique*, 60th edition (1995), Bureau de la statistique du Québec, Les publications du Québec, pg. 213.

TABLE 7 Average Income[1] of Population 15 Years and Over, and for Selected Age Groups, by Gender, Québec, Ontario and Canada, 1985 and 1990

	1985		1990	
	Men	**Women**	**Men**	**Women**
	$			
Québec	**26 879**	**14 927**	**28 001**	**16 512**
15–19 years	4 860	4 074	5 248	4 243
20–24 years	12 662	10 347	13 883	11 019
Ontario	**31 300**	**16 708**	**33 036**	**19 303**
15–19 years	4 277	3 731	4 748	4 219
20–24 years	14 395	11 118	15 238	12 263
Canada	**28 961**	**15 704**	**30 205**	**17 577**
15–19 years	4 475	3 797	4 808	4 084
20–24 years	14 065	10 885	14 619	11 523

[1] In 1990 dollars.

Taken from: *Le Québec statistique*, 60th edition (1995), Bureau de la statistique du Québec, Les publications du Québec, pg. 275.

FIGURE 5 Evolution of the Consumer Price Index and of Average Gross Weekly Salary Québec, 1983–1993

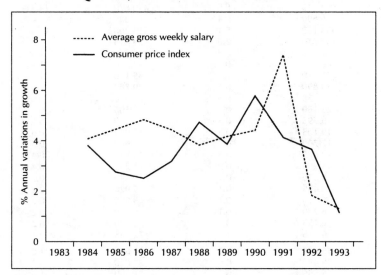

Taken from: *Le Québec statistique*, 60th edition (1995), Bureau de la statistique du Québec, Les publications du Québec, pg. 217.

TABLE 8 Rate of Unionization, Private and Public Sectors
Québec 1988–1993

	Private Sector			Public Sector		
	Total Employees	Unionized Employees	Rate of Unionization	Total Employees	Unionized Employees[1]	Rate of Unionization
	n		%	n		%
1988	2 030 547	646 336	31.8	662 441	531 247	80.2
1989	2 032 868	659 186	32.4	669 052	536 419	80.2
1990	2 024 259	685 684	33.9	671 854	524 768	78.1
1991	1 917 163	673 971	35.2	687 755	530 234	77.1
1992	1 817 147	671 595	36.9	723 130	533 549	73.8
1993	1 826 312	634 757	34.7	723 846	534 692	73.9

[1] The term "unionized employees" designates those whose working conditions are defined.

Taken from: *Le Québec statistique*, 60th edition (1995), Bureau de la statistique du Québec, Les publications du Québec, pg. 215.

TABLE 9 Population by Mother Tongue
Region and Québec Province, 1991

Mother Tongue	Province		Montréal Metropolitan Region	
	n	%	n	%
Single response	**6 735 260**	**98.9**	**3 036 430**	**98.2**
French	5 556 105	81.6	2 080 980	67.3
English	599 145	8.8	440 870	14.3
Native languages	26 890	0.4	380	—
Other single language	553 120	8.1	514 200	16.6
Italian	133 210	2.0	129 615	4.2
Spanish	51 735	0.8	46 570	1.5
Arabic	46 165	0.7	42 230	1.4
Greek	46 110	0.7	45 150	1.5
Portugese	33 890	0.5	29 780	1.0
Chinese	30 755	0.5	20 020	0.6
Creole	25 180	0.4	24 505	0.8
German	19 795	0.3	14 770	0.5
Polish	19 105	0.3	17 075	0.6
Vietnamese	17 790	0.3	15 900	0.5
Armenian	13 875	0.2	13 825	0.4
Yiddish	11 295	0.2	11 255	0.4
Hungarian	9 330	0.1	8 590	0.3
Ukranian	6 455	0.1	5 920	0.2
Persian	6 410	0.1	5 990	0.2
Khmer (Cambodian)	6 290	0.1	5 250	0.2
Romanian	6 155	0.1	5 470	0.2
Others	69 575	1.0	72 285	2.3
Multiple response	**75 040**	**1.1**	**54 680**	**1.8**
French and English	39 485	0.6	23 020	0.7
Others	35 555	0.5	31 660	1.0
Total	**6 810 300**	**100.0**	**3 091 110**	**100.0**

Taken from: *Le Québec statistique*, 60th edition (1995), Bureau de la statistique du Québec, Les publications du Québec, pg. 291.

TABLE 10 Population by Mother Tongue and Language Spoken at Home Québec, 1991

Mother Tongue	Language Spoken at Home								Total Population
	French		English		Others		Multiple Response		
	n	%	n	%	n	%	n	%	n
Single response	**5 579 110**	**82.8**	**702 065**	**10.4**	**356 315**	**5.3**	**97 760**	**1.5**	**6 735 260**
French	5 455 720	98.2	58 040	1.0	10 375	0.2	31 970	0.6	5 556 105
English	54 305	9.1	524 910	87.6	4 810	0.8	15 120	2.5	599 145
Others	69 085	11.9	119 115	20.5	341 130	58.8	50 670	8.7	580 010
Native languages	1 025	3.8	1 020	3.8	24 010	89.3	830	3.1	26 890
Others	68 060	12.3	118 095	21.4	317 120	57.3	49 840	9.0	553 120
Multiple response	**24 910**	**33.2**	**14 090**	**18.8**	**6 645**	**8.9**	**29 385**	**39.2**	**75 040**
French/English	16 825	42.6	7 425	18.8	325	0.8	14 910	37.8	39 485
Others	8 085	22.7	6 665	18.7	6 320	17.8	14 475	40.7	35 555
Total	**5 604 020**	**82.3**	**716 155**	**10.5**	**362 965**	**5.3**	**127 155**	**1.9**	**6 810 300**

Taken from: *Le Québec statistique*, 60th edition (1995), Bureau de la statistique du Québec, Les publications du Québec, pg. 292.

FIGURE 6 Median Number of Years of Education of the Population 15 Years of Age and Older, by Gender Québec, 1971, 1981 and 1991

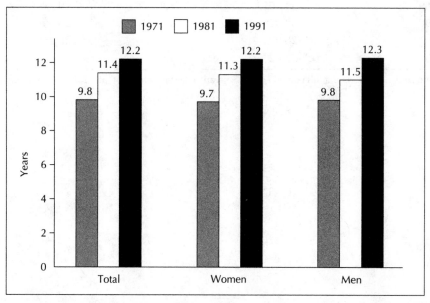

Taken from: Christiane Morin, "Education" in Ministère de la Santé et des Services sociaux, *Le Québec comparé: Indicateurs sanitaires, démographiques et socio-economiques*, Québec, 1995, pg. 59.

TABLE 11 Marriages and Divorces
         Québec, 1971–1992

	Marriages	Marriage Rate	Divorces
	n	o/oo	n
1971	49 695	8.1	5 203
1972	53 967	8.7	6 426
1973	52 133	8.4	8 091
1974	51 890	8.2	12 272
1975	51 690	8.1	14 093
1976	50 961	7.9	15 186
1977	48 182	7.5	14 501
1978	46 189	7.1	14 865
1979	46 154	7.1	14 379
1980	44 849	6.9	13 899
1981	41 006	6.2	19 193
1982	38 360	5.8	18 579
1983	36 147	5.5	17 365
1984	37 416	5.6	16 845
1985	37 026	5.5	15 814
1986	33 108	4.9	18 399
1987	32 588	4.8	19 315
1988	33 469	4.9	19 825
1989	33 305	4.8	19 790
1990	32 059	4.6	20 398
1991	28 922	4.1	20 277
1992	25 821	3.6	19 695

Taken from: *Le Québec statistique*, 60th edition (1995), Bureau de la statistique du Québec, Les publications du Québec, pg. 192.

**TABLE 12 Families[1] by Structure and by Civil Status of Parents
Québec, 1961–1991**

Structure		1961	1966	1971	1976	1981	1986	1991
Two-parent families	n	**1 008 004**	**1 124 833**	**1 222 175**	**1 381 505**	**1 463 105**	**1 498 690**	**1 614 355**
	%	91.3	91.5	90.0	89.7	87.5	85.6	85.7
Of which common-law	n	—	—	—	—	120 885	188 660	306 910
	%	—	—	—	—	7.2	10.8	16.3
Single parent families	n	**95 818**	**104 468**	**135 200**	**158 895**	**208 435**	**252 810**	**268 880**
	%	8.7	8.5	10.0	10.3	12.5	14.4	14.3
Father only	n	23 073	21 352	29 780	26 330	35 120`	44 180	48 760
	%	2.1	1.7	2.2	1.7	2.1	2.5	2.6
Mother only	n	72 745	83 116	105 420	132 565	173 315	208 630	220 120
	%	6.6	6.8	7.8	8.6	10.4	11.9	11.7
Married	n	17 423	19 221	31 945	32 530	39 305	43 080	39 375
	%	1.6	1.6	2.4	2.1	2.4	2.5	2.1
Widowed	n	53 097	60 763	59 810	65 625	66 625	63 585	57 070
	%	4.8	4.9	4.4	4.3	4.0	3.6	3.0
Divorced	n	1 205	1 589	5 920	24 150	45 895	65 780	75 840
	%	0.1	0.1	0.4	1.6	2.7	3.8	4.0
Single	n	1 020	1 543	7 745	10 260	21 490	36 185	47 835
	%	0.1	0.1	0.6	0.7	1.3	2.1	2.5
Total	n	**1 103 822**	**1 229 301**	**1 357 375**	**1 540 400**	**1 671 540**	**1 751 495**	**1 883 230**
	%	**100.0**	**100.0**	**100.0**	**100.0**	**100.0**	**100.0**	**100.0**

[1] All families with or without children.

Taken from: *Le Québec statistique*, 60th edition (1995), Bureau de la statistique du Québec, Les publications du Québec, pg. 295.

FIGURE 7 **Fecundity Index, Canada and Regions,**
1976, 1981, 1986 and 1992

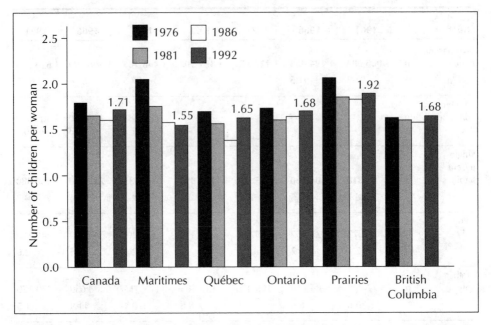

Taken from: Madeleine Rochon, "Fécondité" in Ministère de la Santé et des Services sociaux, *Le Québec comparé: Indicateurs sanitaires, démographiques et socio-economiques*, Québec, 1995, pg. 33.

TABLE 13 Births by Civil Status of Mother
Québec, 1990–1992

Civil Status	Total	%
1990	**98 013**	**100.9**
Single	34 777	35.5
Married	60 661	61.9
Widowed	159	.1
Divorced	1 913	2.0
Separated	503	.5
1991	**97 348**	**100.0**
Single	36 865	37.9
Married	57 593	59.2
Widowed	155	.1
Divorced	2 163	2.2
Separated	572	.6
1992	**96 054**	**100.0**
Single	38 717	40.3
Married	54 350	56.6
Widowed	208	.2
Divorced	2 182	2.3
Separated	597	.6

Taken from: *Le Québec statistique*, 60th edition (1995), Bureau de la statistique du Québec, Les publications du Québec, pg. 191.

FIGURE 8 Proportion of Births Outside of Marriage
Québec, 1970–1992

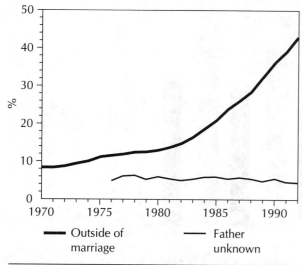

Taken from: Le *Québec statistique*, 60th edition (1995), Bureau de la statistique du Québec, Les publications du Québec, pg. 59.

FIGURE 9 Fecundity Rate for Single People, by Age and Sex
Québec, 1976–1992

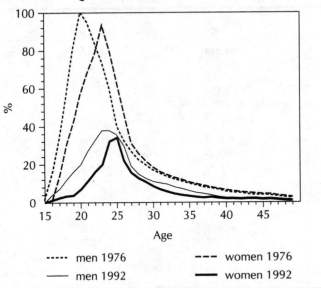

Taken from: *Le Québec statistique,* 60th edition (1995), Bureau de la statistique du
Québec, Les publications du Québec, pg. 59.

FIGURE 10 Life Expectancy at Birth by Sex,
Québec, 1976, 1981, 1986 and 1991

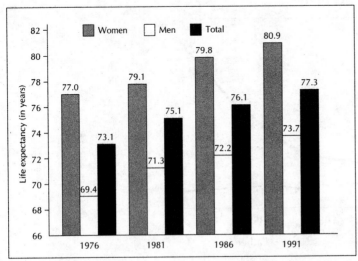

Taken from: Pierre Lafontaine, "Espérance de vie à la naissance"
in Ministère de la Santé et des Services sociaux, *Le Québec comparé: Indicateurs
sanitaires, démographiques et socio-economiques,* Québec, 1995, pg. 25.

TABLE 14 Infant Mortality Rates for Some Canadian Provinces, 1966–1993 (per 1000 live births)

Provinces	1966	1967	1968	1969	1970	1971	1972	1973	1974	1975	1975	1977	1978	1979
Canada	23.1	22.0	20.8	19.3	18.8	17.5	17.1	15.5	15.0	14.3	13.5	12.4	12.0	10.9
Québec	—	—	—	—	—	18.4	17.9	16.4	15.1	14.3	13.5	12.4	11.9	10.5
Ontario	—	—	—	—	—	15.3	15.3	14.1	13.4	12.8	12.3	11.3	11.3	10.3
Alberta	—	—	—	—	—	17.9	17.5	14.2	15.2	14.9	14.2	11.1	11.4	11.4
British Columbia	—	—	—	—	—	18.7	16.8	16.7	16.1	14.4	13.8	13.5	12.7	11.3

Provinces	1980	1981	1982	1983	1984	1985	1986	1987	1988	1989	1990	1991	1992	1993
Canada	10.4	9.6	9.1	8.5	8.1	8.0	7.9	7.3	7.2	7.1	6.8	6.4	6.1	—
Québec	9.8	8.5	8.8	7.7	7.3	7.3	7.1	7.1	6.5	6.8	6.2	5.9	—	—
Ontario	9.5	8.8	8.3	8.0	7.6	7.3	7.2	6.6	6.6	6.8	6.3	6.3	—	—
Alberta	12.6	10.6	9.8	8.4	9.6	8.0	9.0	7.5	8.3	7.5	8.0	6.7	—	—
British Columbia	11.0	10.2	9.9	8.8	8.6	8.1	8.5	8.6	8.4	8.2	7.5	6.5	—	—

Taken from: Sylvie Montreuil, "Mortalité foeto-infantile" in Ministère de la Santé et des Services sociaux, *Le Québec comparé: Indicateurs sanitaires, démographiques et socio-economiques,* Québec, 1995, pg. 124.

FIGURE 11 Total Per Capita Expenditure on Health, Canada and the Provinces, 1991

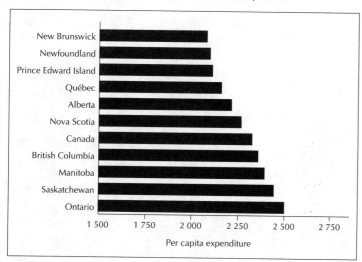

Taken from: Ronald Coté, "Depenses de santé" in Ministère de la Santé et des Services sociaux, *Le Québec comparé: Indicateurs sanitaires, démographiques et socio-economiques,* Québec, 1995, pg. 227.